RENAISSANCE
FLORENCE
The Art of the 1470s

In association with Esso UK plc

RENAISSANCE FLORENCE
The Art of the 1470s

Patricia Lee Rubin and Alison Wright
with contributions by Nicholas Penny

National Gallery Publications Limited, London
Distributed by Yale University Press

Supported by Esso UK plc

This book was published to accompany an exhibition at
The National Gallery, London
20 October 1999 – 16 January 2000

First published in Great Britain in 1999 by
National Gallery Publications Limited
St Vincent House, 30 Orange Street, London WC2H 7HH

ISBN 1 85709 266 x hardback 525313
ISBN 1 85709 267 8 paperback 525454

British Library Cataloguing-in-Publication Data
A catalogue record is available from the British Library.
Library of Congress Catalog Card Number: 99–74591

Authors' abbreviations:
Patricia Lee Rubin PLR
Alison Wright AW
Nicholas Penny NP

MANAGING EDITOR Caroline Bugler
DESIGNER Isambard Thomas
EDITOR Diana Davies
ASSISTANT EDITORS Tessa Daintith, John Jervis
PICTURE RESEARCHERS James Mulraine, Francesca Geens

Full-page illustrations
p. 2   SANDRO BOTTICELLI *Giuliano de' Medici*
        (detail, cat. no. 1).
p. 11   FRANCESCO BOTTICINI *Assumption of the Virgin*
        (detail, fig 28).
p. 33   SANDRO BOTTICELLI *Adoration of the Magi*
        (detail, fig. 38).
p. 77   WORKSHOP OF VERROCCHIO *Tobias and the Angel*
        (detail, cat. no. 21).
p. 123 SANDRO BOTTICELLI *Adoration of the Kings*
        (detail, cat. no. 7).
p. 149 WORKSHOP OF VERROCCHIO *The Virgin and Child with Two Angels*
        (detail, cat. no. 23).
p. 191 ANDREA DEL VERROCCHIO *Head of a youth looking upwards*
        (detail, cat. no. 32).
p. 223 ANTONIO and PIERO DEL POLLAIUOLO *Hercules, Nessus*
        and Deianeira (detail, cat. no. 46).
p. 253 ANTONIO DEL POLLAIUOLO *Prisoner led before a ruler*
        (detail, cat. no. 57).
p. 287 FILIPPINO LIPPI with SANDRO BOTTICELLI *Adoration of the Kings*
        (detail, cat. no. 68)
p. 313 SANDRO BOTTICELLI *Venus and Mars*
        (detail, cat. no. 68)

Printed and bound in Italy by Grafiche Milani.

Sponsor's Preface

Welcome to the eleventh consecutive annual Esso exhibition. It is a pleasure once again to be associated with the National Gallery and to continue our very special partnership.

Following the great success of previous Esso-sponsored exhibitions at the National Gallery, *Renaissance Florence: The Art of the 1470s* continues the theme of putting artists' work into context. This exhibition provides a unique opportunity to raise awareness and understanding of the religious, political and social world of powerful Florentine families during one of the most important and interesting periods in the history of the city.

Any exhibition at the National Gallery can be relied upon to excite and inspire. It is particularly rewarding to us to know that our sponsorship of this exhibition is providing a valuable opportunity for thousands of visitors to appreciate the complexities of the treasures on display, drawn both from the Gallery's Collection and from elsewhere.

K.H. Taylor
Chairman and Chief Executive, Esso UK plc

Director's Foreword

You get good views of the Arno valley from Trafalgar Square. In picture after picture the Tuscan landscape that so beguiled the Victorians beguiles us still today and, thanks above all to their efforts, it is possible to enjoy Florentine painting of the early Renaissance in London as in no other city outside Florence itself.

Building this part of the National Gallery's Collection was a feat of erudition and taste, led by the Gallery's first and greatest director, Charles Eastlake. His scholarship and persistence in identifying the pictures needed if the Gallery was to tell the story of painting in Italy as he understood it, and then in finding the best means to obtain them, laid the foundations of the collection visitors see in the Sainsbury Wing today. At the same time he persuaded the governments of the 1850s to fund his vision, for almost all these pictures were bought with money voted by Parliament so that the British public, many of whom would never be able to travel to Italy, could see some of the finest achievements of the Renaissance here. When necessary, the Government also applied whatever political pressure was required to help solve an export problem – the Pollaiuolos' *Saint Sebastian* required a great deal to get it out of Tuscany – and piece by piece the astonishing narrative took shape on the walls.

Nearly 150 years later, we would still tell the story in roughly the same way. Eastlake's stars are still by and large our stars. But in one major respect the National Gallery is handicapped in attempting to tell a full narrative: it has only pictures. Accidents of British history and habits of British muddle have kept the nation's paintings separate from its drawings, held in the British Museum, and from the related sculpture and decorative arts, shown in the Victoria and Albert Museum. We owe a great debt to these museums, and to many other lenders both at home and abroad, for enabling the organisers of the exhibition to present a view of the overall artistic activity in Florence at one of her richest moments. The lenders are listed later in this volume and it would be invidious to mention one or two of them here, but several institutions within Florence itself have been especially generous to us and we would like to think that this is an exhibition which will be of interest to the increasing number of visitors who have travelled to London from Tuscany in recent years.

It is impossible to discuss Renaissance Florence without mentioning the Medici, whose name has become synonymous with enlightened patronage. And it is pleasing to be able to end this Foreword by thanking our enlightened patrons, Esso UK plc. For many years now they have helped us to present recent research on the Collection to a wide public, believing that deeper understanding of works of art nearly always brings fuller enjoyment. On behalf of all of us who work at the Gallery, and all who will see this exhibition, we thank them.

Neil MacGregor *Director of the National Gallery*

Introduction

One of the special features of Florence is its beauty. This simple statement is not a simple matter. In the course of the fourteenth and fifteenth centuries the beauty, or the beauties, of Florence came to constitute an argument for its status, a form of visual politics. Intrinsic to the city's identity and prestige, its beauty was a key factor in granting its citizens honour, and was the basis of many other forms of exchange – economic, diplomatic and social. That Florence had an aesthetic culture does not make it unique, but that the aesthetic should be consciously articulated as a value in public and private life is noteworthy. The resulting volume of precious and skilfully made objects, impressive at the time, still astonishes today.

Why the 1470s? Any period break is artificial, and ten years have no particular meaning as such. As presented here the decade is a long one and includes works that can be dated to before 1470 and after 1480. Historically the brackets are provided by the death of Piero de' Medici in December 1469 and the rise to ascendancy of his gifted son Lorenzo, whose power was dramatically challenged by an assassination attempt in 1478 and confirmed in 1480 by constitutional changes intended to secure his regime. Exploiting the legacy of two generations of the family's dominance of the city, the young Lorenzo steadily accumulated the materials to fashion his own 'golden age'. He promoted artistic activities that would proclaim and recall his judgement and authority. Friends and rivals responded accordingly, to mark their allegiances or to establish their own territories.

It was an opportune moment for the city's creative workforce, and a peculiar one. A relatively open guild structure had always allowed for exchange between the arts, but the crossover was unusually conspicuous in this period. The highly active shops run by the Pollaiuolo brothers and Andrea del Verrocchio were headed by masters who had trained as goldsmiths and who produced, or supervised the production of, works in a variety of media. These artists were extraordinarily sensitive to the qualities of the different materials which they worked or which they imitated in their works. Not bounded by the traditions or usages of a single craft, they took flexible and exploratory approaches to compositional problems. They tested the boundaries between two and three dimensions. Their goldsmiths' training, and that of others (such as Ghirlandaio and probably also Botticelli), disciplined them in drawing, whose mastery was associated with that craft. Fluency with pen and stylus and an appreciation of linear grace and complexity are resulting features of their works. Love of ornamental intricacy is another. It is often coupled with a striking naturalism based on direct observation of the human figure and of natural phenomena. The artists of the 1470s took advantage of newly acquired knowledge and recent technology: such as the discovery, or rediscovery, of the physical remains and texts of antiquity, which were sources of forms and subjects, and the technologies of printing and copperplate engraving, which were sources of motifs and, as in the case of Antonio del Pollaiuolo, a means of self-publicity (cat. no. 54). These were forces that attracted and stimulated a generation of remarkable students, such as Sandro Botticelli and Leonardo da Vinci.

The National Gallery owns major paintings from this decade produced in its most important workshops, notably those of Andrea del Verrocchio, Antonio and Piero del Pollaiuolo and Sandro Botticelli. The generosity of other institutions allowed the exhibition's organisers to explore their significance by setting them in the wider context of the artistic production of the period. The assumption was that the close comparison of works in different media would provide an opportunity to examine their mutual influence and the processes behind their creation. It was also viewed as essential to challenge the traditional art-historical hierarchy of 'major' and 'minor' arts by displaying the widest possible range of objects, among them a hardstone vessel owned by Lorenzo de' Medici, a cameo and a ceramic vase from the Medici collection, and an embroidered panel from a set of ecclesiastical vestments (cat. nos. 5, 6, 7 and 48). All were highly prized in the Renaissance and their inclusion in this exhibition recognises their historical value as well as their immediate appeal.

Even this diverse grouping is far from complete. The vision of the 1470s available here is necessarily selective. For obvious reasons a number of key works could not be borrowed: they were too fragile, too big or simply immovable. In certain cases exhibitions of the recent past or near future determined the loans. Some limitations created opportunities. For example, a recent exhibition at the Metropolitan Museum of Art dedicated to Filippino Lippi as a draughtsman meant that many of his drawings were not available. Two little-known drawings, not displayed there, were chosen to be shown here. Perhaps less glamorous than others, they are important examples of the young artist's working process and repay careful attention (cat. nos. 73 and 74). Such cases could be multiplied, but it would never have been possible to present the entire decade in all of its richness. The purpose has been to represent some of its aspects in order to provide a tantalising glimpse of the era and a guide to a place and a time that reward visiting and revisiting.

In order to treat the issues raised by this intriguing decade, this volume has been divided into essays and entries – survey and scrutiny. Three introductory chapters give an overview of Florence in the 1470s. They define the city as a physical and political entity and discuss the principal patrons, projects and artistic personalities. These are followed by seven sections, which group the objects under subject headings. The first presents some of the protagonists of the decade – the artists and their clients – to demonstrate their concerns, their pleasures and the types of objects demanded and produced. Subsequently the shops of Andrea del Verrocchio and the Pollaiuolo brothers are considered. The three concluding sections are divided into thematic groups, which show the types of tasks which engaged artists at the time and how they demonstrated their skills and their imagination. The catalogue entries analyse the objects separately in the light of questions raised within each section. They are ordered according to the issues raised by their thematic grouping. They ask the reader and the viewer to see the works both in terms of their specific qualities and in terms of their meaning within the visual culture of the 1470s. They are not exhaustive accounts. Full details of provenance, condition and previous attributions are not given; the bibliography for each work is not comprehensive. The literature involved is large, complicated and full of controversy, and the references chosen here direct the reader as concisely as possible to further discussions of the objects concerned. Study is one feature of the period, and writing about the art of the time stems from the time itself. Even where not explicitly acknowledged, the authors are indebted both to the earlier and most recent literature and want to state that debt here, as well as their gratitude to the colleagues and the institutions who have so kindly helped them in preparing the exhibition and this book. Their hope is to transmit the fascination of the subject and to indicate the many joys that arise by encountering Florence in the 1470s.

Patricia Lee Rubin

1 Florence in the 1470s

Alison Wright

LOOKING ACROSS THE RIVER to the city of London, modern visitors may be disappointed to find the dome of St Paul's now overshadowed by a skyscraper. A visitor to Florence, on the other hand, finds the city still dominated by the cupola of the cathedral (fig. 1) and the crenellated tower of the Palazzo della Signoria, just as it was in the 1470s. Brunelleschi's dome and the bell tower of the town hall, marking the centres of civic worship and republican government, were designed to be the first features visible to anyone, Florentine or foreigner, approaching the city.

The fifteenth-century Florentine map-maker (probably Francesco di Lorenzo Rosselli) reflects this self-conscious pride in the city in his *View with the Chain* that was the largest and most systematic city view to be produced in the period (fig. 2).[1] Dating from the early 1480s, the view shows the city from the south-west in a bird's-eye perspective from outside the walls.[2] From this elevated position the city has a defensive and impressive presence and dominates the valley of the river Arno, the river that served Florence's cloth industry. The valley site also allowed the building of a third set of walls, erected at a time of decisive urban expansion from about 1290. The Rosselli view shows, nonetheless, how Florence's urban fabric (housing a population of about 70,000) was densely packed only within the area of the old twelfth-century walls. The larger mendicant churches and convents of the late thirteenth century are shown spreading into a green, quasi-suburban zone, which was not fully built up until the last century. In fact, the major monuments, especially the churches and convents distinguishing districts and parishes, read more clearly on the map than they would have even then to anyone observing the actual city, and the foreground hill does not exist in reality. But it is significant that the artist includes himself as a witness of the scene, seated on this fictional prominence, as though asserting both the truth of the image and its human perspective.

Apparently documentary in character, the woodcut reflects interest in the specific view that is a feature of Florentine paintings of the 1470s, and it reminds us that the city of Brunelleschi, who was renowned for his theoretical and practical advances in the depiction of rationalised space, was also becoming a centre of cartographic science.[3] The relationship of a Florentine to this cityscape was not just one of aesthetic admiration, still less of cold observation, but one of intense civic pride, and obligation – as part of its tax system, the Florentine state required every citizen to bequeath money for the upkeep of the city walls and for building work on the cathedral. The frequency with which the Florentine cityscape is depicted in paintings of the 1470s owes much to this pride in the city, both its fabric and its government.[4]

Fig. 1 View of Florence cathedral and bell tower, seen from the south.

The description of the city within a broad landscape panorama also reminds the viewer of Florence's position at the centre of its *contado* (the surrounding countryside) and, beyond this, a large territorial state which, by the 1470s, extended from the port of Pisa to the west, where the Arno reached the sea, to Montepulciano in the south. Within the state, local communes retained some areas of jurisdiction and privilege but were subject to Florentine-appointed judicial and military governors and to heavy Florentine taxation.

The visual depiction of Florence in the 1470s was paralleled by an equally strong documentary culture. Proud of their eloquence, Florentines were their own most vivid witnesses, constantly observing and writing about themselves and their city. In particular, the survival of so many family records, *ricordanze*, account books and tax records allows us to know more about Florence's social and economic history than that of any other Italian city of the period. In writing themselves into history Florentines were not only observing, they were selecting and constructing, since history was also a genre of praise. Most types of written records, whether in Latin or the vernacular, were the preserve of men such as notaries, speech makers and members of the patrician class. The voice of the Florentine citizen is thus thoroughly patriarchal and patriotic; a prime subject of humanist writing, for which Florence is renowned, was the fatherland or *patria* and the morality of civic life.

Fig. 2 Attributed to FRANCESCO DI LORENZO ROSSELLI, *View with the Chain*, early 1480s. Woodcut, 58.5 x 131.5 cm. Berlin, Kupferstichkabinett.

A female perspective is more difficult to retrieve. Systematic exclusion from public life has contributed to the obscurity surrounding women's lives, which is only now being illuminated by historians.[5]

A combination of documentary and mythologising history characterises one of the major sources for the Florence of the 1470s – the *Cronica* of Benedetto Dei and his related *Memorie* and *Ricordanze*.[6] His chronicle of 1472, with its obsessive passion for enumeration and lists, presents the political, economic and social fabric of 'Florentie bella', the walls and palaces, the workshops and squares of Florence, as well as its countryside or *contado*, as exemplary. Claiming to know the monetary value of everything and concerned with the activities of Florence's richest families, Dei is also interested in the city's intellectual investment in the Studio (university) and its promotion of Greek studies.[7] If patriotism can be seen as a type of social cement binding the citizens of Florence, Dei was especially implicated in this process as a political agent and servant of the dominant Medici family, as well as other prominent clans, and his glowingly positive picture of Florence tends to support the status quo at every point. A wide variety of sources point to a Florentine information network operating mainly by word of mouth, in the piazza, the public loggias or the workshop, as well as in civic and confraternal meeting places. In this milieu no strict divisions are drawn between public and private realms and in Dei's writings the successes of citizens and their families sit side by side with public events in the fields of trade and diplomacy. Characteristic above all of Dei's Florentine identity is a view of life as an interminable quest for honour (*onore*) for the self, the family and the city, an honour which both tempered and justified an equally strong urge towards profit or self-interest (*utile*).[8]

Dei's concern with the economic picture of the city is significant for a town which prospered on profits from international trade. This mercantile success was dependent on preserving good relations with trading partners and on open trade routes. Dei writes of the later 1460s as a period of peace and plenty: 'bread, wine and oil in very great abundance and peace. 84 parcels of silk came overland from Constantinople.'[9] The manufacture and sale of fine silk and wool cloth were the mainstay of the Florentine economy, facts worth bearing in mind when looking at the meticulous depiction of drapery of all kinds, and especially of luxury cloth, in Florentine art of the 1470s (fig. 51). Certainly Florentines were sensitive to the quality of cloths and their connotations for honour. Dei himself refers to the particularly fine clothing of Florentine aristocratic youth in this period, and he is able to value women's pearl necklaces with precision.[10] Sumptuousness of dress, like other forms of public display, was ostensibly subject to strict controls, but the frequency with which sumptuary laws were reiterated and extended is itself indicative of impotence before a rising tide of conspicuous consumption.[11] That patricians enjoyed surplus capital, the profit of successful trade and international banking, was nothing new in Florence. But the desire for individuals to spend their wealth in increasingly lavish and visible ways is a feature of this period. Florence enjoyed an unusually high degree of social mobility, and spending on the right goods and on semi-public spectacles (especially around the time of marriage) could help confirm a place in the ruling oligarchy.

Dei describes Florence as beautiful, prosperous and admired by other cities; indeed its beauty is seen as an index of prosperity and absolute worth. The view of Florence as a cosmopolitan city of great visual richness and variety is echoed by outside voices. An awestruck witness, Zacchariah of Pisa, reporting in 1460 on the crowds at the Marquis of Mantua's entry into Florence, claims that 'they appeared to me from every nation with a great variety of headdresses, some seemed like angels, some French, some Flemish, some English, some Arabs, Chaldeans.'[12] He continues, 'we found a living paradise full of those visible, palpable forms that speak and respond when others speak, and I wonder that people [in Florence] don't live only to look, smell and speak, without being subject to any other natural passion. I cannot believe that someone who tested this would not end up living just from the power of the visual.'[13]

If Florence could appear like a paradise, the appearance was deceptive for it was, to quote another contemporary, Agnolo Acciaiuoli, 'a paradise inhabited by devils'.[14] The anti-Medicean Acciaiuoli hit upon this telling image in a letter to the exiled Filippo Strozzi. Strozzi found himself at the rough end of the factional strife that was a structural feature of the Florentine republic, and one which constantly threatened political stability in the city. Filippo's family had remained under a cloud since his wealthy ancestor Palla Strozzi had been exiled in 1434 for opposition to Cosimo de' Medici. The Medici position as 'first among equals', secured with the defeat of the Albizzi faction, was based from the outset on the success of the family banking firm with its international interests and privileged position as bankers to the Pope. Filippo himself was eventually allowed to return to Florence in 1466, by which time the Medici family had long since secured control of the government.

The traditional foundation of that government was the Florentine trade guilds, since it was through membership of one of the 21 guilds (7 major and 14 minor) that citizens qualified for office-holding. But since the cloth-workers' uprising in 1378, the lion's share of representation had gone to major guildsmen whose interests as members of the patrician class tended to diminish the power of the guilds within government as a whole. Guild membership (many citizens belonged to more than one guild) nonetheless remained fundamental to a sense of civic belonging as well as a means of social influence.[15] The principal bodies in which those elected for governmental office could serve were the two councils (the Council of the Commune and the Council of the People) and, above these, the two advisory colleges and the Signoria. The Signoria was the highest office, constituted by eight Priors headed by the Standard Bearer of Justice (the Gonfaloniere di Giustizia). All government offices were held in strict rotation (the Priors serving for just two months) in order to avoid the possibility of individuals forming power bases, but, as developments in the 1470s demonstrate, the structures and safeguards of republicanism were not invulnerable and the election of a 'favourable' Signoria could be seen as a chance to forward the interests of particular families and groups. Florentine citizens would have been acutely aware of what was at stake in such political manoeuvring. As a republic – even if one governed by a limited number of the richest citizens (an oligarchy) – Florence was among a tiny minority of North Italian city states, including Siena, which had preserved their independence from lordship into the fifteenth century, partly by expanding their territory to absorb other towns. With the exception of the powerful republic of Venice, which was governed by a fixed number of noble families under the figurehead of the Doge, most Northern Italian states (the largest and most influential being Milan) had long been subject to the rule of a dominant family, with political and cultural life largely centring round a court. At the beginning of the century the greatest threat to the Florentine state came from Milan in the north; in the later 1470s the direction shifted with threats to border territory from the papal state and the kingdom of Naples.

The foundation of the Medici regime in Florence had begun with Cosimo de' Medici's return from exile in 1434. The family's position was consolidated through institutional reform that limited the power of the earlier councils, especially with the formation of a third smaller Council of One Hundred, inaugurated by Cosimo.[16] Cosimo's new palace in the via Larga (built between 1446 and about 1458), by far the largest private house in Florence at that date, was perhaps the most eloquent sign of Medici arrival (fig. 3), and during the frequent illnesses of Cosimo's son Piero the palace became, effectively, a second centre of government.[17] Lacking the traditional authority conferred by princely rule, the state, while fiercely proud of its credentials as a free city, was also eager for recognition from greater powers such as the papacy and the kings of France. Florence referred to its French allegiance by using the Angevin gold lily on a blue ground, so it must have seemed like a resounding endorsement of Medici legitimacy when in 1465 Louis XI granted the family the right to incorporate the French lily within their arms. But the consolidation of Medici power did not go unchallenged. One of the most severe tests of its supremacy after the death of Cosimo in 1464 took the form of a patrician plot, two years later, to unseat Piero. The plot ostensibly aimed to return the city to a purer form of republicanism, the so-called *florentina libertas* of the earlier decades of the century. But this threat to the regime was averted the same year with the support of Milan and of a pro-Medici Signoria that allowed

Medici authority to become hereditary. The 1470s, the first decade of Lorenzo de' Medici's primacy after his father's death in 1469, saw the reinforcement of Medici family domination in Florence, although this was to be gravely threatened in 1478.

Just a few months after Lorenzo's famous joust of 1469 in celebration of his majority, eyes turned to the Medici palace as the site of his wedding to Clarice Orsini, daughter of Jacopo Orsini, and niece of Cardinal Latino Orsini. The political implications of this marriage were considerable. By breaking with tradition to marry into a powerful Roman family capable of providing military support, the Medici both widened their power base outside the city and helped to maintain their position within it. Especially vulnerable immediately after his father's death, Lorenzo succeeded in winning the loyalty of central political figures. His importance for the city's political interests was strengthened in 1471 with the visit of Galeazzo Maria Sforza, Duke of Milan. In political terms the visit bolstered the policy of Milanese alliance, promoted since the 1450s by Cosimo and Piero de' Medici. On an earlier visit Galeazzo had been housed by the state, but he now stayed at the Medici palace, as though the guest of another prince, while his wife, Bona of Savoy, was placed with a cousin, Lorenzo di Pierfrancesco de' Medici. In such circumstances it is perhaps not surprising that the Duke tended to overestimate Lorenzo's autonomy. There is also some evidence of bad feeling within the city, both towards Galeazzo, who failed to turn up to a Pentecost play mounted for his entertainment at S. Spirito, and towards his court which did not observe Lent. Indeed the subsequent fire that gutted S. Spirito was seen as retribution for the Duke's ungodliness. But equally interesting from a social perspective is the claim by the sixteenth-century historian Niccolò

Fig. 3 Medici palace, Florence, seen from the south-east corner.

Machiavelli that the visit had a deleterious influence on Florentine youth, who tended to imitate the courtly (hence decadent) habits of Galeazzo's entourage. Already, it seems, the period of Lorenzo's coming of age was registering a cultural shift.

Lorenzo established himself simultaneously on several fronts. At an informal level, he was able to influence the pattern of alliances within the Florentine élite, making himself indispensable as a match-maker for patrician marriages. The flip side of this policy sometimes meant that those who could not be brought into the net of obligation, or who fell foul of his desires, were made to pay dearly.[18] From the 1470s he was sustained in his position by a loyal coterie of what the historian Francesco Guicciardini called 'new men', patricians such as Antonio Pucci, Girolamo Morelli, Giovanni Lanfredini, Bernardo del Nero and Bartolommeo Scala, whose families were not rooted in the old oligarchy.[19] Not surprisingly, given their privileged position, and a certain cultural expectation raised by Lorenzo's own interests, many of these 'new men' emerge as important artistic patrons in the period.

At an official level Lorenzo's most effective tool was the manipulation of government electoral reform. Innovations of the 1470s included restriction of the numbers of those who became eligible for government and of those who chose them, the *Accoppiatori*. The republican structure remained intact but, more than ever, power was concentrated in the hands of those who were loyal to the regime. More and more non-statutory or 'extraordinary' measures for decision-making were taken and in 1480 a new, smaller, Council of Seventy took over many of the legislative powers from the Signoria. The day-to-day running of the state was gradually put on a new footing with the creation of what amounted to a modern bureaucracy, while the funding of government was addressed through the control of public debt.[20] At the same time Lorenzo extended his influence over the church as can be seen by the appointment in 1474 of a non-Florentine absentee archbishop, Rinaldo Orsini, who was a member of his wife's family. Orsini joined a flood of pro-Medici appointees to powerful and lucrative benefices. Finally, Lorenzo's increasing control over the justice system allowed the exile of enemies of the Medici as enemies of the state.

The conflation of Medici and state interests was demonstrated early in Lorenzo's majority. A dispute over the contract for mining alum (a mineral used in the cloth industry), in which Medici interests were involved, fuelled factional division in the Florentine subject town of Volterra. Lorenzo took an immutable position in favour of mining concessionaries and this prompted the Volterrans to try to liberate themselves from Florentine domination, calling on support from Florence's traditional enemies, Venice and Siena. The revolt of Volterra in 1472 was swiftly put down by troops under the captaincy of Federigo da Montefeltro, Duke of Urbino, but the sacking of the city, despite the signing of a peace agreement, was seen as one of the bloodiest acts of the Medici regime.[21] Nevertheless, Federigo himself was considered a hero and officially honoured by Florence and his godson Lorenzo de' Medici. Among the gifts bestowed on him by the state were a silver helmet made by Antonio del Pollaiuolo with a crest of the warrior hero Hercules victorious over the griffin of Volterra.[22] In the same year the Florentine humanist Cristoforo Landino dedicated his book on the active and contemplative life, the *Disputationes Camaldulenses*, to the Duke who, like Lorenzo, ensured eloquent support by fostering humanist studies.

The more serious threat to Medici hegemony in Florence came from an alliance of forces within and without the city. The Pazzi conspiracy of 1478 was the most dramatic event of the 1470s, and the most far-reaching in its consequences. In this plot the simmering resentment against the regime came to the boil with an attempt to assassinate Lorenzo and his brother Giuliano. The conspirators, consisting of Lorenzo's Florentine opponents, were headed by Jacopo Pazzi, from a patrician family whose position was threatened by Medici dominance, and backed by Pope Sixtus IV. They struck during high mass in the choir of the Duomo on 26 April 1478 (see cat. no. 2).[23] Giuliano was killed and Lorenzo, who received a stab wound in the neck, survived only by escaping into the sacristy. Most of the conspirators were caught and condemned immediately, before being hanged from the windows of the Palazzo della Signoria and the Palazzo del Podestà (headquarters of the chief magistrate and head of policing, now the Bargello Museum).[24] Their fate was further broadcast by the commissioning of a series of defamatory portraits, made by Sandro Botticelli, depicting them as hanged.[25] The images, which were probably painted on the external wall of the Palazzo del Podestà, represented an extension of judicial tradition whereby criminals who had escaped justice could be punished in effigy.[26] These paintings on public view served as a form of visual condemnation intended to blacken the memory of the conspirators. They also provided a vivid warning to anyone disposed to threaten those in power, and it is significant that Botticelli's paintings were destroyed after the expulsion of the Medici in 1494. The late execution of Bernardo Bandini de' Baroncelli, captured in 1479 after being handed over by the Turks, is recorded in a gruesome pen sketch by

Fig. 4 LEONARDO DA VINCI, *Bernardo Bandini de' Baroncelli shown hanged*, 1479. Pen and ink on paper, 19.2 × 7.3 cm. Bayonne, Musée Bonnat, inv. 659.

Fig. 5 Façade of Santa Maria Novella, Florence.

Leonardo (fig. 4).[27] The drawing includes notes of documentary precision on the materials and colours of Baroncelli's exotic dress, raising the possibility that Leonardo was officially commissioned to make a defamatory painting.

At the time Leonardo's drawing was made, Florence was in a state of emergency. Sixtus IV's continuing hostility in the aftermath of the Pazzi conspiracy led to Florence's temporary excommunication, while the King of Naples tried to unseat Lorenzo by force. The so-called Pazzi War, waged to the south of Florence with the help of Siena, once again brought Medici interests into apparent conflict with those of the city as a whole – as Lorenzo was acutely aware. At the height of the crisis he travelled south to plead for peace with Naples, ostensibly putting himself and the regime at considerable risk. But he returned with a peace agreement, and his action was presented as a great diplomatic coup. Indeed it was this diplomatic success, together with his survival of the assassination attempt, that enabled Lorenzo to consolidate his position still further.

Openly ambitious both for himself and for Florence, Lorenzo was eager to be the match of other Italian powers. While Florence could not vie with the kingdom of Naples or the papal state in absolute terms, Lorenzo was a consummate power-broker and he also knew how to exploit Florence's intellectual and artistic achievements on an international stage. As we have seen, Florence's very beauty was an asset. In his miscellany book, or *Zibaldone*, Giovanni Rucellai thanks God for having made him born in Florence, 'which is reputed to be the most worthy and most beautiful *patria* not only of Christendom but of the whole world'.[28] This pride was to a large extent manifested in building, both for public purposes and by wealthy private families (see Chapter 2). Often the two spheres overlapped: while lay boards had long been responsible for ecclesiastical buildings, it is a feature of this period that responsibility for public works and the embellishment of public spaces was increasingly falling into the hands of individuals or families rather than being sponsored by civic bodies. Significantly, the façade of S. Maria Novella (fig. 5), designed by Leon Battista Alberti, not only honours the city but also commemorates and honours its sponsor, Giovanni Rucellai, whose name is written into the design below the pediment.

A view of Florence by Pietro del Massaio, illustrating a contemporary manuscript of Ptolemy's *Geographia*, clearly shows which buildings were considered significant in the 1470s (fig. 6).[29] At the very centre is the geometrical block of the Baptistery, the building that Dei referred to, inaccurately, as the 'big cube'.[30] Believed at the time to have been founded in antiquity as a Roman temple of Mars, the Baptistery was even more important for the city's sense of history and its destiny than the cathedral, shown to the left. Its civic importance was founded on its patron, Saint John the Baptist, who was also patron of the whole city. Placed on the same axis (below the Baptistery on the map) is the recently built family palace of the Medici, and to the south (above) the palace-like guild oratory of Orsanmichele stands as testimony to the power of the trade corporations.

A feature of Florence's urban plan is the separation of governmental and religious centres, with the cathedral physically distant from the town hall. Following the line upwards from Orsanmichele one reaches the centre of civic government (see fig. 6). This developed together with a piazza which is purposefully dominated by the Palazzo della Signoria (later called the Palazzo Vecchio; fig. 7), built from 1299, and the giant Loggia of the Priors (Loggia dei

Lanzi) begun in 1380. On the other side of the town hall from the loggia stands the home of the chief merchant tribunal, the Mercanzia, another fourteenth-century building, in a juxtaposition that underlines the relationship between the government and the guilds (fig. 7). The size and accessibility of the civic and political space of the Piazza della Signoria must have served to emphasise the nature of Florentine government, with its openness to the citizens themselves, but it also aimed to instil respect for the power and authority of the state.

The Palazzo della Signoria is a somewhat aggressive building with a fortified appearance, but in the 1470s a long-planned refurbishment was taking place to provide larger and more sumptuous rooms for the various councils, whose functions and remit were changing.[31] At the same time many new goldsmiths' works are recorded as having been

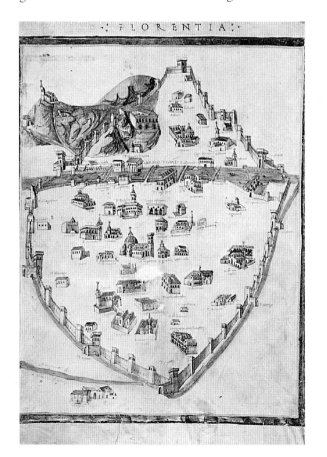

commissioned by the government, including, in 1473, an ornate silver bowl made by Antonio del Pollaiuolo.[32] A surviving piece is Verrocchio's bronze candelabrum for the Sala dell' Udienza, with its inscription recording the period of office of the Priors who commissioned it in 1468 (cat. no. 12).[33] The building work, which gave a new, highly decorative, look to the interior, was funded from a massive fine levied on a Jewish banker and from taxes on foreign traders. Along with the first-floor council room, the major changes of the 1470s occurred on the second floor where a new dividing wall was installed and the adjacent halls, the Sala dell' Udienza and the Sala dei Gigli, were refurbished. The Signoria gave audience three times a week in the first of these two rooms, which also served for meetings of advisory committees, while the two Colleges of the Signoria met in the Sala dei Gigli, which was also used as the

Fig. 6 PIETRO DEL MASSAIO, *Ptolemy 'Geografia': map of Florence*, 1469. Manuscript illustration, 52 x 41.5 cm. Rome, Biblioteca Apostolica Vaticana, Cod. Vat. Lat. n. 5699.

Fig. 7 Piazza della Signoria, Florence, showing from left the palace of the Mercanzia, the Palazzo della Signoria and the Loggia dei Lanzi.

Signoria's dining room.[34] The dominant feature of the restored rooms was their spectacular carved wood ceilings, installed in 1475, which are mentioned admiringly in Dei's *Ricordanze*.[35] Designed and executed by Giuliano da Maiano and, possibly, his brother Benedetto, the ceilings are made up of geometrical coffering freely modelled after the patterns of ancient Roman vaults (fig. 8). The upper walls are ringed by broad friezes bearing arms and emblems of the state, including the Florentine lion or Marzocco, and distinguished by their deep relief carving and the most expensive colours available — gold and blue.[36] Sculpted marble surrounds the door that connects the two chambers (fig. 9). The antique, or *all'antica*, style decoration, here enriched with mythological motifs, is the work of Benedetto da Maiano. On the side looking into the Sala dei Gigli a free-standing sculpture of an elegant young Saint John the Baptist takes a protective position. Beneath him, the Florentine theme is extended in the inlaid design of the wooden doors themselves where the laurel-crowned figures of the medieval poets Dante and Petrarch represent the apogee of Florentine intellectual and creative ability.[37] The manufacture of these doors marks the tribute of Florence's latterday creative talents, involving both the specialist intarsia skills of the woodworkers Giuliano da Maiano and Francione and figure designs attributed to Botticelli and the young Filippino Lippi, then in Botticelli's workshop.[38] On the other side of the door, facing into the Sala dell'Udienza, a female personification of Justice by Benedetto da Maiano sits enthroned.

The primacy of justice as a political virtue directed towards the common good is an old theme that is rehearsed with renewed vigour in the context of the individual's personal responsibility in Matteo Palmieri's book *On Civil Life (Vita Civile)*.[39] For

Fig. 8 Workshop of GIULIANO AND BENEDETTO DA MAIANO, Ceiling of the Sala dei Gigli, installed 1475. Painted and gilt wood. Florence, Palazzo della Signoria.

Fig. 9 BENEDETTO AND GIULIANO DA MAIANO, Doorway of the Sala dei Gigli, after 1476. Marble surround, inlaid wood. Florence, Palazzo della Signoria.

Palmieri, no earthly action is more pleasing to God than just rule, and the just governors of cities and 'conservatori della patria' are guaranteed a place in heaven.[40] The sculpted figure of Justice presiding in the Sala dell'Udienza was the most direct means by which this theme was invoked in contemporary governmental decoration. But it had a wider application. From 1469, the merchants' tribunal or Mercanzia, run by the five major mercantile guilds, chose another variation on the exemplary theme to decorate the audience hall of their palace in the Piazza della Signoria.[41] At a time when Lorenzo de' Medici's plans for judicial reform were beginning to affect their independence as a court they chose Piero del Pollaiuolo and Sandro Botticelli to paint the images of the three Theological and four Cardinal Virtues to preside over the bench of the seven magistrates (figs. 10, 11 and 30). These female personifications were intended to act as an inspiration to the judges themselves and promote confidence in those subject to their judgement.

The depiction of the Virtues at the Mercanzia is a reminder of the deep interpenetration of the religious and the civic in the Tuscan city states, where religious values lent moral weight to the government of the guilds. The way that Christian authority underpinned civic authority is especially apparent in Florence at the wealthy guild church of Orsanmichele where a one-time grain store had become the centre of a cult of the Virgin Mary (fig. 12). Orsanmichele became a locus of political manoeuvring in the 1460s. The Parte Guelfa (Guelph Party), the traditional champion of republican liberty against imperial authority, had been losing influence and was forced to sell its niche on the main façade of the church to the Mercanzia. Donatello's bronze sculpture of the party's patron saint, Louis of Toulouse, made in the early 1420s was

subsequently removed and the Mercanzia commissioned Andrea del Verrocchio to make an ambitious double sculpture of Christ and Saint Thomas, also in bronze, to substitute for it in Donatello's beautiful *all'antica* niche (fig. 29). Documents tell us that Verrocchio had prepared the figure of Christ for casting by 1470, while the Saint Thomas was cast in 1479. The project was completed only in 1483 and the sculpted group, whose subject was chosen to represent justice, was installed in time for the feast of Saint John the Baptist, a move that highlighted the civic significance of the project.[42]

On a city-wide scale the indivisibility of the civic and the religious was embodied in the way Florence referred to its administrative districts. Florence was divided into Quarters, *quartieri*, each named after the major church that dominated the area – S. Giovanni (the Baptistery), S. Maria Novella, S. Croce and S. Spirito (the Oltrarno); these districts were then subdivided into 'standards' or Gonfaloni, making a total of sixteen. Thus the city's sacred geography, identified by the great mendicant and conventual basilicas – the Dominicans at S. Maria Novella, the Franciscans at S. Croce, the Augustinians of S. Spirito – overlaid administrative divisions. While the cathedral itself did not mark a district, it was both a major religious site and a civic site on an immense scale, and as such was administered by the most powerful guild, the Arte della Lana or Wool Guild. In the decade of the 1470s the most important symbolic achievement at the Duomo was the completion of Brunelleschi's cupola with a massive gilded copper ball made by Verrocchio (fig. 13). Seen as a marvel of ingenuity and a literally crowning achievement to the engineering feat of Brunelleschi's dome, the installation in May 1471 must have produced a remarkable effect as the ball was hoisted into place to the singing of the *Te Deum*.[43]

Fig. 10 PIERO DEL POLLAIUOLO, *Faith*, 1470. Panel, 157 × 77 cm.
Florence, Galleria degli Uffizi.

Fig. 11 PIERO DEL POLLAIUOLO, *Prudence*, 1470. Panel, 157 × 77 cm.
Florence, Galleria degli Uffizi.

Verrocchio's success at the Duomo seems also to have won him a commission for sculptures to surround a new choir screen directly beneath the cupola, though this project never got underway.[44] Another cathedral project that was less than entirely successful was the revived attempt to make the Duomo a Florentine pantheon of civic heroes to include those in the artistic realm. In the late 1440s Brunelleschi had been given a monument, with a sculpted portrait and inscription, in the nave. Lorenzo de' Medici also tried to secure the body of Fra Filippo Lippi, who had died in Spoleto in 1469, for the extraordinary privilege of burial in the Duomo. But the Spoletans refused to surrender him and eventually Lorenzo paid for a wall monument designed by the painter's son, Filippino Lippi, in the cathedral of Spoleto.

In the competition for glory between the Florentine Duomo and the adjacent Baptistery, the latter, administered by the Calimala (the international merchants' guild), was in many ways triumphant in this decade. The production of the bronze doors for this site had been the most expensive and, next to the cupola, the most prestigious artistic undertaking in Florence since the beginning of the fifteenth century. During the completion of the second set of doors Lorenzo and Vittorio Ghiberti's shop was a training ground for artists reaching full maturity in the 1470s, including, probably, Antonio del Pollaiuolo. Pollaiuolo and Verrocchio were involved in the many on-going projects to honour Saint John the Baptist, such as the silver altar and its associated treasure (figs. 31, 32 and cat no. 48).

Another major cult site attracting costly, large-scale projects in the 1470s was the Servite church of SS. Annunziata (marked as 'Servi' to the bottom left on the Ptolemy map, fig. 6). Here the cult was attached to a miraculous image of the Virgin considered so powerful that it received votive offerings from the great and the good from all over Italy, as well as massive popular devotion. The Marquis of Mantua, Ludovico Gonzaga, funded the building of a large domed rotunda at the east end of the church, a building campaign that was modified by Alberti and completed in the 1470s.[45] The church also benefited from rich endowments for family chapels and its building committee (the *operai*) included members of the political élite. Piero de' Medici, a member of the committee, had earlier paid for a vastly expensive marble tabernacle to house the miraculous painting of the *Annunciation* at the west end of the church and built a private chapel so close to it as to monopolise the image from one direction. The Medici presence loomed large by the late 1470s for it was in SS. Annunziata, and in two other churches with miracle-working images, that Lorenzo de' Medici chose to

Fig. 12 Orsanmichele, Florence, seen from the north-east corner.

place wax effigies of himself as thank offerings to the Virgin after his deliverance from the Pazzi conspiracy. This kind of individual and familial representation would be emulated by the Pucci in the building of their private oratory next to the atrium of the church. All this patronal activity was carefully controlled by the Servite friars themselves, who negotiated and administered the various endowments to their own advantage. At the same time they began to promote the founding father of their order through the fresco cycle of the life of San Filippo Benizzi begun by Cosimo Rosselli and later extended by Andrea del Sarto in the new atrium.

The church of SS. Annunziata, as a major civic attraction, formed the focus of one of the city's main processional routes. The Signoria processed there on the Feast of the Annunciation (25 March) to mark the beginning of the Florentine year. It is also recorded

that Galeazzo Maria Sforza and his wife Bona of Savoy rode from the Palazzo della Signoria to SS. Annunziata to make a votive offering shortly after their arrival in Florence in 1471. Such ritual routes, which were regularly retraced on feast days, effectively mapped the relation between the city's political and sacred geography.[46] The most important feast, and the principal procession, of the many scores that marked the Florentine calendar, was that of the city's patron Saint John the Baptist, which, since 1454, lasted from 21 to 24 June.[47] On the 21st the major workshops of the city were decked with expensive cloths and displays of their most precious goods. The first procession took place on the 22nd and included the members of the Signoria, high officials, clergy carrying precious relics from their churches, and confraternities. At a later stage the guilds, representatives of the rural parishes and feudal lords trod the same route, showing both their devotion and their allegiance to the commune by making offerings at the Baptistery. The feast day on the 24th concluded with a horse race, the *palio*. Benedetto Dei, who was an organiser of the San Giovanni festival and attuned to the political and diplomatic importance of such public spectacles, refers to the event in his *Ricordanze*. A formal description in a Latin letter of 1475 provides a more explicit account.[48] It describes in detail the miraculous *edifizi* or floats that took part in the procession. The floats, dominated by religious *tableaux* often devised by ingenious designers, lasted no longer than the feast, but they would have had a vivid impact on public memory. They may have resembled the ornamented carts that are featured in illustrated manuscripts of Petrarch's *Triumphs*, which seem to be based on civic processional decoration (cat. no. 3).[49] Such images also appear to reflect a section of the Florentine citizenry, who were required to wear their

Fig. 13 Cathedral lantern, Florence.

27

best attire for the feast. Dei, in fact, perceives the gatherings of young women and young men in their sumptuous and quantifiably costly clothes as part of the collective ornament of the city. Other fancy-dress elements, the fauns and centaurs described by Cennini as roaming the streets of Florence, indicate how the feast could erupt in fantastic secular manifestations that recall the subject matter of popular prints (cat. no. 67).[50]

The civic function of another major festival, the feast of the Epiphany, can be understood in similar terms. The festive procession had, until the late 1460s, been distinguished by a carefully structured re-enactment of the journey of the Magi, organised by the Confraternity of the Magi, which culminated at their fraternal headquarters in the Observant Dominican convent of San Marco, as though at the site of the Nativity. In San Marco, Cosimo de' Medici had his own cell, decorated with a fresco of the Adoration of the Magi, but the importance of the imagery to the Medici is most famously registered in the decoration of the Medici palace chapel where portraits of the family and their allies are placed in the retinue of the philosopher kings. The continued popularity of the theme of the Adoration of the Magi in 1470s Florence is recorded in the work of Botticelli, Antonio del Pollaiuolo, Leonardo and Filippino Lippi, and its dynastic significance was clear for Lorenzo de' Medici himself. Lorenzo was baptised on the feast of the Epiphany 1449. He was to become a leading light in the Confraternity of the Magi, a position that allowed him to cultivate political and social bonds in the flattering light of a young Magus, even though he seems to have suppressed the confraternity's festive activities.[51]

The Magi confraternity was a rather exclusive group, but membership of confraternities – lay brotherhoods dedicated to religious and charitable practices – often crossed social boundaries. One of the new Quattrocento confraternities, that of Saint Paul, was regularly attended not only by Lorenzo de' Medici but also by artists such as Domenico Ghirlandaio (in the 1470s) and Filippino Lippi.[52] Confraternities had a high profile at the major feasts such as the Annunciation and Ascension when they staged sacred plays, or *sacre rappresentazioni*, in the churches of S. Felice in Piazza and the Carmine. The mounting of performances of this type also served the religious and social education provided by some boys' confraternities. The personal discipline and the ability in the civic art of rhetoric fostered by these activities spawned new, specially scripted, moral plays on biblical themes, such as the incredibly popular *Abraham and Isaac*, performed predominantly, but not exclusively, by young men and boys.[53] The 1470s also saw the development of purely secular theatre. For the carnival of 1476 Florence became the stage for the first performances of a revived Latin comedy, Terence's *Andria*, though the pagan character of the text was criticised as inappropriate fare for the boys who performed it.[54]

Public spectacle of a different kind was provided by the aristocratic youth of Florence. For wealthy young men in their early twenties, equestrian games such as jousts (*giostre*), tournaments (*tornei*) and other armed displays (*armeggiarie*) served functions more symbolic than practical. Florence had no standing army and its republican values were incompatible with a strictly knightly ethos. Instead, possession of thoroughbred horses and participation in a joust were indicators of high social standing and a reflection of the youthful allegiances between members of the patriciate in their *brigate* or gangs. Jousts and tournaments such as that organised by the Guelph

Party for carnival often took place at civic feasts as well as on occasions of family celebration.[55] The most famous jousts were those sponsored and 'won' by the Medici, namely that of Lorenzo in 1469 and that of his brother Giuliano in 1475. The poetic praise of the Medici *giostre* by contemporary writers has, as it was intended, given these events added lustre, not to mention a sophisticated interpretative dimension that was probably not obvious to contemporary spectators. Luigi Pulci's thoroughly Medicean account of the 1469 joust gives a detailed picture of the social brilliance of the event as well as of its courtly apparatus. This included the presentation to Lorenzo, as victor, of a silver helmet crowned with a figure of Mars, and the poetic interweaving of Lorenzo's chivalric love for the chaste Lucrezia Donati, mythologised as a nymph. But even before the jousting – a strictly secondary activity – started, the display of splendid and extravagant clothes, of fabulous jewelled caparisons, and of heraldry, mottoes and personal devices, all forged an aristocratic distinction that seemed to reinforce the oligarchy's, and specifically Lorenzo's, right to rule.[56] The same mottoes and emblems continue to appear in Laurentian manuscripts (cat. no. 4) even when his father's death, soon after the joust, forced Lorenzo to put aside the image of gilded youth in favour of the sober, full-length gown worn by the responsible citizen and servant of the republic. Lorenzo's younger brother Giuliano then became his brilliant *alter ego*. It is this chivalric and glamorous Giuliano who gazes serenely beyond us in the portrait bust by Verrocchio (cat. no. 17).

Giuliano's death in the Pazzi conspiracy in 1478 and the expense and danger of the subsequent war ushered in a period of austerity in public spectacles. Horse races continued but major jousts and lavish feast-day plays virtually disappeared from the social calendar until the 1490s.[57] In 1491 Lorenzo sponsored a politically confident and learnedly classicising 'Triumph of Paulus Aemilius', based on the honours awarded to the second-century Roman hero, quite unlike the traditional *feste*. But such public restrictions did not hamper the imaginative development of the new forms of poetic imagery in private display (for example cat. no. 86). The myth of a Florentine, and specifically a Laurentian, golden age – powerfully and purposefully initiated in the 1470s by Lorenzo himself despite the often grim political and social realities of the period – was given tangible form by artists and writers such as Botticelli and Poliziano, and still colours our vision of the city.

NOTES CHAPTER 1

1 G. Fanelli, *Le città nella storia d'Italia*, Firenze, Bari 1980, pp. 77–82, 267–8. M. Chiarini and A. Marabottini, eds., *Firenze e la sua immagine. Cinque secoli di vedutismo*, exh. cat., Forte di Belvedere, Florence 1994, cat. no. 7, p. 69. The woodcut was made after Rosselli's now incomplete multi-sheet engraving.

2 A.M. Hind, *Early Italian Engraving*, vol. 1, London 1938, pp. 145–6 and 292.

3 K. Lippincott, 'The Art of Cartography in Fifteenth-Century Florence', in M. Mallett and N. Mann, eds., *Lorenzo the Magnificent. Culture and Politics*, London 1996, pp. 131–49.

4 The manipulation of the image of the city through the identification of Florence with ancient Rome was one way that the ideological claim of Florence as a New Rome could be invoked. For the increasing practice of comparison with the structure and constitutions of ancient cities brought about by humanist studies see A. Brown, 'City and Citizen: Changing Perceptions in the Fifteenth and Sixteenth Centuries', in A. Molho et al., eds., *City-states in Classical Antiquity and Medieval Italy. Athens and Rome, Florence and Venice*, Stuttgart 1991, pp. 93–111; reprinted in A. Brown, *The Medici in Florence. The Exercise and Language of Power*, Florence and Perth 1992, pp. 281–303.

5 See for example, C. Klapisch-Zuber, *Women, Family and Ritual in Renaissance Italy*, Chicago 1985; E. Rosenthal, 'The Position of Women in Renaissance Florence: neither autonomy nor subjection', in P. Denley and C. Elam, eds., *Florence and Italy: Renaissance Studies in Honor of Nicolai Rubinstein*, London 1988, pp. 369–81; S.K. Cohn Jr, 'Donne in piazza donne in tribunale a Firenze nel Rinascimento', *Studi storici*, no. 3, 22, 1981, pp. 515–33; A. Groppi, ed., *Il lavoro delle donne*, Rome and Bari 1996; T. Dean and K.J.P. Lowe, eds., *Marriage in Italy 1300–1650*, Cambridge 1998.

6 Benedetto Dei, *La Cronica*, ed. R. Barducci, Florence 1984 is based on the manuscript in the Archivio di Stato, Florence, Manoscritti, n.119; a variant manuscript and a set of *Memorie* (Florence, Biblioteca Riccardiana, Codice Riccardiano 1853) are published in G.C. Romby, *Descrizioni e rappresentazioni della città di Firenze nel XV secolo con una trascrizione inedita dei manoscritti di Benedetto Dei e un indice ragionato dei manoscritti utili per la storia di Firenze*, Florence 1976, pp. 56–73. The unpublished *Ricordanze* are in Florence, Biblioteca Riccardiana, MSS Moreni 103.

7 Dei, *La Cronica*, ed. Barducci 1984, p. 79 (f. 30r).

8 A discussion of the interrelation of these two principles in Florentine life appears in M.M. Bullard, 'In pursuit of *honore et utile*, Lorenzo de' Medici and Rome', in G.C. Garfagnini, ed., *Lorenzo il Magnifico e il suo mondo*, Florence 1994, pp. 123–42, esp. p. 124.

9 'El pane, el vino e l'olio in grandissima abbondanza e pace. Vene per terra 84 fardilli di seta di Costantinopoli', Dei, *Ricordanze*, f. 1 v.

10 Dei, *Ricordanze*, f. 20v.

11 C. Kovesi Killerby, 'Practical problems in the enforcement of Italian sumptuary law 1200–1500', in T. Dean and K.J.P. Lowe, eds., *Crime, Society and the Law in Renaissance Italy*, Cambridge 1994, pp. 99–120.

12 'poy le mi parevano d'ogni natione a tanta varietà di aconciature di testa, quale parevano angioli, quale francese, quale fiaminghe, quale inglese e quale inde, arabe e caldee, che so io', letter of 9 May 1460 republished by B.L. Brown in 'L"Entrata" fiorentina di Ludovico Gonzaga', *Rivista d'Arte*, anno XLII, 4th series, 7, 1991, p. 216.

13 'Poy trovammo veramente il paradiso, io dico el vivo e vero, pieno di quelle visibile e palpabile forme e che parlano e respondono, quando altri parla, e maravigliòme assay come che vi sta non vive solamente di veddere, odire e parlare senza essere subiecto ad alcun'altra passione naturale e non posso credere che chi ne facesse prova che non gli venisse ad effetto che si viverebbe solo dela virtù visiva', ibid., pp. 216–17.

14 F.W. Kent, 'Palaces, Politics and Society in Fifteenth-Century Florence', *I Tatti Studies*, vol. 2, 1987, p. 63 and note 109.

15 J. Najemy, *Corporatism and Consensus in Florentine Electoral Politics, 1280–1400*, Chapel Hill 1982, pp. 10–11, and pp. 280–2; N. Rubinstein, *The Government of Florence under the Medici (1434–1494)*, Oxford 1966, pp. 62–5. An attempt to limit the number of minor guilds eligible for representation failed in the 1470s (verbal communication of Prof. Alison Brown).

16 Rubinstein 1966, pp. 112–15.

17 A. Brown, 'Piero's Infirmity and Political Power', in A. Beyer and B. Boucher, eds., *Piero de' Medici 'il Gottoso' (1416–1469). Kunst im Dienste der Mediceer. Art in the Service of the Medici*, Berlin 1993, pp. 9–19.

18 Lorenzo's young cousins, who might have been a potential threat, claimed heavy financial loss at his hands when their inheritance was withheld to fund the Pazzi war. For opposition to Lorenzo see A. Brown, 'Lorenzo and Public Opinion in Florence. The Problem of Opposition', in Garfagnini 1994, pp. 61–85. For a view of Florence in 1470s contrasting political discord there with the 'felice patria' of Naples see the letters of Francesco Bandini published in P.O. Kristeller, *Studies in Renaissance Thought and Letters*, Rome 1956, pp. 406–10.

19 F. Guicciardini, *Storie fiorentine dal 1378 al 1509*, vol. 1, chapter 9, ed. R. Palmarocchi, Bari 1931, pp. 78–9.

20 For these developments see L.F. Marks, 'The Financial Oligarchy in Florence under Lorenzo', E.F. Jacobs, ed., *Italian Renaissance Studies*, London 1960, pp. 123–47.

21 The submission of Volterra is described in some detail as a heroic event by Dei in his *Cronica* (pp. 74–7, f. 27v–28v). Luca Landucci on the other hand registered sympathy with the Volterrans for the sack, see *A Florentine Diary*, trans. A. de Rosen Jervis, London 1927, p.11.

22 Reference to the commission to Pollaiuolo appears in Archivio di Stato, Florence, Dieci di Balìa, 'Libro per l'impresa di Volterra', 1472, f. 37, published by F. Baldinucci, *Notizie degli Professori del Disegno*, Florence 1681–6, vol. 1, p. 544, and M. Cruttwell, *Antonio Pollaiuolo*, London and New York 1907, p. 273. Further documents for the gifts to the Duke of Urbino have been published by D. Carl, 'Addenda zu Antonio Pollaiuolo und seiner Werkstatt', *Mitteilungen des Kunsthistorischen Institutes in Florenz*, 27, 1983, pp. 285–301, esp. p. 296 docs. III and IV.

23 A detailed description of the action and its protagonists appears in Landucci's *Diary*, trans. de Rosen Jervis 1927, pp. 15–17, and p. 28 for Baroncelli.

24 Including Jacopo di Poggio Bracciolini, Francesco Salviati, Bishop of Pisa, Jacopo Salviati, Jacopo, Renato and Franceschino de' Pazzi and about twenty others.

25 On 21 July 1478 the Otto di Guardia paid Botticelli 40 florins for painting the Pazzi conspirators. See S.Y. Edgerton, *Pictures and Punishment. Art and Criminal Prosecution during the Florentine Renaissance*, Ithaca 1985, pp. 104–9, and M.A. Morelli Timpanaro, R. Manno Tolu, P. Viti, eds., *Consorterie politiche e mutamenti istituzionali in età laurenziana*, exh. cat., Archivio di Stato, Florence 1992, cat. no. 6.7, pp. 159–61, for accounts of what was probably depicted.

26 The site is mentioned by an early source, known as the Anonimo Gaddiano, in *Notizie di Pittori, Scultori ed Architetti* (Biblioteca Nazionale, Firenze, Magl. XVII, f. 17), published by C. Frey, *Il Codice Magliabecchiano*, Berlin 1892, p.105. For the tradition of defamatory portraiture see G. Ortalli, '...pingatur in palatio...' La pittura infamante nei secoli XIII–XVI, Rome 1979, and Edgerton 1985.

27 Morelli et al., 1992, cat. no. 6.9, p. 161.

28 'Io ringrazio...d'avermi facto nascere della ciptà di Firenze, la quale è riputata la più degna e la più bella patria che abbi non tanto il Cristianesimo ma tutto l'universo mondo', *Giovanni Rucellai ed il suo Zibaldone*, vol. 1, ed. A. Perosa, London 1960, p. 117.

29 Three versions of this manuscript survive: Paris, Bibliothèque Nationale, Ms. Lat. 14802 dated *c.*1472–8 for Alfonso, Duke of Calabria, which includes the Medici sculpture garden, for Niccolò Perotti dated 1469 (Biblioteca Vaticana, Vat. Lat. 5699), and for the Duke of Urbino dated 1472/3 (Biblioteca Vaticana, Urb. Lat. 277, f. 130v).

30 The 'gran cuba', Dei, *La Cronica*, ed. Barducci 1984, p. 84 (f. 33r).

31 For the most thorough account of the governmental councils, the building and decorative work of the 1470s and those responsible for it see N. Rubinstein, *The Palazzo Vecchio 1298–1532. Government, Architecture and Imagery in the Civic Palace of the Florentine Republic*, Oxford 1995, pp. 36–7 and 58–61.

32 This is probably the same bowl described as decorated with a garland of putti ('con grillanda di bambocci') in an inventory of 1473, published by Carl 1983 (doc. I [H], p. 291), who also details other goldsmiths' pieces commissioned by the government from Pollaiuolo and his partner Attaviano di Antonio di Duccio.

33 Rubinstein 1995, pp. 58–9, 106; A. Butterfield, *The Sculptures of Andrea del Verrocchio*, New Haven and London 1997, pp. 81–2 and 212–13.

34 Rubinstein 1995, pp. 102–3 and 111–12.

35 Dei, *Ricordanze*, f. 20r.

36 For the ceilings and friezes see A. Cecchi, 'Giuliano e Benedetto da Maiano ai servigi della Signoria fiorentina', in D. Lamberini, M. Lotti and R. Lunardi, eds., *Giuliano e la bottega dei da Maiano, Atti del convegno internazionale di studi, Fiesole, 1991*, Florence 1994, pp. 146–52.

37 A similar combination of the religious protector and the secular exemplar would be extended on the opposite wall of the Sala dei Gigli with the addition of murals painted by Domenico Ghirlandaio in 1482. These depicted Saint Zenobius with his deacons flanked by a cycle of six Famous Men of the Roman republic.

38 A drawing in the Musée des Beaux-Arts, Besançon, has been identified as Filippino Lippi's early drawing for the figure of Petrarch for the door of the Sala dei Gigli, see Cecchi 1994, p. 153.

39 Matteo Palmieri, *Vita civile*, ed. G. Belloni, Florence 1982, see especially Book 3 dedicated to justice, pp. 103–48.

40 Ibid., pp. 54–5 (f. 22v).

41 For the Mercanzia under Lorenzo de' Medici's regime see A. Astorri, 'Note sulla Mercanzia fiorentina sotto Lorenzo dei Medici. Aspetti istituzionali e politici', *Archivio storico italiano*, 150, 1992, pp. 965–93.

42 Butterfield 1997, pp. 60–1, and A. Butterfield, 'Verrocchio's Christ and Saint Thomas: chronology, iconography and political context', *Burlington Magazine*, 134, 1992, pp. 225–33. See further, below pp.50–2.

43 The original ball, several times struck by lightning, fell down in 1600 and was replaced by a larger one in 1602.

44 Butterfield 1997, p. 5 and note 25; see also below p.53.

45 B.L. Brown, 'The Patronage and Building History of the Tribuna of SS. Annunziata in Florence: a reappraisal in light of new documentation', *Mitteilungen des Kunsthistorischen Institutes in Florenz*, 25, 1981, pp. 59–142.

46 The festive route via SS. Annunziata, used by visitors to the Medici palace, extended to San Marco before returning south down the via Larga, see C. Elam, 'Il Palazzo nel contesto della città: strategie urbanistiche dei Medici nel gonfalone del Leon d'Oro, 1415–1530', in G. Cherubini and G. Fanelli, eds., *Il Palazzo Medici Riccardi di Firenze*, Florence 1990, pp. 44–57.

47 A recent publication that discusses the major public spectacles of the 1470s is P. Ventrone, ed., *'Le tems revient' – 'l tempo si rinuova'. Feste e spettacoli nella Firenze di Lorenzo il Magnifico*, exh. cat., Palazzo Medici Riccardi, Florence 1992. The changes to the ritual that took place in 1454 were recorded by Matteo Palmieri, see C. Guasti, *Le Feste di S. Giovanni Batista in Firenze descritte in prosa e in rima da contemperanei*, Florence 1884, pp. 20–3.

48 G. Mancini, 'Il bel S. Giovanni e le feste patronali di Firenze descritte nel 1475 da Piero Cennini', *Rivista d'Arte*, 1st series, 6, 1909, pp. 185–227.

49 A detailed description of a 1459 cart with the *Triumph of Love* in the *Terze rime in lode di Cosimo de' Medici* is provided in Ventrone 1992, pp. 108–9.

50 Mancini 1909, p. 224.

51 R. Hatfield, 'The Compagnia dei Magi', *Journal of the Warburg and Courtauld Institutes*, 33, 1970, pp. 107–61; N. Newbigin, 'Piety and Politics in the *Feste* of Lorenzo's Florence', in Garfagnini 1994, pp. 27–8. See also R. Trexler, 'Lorenzo de' Medici and Savonarola, Martyrs for Florence', *Renaissance Quarterly*, 31, 1978, pp. 292–308.

52 For Ghirlandaio's membership of the Compagnia in 1470 see M. Levi d'Ancona, *Miniatura e miniatori a Firenze dal XIV al XVI secolo*, Florence 1962, p. 90, and J. Cadogan, 'Reconsidering Some Aspects of Ghirlandaio's Drawings', *Art Bulletin*, 65, 1983, p. 277, note 23.

53 N. Newbigin, 'Politics in the *Sacre rappresentazioni* of Lorenzo's Florence', in Mallett and Mann eds., London 1996, pp. 117–30. Newbigin makes clear that these plays were not the exclusive preserve of boys' confraternities.

54 P. Ventrone, 'Lorenzo's *politica festiva*' in Mallett and Mann 1996, pp. 111–12; Newbigin 1994, pp. 36–7 and note 62; P. Ventrone, 'La riproposta fiorentina del teatro classico', in Ventrone 1992, pp. 221–2.

55 See L. Ricciardi, '*Col senno, col tesoro e colla lancia'. Riti e giochi cavallereschi nella Firenze del Magnifico Lorenzo*, Florence 1992, chapters 6, 7 and 8.

56 Ventrone in Mallett and Mann 1996, pp. 109–11.

57 For the *palio* see M. Mallett, 'Horse-Racing and Politics in Lorenzo's Florence', in Mallett and Mann eds., London 1996, pp. 253–62. For the chronology of the feast day plays in this period, see N. Newbigin, *Feste dell'Oltrarno. Plays in churches in fifteenth-century Florence*, Florence 1996.

2   Patrons and Projects

Patricia Lee Rubin

WHEN HIS FATHER Piero died on 2 December 1469 Lorenzo was twenty years old. The next day the leading men of Florence asked him to follow his father and grandfather in taking up the care 'of the city and the regime'.[2] This was a heavy burden, assumed, as Lorenzo recalled, reluctantly, but as history records, with extraordinary ability. Still, it was not until the creation of the Council of Seventy in 1480 that his power over the government was secured. As the Pazzi conspiracy of 1478 proved, the situation was volatile, and for Lorenzo threatening to his person as well as his power.

One metaphor used to describe Lorenzo's position at this time was that of the director, or master, of the shop – *maestro della bottega*.[3] The 1470s can be viewed as the period when Lorenzo, already apprenticed to statesmanship by his father, was first crafting his power, affirming and establishing the bonds of obligation and loyalty that assured his authority, that made the city his business.

Just as he had an uncanny talent for shaping the essential forms of rule, the young Lorenzo had a developed appreciation of the visual forms that might express and validate his power. From the early stages of his career he demonstrated an awareness of the role of imagery in conveying and characterising authority. This was accompanied by a genuine interest in things beautiful and precious. It was reinforced by a political sensibility that conditioned all his activities. The selection and sponsorship of artists was another realm of influence – of patronage – which earned him the gratitude of artists and furthered his reputation for good judgement.[4]

Brought up in the palace constructed by his grandfather Cosimo, Lorenzo witnessed its decoration as its interior spaces were filled with paintings and sculptures emblematic of the family's dominant position: a chapel with murals showing the procession of the Magi by Benozzo Gozzoli, bronze statues of *David* and *Judith* by Donatello, canvases of the *Labours of Hercules* by Antonio del Pollaiuolo. Lorenzo had a unique cultural as well as material inheritance. His father Piero was passionate about the precious cameos, gems and manuscripts that he assembled in his study. His grandfather was celebrated for the fact that 'he had dealings with painters and sculptors and had in his house works of divers masters. He was … liberal to all men of worth through his great liking for them. He had good knowledge of architecture … moreover, all those who were about to build would go to him for advice.'[5]

Lorenzo was educated in and by these traditions. From his early teens, well before the legal age of office-holding, he served on the boards of works (*opere*) supervising major building and decorative projects. In 1463, for example, when he was fourteen, he replaced his uncle Giovanni on the board of works of the Bridgetine convent known as the Paradiso. That this was a deliberate policy is indicated by Piero's nomination of Lorenzo to replace him in 1466 on the board of the Merchants' tribunal responsible for the commission of Verrocchio's *Christ and Saint Thomas* (fig. 29).[6] After Piero's death, Lorenzo took his place on the board of works of the Guelph Party and in 1468 Lorenzo was among the citizens commissioning the cupola ball for the Duomo from Verrocchio.

This consultative role continued officially and unofficially through the 1470s. When debates arose over the plans for the tribune for SS. Annunziata,

Lorenzo was called upon in an attempt to resolve the matter. In this case his official response (in a letter of May 1471) was diplomatically to advise the Marquis of Mantua, Lodovico Gonzaga, to pursue the project according to his taste, because he was paying for it, saying that 'everyone would praise it'.[7] At just about the same time, after a fire laid waste the convent at Le Murate, Lorenzo became involved in sponsoring its rebuilding, ultimately spending 5000 florins there and effectively becoming its chief patron.[8] In 1473 he acquired properties to the west of Florence, in the plain around the Ombrone river, including a country estate at Poggio a Caiano that belonged to Giovanni Rucellai. He set about developing this property as an innovative agricultural venture, including a dairy farm. A year later he was sent a drawing for a villa, and it seems that he was involved in discussions about designing a totally unprecedented type of country

palace on the site, which was begun in the mid-1480s.[9] Although most of Lorenzo's own major building projects – both institutional and familial, such as the Augustinian convent at San Gallo or the villa at Poggio a Caiano – date from the 1480s, he came to those projects with considerable experience of the practice and theory of architecture and respect for its role in expressing public interest and honour.

Lorenzo's precociously established position as arbiter is demonstrated by his role in the dispute over the monument that the town council of Pistoia wished to erect to honour their illustrious citizen and municipal benefactor, Cardinal Niccolò Forteguerri.[10] Forteguerri died on 21 December 1473 and on 2 January 1474 the council voted to spend 30 florins on a service of commemoration and to commission a cenotaph. An appointed board of works held a competition for its design, which was won by Andrea

Fig. 14 ANDREA DEL VERROCCHIO and LEONARDO DA VINCI, *Sleeping nymph and a cupid*, 1475. Metalpoint, black chalk, brown ink on paper, 14.8 × 25.9 cm. Florence, Galleria degli Uffizi, Gabinetto Disegni e Stampe, inv. 212E.

del Verrocchio on 15 May 1476. There seems to have been debate about this decision and the board of works also asked for a model from Piero del Pollaiuolo, at that time in Pistoia. Piero was awarded the commission in 1477. Pistoia was a subject city of Florence, and the decision of the board was overturned by the Florentine commissioners appointed to settle factional disputes in the city. At this point the board appealed to Lorenzo – proof that his judgement was valued and that his influence, if not direct power, was viewed as absolute. In the event, he decided in favour of Verrocchio's model. Pollaiuolo's model does not survive, so it is not possible to guess at the aesthetic, or even practical, factors that might have affected Lorenzo's decision. It was not a bias for Verrocchio. Both the Pollaiuolo firm and the Verrocchio shop had produced works for the Medici, and Lorenzo continued to sponsor both, in direct commissions and in indirect recommendations for other projects.

Lorenzo's spectacular and semi-official debut as a public figure in his joust of February 1469 had taken place under a standard designed by Verrocchio. Its imagery prophesied a golden age of rejuvenation and renewal. It showed a sun and rainbow and a young woman in a gown embroidered with flowers. Standing in a meadow with a partly withered laurel tree, she gathered laurel to make a garland from its one green branch: a play on Lorenzo's name as Laurentius = *lauro* = laurel. Suiting the tone of the event, its motto ('Le tems revient') was in French, the language of chivalry, and it was to be interpreted, as explained in the contemporary poem by Luigi Pulci, to mean that 'time returns and the century is renewed'.[11] Although the imagery of the event was fixed in poetry, there is no record of Verrocchio's design for this intricate emblem. However, a drawing by him survives that can be related to a standard painted for a member of the entourage of Lorenzo's younger brother Giuliano in his joust of 29 January 1475 (fig. 14). It shows a sleeping nymph with a cupid stealing up behind her and taking an arrow from a quiver as if about to pierce her heart. She seems to have flowers gathered in her skirt. The drawing departs from the standard as described by a contemporary, where both the nymph and the cupid (or *spiritello*) were more actively strewing flowers and the nymph displayed a shield. The carefully worked drawing may be Verrocchio's early idea for the composition. It could also be a poetic reworking of the theme: a visual parallel with the verses inspired by the joust written by Lorenzo's friend, the humanist Angelo Poliziano.[12] Giuliano's own standard, also lost, was painted by Botticelli. It showed Pallas along with Cupid who was bound to a tree. Elements of its invention and of Poliziano's verses about it were to recur in other paintings by Botticelli, notably the *Primavera* (fig. 15).

The web of amorous verse and imagery spun around these occasions by poets and artists should not and did not disguise the fact that their splendour had serious purposes. The first joust both celebrated a peace treaty with Venice and signalled the transition from Piero to Lorenzo as head of the family. The second was to publicise the alliance agreed between Venice, Milan and Florence in November 1474. It was important to the Medici that such celebrations be 'most sumptuous and worthy'.[13] No expense was spared to make the greatest impression of magnificence, with the Medici triumphantly taking the prizes. Although ephemeral, Verrocchio's tasks were not trivial.

The standards are among fifteen items in a list dated 27 January 1496 which was submitted by Verrocchio's brother to claim payment from the

Fig. 15 SANDRO BOTTICELLI, *Primavera*, early 1480s. Tempera on panel,
203 × 314 cm. Florence, Galleria degli Uffizi.

materials, the originality of the design, and the extraordinary quality of its execution (fig. 16). The inscription is an important reminder that Giuliano was a protagonist in the artistic policies and politics of the family. His junior position and early death have tended to obscure his role. In broad terms it can be said that Lorenzo played a greater part than Giuliano in commissions that were directly related to his position as unofficial head of state, but that Giuliano was an active participant in projects regarding the family's reputation.

One occasion that documents the joint decision-making of the brothers is the sale of Verrocchio's bronze statue of *David* to the Signoria on 10 May 1476 (fig. 17). The board of works responsible for the Palazzo not only accepted the price of 145 florins, but also a stipulated site outside the door leading to the Sala dei Gigli.[17] Bronze statues were one of the special features of the decoration of the Medici palace, expressive of the family's wealth and status and of the ambiguous boundaries of the role of the Medici as private citizens. Their courtyard statues of *David* and *Judith* by Donatello both had inscriptions on their bases urging the citizenry to see them as exemplars of civic virtue. Thus to place a *David* of Medici provenance in the Palazzo della Signoria was an unmistakable fusion of public and private, linking the state palace and the Medici palace. Lorenzo did not in fact serve on the board of works at the Palazzo della Signoria until 1479, and his intervention in the works in the Sala dei Gigli seems to have been limited before then. But by engineering this sale at a price that must have been well below the actual cost of the statue, the brothers forestalled resistance. The victorious David was an accepted figure for the virtuous defense of liberty and of good government. The sculpture offered to the Signoria was unarguably

officials in charge of the confiscated Medici possessions and the settlement of their debts after the family's exile in 1494. The works listed range from the celebratory and festive, such as the standards and the decorations made for the visit of Duke Galeazzo Maria Sforza in 1471, to the monumental and commemorative, such as Cosimo's tomb in the crossing of S. Lorenzo, which was completed by 22 October 1467.[14] The tomb is the first securely datable work that Verrocchio made for the Medici.[15] An inscription on the pier in the crypt records that it was Piero's commission. After Piero's death, Lorenzo and Giuliano in their turn commissioned the 'most honourable' tomb possible for their father and uncle from Verrocchio.[16] Their filial devotion is recorded explicitly by the names inscribed around the base (LAVRENT ET IVL PETRI F/POSVER/PATRI PATRVO QUE/MCCCCLXXII) and implicitly by the costly

Fig. 16 ANDREA DEL VERROCCHIO, Tomb of Piero and Giovanni de' Medici, seen from the Old Sacristy, completed 1473. Bronze, red and green porphyry, white marble, pietra serena, 582 × 245 cm. Florence, San Lorenzo.

an appropriate and beautiful addition to the decoration of the palace.

The diplomatic use of works of art became a feature of Lorenzo's foreign as well as domestic policy. Verrocchio produced, for example, reliefs of Alexander the Great and Darius which Lorenzo sent to King Matthias Corvinus of Hungary. They are lost, but the compositions inspired variants in different media (cat. nos. 61 and 62). Like the poetic inventions for the jousts, these heroic subjects from antiquity, made for one purpose, generated a further production and widened the markets for artists inside the city and abroad.

Both Lorenzo and Giuliano followed their grandfather in his liberal promotion of talented artists and in his loyal friendships with some of them. In addition to the works mentioned above, the Verrocchio list of 1496 also documents works done for the palace and the villa at Careggi, including a relief thought to be the terracotta *Resurrection* now in the Bargello (fig. 18), the bronze *Putto with a Dolphin* (fig. 66), and a lost painting of Lucrezia Donati – the ideal lady-love of Lorenzo's joust. There is also named a 'red nude', an antique torso of the flayed Marsyas, which Verrocchio restored by adding arms and legs.[18] He supplied twenty masks from life ('maschere ritratte al naturale'), whose purpose cannot be determined, and he restored or mounted antique busts over the doors of the courtyard. The latter formed a historical comparison with contemporary sculpted busts of family members, such as those by Mino da Fiesole of Piero, his brother Giovanni and his wife Lucrezia, so that ancient exemplars were combined with contemporary memory as part of the palace's decoration.[19] Lorenzo's understanding of this programmatic use of portraiture is indicated by the commission given to Piero del Pollaiuolo to portray

Fig. 17 ANDREA DEL VERROCCHIO, *David*, before 1476. Bronze, height 126 cm. Florence, Museo Nazionale del Bargello.

three-dimensional complement to a subject treated in one of the canvases (figs. 62 and 64), the statuette was a revival of an ancient genre and it was designed to appeal to Lorenzo's taste as a collector as much as to his impulses as a patron. Equally it is to Lorenzo and his ancestors as collectors that Antonio seems indebted for his stylistic formation. Medici protection and promotion are registered indirectly through Antonio's imaginative response to the ancient gems and Netherlandish paintings that he knew from the Medici palace and villa at Careggi (see, for example, figs. 21 and 46). Antonio was also probably among the numerous goldsmiths, not all of whom are named in documents, who framed and adorned many of the precious objects in Lorenzo's collection (cat. no. 5). The silver cover of the bound copy of Petrarch's *Triumphs*, whose enamelled roundels depict Apollo and the Muses, may be his work (cat. no. 3).

Galeazzo Maria Sforza (fig. 19), made in connection with the Duke's visit in 1471. The portrait shows Galeazzo in an animated three-quarter view, gesturing authoritatively. Its presence alongside a portrait of the Duke of Urbino placed on display Lorenzo's alliances with important Italian powers.[20]

The Medici family had helped to launch the Pollaiuolo brothers' careers as painters in about 1460 with the *Labours of Hercules* canvases for the great hall of their palace. Scholars have sometimes tried to link all of Antonio del Pollaiuolo's works on the subject of Hercules to Lorenzo's patronage, claiming that Lorenzo wanted to identify himself with the mythological hero.[21] Antonio's remarkable bronze statuette of *Hercules and Antaeus*, apparently mentioned in the Medici palace inventory, is, however, the only work of this kind that may be safely related to Lorenzo's patronage in the 1470s.[22] A sophisticated

Fig. 18 ANDREA DEL VERROCCHIO, *Resurrection*, c.1480. Painted terracotta, 135 × 150 cm. Florence, Museo Nazionale del Bargello.

Fig. 19 PIERO DEL POLLAIUOLO, *Galeazzo Maria Sforza*, 1471. Panel, 65 × 42 cm. Florence, Galleria degli Uffizi.

The lively engraving of the music-making figures is typical of his draughtsmanship, while the subject represents a flattering allusion to Lorenzo as poet and protector of the creative muse.

The luxury and learning of the house of Medici are also expressed in the bronze relief of a battle produced in about 1476 by the sculptor Bertoldo di Giovanni and set over a fireplace in a room opposite the great hall of their palace (fig. 20).[23] Based on an antique marble sarcophagus in Pisa, it completes the missing parts in a way that is comparable to the textual scholarship of the humanists. Not only does it ask for comparison with its source, it enters into competition with it and does so in a more valuable material than the original. In Bertoldo's case the favours of friendship or patronage were extended to those of becoming part of the *famiglia* or household.[24]

Acute and astute recognition of the prestige of possession was inherited by the younger Medici along with their ancestral legacy. In addition to commissioning new works for their palace, both Cosimo and Piero had purchased ancient gems and cameos, precious items that had more usually belonged in ecclesiastical treasuries and the collections of princes, popes and cardinals than in the possession of private citizens. In his lifetime Lorenzo more than doubled the family's collection, which, in monetary terms, contained the most valuable items in the palace. His official initiation as a collector came at the time of his mission to Rome as ambassador to the newly elected Pope Sixtus IV in September 1471. In his memoirs, Lorenzo recalled that he was 'much honoured' by the Pope who gave him ancient marble busts of Augustus and Agrippa. While in Rome he also acquired a number

Fig. 20 BERTOLDO DI GIOVANNI, *A battle scene, c.1476*.
Bronze, 45 × 99 cm. Florence, Museo Nazionale del Bargello.

of medals and cameos. Among them was the most famous surviving cameo from antiquity, which he called 'la scudella nostra' ('our bowl'), and is now known as the 'tazza Farnese' (the Farnese Cup), and which was valued at the astronomical sum of 10,000 florins in the 1492 inventory of the palace.[25] Lorenzo's guide to the antiquities of Rome had been the humanist Leon Battista Alberti and Lorenzo became an avid collector of antiquities of all sorts: sculptures as well as coins, vases and cameos. Such was his identification with them that he had a number of them engraved with his own name (LAV.R.MED; cat. no. 6 and fig. 21). These objects were a facet of his learning, as well as becoming an extension of his power and politics. Even as he gained two busts from Pope Sixtus, Lorenzo dispatched a colossal bronze horse's head to Count Diomede Carafa in Naples; Carafa was King Ferrante's closest and most

powerful adviser as well as a friend to Alfonso, Duke of Calabria.[26]

There were other rarities. Learning could become a luxury good in the form of sumptuously produced manuscripts (cat. no. 3). Every aspect of life could be shaped by exquisite craftsmanship and adorned with precious materials, as the devotional Book of Hours made for Lorenzo's bride, Clarice Orsini, exemplifies (cat. no. 4). While assiduously promoting the excellence of Florentine artists, Lorenzo also showed an appreciation for foreign works. The Medici palace inventory records paintings by Netherlandish masters, including, for example, a (now lost) *Saint Jerome in his Study* by Jan van Eyck probably similar to the panel now in Detroit (fig. 22). Medici commissions and collections not only gave artists opportunities to demonstrate their skills, they created a realm of competition and curiosity. Imported paintings like

Fig. 21 *Dancing Satyr*, 40–30 BC. Agate-onyx, 3.6 × 2.8 cm. Naples, Museo Nazionale, inv. 25873.

Fig. 22 FOLLOWER OF JAN VAN EYCK, *Saint Jerome in his Study*. Oil on panel, 20 × 13 cm. Detroit Institute of Arts.

the van Eyck were admired and imitated for their mastery of oil technique and for their motifs. As that great chronicler of artists' lives, Giorgio Vasari, recognised, when Verrocchio restored the Marsyas, he had a chance to study its anatomy and to learn from a classical model.[27] The ancient cameos and medals, which Lorenzo had mounted and engraved by contemporary goldsmiths, similarly provided lessons: examples of figures in dramatic and graceful poses and of dynamic drawing and design. In Poliziano's *Stanze* Venus tells Cupid that Giuliano is 'singing of arms like those of strong Achilles and is renewing the ancient times in his own style'.[28] This association of poetic style with renewal had a wider resonance in the practice and the appreciation of the visual arts.

In the 1470s Lorenzo and his brother were obviously key figures in creating a special climate for the visual arts in Florence, through the artists they favoured and the objects they collected. Certain features of their behaviour can be regarded as exceptional. Atypical, obviously, was their position in the city, especially Lorenzo's as the unofficial head of state. And Lorenzo's remarkable character is not in doubt; even as a youth he was noted for his 'dextrous intellect', competitive spirit and desire for glory.[29] But his activities and those of Giuliano can be situated within conventions followed by other leading citizens who saw to the honourable equipping of their households, and who worried about the fate of their souls and those of their ancestors, and about their reputations and welfare in this life and the next. They too were involved in the boards of works that deliberated upon the commissions that would meet the practical needs of the city's institutions while expressing their own honour and prestige.

A letter written by Filippo Strozzi (1428–91) to his brother in Naples is explicit about priorities: 'since

God has granted me temporal goods, I want to show my gratitude. And beginning with His things, we can one day come to ours.'[30] Filippo (fig. 23) came from a branch of the Strozzi family that had been exiled since 1434 as rivals of the Medici. He made a considerable fortune in banking and trade in Naples and when he was allowed to return to Florence in 1466 he was concerned to re-establish his family's position. The projects he undertook are, therefore, valuable indicators of expectations. He donated hangings and vestments to his local church, S. Maria degli Ughi (1472–6), as well as two windows, one bearing his coat of arms along with those of his wife's family, the Adimari (1472).[31] As its name states, the patronage rights of the church (destroyed in 1785) belonged to the Ughi family. Even though such emblazoned donations allowed Filippo to mark his piety and his

Fig. 23 BENEDETTO DA MAIANO, *Filippo Strozzi*, 1475. Marble, height 52 cm. Paris, Musée du Louvre.

43

presence in the parish, he was not able to take precedence. Consequently he initially directed his energies, and his resources, 'in gratitude to God', towards churches and oratories outside the city, both where the Strozzi already had the patronage rights, at Santuccio, and where he could more readily acquire them, as at the church of the Carmelite monastery of Santa Maria delle Selve (in November 1476) and at the Dominican oratory at Lecceto. At Le Selve he built two chapels (in 1477), gave vestments and hangings (1477–8), and in 1482 supplied an altarpiece by Neri di Bicci. At Lecceto, among other things, he built the high altar chapel (between 1478 and 1489), specifying that it be modelled on that of S. Maria degli Ughi – thereby bringing the town to the country. Not only are the Strozzi arms displayed in various places inside and outside the oratory, but the choir bears a bold inscription commemorating Filippo's donation, 'dedicated to the life-giving Virgin' for his salvation (VIRGINI GENITRICI PHILIPPUS STROZZA SUI IN SALUTEM CONDIDIT).[32]

The traditional burial place of Filippo's branch of the family was in the Florentine church of S. Maria Novella, and from the late 1470s he and his brother began to think of endowing a new funerary chapel there.[33] Filippo was not able to secure patronage until 1486, and the chapel decoration was only completed in 1502, eleven years after his death. Filippo was not indifferent to his splendid chapel, as the provisions of his will demonstrate, but he had faith in his heirs to complete the projects he had begun for the benefit of his soul and the honour of his family.

Pious concerns preceded, but did not pre-empt the secular expression of family glory – a palace. As with the chapel, however, posterity was as much, or more, in view as present satisfaction. Just as acquiring patronage rights involved balancing institutional and

personal interests and could take years of careful negotiating, acquiring a site for a palace could be a long drawn-out matter. Filippo, like most Florentines, chose to build in his ancestral neighbourhood. He began buying properties in the 1470s to clear the space. The construction of the enormous new palace, which gained the reputation of being even grander than that of the Medici, began in 1489 and lasted until 1504.[34]

In 1475 Filippo had a marble portrait bust of himself made by Benedetto da Maiano (fig. 23).[35] Literally warts and all, the bust depicts him with a forthright gaze, but thoughtful expression. He is wearing sumptuous, fur-lined robes with brocade sleeves. This is one of a number of works Filippo commissioned from the da Maiano firm, both in stone and intarsia woodwork. His tomb was also made by Benedetto. Strozzi's respect for the craftsman as well as his craftsmanship is recorded by a gift of valuable cloth that he made to Benedetto in 1478.[36] He seems to have had similar trust and respect for the sculptor Antonio Rossellino, who advised him about a tomb planned for his youngest brother, who was buried in Naples.[37]

Although Filippo was not a collector on the scale of the Medici, he too supported Florentine excellence and learning and showed a love for expensively and elaborately ornamented objects. In 1479 the miniaturist Monte di Giovanni received payments from Filippo for illuminating manuscripts, including a work by the humanist Lorenzo Valla, the *Triumphs* of Petrarch and, most ambitiously, a deluxe version of Cristoforo Landino's translation of Pliny the Elder's *Natural History*, 'my Pliny' as Filippo called it.[38] Pliny's text was one of the chief sources of knowledge about the ancient arts and Landino's translation, also sponsored by Filippo and his brother, was an

Figs. 24 and 25 MONTE DI GIOVANNI, *Pliny the Elder 'Natural History': 'Sculpture'*, 1479, incipit of Book 36, detail, *'Painting'*, 1479, incipit of Book 35, detail. Manuscript illuminations. Oxford, Bodleian Library, Douce 310.

important mode of transmitting that knowledge (figs. 24 and 25).[39] The manuscript, which took four years to complete, was bound in a gold-threaded brocade with enamelled clasps. Its illuminated borders include a portrait of Filippo and his son as well as one of King Ferrante of Naples (the dedicatee of the Landino translation). They further include famous gems from the Medici collection. The illuminations do more than illustrate the text, they indicate a web of loyalties, alluding to Filippo's history, while also complementing and appropriating the Medici's most prized treasures.

Filippo Strozzi's carefully plotted re-entry to Florence made relatively little impact on the city in the 1470s and has left few surviving traces from that decade. Giovanni Rucellai (1403–81) presents an interesting comparison. By the 1470s he had reshaped significant portions of his neighbourhood, in both its sacred and secular realms. Approaching his seventies, he was seeing the results of twenty years of spending for himself, his lineage, and above all, for the grace of God. Like Strozzi, he repeatedly gave thanks to God for the many favours bestowed upon him, and for his good fortune in his commercial enterprises.[40] A loyal son-in-law to the exiled Palla Strozzi, his political position in the city was equivocal until the betrothal of his son Bernardo to Piero de' Medici's daughter Nannina in 1461 (they were married in 1466). His economic status had been established since the 1450s when he was among the wealthiest men in the city and eager to embark on an extensive programme of building and benefaction.[41] In his *Zibaldone* or chapbook he noted that earning and spending were ranked among the greatest pleasures in life, and it was his personal opinion that of the two, to spend was the more rewarding.[42] He contemplated and summarised his expenditures with great satisfaction. He listed his

Fig. 26 Façade of the Rucellai palace, Florence.

house (fig. 26) and the adjacent loggia (c.1463–6), his villa (c.1448–64), the façade (c.1457–70) and portal of the church of S. Maria Novella (fig. 5), and the chapel of the Holy Sepulchre in his parish church of S. Pancrazio, with all of its liturgical furnishings (c.1458–67).[43] He also noted the 'many sculpted, painted and intarsiaed works' that decorated his house 'by the best masters … not only in Florence, but in Italy'.[44]

Rucellai's writings also chronicle a generally increased investment in household luxury.[45] Traditional objects for the domestic setting, such as images of the Virgin and Child, were crafted using more expensive materials (fig. 68) or in new forms (cat. no. 23). New types of subjects and objects also came into vogue, such as paintings of poetic subjects (cat. nos. 86 and 88) and portraits, both painted and sculpted. It is likely that the courtly style of the Medici palace interior had some influence on this, but Rucellai's note suggests that ambitious artists had a place in crafting these new desires. Furthermore, as the independent style of Rucellai's major commissions demonstrates, the impetus to acquire beautiful things came from many directions.

Many of Rucellai's musings are adaptations of passages from ancient authors. He was aware of the model of the good man and good citizen proposed in the writings of Cicero and Seneca. He was also convinced that 'in this age there have been more distinguished learned men than in [recent] past times … who have returned to light the lost and extinguished beauty of ancient style.'[46] His house (fig. 26), his funerary chapel and the façade of S. Maria Novella (fig. 5) can be seen in this context as conscious efforts to participate in the recovery of ancient beauty. Rucellai does not name an architect in his *Zibaldone*. In his *Lives of the Artists* (first edition 1550)

Vasari attributed all of Rucellai's projects to Leon Battista Alberti. There is, however, no documentation to prove Alberti's authorship.[47] In any event, the person who 'signed' the S. Maria Novella façade was Giovanni Rucellai. Rucellai's name, with the date 1470, is spelled out in Latin in *all'antica* lettering just below the pediment. The Rucellai arms appear at the top of the framing pilasters on the upper level and one of his emblems, the full sail, adorns the cornice and the framing pilasters of the first level. The design was determined by a number of factors, in addition to the principal one of arriving at a beauty befitting both the Rucellai name and the principal Dominican church of Florence. The ground level was already clad in the mid-fourteenth century and this established the use of green serpentine and white marbles, and geometric patterns. Another given was the large round window and the roofs of the aisles. The designer of the façade had to create a unified whole from ungainly parts. This was done by dividing the façade with an attic storey and by finding a proportional system to balance architectonic elements against ornamental motifs. The result pays tribute to Florentine antiquity – the Romanesque façade of San Miniato al Monte for example – while proposing a critical reformulation in an ancient Roman key. There is no reason to believe Rucellai himself capable of arriving at this ingenious solution to the problems posed by the task; but it is equally clear that he was, in the end, to be remembered as responsible and that was, of course, part of what inspired him and others to compete for such honours.

Filippo Strozzi's correspondence and Giovanni Rucellai's *Zibaldone*, as well as scores of letters, wills and records by other members of the élite document just how much determination, patience and skilful negotiation it took to realise such projects – to clear a building site, for example, or to procure patronage rights, to arrive at designs and to see through their execution. But immediate gratification was held to be far less important than the benefits to one's descendants and one's soul that were the lasting results of such investments. With their expenditures for endowments and embellishments to churches, and for building and furnishing their palaces and villas, such men were, moreover, not merely or not simply showing off their accumulated wealth or creating monuments to their mercantile ability. According to contemporary definition, they were behaving 'magnificently'.

History has dubbed Lorenzo 'the Magnificent' and he was, in his day, addressed as *magnifico*. This was a general title of respect accorded to powerful men who were not of noble birth. Lorenzo undoubtedly cultivated the magnificence attached to his name, for it had important implications. Magnificence was a virtue, first defined by Aristotle in his *Nichomachean Ethics* as 'an excellence concerned with wealth ... [A] fitting expenditure involving largeness of scale [it] is an attribute of expenditures of the kind which we call honourable, e.g. those connected with ... any form of religious worship, and all those that are proper objects of public-spirited ambition.'[48] The theory of magnificence was developed in the fifteenth century in connection with ideals of civil or civic life. One of its notable exponents was Matteo Palmieri (1406–75; fig. 27).

The fourth book of his treatise *On Civil Life* is dedicated to 'the useful'. Its topics include wealth, which was defined as a means for worthy men to act virtuously.[49] In a preceding section 'on magnificence' Palmieri paraphrases Aristotle's definition.[50] Such theories were convenient to the citizens of a mercantile republic, suggesting how earnings could be

a facet of private merit and public benefit. Most importantly, private splendour was part of the general embellishment of the city and contributed to civic beauty.[51]

Palmieri's conviction was that 'private citizens' made cities glorious by working for the common good. The general prescription is also a specific description of Palmieri's own behaviour. He was active in public service and was a frequent office-holder. He was celebrated by the contemporary bookseller and biographer Vespasiano da Bisticci as one of relatively modest birth who 'was a founder of his house and ennobled it by his worthy life [and] won a high position in the city, and ultimately enjoyed all the honours it could give'.[52] Palmieri's estimate of his own value is expressed by his commission of a marble portrait bust from Antonio Rossellino in 1464,

Fig. 27 ANTONIO ROSSELLINO, *Matteo Palmieri*, 1464.
Marble, height 54 cm. Florence, Museo Nazionale del Bargello.

which was displayed over the door of his house (fig. 27). Made when he was 62 years old, this candid and now weatherbeaten bust, shows him as a citizen (through his dress), dignified and confident. Just as his treatise took ancient precepts and rendered them in modern language for modern usage, his portrait took up ancient precedents in Roman senatorial portrait busts and the custom of displaying busts over doors described by Pliny in the *Natural History* (Book xxxv, chapter 2). Where Pliny lamented the lapse of transmitting exact likenesses, Florentine citizens, like Palmieri, revived them. He became an ornament to his city, not for his beautiful features, but for being among those to be counted of honourable reputation ('honoratamente notabili').[53]

In his funerary oration, Palmieri's eulogist made his construction of magnificent buildings a topic of praise, but Palmieri's means did not allow for the magnitude of spending required of true magnificence.[54] He was not a palace builder, nor could he sponsor large-scale building projects. His patronage presents an instance of the behaviour of a well-to-do and influential citizen. He had a house in town and a country house and farms near Fiesole. He had the patronage rights to a chapel in the Badia at San Domenico, near that property.[55] His most lavish expenses were directed towards the afterlife in a funerary chapel constructed in his parish church, attached to the Benedictine nunnery of S. Piero Maggiore. This included not only its decoration with the massive altarpiece of the *Assumption of the Virgin*, by Francesco Botticini, painted between 1475 and 1477 (fig. 28), but, necessarily, the endowment of its liturgical programme and the provision of altar furnishings.[56] The project was initiated by Palmieri shortly before he died. It was left to his heirs – his wife and nephews – to see to its completion.

The altarpiece shows Matteo and his widow, Niccolosa de' Serragli, in profile and in prayer, the conventional pose for donors. Matteo has the position of honour – the viewer's left, which is the liturgical right of the holy scene. As in his portrait bust, he is in the dress of a Florentine citizen. His wife wears dark matronly garments. The composition of the scene demonstrates how such donations represented the interests of all parties concerned: in this case the nuns at S. Piero and Matteo Palmieri and his family. The chief image must relate to the dedication of the altar. The prominence given to Saint Peter standing at the liturgical right in the crowd of apostles refers to his patronage of the church and convent, as its titular saint. Peter's attribute of the key of heaven touches the rim of the empty tomb. The reception of Mary in heaven, as queen of heaven and bride of Christ, would remind the nuns of their roles as brides of Christ on earth. Her attitude presented them, and all worshippers, with a forceful example of humility. Matteo, portrayed against a background of hills with the Badia at S. Domenico and a view of Florence, exemplifies the virtuous citizen. In his treatise on civil life, Palmieri describes a dream vision of heaven that promises salvation to all those who have dedicated their lives to the good of the republic. In the altarpiece heavenly vision is united with earthly projection, allowing the viewer to experience them simultaneously and to see the devout attitudes of Palmieri and his wife as models for emulation as well as invitations to remember them in prayer.[57]

Palmieri's bequests are typical for one of his status. His writings supplied an ethics of display. He devoted part of his treatise to 'the beauty and the embellishment of the city'.[58] This section provides useful categories for considering how and by whom this was achieved in the 1470s.

Fig. 28 FRANCESCO BOTTICINI, *Assumption of the Virgin*, c.1475–7.
Tempera on panel, 228.6 x 337.2 cm. London, National Gallery.

Fig. 29 ANDREA DEL VERROCCHIO, *Christ and Saint Thomas*, 1467–83. Bronze. Florence, Orsanmichele.

PUBLIC BUILDINGS

'The beauty and the unique embellishment of buildings resides in the first instance in public constructions . . . in the lofty and proud palaces [built] for the outstanding glory of the magistrates.'[59]

That proudest of palaces, the Palazzo della Signoria, was the focus of much activity in the decade, but it was far from the only place where public interest took the form of decorative projects. Nor was it the only arena where citizens like Matteo Palmieri subsumed their private identities in civic or corporate endeavours, acting as members of the government, of guilds and of confraternities, where they were called upon to plan and to see to the completion of works that expressed common or communal ideals.

Matteo, for example, was one of those named in the board of works elected by the Mercanzia in March 1463 to oversee the making of a 'worthy figure' for the niche that it had just acquired at Orsanmichele.[60] The result was the bronze group of Christ and Saint Thomas by Verrocchio (fig. 29), unveiled more than twenty years later in June 1483. The first surviving document mentioning Verrocchio in connection with the commission dates from 15 January 1467 when he was paid 300 *lire* for making a bronze statue.[61] The plural 'figures' does not occur until 24 April 1468, when the Mercanzia agreed to pay Verrocchio a monthly salary of 25 *lire* for his work on them. The modelling, casting and chasing of the figure of Christ can be dated between then and 1479, and of Saint Thomas from 1476 to 1480, with some further work in the spring of 1483.[62] The total of fifteen years (1468–83) that Verrocchio devoted to the project indicates the complexities of designing and executing a monumental two-figure group in bronze, of doing so while running a firm that was producing painted, modelled and sculpted works, and of dealing with a committee. Over time the rate of work may have been determined by the rate of payments, but in observing the fitful beginnings of this commission one gets the sense that this is an instance where management of magnificence suffered delays due to complications in committee work. Indeed, three years after the first board had been appointed, Piero de' Medici stepped down in favour of his son Lorenzo, because ill-health and affairs of state prevented him from serving conscientiously.[63] It is from that time (December 1466) that the project really began to advance. It is not known whether the young Lorenzo's greater energies helped; what is sure is that the appointment of Piero's teenage son is a clear demonstration of Piero's concern to have family representation in this project and of his power to do so.

The Mercanzia was a corporation made up of representatives from the five major commercial guilds. It acted as a tribunal to try disputes between merchants. Its executive board was made up of six men – the Sei – and a foreign chief magistrate who served as judges. This board had significant impact on financial matters in the city and Piero and subsequently Lorenzo took care to have their allies elected to its governing bodies and to promote its juridical powers. One sign of its importance in the fifteenth century was the acquisition of the Guelph Party niche, finalised in March 1463. The removal of the statue of the party's patron, Saint Louis, gave the Mercanzia the opportunity to set an emblematic figure in a dominant position on one of the city's most important shrines overlooking one of its busiest streets.

In appointing a board of works, the Mercanzia was following standard practice for a corporate commission. However threatened by group dynamics, this mechanism allowed for a combination of

collective representation and individual responsibility. One result of this practice was that there was significant experience in Florence of discussing and evaluating projects, in deciding on suitable subjects, on what form they should take, what material, what scale, by which artist and at what cost. Like all electoral processes in Florence, the election of the board of works could be and was engineered to serve more particular interests. In this case there were five members, one from each of the member guilds. Although the composition changed over time, all those selected (at least at the time of their appointment) were sympathetic to the Medici regime and both the choice of artist and the choice of subject can be connected to Medici patronage. The Medici were the patrons of the church of Saint Thomas the Apostle in the Mercato Vecchio (which was just to the west of Orsanmichele) and Cosimo had actively promoted the saint's feast day.[64] Verrocchio, as discussed above, was consistently employed by the Medici. Their support of his skill and his style meant that as his career advanced that skill and style might have been recognised as having a Medicean imprint. It certainly meant that there was a degree of private influence being expressed in the public beauty of Florence. But the glory of the magistrates was also given 'suitable' and 'worthy' form.[65]

The subject of the sculpture for the niche does not seem to have been taken for granted (the Mercanzia had no patron saint as such), but as an image of doubt and of the necessity of proof in the search for truth and of the divine grace that confers it, the encounter of Saint Thomas and Christ is entirely appropriate as an emblem for the Mercanzia. It was a subject associated with justice and courts. There was an image of Christ and Saint Thomas in the Palazzo della Signoria and the Mercanzia already had a panel of the

Incredulity of Saint Thomas in their palace. The search for
truth that it embodied was also connected with good
government: a happy connection both for the Medici
and the Mercanzia.

The Sei seemed to have had Verrocchio in mind
when in August 1469 they resolved to commission a
painting of Charity for the wall above the bench in
their audience hall where they sat in judgement,
naming the artist 'Piero del Verrocchio'.[66] This was a
slip for Piero del Pollaiuolo, who was awarded the job
on the basis of a large-scale drawing. The drawing
must have been similar to, if not the same as, the
design that is on the back of the Charity panel, which
may be attributed to his brother Antonio, who is
mentioned as guarantor in September 1469. The
choice of Charity as the subject of the trial piece
reinforces the themes of mercy and love that were
embodied in the *Christ and Saint Thomas* group.

The figure of Charity was to be one of a set of
seven Virtues, corresponding to the seven judges of
the Mercanzia. The error in the document is revealing,
because the project continued to be debated. Other
artists were eager to be involved. On 18 December
there was a meeting with consuls of the five guilds
affiliated with the Mercanzia to discuss how to
proceed. The minutes record that a drawing by
Verrocchio was seen and that the views of Piero and
Antonio del Pollaiuolo were heard. Verrocchio was
paid eight *lire* for a drawing of Faith, but Piero was
confirmed in the commission, to be paid 20 florins for
each figure (the sum included materials as well as
workmanship). He was to be held to a strict deadline
and equally strict quality control. Two figures were
to be produced every three months starting from
1 January. They were to be at least as good as the
first figure, as would be judged by four delegates from
the Sei.

This was a demanding task, given the life-size scale of the figures (the panels average 1.67 metres in height), their regal settings and their rich robes as rendered by Piero. It is hardly surprising that Piero fell behind the stipulated schedule. It was not unusual for projects to take many more years than contracted. The fact that when the next two paintings were not completed by May 1470 one of the appointed deputies, Tommaso Soderini, convinced the Sei to commission a figure from Botticelli, suggests that Soderini was exerting special pressure for a protégé. Documents do not survive that tell the rest of the story in detail, but committee consultation and artistic competition resulted in Piero del Pollaiuolo delivering the second and third panels, *Temperance* and *Faith*, by 2 August, and Botticelli *Fortitude* by 18 August (fig. 30). Despite the undoubted strengths of Botticelli's figure – solid, exquisite and thoughtful – Piero finished the series, producing Virtues that demonstrated his own *virtù*, or excellence, as a painter of elegant and ornate figures.

SACRED BUILDINGS

'The beauty and the unique embellishment of buildings . . . includes the sublimeness and the remarkable magnificence of the sacred temples.'[67]

The sacred centre of the city – the Duomo and the Baptistery – had been the focus of constant, competitive embellishment for centuries. Dedicated to the patron-protectors of the city, the Virgin and the Baptist, those 'temples' were symbols of civic pride as well as sites of intense devotion. Their magnificence was a direct expression of the magnitude of their grace. As mentioned above every will drawn

up in Florence contained a donation to the construction of the cathedral as well as to the maintenance of the city walls. The wool guild was responsible for the cathedral and the merchants (or Calimala) for the Baptistery. Given the scale of the operation, the board of works supervising the building and decoration of the cathedral – its *Opera* – had evolved into a highly developed organisation, one that survives to this day. The enormous enterprise of creating the architectural and decorative works for both had effectively produced schools for the sculptors and goldsmiths of the city, not only supplying work and materials, but also a training ground, a showcase and a reference point.

Work on the cathedral dome was completed and the copper ball placed atop it in May 1471. Inside, beneath the cupola, the intarsias of the north sacristy, the Sagrestia delle Messe, had recently been finished (1463–5) by Giuliano da Maiano and his collaborators and, after thirty years of work, the sacristy's bronze doors by Luca della Robbia were installed in 1475.[68] There were plans (subsequently abandoned) for a choir beneath the dome with woodwork by Giuliano da Maiano and sculptures in bronze and marble by Verrocchio. Instead, tapestries were woven for the site by Giovanni d'Alemagna.[69]

The Calimala took care not to be outdone by the vast enterprise of the cathedral, ensuring that the splendour of the Baptist's shrine was never dimmed by the shadow of the cupola. Indeed one feature of the Baptistery projects is their emphatic preciousness: from the gilt bronze doors of the exterior to the silver altar and altar furnishings and richly embroidered liturgical vestments that would glimmer inside beneath the thirteenth-century gold mosaics of its dome. Whereas the cathedral was a monument in the process of coming into being, the Baptistery had been

at the centre of the city's consciousness for so long that its actual origins (it was built in the twelfth century) had been forgotten in favour of a mythical beginning as a Roman temple of Mars. The assertion of history is another feature of Baptistery commissions: not ancient history, but the history of salvation and particularly the Baptist's place in that history, which was told repeatedly in the decorations of the building. The 1470s saw significant additions to that repertoire.

At this time it was decided to complete the scenes from the life of Saint John on the silver altar. Begun in 1367, the front panels were finished by various goldsmiths by 1410. The central tabernacle was commissioned in 1445 and its figure of Saint John was cast by Michelozzo in 1452, but the altar still lacked the side panels telling the beginning and the conclusion of the Baptist's story. On 24 July 1477 the Calimala announced that it would commission the four panels. This prompted a number of goldsmiths to submit models in terracotta. The commissions were awarded on 13 January 1478, with Bernardo Cennini assigned the panel of the *Annunciation to Zachariah* and the *Visitation*, Antonio del Pollaiuolo the *Birth of the Baptist* (fig. 31), Antonio Salvi and Francesco di Giovanni the *Feast of Herod*, and Verrocchio the *Beheading of the Baptist* (fig. 32). The reliefs were finished by the end of the year. It took another year for the frame with figures in niches to be completed. The artists were paid for most of the work and materials in 1480. The deliberations state that the reliefs were to be in the 'shape and form' ('nel modo e forma') of the front panels.[71] In terms of measurement and framing, this is true, but the artists shaped the stories according to their own styles, probably stimulated by the competitive context – as the Calimala might have expected.

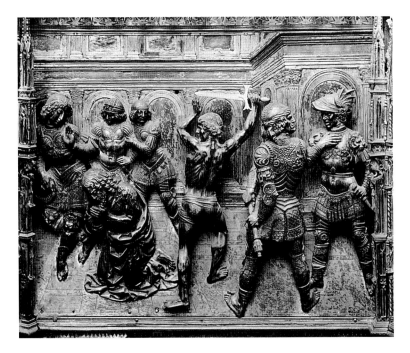

Fig. 31 ANTONIO DEL POLLAIUOLO, *Birth of the Baptist*, 1478–80. Silver, 31.5 × 42 cm. Florence, Museo dell'Opera del Duomo.

Fig. 32 ANDREA DEL VERROCCHIO, *Beheading of the Baptist*, 1478–80. Silver, 31.5 × 42 cm. Florence, Museo dell'Opera del Duomo.

Between 1466 and 1480 one of the most extensive, and expensive, cycles ever devoted to the Baptist's life was woven in the panels that were embroidered in gold and silk by a dedicated team of master embroiderers after drawings by Antonio del Pollaiuolo (cat. no. 48). Twenty-seven scenes survive from the set of ecclesiastical vestments, two dalmatics, a chasuble and a cope, whose total cost apparently came to 3179 florins.[70] There are two payments of 90 florins each to Antonio, in 1469 and 1480, for his designs.

Antonio del Pollaiuolo's privileged status as a designer for the Baptistery was confirmed by other commissions he received from the Calimala as part of their long-term project to revive and augment the Baptistery's liturgical treasure. At the end of the 1450s and continuing in the 1460s he had made the lower part of the great silver cross intended initially to display a relic of the True Cross (fig. 58).[72] In 1465 he was commissioned to make the pair of equally enormous silver and enamelled candlesticks to flank the cross on the silver altar on feast days.[73] Shortly after the altar relief commission, in 1478, he also took on the project to house what was, for the Baptistery, perhaps a still more precious relic, Saint John the Baptist's prophetic right index finger.[74] Like Antonio's coloured *modello* for an altar image with the Baptism of Christ, referred to by an eighteenth-century source, reliquary and candlesticks no longer survive.[75]

The 'sublimeness' of the Baptistery owed much to its status as a public shrine. But the 'sacred temples' of Florence were many and various, and their beauty depended in great part upon the pious undertakings of its private citizens. The building and decoration of churches were first on Matteo Palmieri's list of the honourable and glorious expenditures of the 'magnificent' man.[76]

One instance of a such a project from the 1470s is the sacristy of S. Felicita (fig. 33). In his will dated 15 March 1474 the 'magnificent and generous knight' Giovanni di Antonio Canigiani (1404–77) left property to the value of 550 florins to complete the construction of the sacristy and its chapel and to endow daily masses in perpetuity.[77] Although he had moved a few streets away from his ancestral parish church of S. Felicita, he reverted to it for the eternal remembrance of his soul. He did so in terms that might have been inspired by his lifetime allegiance

Fig. 33 View of altar chapel, sacristy of Santa Felicita, Florence.

to the Medici, by imitating their construction of a sacristy chapel at S. Lorenzo.

Antonio di Puccio Pucci (1418–87) was another prominent Medicean whose concern for his soul and those of his ancestors involved him in a magnificent project in the 1470s. He supplied the altarpiece of the *Martyrdom of Saint Sebastian* (cat. no. 43) to the oratory dedicated to that saint at SS. Annunziata, which was also the Pucci funerary chapel. The family burial chapel was first established in the choir of SS. Annunziata by Antonio's father and uncles in the 1440s. In the early 1450s it was moved to the new oratory built at Antonio's expense. In terms of ecclesiastical patronage the move to SS. Annunziata was a move away from the Pucci's parish church of S. Michele Visdomini. SS. Annunziata was still in the Pucci's neighbourhood, however, and it was a church of greater prestige, being the site of a miraculous

image of the Annunciation and one of the city's most important pilgrimage shrines. From the mid-1440s it had also become the site of Medici patronal intervention. An ambitious scheme of expansion was begun there, and Pucci involvement in the church must be viewed in tandem with that of the Medici.[78] By the 1470s Antonio was indisputably the most prominent member of the family – and also an ageing one. Recently discovered payments from 1474 to Piero del Pollaiuolo for part of his work on the altarpiece prove that it dates from this time.[79] The extremely high price that Vasari cites for the panel (300 *scudi*) has not been confirmed. Even if the figure is exaggerated, Vasari's statement accurately recalls the reputation achieved by a work whose singular scale and ambition set new standards in altarpiece design.

The Pucci family, particularly Antonio's branch, owed its fortune and its rise in the social and political scale to its constancy to the Medici cause from the time of Cosimo. Antonio's second marriage had been arranged by Cosimo and those of the children from that marriage were arranged by Lorenzo. His letters to Lorenzo report on 'our affairs', meaning those of the state and of their families.[80] His choice of the Pollaiuolo brothers to paint this altarpiece shows his sympathy for Lorenzo's judgement in matters of style as well as those of state. The discreet inclusion of the Medici emblem of the diamond ring on the trappings of a horse in the background of the painting represents a subtle acknowledgment of the enduring alliance between the families (fig. 34).

Whereas Antonio Pucci may be described as Lorenzo's right-hand man – as he is placed in the portraits in the chapel of Francesco Sassetti, another Medici ally (fig. 35), Tommaso Soderini's position with regard to Lorenzo could not have been so easily depicted.

Fig. 34 ANTONIO AND PIERO DEL POLLAIUOLO, *The Martyrdom of Saint Sebastian*, detail of cat. no. 43.

Soderini (1403–85) was a senior statesman, with considerable influence both in the city and outside it. Lorenzo's uncle by marriage (to his second wife, Dianora Tornabuoni), he had been among those whose arguments in favour of Lorenzo secured his coming to power in 1469. But he was independently ambitious and could be as dangerous as he was influential. Although by 1476 Lorenzo could say that he 'knew he could trust him freely' as one of the 'most prudent and wisest' men of Florence, that trust was hard won.[81] Unlike Pucci, who was a 'new man', Soderini had no need to make friendship with the Medici a feature of his commemorative schemes. In 1431 he had moved with his brother and his mother into a house in the S. Spirito quarter, returning to a part of the city traditionally inhabited by the Soderini, on the other side of the Arno from the Medici enclave. He contributed

to the renovations of his parish church of S. Frediano and of the Carmelite church of S. Maria del Carmine.[82] It was the latter that Tommaso and his brother Niccolò had chosen for their burial place ('among their ancestors'), taking up the patronage rights of the Soderini chapel.[83] Niccolò had been exiled in 1466 and was a declared enemy of the regime, so Tommaso assumed entire responsibility there. Although of undisputed status, Tommaso was not as wealthy as the Medici or as some of the other leading men of the city, but he had every reason to want to maintain his reputation as being among the *magnifici*. He did this by shrewdly concentrating his expenditures locally, spending more on renovation than on lavish new buildings, and reasserting family traditions and privileges.

Tommaso was foremost among those acquiring the patronage rights to the church of S. Frediano, arguing ancestral connections there in petitioning the pope about this matter. In the 1470s he spent 280 florins on its restoration and donated income-yielding property for its maintenance.[84] The renovation policy was also applied to the church's altarpieces. On 26 July 1469 the painter Neri di Bicci recorded a commission to make a new-style frame with columns, architrave, frieze and cornice for an old panel ('una tavola antica'). He added four saints in the spandrels and a predella with the *Pietà* (for a total of 70 *lire*, or about 21 florins).[85] A subsequent entry records a commission from August 1471 for the reworking of an old altarpiece for a new altar next to the sacristy. This not only included re-fashioning the frame to current taste ('a l'uso d'ogidi'), but also the total repainting of one of the saints to change a Saint Fredianus, the titular saint of the church, into a Saint Margaret, the titular saint of the new

Fig. 35 DOMENICO GHIRLANDAIO, *The Confirmation of the Rule of Saint Francis*, detail showing Antonio Pucci, Lorenzo de' Medici, Francesco and Teodoro Sassetti, 1479–85. Mural painting. Florence, Santa Trinita, Sassetti Chapel.

altar (fig. 36). He also freshened-up the other saints, one of which survives, a Saint Blaise, attributed to Agnolo Gaddi. The total cost of this transformation was 40 *lire* (12 florins).[86] This was an extremely thrifty way to supply an altarpiece, not only when measured against the reputed price of the Pucci altarpiece, but against others. The normal price for such an altar panel ranged from 40 to 70 florins. Even the additional costs of the curtain and the dossal, which came to between three and four florins, were hardly extravagant, still less the four *lire* (about one florin) given to Neri for repairing the 'broken' and 'ruined' altar cross and candlesticks for the high altar on 26 September 1472.[87] What Soderini seems to have done was to re-use extant altar furnishings in the church, putting them in good order and making them look less archaic. This had the benefit of economy and it was also in line with what seems to have been his

policy of affirming traditions. It proves a general awareness of what was old and out-of-date, accompanied by a respect for venerated works. By calling upon Neri di Bicci, Soderini also increased the effects of his patronage at S. Frediano by giving work to an artist who was a resident of the parish and who, like himself, was active in the confraternity located at the church. He had supported Botticelli for the Mercanzia commission, but in his own quarter Soderini did not demonstrate a need to ally himself with new trends in taste. He kept familiar works in familiar places. This suggests that there could be alternative strategies for choosing among artists' styles and styles of patronage.

Soderini also sponsored renovation at the convent of the Carmine. In the 1460s following the request of the friars, he financed the restoration of the novices' dormitory, the chapter-house and the refectory. The work took a year. At its conclusion Neri di Bicci was called upon to paint the sculpted Soderini coat of arms in those places and on the organ loft.[88] In 1472 Antonio del Pollaiuolo began a silver cross for the convent church, paid for principally by a relative from another branch of the Soderini family, Madonna Tommasa di Luigi Soderini in 1473.[89] On 7 March 1474 Tommaso added a codicil to his previous wills, instructing his heirs to spend 500 florins on a library, placing his arms there.[90] Taken as a whole, the similarity of Tommaso's donations to the Observant Carmelites with Cosimo de' Medici's patronage of the convent of the Observant Dominicans at S. Marco would have been unmistakable, although achieved at less cost. Cosimo was reputed to have spent 'more than forty thousand florins.'[91] However calculated their nature, Soderini's benefactions to the churches of his neighbourhood were also genuine expressions of devotion. As a

Fig. 36 NERI DI BICCI, *Saint Margaret*, 1471. Tempera on panel, 55.9 × 29.2 cm. Cambridge, Mass., Harvard University Art Museums, Fogg Art Museum, Gift of Miss Margaret Whitney.

programme of patronage they comprehensively manifested the exercise of that virtue connected with wealth: 'fitting expenditure involving largeness of scale'.[92]

Even those who did not have the means to be magnificent were devout and regularly made donations 'for the good of their souls' (as expressed in their wills) while participating in neighbourhood projects.

In Soderini's own quarter, for example, the apothecary Mariotto di Marco commissioned an altarpiece for S. Spirito. He was not from one of the grand families of the quarter, or the parish. He, too, chose Neri di Bicci for the task – possibly on the recommendation of the friars of S. Spirito, for whom Neri had worked, possibly from personal knowledge, or a combination of both. Neri's shop was in the same street as Mariotto's, the Porta Rossa on the other side of the Arno. On 7 May 1471 Neri noted that he undertook to paint an altarpiece for Mariotto, which 'he [Mariotto] said he wanted to place in the church of Santo Spirito … in his chapel, or wherever he decided.'[93] The location was left open, but the subject was specified as the archangel Raphael and Tobias, with the archangel Michael to the liturgical right and Gabriel to the left, and below a small fictive panel of the Crucifix with Mary and Saint John, flanked by angels, with a fine gold background and best quality ultramarine: instructions that Neri followed to the letter (fig. 37). Given the precision of the commission, Mariotto's indecision over the location might seem strange, but it was probably caused by the dynamics of patronage at S. Spirito at that moment. The new church, designed by Brunelleschi, had been under construction since the 1430s. On 21 March 1471 there was a fire in the old church, after an ill-fated

attempt to amuse Galeazzo Maria Sforza with an out-of-season (it was Lent) production of the church's famous Pentecost play. The Duke never arrived, but the fireworks exploded nonetheless. A contemporary reported that all of the altars were destroyed.[94] Mariotto was the first to order a replacement, perhaps eager to gain his altar a more prestigious position in the old church (which was restored) or in the new one when it was completed. This was not to be so, Mariotto's family chapel ultimately was in the nave (the seventh chapel on the right), even though, as Mariotto's son complained to the *operai*, they were paying more than others with chapels near the high altar.[95]

Mariotto seems to have been willing to spend. His altarpiece from Neri cost 85 florins, and Mariotto paid directly for the fine pigments Neri had required.[96] The resulting work is indeed sumptuous

Fig. 37 NERI DI BICCI, *Archangel Raphael with Tobias flanked by Saints Michael and Gabriel*, 1471. Tempera on panel, 183.5 × 174.6 cm. Detroit Institute of Arts.

Fig. 38 SANDRO BOTTICELLI, *Adoration of the Magi*, c.1475.
Tempera on panel, 111 × 134 cm. Florence, Galleria degli Uffizi.

not only in the colours used and the gold background, but in the depiction of the brocades in the fashionable clothing and the elaborate dress of the figures. Since 1455 S. Spirito had been the meeting-place of a confraternity dedicated to Archangel Raphael, one of two in Florence dedicated to the saint. Mariotto's altar might originally have been intended to replace the first altarpiece lost in the fire, but Francesco Botticini later produced yet another version of the three archangels (now in the Uffizi) for the church's 'Raphael altar'. The subject of Raphael and Tobias was a popular one; Neri himself painted at least nine versions of different sizes.⁹⁷ Mariotto's panel had a (now lost) predella showing miracles of the Angel Raphael, who was known as a healer and as an angel of revelation. Even though the subject of the altarpiece contained no direct reference to a name saint, it placed Mariotto under the patronage or protection of three powerful figures, whose presence on his altar would invite others to remember him in their prayers as well.

Botticelli's *Adoration of the Magi* (fig. 38) commissioned by Guasparre del Lama (*c.*1411–81) for his funerary chapel at S. Maria Novella represents another instance of the way that the patronage of altarpieces could be connected with wider patronage interests. Mariotto may well have hoped that in addition to acting for the benefit of his soul, his gift to S. Spirito would advance his status in that quarter at a time when the greatest families of that neighbourhood were involved with the church. It also answered devotional interests of the convent itself. In Del Lama's case the imagery of the Magi was related to the dedication of the altar to the Epiphany, the feast of the Three Kings on 6 January. Guasparre's name – Caspar – was that of the youngest of the three kings. The kings are shown in the altarpiece at the destination of their journey,

kneeling in homage to the infant Christ. A golden shower pours down towards Christ, who blesses the oldest king, who in turn pauses thoughtfully as he seems about to kiss the child's feet, which he supports with a veil. The mood of the whole painting is subdued. This is not the tumultuous gathering of the *Adoration* tondo painted by Botticelli for Antonio Pucci (cat. no. 7). The centralised composition of Del Lama's painting emphasises the liturgical aspects of its function as an altar image. The careful gestures of the kings as they make their offerings are a reminder of the rituals of the mass. Rather than telling the story as a pageant and procession, which was one popular way of depicting the subject in Florence, the scene was organised to bring out its eucharistic significance.⁹⁸ As such it referred in general to the Dominican order's interest in the feast of Corpus Christi and specifically to the fact that in Florence the cults of Corpus Christi and the Epiphany were under the care of the Dominicans of S. Maria Novella. That alone would make Guasparre's an important altar in one of the city's principal churches. Its placement in the church, on the façade wall to the right of the main door, had the added benefit of making it a pendant to the mural of the *Annunciation*, also on that wall, which was a version of the miraculous image at SS. Annunziata. This meant that two of the city's most important feasts were represented there.

But the feast of the Epiphany had further resonance. Every five years a procession of the Magi was staged in Florence and hundreds of Florentines dressed up as the kings and their entourage and paraded around the city re-enacting the journey. This festival was organised by a confraternity dedicated to the Magi, which had come under Medici protection.⁹⁹

The three kings personified Christian devotion, the high become humble – but they were still kings, and the Medici had made the imagery part of their own mythology. This, too, seems to be acknowledged in the Del Lama altar, where the oldest and middle kings are respectively idealised likenesses of Cosimo and Piero de' Medici (fig. 38). Both in profile, they resemble the fictive medallic images of the deceased Medici that decorated a deluxe manuscript of Aristotle's *Physics*, produced in the mid-1470s, with illuminations by Francesco Rosselli. In the manuscript they are placed among cameos of Roman emperors, emblematically joining them as examples of rulership.[100] There is no reason to suggest that Guasparre had access to this manuscript. On the contrary. There is no proof, not even in Lorenzo's vast correspondence, that he had any direct contact with him. Del Lama was an exchange broker, registered with the bankers' guild – a tenuous professional tie to the Medici. Son of a barber, his career was distinguished by as many setbacks as successes. Botticelli's painting may be read as a form of hopeful tribute – a bid for Lorenzo's patronage. Lorenzo can be identified in the painting as the pensive young man standing above the youngest king, Caspar. Rather than referring directly to the manuscript medallions, the eulogistic portraits of the painting relate to a more general tendency in Florence to praise the Medici in terms of ideal rulers and to develop a commemorative iconography for them. Botticelli, for example, portrayed a young man holding a medal of Cosimo to his heart at about the same time (*c*.1475) as Del Lama's altarpiece can reasonably be dated (fig. 82). Del Lama's choice of Botticelli might also have been influenced by his aspirations. Guasparre is not among known Medici supporters, but the executors of his first will were part of the regime. In addition,

Francesco di Niccolò Cocchi, who was left 100 florins in the will, was Gonfaloniere di Giustizia in 1469, and was a strong supporter of Lorenzo.[101] It seems as though Guasparre was moving among the Mediceans, even though he ultimately failed to profit from these connections.

However futile these earthly hopes, the chief message of the painting is one of salvation through devotion. As patron of the chapel, Del Lama brought the magnificence of kings to his hopes for posterity while also embellishing the church of S. Maria Novella with a small (111 x 134 cm) but intensely beautiful altarpiece.

Portraits are also a feature of the mural that Amerigo di Nastagio Vespucci (1394–1472) commissioned for his funerary chapel (figs. 39 and 40). The figures kneeling in prayer to the far left and right of the upper portion can probably be identified as Amerigo and his wife. A tomb marker on the floor to the left of the wall has the date 1472. Amerigo was an eminent notary and jurist and a faithful Medici servant. The Vespucci clan were prominent in the parish of Ognissanti and in the 1470s and 1480s were benefactors of their local church and of its local painters. Amerigo commissioned these murals from Domenico Ghirlandaio and a few years later his son, the learned cleric Giorgio Antonio, commissioned murals of two of the Fathers of the Church, Saints Jerome and Augustine, from Ghirlandaio and Botticelli respectively. Both artists were neighbours of the Vespucci.

The Vespucci chapel combines images of comfort and sorrow. Above, the Virgin extends her mantle to protect representatives of various ages and conditions of man and womankind – youth and old age, lay and religious (fig. 39). Most of them are intentionally generic, as was normally the case in such images.

However, the high-ranking cleric in profile can be reasonably identified as a posthumous tribute to the distinguished theologian and reformer, the Florentine archbishop Antoninus (d. 1459).[102] The figure who looks outwards between Amerigo and the archbishop has the eye-catching glance of a portrait figure, but cannot be firmly identified.

The same is true of the portly saint who stares fixedly towards the nave from the group below (fig. 40). His martyr's palm is held as though it were a pen, about to record a commentary on the pitiful scene his glance invites the worshipper to witness. Neither the saint nor a potential sitter have been convincingly named, but the figure has been made a protagonist and a change in the position of Saint John the Baptist was required to do this.[103] The other saints demonstrate different states of sorrowful meditation and prayer, except for Mary, Mary Magdalene and John the Evangelist who tenderly lower the crumpled body of Christ towards the ground. Flemish inspiration has been cited as source for this image of mourning.[104] The insistent, even awful, physicality of the bleeding figure of Christ may refer to Ghirlandaio's study of the slumping Marsyas of the type restored by Verrocchio in the Medici collection. The gracefully entwining arms of Mary and Christ and the delicately counterposed hands of Christ and John the Evangelist also suggest Verrocchio's influence on the younger painter. Above all, the crystalline sculptural forms, legible even from a distance, show Ghirlandaio responding in paint to what he had learnt from sculpture.

As these instances show, private benefaction took many forms and involved many interests: those of the donor, those of the receiving institution, and those of the administering body (the board of works that might be appointed directly by the church involved,

Figs. 39 and 40 DOMENICO GHIRLANDAIO, *Madonna della Misericordia*, and *Pietà*, both c.1472. Detached murals. Florence, Ognissanti, Vespucci Chapel.

by the commune or by a supervising guild). Individuals making bequests usually did so with the purpose of representing their lineage as well as themselves, expressly including their ancestors and their descendants, all held to share a common concern for pious remembrance and family honour. Expenditure was generally concentrated in neighbourhood churches, both those near town houses and those near country estates. But the principal churches of the mendicant orders, particularly the Franciscan church of S. Croce and the Dominican church of S. Maria Novella, held considerable prestige, and could take precedent over parish. This was also true of the major shrines, such as SS. Annunziata, or pet projects, such as Cosimo de' Medici's foundation, the Badia at S. Domenico, where the chapels were purchased and equipped by Medici supporters (all but one of them employees in their bank).[105]

Monumental, or magnificent, patronage was rarely undertaken by women, whose personal property or wealth was usually tied up in their dowries and whose financial independence was restricted. Widows acted as executors of their husbands' wills (as in the cases of Matteo Palmieri and Guasparre del Lama). Women could and did make bequests, usually to established sites of family piety. The endowments made by their husbands and fathers were also viewed as representing their good, as their inclusion beneath the Virgin's open mantle and the donor portraits in the Vespucci mural illustrate.

One direct form of female patronage was that of the female religious orders. The nuns at S. Apollonia offer an example of this in the 1470s. Observant Benedictines, they had received special protection and financial privileges from Pope Eugene IV in the 1440s because of their strict behaviour. Though cloistered,

they were not removed from the cares of maintaining their convent and its ritual life. They had the responsibility of managing the resources and revenues that came to them from bequests, from the dowries of the young women who entered the convent, and from gifts from their families. In the 1470s they directed some of these funds towards altarpieces. On 8 June 1472, Neri di Bicci recorded that he had agreed to 'have made and to paint a wood panel' for the abbess and nuns showing the Virgin and Child with four saints.[106] The details of the transaction show that they determined the programme and the look of their altarpiece as well as its cost. They must have been satisfied with the result, because subsequent commissions were given to Neri, including one for a (now lost) altarpiece with the *Coronation of the Virgin*.[107] The nuns of S. Apollonia seem to have had visual literacy as well as business sense. They chose an artist

Fig. 41 ANDREA DEL VERROCCHIO, *Crucified Christ*, mid-1470s. Painted, stuccoed and gessoed limewood, cork and painted and gessoed linen, height 87 cm. Florence, Museo Nazionale del Bargello.

In the mid-1470s Verrocchio made a wooden sculpture of the Crucified Christ for S. Maria della Pietà (fig. 41).[108] Gessoed and painted, it must have been intended to stress the reality of Christ's sufferings and sacrifice in order that they be vividly remembered by the gathered brothers of the confraternity. In 1478 the company of woolcarders had Cosimo Rosselli paint an altarpiece for their meeting place in the chapel of S. Andrea in the church of S. Candida (fig. 42).[109] It was a *laudesi* company, that is, one devoted to singing hymns of praise (lauds) to the Virgin Mary, who is the central figure of the altarpiece. The angels holding flowers and the star on the Virgin's robe allude to verses of the songs that would be chanted in her praise. She is further honoured by the sumptuous setting of multi-coloured marbles. Around her gather saints who would remind the confraternity of its august patrons and protectors, the city's saints John the Baptist and Zenobius at the far left and right, and, nearest to the Virgin, Andrew (the titular saint of the chapel) and Bartholomew (the patron saint of the company's chaplain, Ser Bartolommeo di Matteo). The lower social rank of the confraternity's members did not prevent them from representing their corporate interests in the richest terms. In choosing Cosimo Rosselli, they were opting for an artist who had recently done important works for SS. Annunziata (including the mural of about 1475 in its entrance cloister showing the order's founder Saint Philip Benizzi donning the Servite habit), as well as altarpieces for a number of other confraternities. Although now relatively neglected, Rosselli was at that time much in demand for the adornment of the 'sacred temples' of the city.[110]

of considerable technical skill, and one who must have been known for reliability and efficiency and for his ability to combine *all'antica* motifs with traditional formulas at very good prices (40 florins for the first and 20 florins for the second painting). One wonders if they did not bargain to a certain extent on Neri's piety.

Another form of patronage was that of religious confraternities – lay associations whose members gathered for purposes of prayer, penitence and charity. Among those commissioning major works for ecclesiastical sites, confraternities represented the widest social range. Some, like the confraternity of S. Maria della Pietà, drew a high proportion of their membership from the élite. Others, like that of S. Andrea dei Cardatori (woolcarders), were made up of artisans. They all required images to focus their meditation and to express their communal identity.

Fig. 42 COSIMO ROSSELLI, *Virgin and Child with Saints John the Baptist, Andrew, Bartholomew and Zenobius*, 1478. Tempera on panel, 190.5 × 175.2 cm. Cambridge, Fitzwilliam Museum.

PRIVATE BUILDINGS

*'The beauty and the unique embellishment of buildings . . . resides
. . . in the decorous and most fitting beauty of private dwellings.'*
111

The Florentine cityscape, now so solidly set in stone,
was constantly evolving throughout the fifteenth
century. In every neighbourhood, if not every street, a
major construction project was underway at some
time. 'There are two principal activities in life: one is
to procreate, the other to build' was a maxim Giovanni
Rucellai quoted in his chapbook.[112] Both were
connected with family identity and survival, as the
painstaking inheritance provisions of wills
demonstrate. The suitable 'composition' of a private
dwelling related to the correct projection of a family's
image in the city, one that it was hoped would become
a matter of permanent presence. Not only did the
family's arms conspicuously mark the house, but its
chosen style could qualify or characterise the family's
status.[113] Almost none of the great palaces of
Renaissance Florence has a secure attribution to an
architect in the modern sense. Today's architecture is
most often remembered according to architects whose
styles bear the signature of their originality: in the
fifteenth century the palace builders were the palace
dwellers. The 'great houses' were remembered
according to their owners. Those owners might
sometimes wish to assert independence, and favour
novel motifs, or they might want to find 'the most
fitting beauty' in well-tried forms. In order to do so
they undoubtedly relied upon the expertise of
professionals versed both in design and construction,
but the fame or reputation of the resulting building
was intended to become part of family history, not an
architect's portfolio.

As has been observed in the case of Filippo Strozzi
planning a palace could take decades. Because
neighbourhood was a key element in family identity
and importance, assembling and acquiring a suitable
site in a traditional (and often densely occupied) area
could be a matter of prolonged negotiations. It could
happen that construction and acquisition overlapped.
Sometimes existing houses, or foundations, were used,
renovated and reordered behind unifying façades, as in
Giovanni Rucellai's palace. Other times the site was
cleared, as with the Medici and the Strozzi palaces.
Conception of a project, therefore, might have
preceded its detailed design, and design might have to
be modified according to circumstance.

All of these factors complicate chronology and
enrich notions of authorship and style. The
appearance of private dwellings in this period is best
understood as an accumulation of possibilities rather

Fig. 43 The Pitti palace, Florence, detail showing the original seven-
bay façade.

Fig. 44 Façade of the Pazzi palace, Florence.

than as resulting from a sequence of stylistic development. The palaces that can be dated to the 1470s – including those just completed, those underway, and those started – demonstrate a range of choices. The contrasting forms taken by the houses of Luca di Buonaccorso Pitti (1395–1473) and Jacopo di Andrea Pazzi (1422–78) are good examples (figs. 43 and 44).

When he began planning his palace in the 1450s, Luca Pitti was one of the most powerful men in the city. In his *Florentine Histories* Niccolò Machiavelli wrote that when Luca was Gonfalonier of Justice (1458), he had risen 'to such a reputation that not Cosimo but Messer Luca governed the city. He gained such confidence from this that he began two buildings, one in Florence, the other in Rusciano … both splendid and royal, but the one in the city

was altogether greater than any other that had been built by a private citizen until that day.'[114]

Machiavelli, whose ancestor Girolamo had been first banished, then arrested and finally put to death during Pitti's tenure in that office, had reason to see the massive palace as a strongbox of corruption and a symbol of all that was wrong in those days. But he also conveys its unabashed grandeur. Set against the hillside that provided the quarry for the huge blocks of stone used to build it, its three equal storeys of rustication make it more formidable than the Palazzo Medici with its gradations of worked stone and ally it even more closely to the masonry of the Palazzo della Signoria (figs. 3 and 7). As with Cosimo's palace, the knowledgeable viewer could understand a reference to ancient precedent in the type of rustication, which was based on the remains of a wall in the forum of Augustus in Rome.[115] All could admire the order of the whole and the innovative elements such as the Ionic balustrades in front of the top storeys. Luca's house was built on a site that, unusually, was separated from the street, and where (more typically) the extended family had been living in a group of older houses that had been joined together.[116] When Luca decided to build, probably around 1450, he added to the properties, buying houses that he cleared away, intentionally extending the site to create a piazza that would enhance the building's monumentality by its imposing isolation. Even in its original form (with seven window bays), the palace was a colossus towering over the neighbourhood and demanding recognition of its magnificence. It was still being built when Luca made his will, just before his death in February 1473.

Whereas Pitti was of established citizen stock, with a solid tradition of office-holding, the Pazzi were a family of proud feudal origins. Jacopo Pazzi's palace, which dominates the street with elegant assurance, is usually dated from after 1458 to around 1469 (fig. 44).[117] Jacopo's new palace was built on the site of an extant family house (inherited with his two brothers from his father in 1445), which he enlarged, not to create a piazza like Luca Pitti but, like Cosimo de' Medici, to exploit a corner, with perspectives along two streets. The family's arms are on the edge of the palace and are visible from both sides. The ground floor is rusticated stone, but the upper storeys are stuccoed, so that the emblematic decorative stonework of the window frames is thrown into relief. The refinement of the carved decoration of the palace exterior and its courtyard can be related to an ornamental style developed in prominent goldsmiths' shops like that of Maso Finiguerra and by associated woodworkers, as in the intarsia work of Giuliano da Maiano (Finiguerra's brother-in-law) and his firm. A few months after the Pazzi conspiracy, Giuliano made a claim to the Ufficiali dei Ribelli for 2149 *lire* owed to him by the Pazzi for work on the palace, the chapter-house at S. Croce and their villa.[118] It is not known whether this sum was for furnishings or for construction and sculpting, but Jacopo Pazzi's taste was in accordance with that of Giuliano's firm and of a sort that would be viewed as both *all'antica* and up-to-date. It was conspicuously different from the Medici model and a civilised declaration of the proud independence that was to be played out so violently in the conspiracy of 1478.

Yet another stylistic strategy was adopted by the banker Giovanni di Bono Boni. Giovanni began to acquire property on a site near his father's house at the end of the present-day via Tornabuoni in 1461. Building was in progress by the mid-1460s (fig. 45).[119] Although affluent, the Boni family did not have a long heritage of office-holding – of status (*stato*) in the city.

Giovanni's father was the first of the lineage to be elected to the Signoria, in 1442.[120] Rather than choose a style of building that would appear assertively novel or grandiose, Giovanni and his father (after Giovanni's death in 1466) opted for an updated version of recognised forms, as though constructing a family history in the new house. The pointed arches of the door frame and of the window frames that rest directly on the mouldings dividing the storeys echo the forms and the arrangements found on the thirteenth-century palace of the Spini family and the fourteenth-century Minerbetti palace at the other end of the street. These old-fashioned motifs are complemented by *all'antica* detailing, notably the differentiated mouldings that divide the first two storeys and the egg and dart course beneath the cornice. The stone blocks are evenly cut, as if commenting on the rough walls of the earlier palaces.

Fig. 45 Façade of the Boni palace (now Palazzo Antinori), Florence.

Though restrained, the palace façade is still magnificent – its carefully worked masonry must have been extremely costly. Perhaps too costly. The Boni fortunes declined sharply, ending in bankruptcy in 1474. On 11 July 1475, Lorenzo de' Medici bought the 'great house'; in August he gave it to the loyal Medici friends Carlo and Ugolino Martelli.[121]

Neither the fate nor the conservatism of the Boni palace was exceptional. In 1469, in the Medici palace, and on the eve of becoming a partner in the Florentine branch of the Medici bank, Francesco di Antonio Nori (1430–78) signed the contract to buy a 'venerable palace' that had become available in his family neighbourhood.[122] Although Nori's career was advancing, and he had been married to one of Lorenzo's Tornabuoni cousins, his own lineage lacked prestige in the city. When he renovated and enlarged the palace in the 1470s, he retained its old-fashioned look, perhaps out of a desire to associate himself and his family with a longer history. It is also as though, by placing their supporters in impressive, but conservative, houses around the city, the Medici were demonstrating that their magnificence was solidly traditional.

This does not mean that Medici patronage, in the political sense, encouraged reactionary patronage in an artistic or aesthetic sense. It shows, in palaces as in paintings or sculpture, that style had meaning. It provoked variety and enterprise and resulted in significant novelty as often or as well as meaningful references to the past. The commission to Antonio del Pollaiuolo to fresco a public room of the Lanfredini villa at Arcetri, to the south of the city, represents a case in point.

The villa La Gallina is now a hotchpotch of late medieval and nineteenth-century historicist features, obscuring what was probably a modest two-storey country dwelling, suited to the middling status of its owners, the brothers Jacopo and Giovanni di Orsino Lanfredini.[123] Jacopo and Giovanni made their careers as loyal servants of the Florentine state, serving variously as ambassadors (and even as spies) in Venice, Ferrara, Naples and Rome. Both were staunch Mediceans. Not wealthy and not in a position to spend lavishly on building, they commissioned a mural from Antonio del Pollaiuolo (fig. 46), whom Jacopo, in a letter of the 1460s, declared to be 'the greatest master in Florence … in the opinion of all those who know about such things'.[124] A commission to Antonio could be read as an indirect statement of Medici allegiance, given the family's traditional support for him. The extraordinary frieze of dancing nude figures in the large ground-floor hall of their villa (now badly damaged) gave Antonio the opportunity to demonstrate his abilities in the terms that first made him famous in the *Labours of Hercules* canvases for the Medici palace. The dancers are depicted, like Hercules, as *all'antica* nudes in dramatic action, though their joyful bearing would have been

Fig. 46 ANTONIO DEL POLLAIUOLO, *Dancers and architectural perspectives*, 1470s. Mural. Florence, Arcetri, Villa La Gallina.

opposite the church (fig. 47). The brothers had purchased a house in 1463; Francesco's tax declaration of 1469 states that it was to be renovated. The timing of the work (probably completed by 1474) coincides with Lorenzo's joust, which was held in the piazza, as was Giuliano's in 1475. The project might be connected with the 1469 joust: as a lasting contribution to its decoration, it could be seen as a manifestation of the ideal of the golden age being proclaimed by the festivities. The sculptural use of arches and pilaster orders on the façade shows direct study of ancient prototypes and suggested a new order of beauty for the city.[125]

Bartolommeo Scala's house was equally original (fig. 48). Scala (1430–97) was the city's chancellor and a Medici 'new man'. Having risen to the highest offices in the city, Scala could write candidly of himself that he 'came to the republic naked,

seen as appropriate for a country property. Those who knew the Medici collections might also have been able to appreciate Antonio's artful adaptation to a classicising bacchic form of the *moresca* dancers seen on Netherlandish cloth paintings of the type found in the Medici villa at Careggi. The overall aesthetic of the mural, with its pale figures isolated against a dark foil, is indebted to ancient cameos of the kind owned by Lorenzo (fig. 21). The Lanfredini mural thus succeeded in being both sophisticatedly referential and completely new.

The city palace built by the brothers Francesco and Borghino di Niccolò Cocchi and the suburban villa built by Bartolommeo Scala could be described in similar terms. In both cases the patrons were loyal Mediceans and in both cases the young Giuliano da Sangallo was probably the architect. The façade of Palazzo Cocchi dominates the end of Piazza S. Croce

Fig. 47 Façade of the Cocchi-Serristori palace, Florence.

Fig. 48 Courtyard of the Scala palace (now Palazzo Scala della Gherardesca), Florence.

disadvantaged, of the lowest parentage, full of confidence, but absolutely penniless, without reputation, patrons, or kinsmen.'[126] Ambition, intelligence and Medici support guaranteed his success, and in turn his support for Lorenzo in the key years of the 1470s helped guarantee the young leader success in establishing his regime. Scala was more than a political ally, he was a learned man who shared Lorenzo's cultural enthusiasms. His erudition was built into his extraordinary house.

Scala had no ancestral neighbourhood in Florence – he was born in Colle Val d'Elsa. He chose to build his house in an area of monastic gardens and farms in a zone just inside one of the northern gates of the city, which Lorenzo was soon to make part of an urban development project.[127] This allowed him to create a building that was at once both ancient and new. It was a type described by Leon Battista Alberti in his treatise *On Architecture*, as requiring 'both the dignity of a town house and the gaiety of the villa . . . the suburban garden'.[128] It combines notions of villa life derived from Pliny the Younger with the form of the Roman house as defined in Book 6 of Vitruvius's *Ten Books on Architecture*. The house was remodelled in the late sixteenth century and was subsequently absorbed into an eighteenth-century palace, but its original plan has been reconstructed as a square with a large courtyard, or atrium, at the centre. The obvious inspiration for its architecture is not the colonnades of Florentine courtyards, but the triumphal arches found in Rome. Such arches incorporated panels with figured reliefs and similarly in Scala's courtyard there is a stucco frieze with fables taken from a collection (the *Hundred Apologues*) written by Scala in imitation of Aesop. Imbued with Stoic philosophy and subtle wit, they are reminders of Scala's belief in the hard work and virtuous effort that he put into climbing the ladder

(the *scala*) of success.[129] An emblematic ladder is on the pediment of the temple in the panel showing Poverty pleading to Mercury, the god of trade (fig. 49). Scala's palace was clearly a studied work, a statement about his character and his achievements. It anticipates Lorenzo's equally studied and innovative villa at Poggio a Caiano and indicates a developing interest in expanding the expressive as well as the functional possibilities of buildings. While the concepts might have been his, the realisation of his ideas required skilled artisans. As with the Cocchi palace, the most likely candidate for the building is Giuliano da Sangallo, later Lorenzo's favourite architectural collaborator. Giuliano avidly studied the ruins of ancient Rome and brought passion and knowledge to the enterprise of rivalling Rome in Florence. But he needed guidance from the learned men, the amateurs, who owned and could read the architectural treatises – which were in Latin and still in manuscript form – so that the ideas they contained could become realities.

The creative community of interest informing Scala's palace project is representative of the 1470s. In this decade both traditions and new enthusiasms encouraged patrons to make ambitious demands upon an artisan population that was more than prepared to meet them and in turn to stimulate ever more adventurous requests for their skills.

Fig. 49 Attributed to BERTOLDO DI GIOVANNI, *Allegory of Negligentia*, 1480s. Stucco relief, 140 × 400 cm. Florence, Scala palace.

In Florence there were copper- and silver-based coins used locally for general circulation (*monete di piccioli*) and the internationally famed gold coin, the florin. The *lira* was the money of account, used for recorded transactions. The *lira* was divided into twenty *soldi*. There were twelve *denari* to a *soldo*. The value of the *lira* fluctuated with regard to the florin. It fell slightly overall during the 1470s moving between 5.5 and just under six *lire* to the florin in the course of the decade.

1 F. Guicciardini, *Storie fiorentine dal 1378 al 1509*, ed. R. Palmarocchi, Bari 1931, chapter 3, p. 24: 'In questo tempo ed anno 1470, Lorenzo de' Medici cominciò in Firenze a pigliare piede.'

2 N. Rubinstein, *The Government of Florence under the Medici*, Oxford 1966, p. 175, quoting from Lorenzo's *Ricordi*: 'principali della città e dello stato'.

3 See for this expression and its meanings, F.W. Kent, 'Patron-Client Networks in Renaissance Florence and the Emergence of Lorenzo as "Maestro della Bottega"', in *Lorenzo de' Medici. New Perspectives*, ed. B. Toscani, New York 1993, pp. 279–314. For this period, see also his article, 'The Young Lorenzo, 1449–69', in *Lorenzo the Magnificent. Culture and Politics*, M. Mallett and N. Mann eds., London 1996, pp. 1–22.

4 For the definition of Lorenzo as 'arbiter of taste', see E.H. Gombrich, 'The Early Medici as Patrons of Art', in *Norm and Form. Studies in the Art of the Renaissance*, London 1966, p. 54; see Kent, 1993, pp. 280–1 and *passim*, for the role of arbiter or broker in a wider social and political context.

5 Vespasiano da Bisticci, *The Vespasiano Memoirs. Lives of Illustrious Men of the XVth Century*, trans. W.G. and E. Waters, New York 1963, p. 224.

6 See below, p. 51. For an account of Lorenzo's early patronage, see F.W. Kent, 'Lorenzo de' Medici, Madonna Scolastica Rondinelli e la politica di mecenatismo architettonico nel convento delle Murate a Firenze (1471–72)', in *Arte, committenza ed economia a Roma e nelle corti del Rinascimento*, A. Esch and C.L. Frommel, eds., Turin 1995, pp. 353–82. A more detailed consideration will be given by F.W. Kent in *'A Hunger for Beauty': Lorenzo de' Medici, Amateur and Patron of Art* (forthcoming).

7 B.L. Brown, 'The Patronage and Building History of the Tribuna of SS. Annunziata in Florence: A reappraisal in light of new documentation', *Mitteilungen des Kunsthistorischen Institutes in Florenz*, 25, 1981, p. 129, and R. Fubini, ed., *Lorenzo de' Medici. Lettere*, Florence 1977, I, no. 78, p. 277 (22 May 1471): 'il parere mio … è questo, che havendo epsa Vostra Signoria a spendere e sua danari qua, per nessuno modo si debbe ritrarre dalla impresa sua, ma seguitarla a punto secondo il gusto e appetito suo, al quale ognuno qui s'accorderà volentieri et lauderallo come ragionevolmente si debbe fare.'

8 See Kent 1995.

9 See P. Foster, *A Study of Lorenzo de' Medici's Villa at Poggio a Caiano*, PhD thesis, Yale University, New Haven 1973. For the 1474 letter from Bernardo Rucellai to Lorenzo, see F.W. Kent, 'Lorenzo de' Medici's Acquisition of Poggio a Caiano in 1474 and an Early Reference to His Architectural Expertise', *Journal of the Warburg and Courtauld Institutes*, 42, 1979, pp.250–7.

10 For the documents relating to this project, see E. Wilder, C. Kennedy, P. Bacci, *The Unfinished Monument by Andrea del Verrocchio to the Cardinal Niccolò Forteguerri at Pistoia*, Northampton, Mass. 1932; for further discussion see A. Butterfield, *The Sculptures of Andrea del Verrocchio*, New Haven and London 1997, pp. 137–54, and cat. no. 21, pp. 223–8.

11 Luigi Pulci, 'La Giostra', in *Opere Minori*, ed. P. Orvieto, Milan 1986, verse 64, p. 86: 'che può interpretarsi/Tornare il tempo e 'l secol rinnovarsi'. For a description of the joust and its equipment, including the standard, see P. Ventrone, *'Le tems revient – 'l tempo si rinuova'. Feste e spettacoli nella Firenze di Lorenzo il Magnifico*, exh. cat. Florence 1992, pp. 167–87.

12 See M. Cruttwell, *Verrocchio*, London and New Haven 1904, p. 86, for the description of the banner carried by Giovanni di Papi Morelli in the joust, but supplied by the Medici. D.A. Brown, *Leonardo da Vinci. Origins of a Genius*, New Haven and London 1998, pp. 124–6, attributes the Uffizi drawing to a collaboration between Verrocchio and Leonardo, and refers to other discussions of the attribution.

13 Filippo Sacramoro, reporting Giuliano's words to the Duke of Milan, quoted by E. Fumagalli, 'Nuovi documenti su Lorenzo e Giuliano de' Medici', *Italia medievale e umanistica*, 23, 1980, p. 144, who also discusses the context of the correspondence and the preparations for the joust (pp. 141–64). See further Ventrone 1992, pp. 189–205.

14 The list was published and glossed by C. de Fabriczy. 'Andrea del Verrocchio ai servizi de' Medici', *Archivio storico dell'arte*, 2nd series, I, no.3, 1895, pp. 163–76; for an English translation, see Cruttwell 1904, p. 243.

15 See Butterfield 1997, pp. 205–6, quoting the document from the archive of S. Lorenzo recording the service held on that day when Cosimo was reburied in the new tomb: 'adi 22 [October 1467] facemo un magnificho ossequio per buona e felice memoria di Cosimo de' Medici che fu sepellito nella nuova sepoltura …'

16 Ibid., p. 208, quoting from Lorenzo's *Ricordi*: 'si fa la sua sepoltura e di Giovanni suo fratello, più degna che sappiamo per mettervi le loro ossa.'

17 Ibid, p. 204: 'apud hostium catenae pro ornamento et pulchritudine ac etiam magnificentia palatii.'

18 de Fabriczy 1895, p. 167. The restoration of the Marsyas is described by Vasari in the Life of Verrocchio, *Le opere di Giorgio Vasari*, G. Milanesi, ed., Florence 1878–85, III, pp. 366–7, and in the Preface to the third section, IV, p. 10. The statue has been mistakenly identified with a Marsyas in the Uffizi, but it is now lost, see L. Beschi, 'Le antichità di Lorenzo il Magnifico', in P. Barocchi and G. Ragionieri, eds., *Gli Uffizi quattro secoli di una galleria. Atti del Convegno Internazionale di Studi (Firenze 20–24 settembre 1982)*, Florence 1983, p. 169, and F. Caglioti: 'Due "restauratori" per le antichità dei primi Medici: Mino da Fiesole, Andrea del Verrocchio e il "Marsia rosso" degli Uffizi. I', *Prospettiva*, 72, 1993, pp. 17–42.

19 The bust of Piero, from 1453, is the earliest dated Florentine portrait bust. It is in the Bargello in Florence. The bust of Giovanni, who is shown in *all'antica* armour, is also in the Bargello. Lucrezia's portrait, documented in the 1492 Medici inventory, is now lost.

20 The portraits are listed together in the 1492 Medici palace inventory; for the Galeazzo portrait see A. Wright, 'A Portrait for the Visit of Galeazzo Maria Sforza to Florence in 1471', in Mallet and Mann eds., London 1996, pp. 65–92.

21 See L.D. Ettlinger, 'Hercules Florentinus', *Mitteilungen des Kunsthistorischen Institutes in Florenz*, 16, 1972, pp. 135–7, and *idem.*, *Antonio and Piero Pollaiuolo*, Oxford 1978, p. 165.

22 M. Spallanzani and G.G. Bertelà, eds., *Libro d'inventario dei beni di Lorenzo il Magnifico*, Florence 1992, p. 72 (fol. 38v), in the room then used by Lorenzo's son Giuliano ('Nella chamera che risponde in sulla via chiamata la camera di monsignore, dove sta Giuliano'): 'Uno Erchole che schoppia Anteo, di bronzo tutto, alto br. 1/3', valued at 2 florins.

23 In the 'saletta rimpetto alla sala grande', described as 'Una storia di bronzo sopra il chammino, di più chavagli e gnudi, cioè una battaglia lunga br. uno e 2/3, alta br. 2/3' and valued at 30 florins; see Spallanzani and Bertelà 1992, p. 71 (fol. 38r).

24 See for this J. Draper, *Bertoldo di Giovanni, Sculptor of the Medici Household. Critical Reappraisal and Catalogue Raisonné*, Columbia, Missouri, 1992.

25 See Beschi 1983, p. 165, where he quotes from Lorenzo's *Ricordi* about his mission and these gifts and acquisitions. See also *Il Tesoro di Lorenzo il Magnifico. Repertorio delle gemme e dei vasi*, N. Dacos, A. Grote, A. Giuliano, D. Heikamp, U. Pannuti, eds., Florence 1980, p. 4 for the visit and pp. 69–74 for the 'tazza farnese'.

26 See Beschi 1983, p. 163.

27 Vasari/Milanesi, vol. 4, p. 10.

28 *The 'Stanze' of Angelo Poliziano*, trans. D. Quint, Amherst, Mass., 1979, pp. 74–5: 'tal del forte Achille or canta l'armi/e rinnuova in suo stil gli antichi tempi.'

29 This characterisation ('dextrissimo ingenio') was made in a letter to the Duke of Milan by his ambassador Sacramoro dei Mengozzi da Rimini, see *Lorenzo de' Medici. Lettere*, ed. Fubini 1977, I, p. 41.

30 Quoted by E. Borsook, 'Documenti relativi alle cappelle di Lecceto e delle Selve di Filippo Strozzi', *Antichità Viva*, vol. 9, no. 3, 1970, doc. 18, p. 15, from a letter to Lorenzo Strozzi (22 April 1477): 'Avendomi chonceduto Iddio de' beni temporali, liene voglio essere ricordevole. E principiando dalle chose sua, potreno venire uno dì alle nostre.' See further E. Borsook, 'Ritratto di Filippo Strozzi il Vecchio', in *Palazzo Strozzi, metà millenio. 1489–1989. Atti del convegno di studi, Firenze, 3–6 luglio, 1989*, Rome 1991, pp. 1–14, for a succinct characterisation of Filippo and his projects.

31 See J.R. Sale, *The Strozzi Chapel by Filippino Lippi in Santa Maria Novella*, PhD thesis, University of Pennsylvania, Philadelphia 1976, Appendix A, doc. 2, pp. 20–1.

32 Borsook 1970, pp. 4, 6, fig. 2.

33 Sale 1976, for this chapel and its decoration.

34 For a summary of the project, see A. Lillie et al., 'The Palazzo Strozzi and Private Patronage in Fifteenth-Century Florence' in H. Millon and V. Lampugnani, eds., *The Renaissance from Brunelleschi to Michelangelo. The Representation of Architecture*, London 1994, pp. 518–21. See further R. Goldthwaite, 'The Building of the Strozzi Palace: the Construction Industry in Renaissance Florence', *Studies in Medieval and Renaissance History*, 10, 1973, pp. 97–194 and F.W. Kent, '"Più superba di quella di Lorenzo": Courtly and Family Interest in the Building of Filippo Strozzi's Palace', *Renaissance Quarterly*, 30, 1977, pp. 311–23.

35 Borsook 1970, p. 9, doc. 12 (15 July 1475), a payment of 15 florins, 'per una testa di marmo fatta fare al mio naturale da Benedetto da Maiano.' The terracotta model for this bust is in Berlin, see Borsook 1991, p. 9 and fig. 9.

36 Borsook 1970, p. 9, doc. 3 (21 October 1478), four *braccia* 'di raxo lionato donato a Benedetto da Maiano'.

37 Ibid, pp. 14–15, docs. 16–18, for the letters about this to Lorenzo Strozzi in Naples, dating from 29 January 1475, 20 April 1477 and 22 April 1477.

38 Now in the Bodleian library, Oxford, Douce 310; see Borsook 1970, p. 9, and Borsook 1991, pp. 8–9.

39 F. Edler de Roover, 'Per la storia dell'arte della stampa in Italia', *La Bibliofilia*, 55, 1953, pp. 109–10, for the payment of 50 florins made by the Strozzi brothers in 1476 to Landino. The translation was for a printed edition of 1025 copies; not only was it among the earliest printed books in Italy, but it became a bestseller.

40 *Giovanni Rucellai ed il suo Zibaldone*, vol. 1, ed. A. Perosa, London 1960, pp. 117–21.

41 For Giovanni's career, see F.W. Kent, 'The Making of a Renaissance Patron of the Arts' in *Giovanni Rucellai ed il suo Zibaldone*, II, London 1981, pp. 9–98.

42 *Zibaldone*, vol. 1, ed. Perosa 1960, p. 121.

43 Ibid, pp. 117–18.

44 Ibid, pp. 23–4: 'Memoria che noi abiamo in chasa nostra più chose di scholtura e di pitura di tarsie e comessi, di mano de' migliori maestri che siano stati da buono tenpo in qua, non tanto in Firenze ma in Italia.'

45 For this phenomenon see J.K. Lydecker, *The domestic setting of the arts in Renaissance Florence*, PhD thesis, The Johns Hopkins University, Baltimore 1987, and R. Goldthwaite, *Wealth and the Demand for Art in Italy 1300–1600*, Baltimore 1993.

46 *Zibaldone*, vol. 1, ed. Perosa 1960, p. 60: 'Sono stati nella detta età … più singulari huomini inn iscienzia che ne' tenpi passati … i quali à rivochato a lucie [l']anticha leggiadria dello stile perduto e spento.'

47 Vasari/Milanesi, vol. 2, pp. 541–4. For the problems of attribution, see B. Preyer, 'The Rucellai Palace', in *Zibaldone*, II, London 1981, pp. 192–7, who notes that another sixteenth-century source, the *Libro di Antonio Billi*, credits Bernardo Rossellino with the model for the palace (p. 192).

48 *Nichomachean Ethics*, ed. J. Barnes, *The Complete Works of Aristotle*, Princeton 1984, vol. 2, Book IV, chapter 2, pp. 1771–2.

49 M. Palmieri, *Vita civile*, ed. G. Belloni, Florence 1982, p. 153.

50 Ibid., p. 147.

51 Ibid., p. 194.

52 *The Vespasiano Memoirs*, trans. Waters, New York 1963, pp. 416–17.

53 *Vita civile*, ed. Belloni 1982, p. 195.

54 A. Rinuccini, *Lettere ed orazioni*, ed. V. Giustiniani, Florence 1953, p. 81.

55 P. Nuttall, 'The Patrons of Chapels at the Badia of Fiesole', *Studi di Storia dell'Arte*, 3, 1992, p. 97, ceded before his death to Francesco Nori.

56 See R. Bagemihl, 'Francesco Botticini's Palmieri altar-piece', *The Burlington Magazine*, 138, 1996, pp. 308–14, for the relevant documents. The altarpiece measures 228.5 × 377 cm.

57 For further discussions of this painting and its unusual iconography, see M. Davies, *National Gallery Catalogues. The Earlier Italian Schools*, London 1961, no. 1126, pp. 122–7, and P. Rubin, 'Art and the Imagery of Memory', in *Art, Memory, and Family in Early Renaissance Florence*, G. Ciappelli and P. L. Rubin, eds., Cambridge 1999.

58 *Vita civile*, ed. Belloni 1982, p. 194: 'Della bellezza et Ornamento della città'.

59 Ibid., p. 195: 'La belleza et singulare ornamento degli edificii prima è posto in ne muramenti publici … gli elevati et superbi palagi, per insigne gloria de' magistrati.'

60 See C. von Fabriczy, 'Donatello's Hl. Ludwig und sein Tabernakel an Or San Michele', *Jahrbuch der Königlich preussischen Kunstsammlungen*, 21, 1900, pp. 255–6 (29 March 1463).

61 Butterfield 1997, p. 209.

62 For these dates see Butterfield 1992, p. 228. For a more detailed discussion, see Butterfield 1997, chapter 3 (pp. 57–80), and cat. no. 8, pp. 209–12.

63 Butterfield 1992, p. 233, Doc. 1 (19 Dec. 1466): 'quod ipse Pierus est adeo infirmitate gravatus et in negociis rei publice adeo versatus et occupatus quod comode sine scandalo tali officio vacare non potest.'

64 See J.T. Paoletti, '"… ha fatto Piero con voluntà del padre…", Piero de' Medici and Corporate Commissions of Art', in A. Beyer and B. Boucher, eds., *Piero de' Medici 'il Gottoso' (1416–1469). Kunst im Dienste der Mediceer. Art in the Service of the Medici*, Berlin 1993, pp. 232–6.

65 von Fabriczy 1900, p. 255: 'statua et seu figura digna et venerabilis'.

66 J. Mesnil, 'Les Figures de Vertus de la Mercanzia. Piero del Pollaiuolo et Botticelli', *Miscellanea dell'arte*, 1, 1903, p. 43. A detailed account of this project based on the Mercanzia documents is in A. Wright, *Studies in the Paintings of the Pollaiuolo*, PhD thesis, University of London, 1992, chapter 6 and Appendix V.

67 *Vita civile*, ed. Belloni 1982, p. 194: 'La belleza et singulare ornamento degli edificii … contiene la sublimità et notabile magnificentia de' sacrati templi.'

68 For the sacristy intarsias, see M. Haines, *La Sacrestia delle Messe del Duomo di Firenze*, Florence 1983. For the della Robbia door, see J. Pope-Hennessy, *Luca della Robbia*, Oxford 1980, pp. 67–72 and cat. no. 47, pp. 258–61.

69 G. Poggi, *Il Duomo di Firenze*, Florence 1909, I, pp. 241–3, doc. 1206, for the choir commission. For the tapestry *spalliera*, see M. Wackernagel, *The World of the Florentine Renaissance Artist*, trans. A. Luchs, Princeton 1981, p. 31.

70 The documents are published by G. Poggi, *Catalogo del Museo dell'Opera del Duomo*, Florence 1904, pp. 69–72. See also L. Becherucci and G.Brunetti, *Il Museo dell'Opera del Duomo a Firenze*, Florence (n.d[1969?]), vol. 2, pp. 259–67 and figs. 205–37. The transcription of the 1487 document of the total cost mentions two different sums, 3179 florins and 7646 *lire, 10 soldi, 8 denari*.

71 For the documents see Poggi, *Catalogo* 1904, pp. 75–8. A useful summary of the commission is in Butterfield 1997, pp. 218–20. See also Becherucci and Brunetti [1969?], vol. 2, pp. 215–29 and figs. 3–77.

72 See below, p.88. See also Becherucci and Brunetti [1969?], vol. 2, pp. 229–36, figs. 78–104.

73 Archivio di Stato, Carte Strozziane, I, fol. 230v, Carte Strozziane, II, fol. 112v and fol. 120, published in G. Vasari, *Le vite de' più eccellenti pittori, scultori ed architettori*, ed. K. Frey, Munich 1911, p. 372.

74 Archivio di Stato, Florence, Deliberazioni dei Consoli dell'Arte della Calimala, 1476–82, fol. 36 and fol. 47v, published by Poggi 1909, II, p. 87, docs. 1869 and 1871.

75 A.F. Gori, *Thesaurus, veterum diptychorum*, Florence 1750, vol. 3, p. 316.

76 *Vita civile*, ed. Belloni 1982, p. 147.

77 F. Fiorelli Malesci, *La chiesa di Santa Felicita a Firenze*, Florence 1986, pp. 328–9, see also pp. 257–8, and figs. 246–50, figs 56–7 for general views of the sacristy and the vault of the sacristy chapel and figs. 246–50 for details. See further F.W. Kent, 'Individuals and Families as Patrons of Culture in Quattrocento Florence', in A. Brown, ed., *Language and Images in Renaissance Italy*, Oxford 1995, p. 186, for Canigiani's bequest.

78 See D.F. Zervas, '"quos volent et eo modo quo volent": Piero de' Medici and the *Operai* of SS. Annunziata, 1445–55', in P. Denley and C. Elam, eds., *Florence and Italy. Renaissance Studies in Honour of Nicolai Rubinstein*, London 1988, pp. 465–79.

79 These important documents were found by Rolf Bagemihl and will be published in a forthcoming issue of *Prospettiva*.

80 As in letters written in January 1480 to Lorenzo, in Naples, Archivio di Stato, Florence, Mediceo avanti il Principato [MAP], busta 61, nos 68, 70.

81 P.C. Clarke, *The Soderini and the Medici. Power and Patronage in Fifteenth-Century Florence*, Oxford 1991, p. 217; for Tommaso and Lorenzo in the 1470s, see chapters 7–9.

82 Ibid., p. 123 (for the move to the quarter of S. Spirito from S. Maria Novella) and pp. 131–2, 145 (for the involvement with the quarter's churches). See further N. Eckstein, *The District of the Green Dragon. Neighbourhood Life and Social Change in Renaissance Florence*, Florence 1995, pp. 200–5.

83 Clarke 1991, p. 131, note 28, for Niccolò's will of 19 October 1444 and Tommaso's of 10 March 1462, making this provision.

84 For the petition, see ibid., p. 131 and note 29; for the 1470s benefactions, see Eckstein 1995, p. 201.

85 Neri di Bicci, *Le Ricordanze 1453–1475*, ed. B. Santi, Pisa 1976, pp. 332–3, no. 627 (26 July 1469).

86 Ibid., pp. 382–3, no. 717 (31 October 1471). The *Saint Margaret* and *Saint Blaise* are now in the Fogg Art Museum. See A. Thomas, 'Neri di Bicci in the Compagnia di San Frediano detta la Bruciata and a painting of a deacon saint', *Arte Cristiana*, 85, no. 778, 1997, pp. 27–34. See also her article 'Restoration or Renovation: Remuneration and Expectation in Renaissance "acconciatura"', in C. Sitwell and S. Staniforth, eds., *Studies in the History of Painting Restoration*, National Trust, London 1998, pp. 5–9.

87 *Ricordanze*, ed. Santi 1976, pp. 397–8, no. 742 (26 Sept. 1472).

88 For this project, see Eckstein 1995, pp. 204–5, and P. Giovannini, *Il convento del Carmine di Firenze: caratteri e documenti*, Florence 1981, pp. 86–7 and p. 94 (document 3.49), and Neri di Bicci, *Ricordanze*, ed., Santi 1976, pp. 241–2, no. 470 (17 May 1465).

89 Vasari/Milanesi, vol. 3, p. 288, n. 4. The payment, hitherto known only through secondary sources, was discovered and published by D. Carl, 'Addenda zu Antonio Pollaiuolo und seiner Werkstatt', *Mitteilungen des Kunsthistorischen Institutes in Florenz*, 27, 1983, p. 306, note. 48.

90 The library endowment is in Archivio di Stato, Florence, Notarile Antecosimiano 14200, fol. 90r.

91 *The Vespasiano Memoirs*, trans. Waters 1963, p. 219.

92 *Nichomachean Ethics*, ed. Barnes 1984, vol. 2, Book IV, chapter 2, p. 1771.

93 *Ricordanze*, ed. Santi 1976, no. 698, p. 372.

94 C. Botto, 'L'edificazione della Chiesa di Santo Spirito in Firenze', *Rivista d'Arte*, 2nd series, 3, 1931, p. 483.

95 The complaint dates from 1490 and is documented in the S. Spirito archives, as is the agreement of the board of works in charge of allocating chapels. The position of the della Palla chapel was not changed, however; the more prestigious places near the high altar were given to members of more prominent families. I want to thank Jill Burke for this reference, which is included in her discussion of the hierarchical division of space in the church in her PhD thesis on *Form and Power. Patronage and Visual Arts in Florence 1480–1512*, Courtauld Institute, London 1999.

96 *Ricordanze*, ed. Santi 1976, no. 686, p. 366 (8 July 1471). See also the comments by A. Thomas regarding this commission, *The Painter's Practice in Renaissance Tuscany*, Cambridge 1995, pp. 311–13.

97 For the S. Spirito altars see C. Acidini Luchinat, ed., *La Chiesa e il Convento di Santo Spirito a Firenze*, Florence 1996, pp. 240–2, for Neri and Botticini's paintings, plates 2 and 3, and L. Venturini, *Francesco Botticini*, Florence 1994, p. 54. More generally see E.H. Gombrich, 'Tobias and the Angel', in *Symbolic Images. Studies in the Art of the Renaissance*, London 1972, pp. 26–30.

98 For a detailed treatment of this painting and its iconography, see R. Hatfield, *Botticelli's Uffizi 'Adoration'. A Study in Pictorial Content*, Princeton 1976.

99 R. Hatfield, 'The Compagnia de' Magi', *Journal of the Warburg and Courtauld Institutes*, 33, 1970, pp. 107–61. See also above, p.28.

100 The manuscript, now in the Biblioteca Laurenziana, and its dating, are discussed by A. Garzelli, *Miniatura fiorentina del Rinascimento 1440–1525. Un primo censimento*, Florence 1985, I, pp. 176–7, and II, figs. 501–6.

101 G. Trotta, *Palazzo Cocchi Serristori a Firenze*, Florence 1995, pp. 18–21. For this bequest and the names of the executors of the will (Giovanni di Lorenzo Benci, Bernardo di Stoldo Rinieri and Piero di Lorenzo Capelli), see Hatfield 1976, p. 118 (29 May 1469).

102 See H. Brockhaus, *Forschungen über Florentiner Kunstwerke*, Leipzig 1902, pp. 118–19, for a comparison with a medal of Antoninus. In the chapter on 'Die Familienbild der Vespucci in der Kirche Ognissanti', pp. 85–134, Brockhaus identifies all the other figures beneath the Virgin's mantle as members of the Vespucci family, with very little evidence.

103 J. Cadogan, 'Reconsidering Some Aspects of Ghirlandaio's Drawings', *Art Bulletin*, 65, 1983, pp. 274–5, notes 13–14, describes changes between a drawing in the Uffizi for Saint John (263S), the *sinopia* for the figure and the figure as painted, probably made to accommodate the larger saint in front.

104 See M. Rohlmann, 'Ein Flämisches Vorbild für Ghirlandaios "prime pitture"', *Mitteilungen des Kunsthistorischen Institutes in Florenz*, 36, 1992, pp. 388–96.

105 Nuttall 1992, pp. 97–113.

106 *Ricordanze*, ed. Santi 1976, no. 736, p. 393–4. The price was 40 florins. The altarpiece with the Virgin and Child with Saints Benedict, Louis, Catherine and Appollonia, no. 3463, Depositi, Gallerie di Firenze, is at the former convent of S. Apollonia, the Museo di Andrea del Castagno, Florence.

107 Ibid., no. 771, p. 414, recording delivery of the altarpiece on 17 July 1473, whose cost was 20 florins paid in three instalments and no. 780, pp. 419–20 (6 November 1473) for delivering a pair of gilded clasps, for which he was paid 62 *lire* and 4 *soldi*.

108 Discovered by B. Paolozzi Strozzi, 'An unpublished crucifix by Andrea del Verrocchio', *Burlington Magazine*, 126, 1994, pp. 808–15.

109 The panel, now in the Fitzwilliam Museum in Cambridge, was identified by A. Padoa Rizzo, 'Cosimo e Bernardo Rosselli per la Compagnia di Sant'Andrea dei Purgatori a Firenze', *Studi di Storia dell'Arte*, 2, 1991, pp. 265–70.

110 See A. Padoa Rizzo, 'La cappella della Compagnia di Santa Barbara della "nazione tedesca" alla Santissima Annunziata di Firenze nel secolo XV. Cosimo Rosselli e la sua "impresa" artistica', *Antichità Viva*, 20, no. 3, 1987, pp. 3–18, for the activities of the Rosselli shop at that convent.

111 *Vita civile*, ed. Belloni 1982, p.194 : 'La belleza et singulare ornamento degli edificii … è posto … [nel]la conveniente compositione et attissima belleza de' privati habituri.'

112 'Due cose principali sono quelle che gl'uomini fanno in questo mondo: La prima lo'ngienerare: La seconda l'edifichare', *Zibaldone*, f. 83v; quoted by F.W. Kent in *Zibaldone*, vol. 2, London 1981, p. 13.

113 See for this B. Preyer, 'The "chasa overo palagio" of Alberto di Zanobi: A Florentine Palace of About 1400 and Its Later Remodeling', *Art Bulletin*, 65, 1983, pp. 387–401, and 'Florentine Palaces and Memories of the Past', in Ciappelli and Rubin 1999. See also F.W. Kent, 'Palaces, Politics and Society in Fifteenth Century Florence', *I Tatti Studies*, vol. 2, 1987, pp. 41–70.

114 *Florentine Histories*, trans. L. F. Banfield and H. C. Mansfield, Jr, Princeton 1988, Book VII, chapter 4, pp. 279–80.

115 See for this B. Preyer in G. Cherubini and G. Fanelli, eds., *Il Palazzo Medici Riccardi di Firenze*, Florence 1990, pp. 61–2.

116 L. Baldini Giusti and F. Falchinetti Bottai, 'Documento sulle prime fasi costruttive di Palazzo Pitti', in *Filippo Brunelleschi. La sua opera e il suo tempo*, Florence 1980, II, pp. 704–10.

117 A. Moscato, *Il Palazzo Pazzi a Firenze*, Rome 1963, pp. 41–78, and F. Quinterio, *Giuliano da Maiano 'Grandissimo Domestico'*, Rome 1996, pp. 312–30.

118 Quinterio 1996, p. 316, on 9 June 1478. See also Haines 1983, pp. 168–9, for a discussion of the attribution to Giuliano.

119 M. Trionfi Honorati, 'Il Palazzo degli Antinori', *Antichità Viva*, 7, no. 2, 1968, p. 65, citing Giovanni's father: 'Quaesto dì 2 dicembre 1465, sendo io su la Piazza di S. Michele Berteldi allato alla Porta dell'Uscio mio su la piazza, e stavo a murare la mia casa.'

120 For this and for the question of style, see Preyer 1983, p. 399.

121 Trionfi Honorati 1968, p. 72.

122 Preyer 1983, p. 398.

123 For the Lanfredini and the Pollaiuolo mural, see A. Wright, 'Dancing Nudes in the Lanfredini villa at Arcetri', in E. Marchand and A. Wright, eds., *With and Without the Medici. Studies in Tuscan Art and Patronage 1434–1530*, Aldershot 1998, pp. 47–77. For the mural, see also E. Borsook, *The Mural Painters of Tuscany*, 2nd ed., Oxford 1980, pp. 111–13.

124 E. Borsook, 'Two Letters concerning Antonio Pollaiuolo', *The Burlington Magazine*, 115, 1973, p. 468.

125 The connection with the 1469 joust was suggested by Caroline Elam; the documents, with some eccentric interpretation, are published in Trotta 1995. Francesco di Niccolò, as noted above, was a legatee in Guasparre del Lama's will that year, which was also the year that he was Gonfaloniere di Giustizia. This branch of the Cocchi family is often identified as Cocchi Donati. For the prototypes in Roman architecture see D. Hemsoll, 'Giuliano da Sangallo and the new Renaissance of Lorenzo de' Medici', in *The Early Medici and their Artists*, ed. F. Ames-Lewis, London 1995, pp. 190–1.

126 In a letter to Agnolo Poliziano, quoted from A. Brown, *Bartolommeo Scala, 1430–1497, Chancellor of Florence. The Humanist as Bureaucrat*, Princeton 1979, p. 3.

127 C. Elam, 'Lorenzo de' Medici and the Urban Development of Renaissance Florence', *Art History*, 1, 1978, pp. 43–66.

128 Quoted by L. Pellecchia, 'The Patron's Role in the Production of Architecture: Bartolommeo Scala and the Scala Palace', *Renaissance Quarterly*, 42, 1989, pp. 265–6, as part of an illuminating discussion and reconstruction of the building and its sources. See also A. Bellinazzi, ed., *La casa del cancelliere. Documenti e studi sul palazzo di Bartolommeo Scala a Firenze*, Florence 1998.

129 For the courtyard reliefs, Brown 1979, pp. 234–5, 317–18, and A. Parronchi, 'The Language of Humanism', *Journal of the Warburg and Courtauld Institutes*, 27, 1964, pp. 108–36.

3 Artists and Workshops

Patricia Lee Rubin and Alison Wright

In a famous early Florentine engraving (fig. 50), sculptors, painters, goldsmiths, clock-makers and astrologers ply their trades under the influence of the planet Mercury. Despite this planetary association, in Renaissance Florence none of them would have been described as an 'artist' in the modern sense of the word. They were all professional craftsmen, identified by particular skills and materials, who, more often than not, worked collaboratively. In his *Zibaldone*, Giovanni Rucellai registers Florentine pride in the abundant talents of those who embellished the city in the fifteenth century, noting:

architects, sculptors, carvers supplying all Italy, [...]
woodworkers, marquetry workers with such skill in perspective
that one could not do better with a brush, painters, outstanding
designers of great skill, measure and order such that Giotto
and Cimabue would not have been adequate pupils; most
notable embroiderers and goldsmiths.[1]

Extending the association with embroiderers and goldsmiths, he then praises the quality of Florentine dress and the strength of the silk industry.[2]

What is remarkable in Rucellai's book is his interest in painters, sculptors and designers as outstanding individuals. When noting the contents of his palace he records the names of the men who made the works rather than the objects themselves.[3] Significantly he ranks the architect/engineer Brunelleschi alongside the humanist Leonardo Bruni among the four exceptional Florentines of his age.[4] In a republic that heroised famous men, this association implicitly attached Brunelleschi's achievements to a reputation for intellectual acumen (*scienza*) equivalent to that of other worthies. An appreciation of intellectual as well as artistic ability lies behind the prominence and status given to such craftsmen as

Andrea del Verrocchio, Antonio del Pollaiuolo, Leonardo da Vinci and Botticelli, now regarded as among the greatest artists of the Renaissance.

The products of the Florentine wool and silk industry were known all over Europe and beyond. Rucellai's memorandum reminds us that the fame of the city's painters, sculptors and architects was also widely celebrated. Lorenzo de' Medici and others, like Filippo Strozzi, exploited Florentine artistic skill for diplomatic purposes, sending Florentine goods as gifts and Florentine artists as emissaries of the city's excellence. It is worth asking here what underpinned this reputation. As in other European cities, Florentine production was controlled by the guilds whose regulations were intended to enforce standards of business practice and of production that would ensure strength in the market. In Florence these standards seem to have been upheld without great

Fig. 50 BACCIO BALDINI, *Mercury*, 1460s. Engraving from a series of the Planets, 32.4 × 21.7 cm. London, British Museum.

restrictions on practice: experimentation and novelty were at a premium and many artists pursued different occupations simultaneously. Guild membership was linked to political rights. While this increased the civic identity of the city's artists, it also loosened their craft identity. The number of guilds was limited to twenty-one, divided into seven major and fourteen minor guilds; this meant that some professions were grouped together. Florentine painters formed a branch of the Guild of Doctors and Apothecaries (Arte dei Medici e Speziali), being related to the latter not by their products but by their materials – pigments were traded by druggists. There was a painters' confraternity dedicated to Saint Luke (who had reputedly painted a portrait of the Virgin Mary) and painters were required by the guild to belong to it. This presumably helped to promote social cohesion within the profession. Sculptors or carvers were generally inscribed in the Guild of Stone and Woodworkers (Arte dei Maestri di Pietra e Legname) while goldsmiths were part of the more important Silk Guild (Arte della Seta) because of their common use of luxury materials. The Florentine silk industry specialised in cloths of gold, which were made by wrapping silk thread with ribbons of beaten gold made by goldbeaters (*battilori*). Botticelli's brother Antonio was at one time a *battiloro* and supplied gold leaf for Botticelli's paintings and their frames.[5] According to Vasari, Botticelli himself was first apprenticed as a goldsmith.[6] Indeed the links between the different trades are intrinsic to an understanding of how works were made and how they were seen.

The passage from goldsmith to painter that in all likelihood occurred in Botticelli's career was not uncommon in Florence. The ties between a goldsmith's training and painting probably nourished the fascination with evoking the precious and

luxurious in the depiction of sumptuous cloth and jewellery that is characteristic of Florentine painting of the 1470s (fig. 51). High-quality Florentine products with their own allure, such as silk cloth and embroidery, could transfer their value to paintings, conferring worth on the paintings as objects and honouring the exemplary subjects they depicted.

The guilds formulated regulations about the length of training for would-be masters and the qualifications for matriculation.[7] Goldsmiths were required to study for six years as a *discepolo* before they could become a master.[8] The statutes for the Arte dei Medici e Speziali stated that each master was allowed one pupil, whose term was nine years: three years to be paid by the pupil, and six by the master.[9] Surviving apprenticeship documents indicate that in practice the latter was the outside limit, not a fixed term of study. Indeed, it was up to the master to decide when a pupil

Fig. 51 ANDREA DEL VERROCCHIO, *Virgin and Child with Two Angels*, detail of cat no. 23.

was ready to exercise the profession on his own 'for gain'. Neri di Bicci's *Ricordanze*, the most complete surviving records of a fifteenth-century painter's practice, show that apprenticeship contracts actually varied and that the terms *garzone* (shop boy) and *discepolo* (student) were applied to those contracted regardless of the level of training or their years of service. The difference of grade was marked by their wages. Neri's apprentices were paid, with the exception of the most inexperienced boys, some of whom were taken on for a year without stipend. His apprenticeship agreements varied from one to three-year terms, and pay ranged from just over two florins a year to thirty-four florins (Neri's female domestic servants earned nine florins a year). In general Neri had two *garzoni* – one a trainee, the other a senior assistant. The time and labour of both, however, were totally at Neri's disposal and their output would have been regarded as his.[10] It is misguided to think of artists' shops as bustling academies. They were businesses, focused on meeting deadlines and maintaining a reliable and well-regarded output. Over the twenty-two years documented in the *Ricordanze*, nineteen *discepoli* are mentioned, some leaving after a few days, others staying for several years. Four were sons of painters and two (Cosimo and Bernardo Rosselli) came from a family of stoneworkers who developed into a diversified group of artisans collaborating on artistic projects. There was, therefore, plenty of opportunity for Neri's teachings and techniques to be disseminated among a wider artistic community. Neri's records also show that a senior student might take leave to work with other masters, an arrangement that encouraged the exchange of ideas, or 'trade secrets', between shops.

Artists also moved between disciplines and evidence suggests membership in one guild might allow practice in the field regulated by another – it certainly did not prohibit it. As noted above, Cosimo Rosselli's father was a stonemason and, saving a matriculation fee through this connection, Cosimo joined the Arte dei Maestri di Pietra e Legname, calling himself a painter. Verrocchio is listed as a painter and sculptor in the register of the confraternity of Saint Luke, while he was also matriculated as a sculptor in the Arte dei Maestri di Pietra e Legname.[11]

Some artists, unwilling or unable to afford both the guild matriculation fees and the capital costs of setting up in trade, postponed opening their own shops, remaining as assistants to established masters or working for hire. Even after becoming registered masters, Leonardo da Vinci and Lorenzo di Credi still preferred to stay in their former master's studio, where their talents seem to have been acknowledged and fostered as part of Verrocchio's highly successful business.

Goldsmiths are also known to have worked on their own account within another master's *bottega*. Sometimes a pupil might go on to form a partnership with a former master. In the case of the goldsmith Paolo Sogliani this move seems to have taken place prematurely according to guild regulations. We find Sogliani running into trouble in his attempt to matriculate into the Arte della Seta in 1484, having already formed a business partnership or *compagnia* with Antonio del Pollaiuolo in the 1470s. Sogliani had acted as an independent master when he was still technically a student and it was presumably considered that his training was incomplete.[12]

Apprentices were expected to fulfil menial, mechanical and time-consuming tasks diligently. In the case of painters' practice, which is most fully documented, this included the groundwork of making gesso and applying it to panels, preparing raw materials and grinding pigments. In many workshops they acted as errand boys and studio models. They were delegated portions of work. Training in craftsmanship was accompanied by the challenge of learning design. Indeed, it was above all the mastery of the latter that allowed artists such as Verrocchio and Pollaiuolo to move between the arts. We know from the writings of the painter Cennino Cennini and the goldsmith/sculptor Lorenzo Ghiberti that exceptional importance was attached to drawing – which Ghiberti calls the 'foundation and theory' of sculpture and painting.[13] Its primacy is confirmed by the guild documents of the 1470s that refer to the 'Guild of Painting and Drawing (*disegno*)'.[14] Goldsmiths like Antonio del Pollaiuolo were sometimes called *maestri di disegno*, master draughtsmen. The embellishment of precious wares, especially silver, with figures and scenes required great manual dexterity and security of draughtsmanship. The engraved design might be left as a low relief, enamelled, or, in the technique of niello perfected by Maso Finiguerra (1426–64), Antonio del Pollaiuolo's fellow *maestro di disegno*, the incised drawing, shaded with fine hatching strokes, would be filled with a black metal alloy. The alloy was then fired onto the surface and polished flat, producing an emphatically linear design that also has great delicacy of relief. These same qualities characterise Maso's many surviving drawings, which insist upon a standard of legibility achieved through a continuously penned contour and luminous internal modelling made with an ink wash (fig. 52). In the case of niello work, a record of the design might be kept in the form of a sulphur cast or a print taken from the plate before it was filled with alloy. This practice further encouraged the emulation of Maso's drawing style by other artists, as well as the

commercial production of figurative prints. Antonio del Pollaiuolo developed both Maso's pen technique and his interest in figural compositions displaying the male nude (cat. no. 57). Maso's pupil Baccio Baldini continued to produce nielli and prints in this style long after his master's death.

Disegno in its widest definition – covering design as well as drawing – was considered an intellectual activity. Increased availability of paper, the tendency to keep and reuse drawings within the workshop, as well as subsequent collecting practices, have helped to preserve large numbers of Florentine drawings from the 1470s. Mostly cut down from larger sheets and extracted from drawing books, these survivors testify to the manifold uses of drawing: as exercise, as study, as preparatory tool and as record.

Lorenzo Ghiberti, writing in the 1450s, enumerated the intellectual attainments that needed to be mastered by artists. Ghiberti was concerned to raise the status of work traditionally considered as craft, but he was also reflecting the actual skills, notably in

Fig. 52 MASO FINIGUERRA, *The Flood*, before 1464.
Pen and brown ink and wash on parchment, 27.5 × 40.9 cm.
Hamburg, Kunsthalle, Kupferstichkabinett, inv. 21080

geometry and mathematics, displayed in the work of innovative artists. Leonardo's drawing for the background of his *Adoration of the Magi* altarpiece, with its tight net of construction lines, demonstrates his competence in these areas (fig. 53) and seems to satisfy a technical curiosity that exceeds the immediate requirements of picture-making. It also demonstrates the value of geometry and mathematics in the representation of regular bodies and the mapping of figures in space. The type of knowledge displayed in the drawing underlies the organisation of compositions such as Verrocchio's *Virgin and Child* now in Edinburgh (cat. no. 25). Such skills, moreover, were made familiar – indeed fashionable – to laymen through the work of specialists who designed *trompe l'oeil* marquetry (often called *prospettive*), most famously in the workshop of Giuliano da Maiano, Rucellai's 'master of intarsia'.[15]

Workshops were such a fundamental unit of social organisation for the Florentine citizen that Benedetto Dei could even describe God as 'maestro di bottega', master of the workshop.[16] This title – also bestowed on Lorenzo de' Medici – suggests the authority granted to those heading a successful business. That authority also created a powerful tradition of mastery within the city – an important element of artists' studies. Surviving drawings and completed works testify to lessons absorbed from the work of earlier artists still visible in the city's streets and churches. The earlier frescoes of Giotto and Masaccio, the recent sculptures of Donatello (d. 1466), Ghiberti (d. 1455) and Desiderio da Settignano (d. 1464) and the paintings of Fra Filippo Lippi (d. 1469) constituted an open workshop that could be visited in actuality and revisited imaginatively in contemporary painting, sculpture and goldsmith work. Antonio del

Fig. 53 LEONARDO DA VINCI, *Study for the background of the 'Adoration of the Magi', c.*1481. Metalpoint ruled lines, black chalk, pen and brown ink and brown wash on paper, 16.2 × 29 cm. Florence, Galleria degli Uffizi, Gabinetto Disegni e Stampe, inv. 436E

Pollaiuolo's art, for example, was deeply indebted to the publicly displayed works of Donatello, though he is unlikely ever to have been taught by the sculptor (see cat. no. 58). While Pollaiuolo's stylistic affinities to Lippi are weak compared to those of Verrocchio, Antonio is recorded as having visited the ageing Lippi at Spoleto shortly before his death in 1469.[17] Such an episode reminds us of the important role of informal contacts between artists who were natives of a city where everyone seems to have known everyone else.

The task of understanding how artists worked and what was required of them is greatly helped by the wealth of legal and other records kept by this city of businessmen and notaries. Surviving documents include formal, that is, notarial, contracts (usually for large-scale altarpieces and public or semi-public works), non-notarised agreements and notes of expenditure in account books and family records. The form given to transactions varies little over time, despite the great changes in artistic style. What emerges from the archive for the 1470s confirms the continuation of the craft traditions and standard practices structuring the business of art and integrating it with other business procedures in the city.

Contracts and commission agreements typically specify the subject and size or scale of the work. Their concern is to fix the cost of the materials, the quality of precious and/or variable materials to be used (notably gold and ultramarine blue for painters), the price of labour and the duration of the job. Sometimes a price is stated, sometimes it is allowed to depend on a judgement of the value of the finished work, which indicates the confidence of artists to meet a desired standard, as well as the existence of an informed and discerning clientele. Some documents state the parts to be executed by the master – whole

figures, or the heads and hands of figures.[18] This acknowledges the realities of the workshop where the master's contribution was sought above all in the qualities of design and finish, while other more routine tasks were delegated to assistants, some of whom are now completely unknown.

The issue of fair pricing is addressed by the regulations of the Arte dei Medici e Speziali of 1470, which provided for members to act as judges, deciding the cost of their fellow guildsmen's wares.[19] However, the regulations say nothing about the particular considerations that controlled prices, and these can be difficult to gauge. Sometimes the size of a work and the number of figures were significant, although this was by no means the rule.[20] A frame, usually gilt, could cost about a third of the total. At least half of the expenditure for any work was for its materials. There is some evidence that artists priced their work according to the client involved, as Neri di Bicci may have done when negotiating with the nuns of S. Apollonia. There is no marked increase in prices over the course of the fifteenth century, though there was perhaps some increase in the value granted to reputation. Competitive pricing was the norm in the 1470s as in other times; it might happen, however, that an artist charging a higher price could be considered, as was possibly the case with Piero del Pollaiuolo's bid for the Forteguerri commission.[21]

Most works were made to order as they were intended for a specific site. The exceptions were the images of the Virgin and Child and smaller devotional works made for domestic settings, which as fundamental household items were always in demand. Most were likely to have been produced and sold as stock items, perhaps with a client's coat of arms added to the frame at the time of purchase. Clearly some workshops had best-selling formulas –

trademarks as it were – like the half-length Virgin with standing infant available in painted, sculpted or modelled versions from the Verrocchio shop (cat. nos. 27 and 28). Botticelli had great success in this field and was also, Vasari records, known for producing tondi, or circular paintings.[22] Deluxe items, often elaborately framed, the larger tondi were probably made on request and Botticelli seems to have been asked to repeat popular or admired compositions, as in the case of the *Madonna of the Magnificat* (cat. no. 84).

Individual workshop structure varied considerably. As Neri di Bicci's records show, workshops were inherently dynamic. Once his basic apprenticeship was finished, a pupil could stay on as a salaried assistant. Masters also formed partnerships or companies (*compagnie*) for fixed periods in a bid to win better commissions and provide one another with social and financial insurance. For goldsmiths, the high cost of the materials of their trade demanded concomitantly high investment in order to set up in business. Many master goldsmiths, like Antonio del Pollaiuolo, worked in partnerships as a way of spreading not only the burden of work but of capital risk. Such *compagnie* would not always be renewed and personnel changed over time.[23] Experienced help could also be taken on for big or pressing projects, and specialist collaborators were called upon as necessary. This movement resulted in a circulation of ideas and techiniques between shops. Artists also commonly travelled to places of commission. This was necessarily the case for mural painters. Thus the young Domenico Ghirlandaio was frequently absent from his native city in the 1470s, occupied with commissions such as the narrative frescoes in the chapel of Santa Fina in San Gimignano (fig. 54).

The ability to work in a variety of media, as did Verrocchio and the Pollaiuolo brothers, enabled artists to be responsive to a demanding, and shifting, market.[24] They also had to shape their careers in competition with one another. Competition could be direct, as in the case of the panels for the Baptistery silver altar described in Chapter 2. Sometimes a sponsored bid was introduced for a work, or part of a work, already commissioned. Piero del Pollaiuolo was the victim of this practice on more than one occasion in the 1470s. As noted earlier, Botticelli, backed by Tommaso Soderini, took over one of the paintings of the Virtues for the Mercanzia (fig. 30) and the commission for the altarpiece of the Signoria's chapel dedicated to Saint Bernard in the Palazzo Vecchio, given to Piero on 24 December 1477, was reallocated to Leonardo da Vinci just a week later. The fact that Leonardo's father was a notary of the Signoria may have played a part in this.[25] Competition could also operate tacitly once commissions were secured. One

Fig. 54 GIULIANO DA MAIANO (architecture), BENEDETTO DA MAIANO (altar wall sculpture), DOMENICO GHIRLANDAIO (murals), c.1471–5. San Gimignano, Collegiata, Chapel of Santa Fina.

can imagine, for example, that Verrocchio's work on Lorenzo de' Medici's pageant equipment for his joust in 1469 would have stimulated the Pollaiuolo brothers' competitive instincts in their work for Benedetto Salutati for the same occasion.

Paradoxically, some competition could also promote collaboration. Working in partnerships or teams was for most craftsmen in Florence, as elsewhere, a necessity of production, especially when there was an inflexible deadline, as was the case for Lorenzo's joust. Collaboration could be familial: for the Salutati commission Antonio del Pollaiuolo was engaged as the goldsmith/designer, while his brother Piero painted Salutati's banner.[26] It could also involve other co-workers and sub-contracting for specialist jobs (the sculptor Antonio Rossellino was brought in to make the figure of a goddess for the crest of Salutati's helmet). Neri di Bicci's records document

Fig. 55 LUCA DELLA ROBBIA, Vault, 1461. Glazed terracotta. Florence, San Miniato al Monte, Chapel of the Cardinal of Portugal.

Fig. 56 ANTONIO AND BERNARDO ROSSELLINO, Tomb of the Cardinal of Portugal, 1461–6. Marble.

Fig. 57 ANTONIO AND PIERO DEL POLLAIUOLO, Altar wall, 1466; mural of angels holding back curtains, with copy of altarpiece, *Saints Vincent, James and Eustace* (original in the Galleria degli Uffizi). Panel, 199 × 166 cm., Chapel of the Cardinal of Portugal.

steady traffic between his shop and those of woodworkers and sculptors. The da Maiano brothers regularly supplied the panels and frames for Neri's paintings and he routinely coloured Virgin and Child reliefs by Desiderio da Settignano.

Among projects that involved artistic collaboration at a single site, the most influential was that of the burial chapel of the Cardinal of Portugal in San Miniato al Monte, completed at the end of the 1460s (figs. 55–7). It provided the model for the chapel dedicated to S. Fina in San Gimignano, decorated with murals by the Ghirlandaio firm and sculptures by Benedetto da Maiano in the 1470s (fig. 54). It also inspired the tomb chapel of Maria of Aragon in S. Anna dei Lombardi in Naples, begun by Antonio Rossellino and completed by Benedetto da Maiano.

The Cardinal of Portugal's chapel was devised as a purpose-built space on a centralised plan. Its decoration was conceived as a multi-media extravaganza involving at least five different workshops.[27] The murals were mostly the work of Alesso Baldovinetti, with the exception of the prestigious altar wall with its altarpiece in oil and frescoed angels by the Pollaiuolo brothers (fig. 57). The sculptor brothers Antonio and Bernardo Rossellino carved the extraordinarily refined tomb of the young cardinal (d. 1459), with a recumbent effigy, angels, and a tondo of the Virgin and Child revealed by a marble curtain (fig. 56). The Rossellino brothers also supplied other marble revetments and furniture for the chapel. The dazzling polychrome ceiling by Luca della Robbia, showing the Cardinal Virtues and the dove of the Holy Spirit, used the glazed terracotta technique that Luca pioneered and perpetuated in his family shop (fig. 55). The geometrical inlaid marble of the floor was executed by a specialist team brought from Rome and recalls the grandeur of early

Christian basilicas. Even though each workshop was operating to the limits of contemporary artistic ambitions, the result is no battle of separate voices, but a harmoniously integrated polyphony. Dominated by principles of geometrical and decorative design that emphasise the interrelation of square and circle, the Brunelleschian architecture by Antonio Manetti frames a coherent ensemble. Each workshop operated with the same controlling design in mind and extended the architectural principles to the different tasks in different media. By responding to one another's work, they also succeeded in setting up a sophisticated play between actual and fictive space.

The dialogue between painting and sculpture, so richly articulated in the Cardinal of Portugal's chapel, was enthusiastically pursued by artists of the 1470s. Two of the leading firms of the city were those of Andrea del Verrocchio and Antonio del Pollaiuolo, who had both begun their careers as goldsmiths, working for branches of the Dei goldsmith family (relatives of the chronicler Benedetto) in the later 1450s.[28] Both subsequently became expert in other media. Florentine goldsmith shops had a reputation for offering rigorous training in draughtsmanship and design, skills that provided the springboard for all sorts of careers. Vasari claims that there was a particular bond between goldsmiths and painters in the fifteenth century. Painters who started their training as goldsmiths, such as Botticelli and Ghirlandaio as well as Verrocchio and Antonio del Pollaiuolo, were a distinctive feature of the Florentine milieu, almost unknown in other cities with strong traditions of art production.

Early, and highly plausible, tradition also has it that Antonio del Pollaiuolo had experience in the Ghiberti shop in the making of the Baptistery portals. The bronze doors – the costliest and possibly the greatest

sculpture project of the first half of the fifteenth century – were finally completed with the manufacture of the jambs in the shop of Ghiberti's son Vittorio in the 1450s and 1460s. The garlands of these door surrounds reveal the breathtaking naturalism and subtlety of relief that is so characteristic of Florentine art of the 1460s and 1470s. In his *Commentaries*, Ghiberti states that for the second set of doors he was granted the freedom (*licentia*) to do as he thought would 'turn out most perfect and ornate and richest', and that in the narrative panels he sought to observe the due proportions and principles, to imitate nature 'with excellent compositions ... rich with very many figures'.[29] Certainly the exploration of the principles of nature, in the geometrical description of space and in the varied movements of figures, as well as the search to arrive at perfected forms and complex – or ornate – compositions are key aspects of the 1470s. A brief look at some of the major artists active in that decade shows how they developed and promoted their diverse talents in competition and collaboration and as masters and pupils.

ANTONIO AND PIERO DEL POLLAIUOLO

The career of Antonio del Pollaiuolo (1431/2–98), whose staple activity was goldsmithing, encompassed painting, domestic and monumental sculpture, and design. He was a frequent collaborator and supporter of his painter and sculptor brother Piero (1441–96) and the Pollaiuolo could be defined as a family firm for certain types of product. Antonio was the eldest of six siblings living in the parish of S. Maria Maggiore, to the west of the Baptistery. His younger brother Giovanni took over their father's poultry business but it was Antonio who bought the family house – for himself, Piero and Giovanni – with the

Fig. 58 ANTONIO DEL POLLAIUOLO AND BETTO BETTI, *Baptistery Cross*, begun 1457. Silver, height 250 cm. Florence, Museo dell'Opera del Duomo.

Fig. 59 ANTONIO DEL POLLAIUOLO, *Design for an incense burner*, 1460s. Pen and brown ink and brown wash on paper, 29.1 × 20.3 cm. Florence, Galleria degli Uffizi, Gabinetto Disegni e Stampe, inv. 942E recto.

proceeds of his wife's dowry in 1472. Antonio's success as a goldsmith was already sealed in 1457 when, together with Betto Betti, he was awarded the commission for the massive silver reliquary cross for the Baptistery (fig. 58).[30] Antonio was not inscribed into the goldsmith's guild, the Arte della Seta, until 1466 but his reputation in the field can be gauged by the large number of documents relating to his goldsmith commissions.[31] Some idea of his ability and acute promotional skills can also be gained from his double-sided design for a thurible (incense burner) (fig. 59) and incense boat to which he precociously appended his signature and profession, 'Antonio del Pollaiuolo horafo'.[32] Liturgical objects of this kind were a mainstay of his goldsmith business, but prestigious secular commissions also flowed from the government in the 1470s, including the presentation helmet for the Duke of Urbino and silverware for the Palazzo Vecchio.[33] As noted earlier the coffers of the Baptistery were very generous to Antonio del Pollaiuolo, but the curse of goldsmith's work – that it is easily melted down – has left us with hardly any finished work by him, apart from his relief of the *Birth of the Baptist* for the great silver altar itself (fig. 31). Antonio's silver cover for a Gospel book for the Duomo made in 1476 was thought, by 1500, to make the book to heavy to carry. His work was destroyed and the silver recycled in the form of candlesticks.[34]

Like most goldsmiths, Antonio del Pollaiuolo operated in partnerships and he is documented early on as involved with commissions given to the *compagnia* of Maso Finiguerra and Piero Salì. His interests and techniques as a draughtsman, concentrating on the active male figure, were very close to those of Finiguerra who shared with him the epithet *maestro di disegno* in the *Zibaldone* of Giovanni Rucellai.[35] Like Finiguerra, Antonio may have contributed figure designs for the marquetry decoration completed in the 1460s in the North Sacristy of the Duomo, under the direction of Giuliano da Maiano. By the 1470s he had his own thriving workshop in the via Vaccherecchia, a street dominated by goldsmiths near the Palazzo della Signoria, and with the security of several partnerships, his work influenced goldsmiths' production in Florence and beyond until well after his death.

Vasari claims that Antonio del Pollaiuolo's younger brother Piero trained with the painter Andrea del Castagno (d. 1457) and then passed on his knowledge to Antonio.[36] In reality, Antonio anticipated his brother's work as a painter and was almost certainly the senior partner in collaborative works such as the *Labours of Hercules* canvases for the Medici palace (which Antonio said he painted with his brother in 1460) and the paintings on the altar wall of the Cardinal of Portugal's Chapel (fig. 57). In the altarpiece, Piero del Pollaiuolo carefully adapted his style to harmonise with that of his brother, but his hand is apparent in the saint to the right. A similar pattern of collaboration can be traced in the Pollaiuolo's major painted work of the 1470s, the Pucci *Martyrdom of Saint Sebastian* (cat. no. 43), in which the figure of Sebastian himself was both designed and, apparently, painted by Piero, though individual hands are less easy to detect in the archers. Seen in its entirety, this altarpiece represents a manifesto of the concerns of the Pollaiuolo shop – especially those of Antonio. Its combination of active, muscular figures that appear to turn in space, but that are nonetheless locked into a strong two-dimensional geometry, can be compared with Antonio's signed engraving (cat. no. 53). The ambitious design of the figures and the fine textural detail of the foreground features achieved in oil is matched with an acutely observed and atmospheric Tuscan panorama receding in aerial perspective.

Piero's known independent works, exclusively paintings, tend towards less active subjects and include the exemplary female figures that were somewhat antithetical to Antonio's more robust aesthetic. Nonetheless, Piero was able to use his brother's influential support to gain an advantage in Florentine painting commissions. Antonio acted as a guarantor for the *Charity* for the Mercanzia and apparently gave his brother a head start by providing a full-scale drawing of the figure on the panel. Similarly, Antonio's draughtsmanship is not far below the surface in Piero's Turin *Tobias and the Angel* (fig. 60). That Piero enjoyed a certain prestige as a painter is signalled by his ambitious portrait of Galeazzo Maria Sforza, probably commissioned by Lorenzo de' Medici (fig. 19), but he was also beaten to commissions by Leonardo and his record of success was greater outside Florence. It was his work on a now lost Corpus Domini altarpiece for the cathedral of Pistoia that probably drew him to the attention of the commissioners of the Forteguerri monument in 1477, though he must also have been advertising himself as a sculptor to qualify for consideration. Piero's only independent surviving altarpiece, signed and dated 1483, is in the convent church of S. Agostino in San Gimignano. His Pistoia work, described as '*elegantissimo*' may again have provided the catalyst for this commission.[37] Interestingly, Piero's Florentine tax return of 1480 implies that his painting commissions were either intermittent or executed near their destination – it emerges that he had no painting workshop *per se*, but a room in his part of the Pollaiuolo family house in Piazza degli Agli, used 'when I have something to paint'.[38]

Antonio del Pollaiuolo was more emphatically in demand as a painter within Florence, though again

Fig. 60 PIERO DEL POLLAIUOLO, *Tobias and the Angel*, late 1460s. Oil on panel, 187 × 118 cm. Turin, Galleria Sabauda.

in the same medium. The *Hercules, Nessus and Deianeira*, possibly painted with Piero, exemplifies Antonio's specialisation in the Hercules subject and the movements of man and nature, while the *David* presents a rather domesticated and courtly version of the youth who, like Hercules, was promoted as a Florentine civic hero. A further, or rather, overlapping strand to the civic themes commissioned from Antonio is that of the antique and secular. Among these, the highly inventive scheme of dancing adult nudes cavorting above a perspectival architecture that he painted for the villa of his Lanfredini patrons almost certainly dates to the 1470s (fig. 46). In several ways, the themes and interests of Antonio's paintings are comparable to those of Verrocchio in sculpture. Unlike Verrocchio, Antonio had no painting workshop in the sense of a place where assistants could learn the trade under the master's *aegis*, but he

there is no evidence for a separate painting workshop. We do not know who trained him as a painter. His earliest altarpiece of the *Elevation of Mary Magdalene* for the parish church in Staggia and the record of his lost *Hercules* canvases in the Uffizi panels (figs. 61 and 62) show a strong affinity with the palette, as well as the expressive and dynamic interests of Andrea del Castagno (*c*.1421–57). It may be significant that he was chosen for similar commissions to Castagno and worked at the same sites. The patrons of Antonio's smaller works are also unknown, though the *Apollo and Daphne* (cat. no. 88), his profile portraits of patrician women such as that now in Milan (fig. 63), the *Hercules, Nessus and Deianeira* (cat. no. 46) and the earlier *David*, now in Berlin, are all works designed for the domestic chambers of a cultivated élite. The first of these is an exquisite secular work in oil that presents itself as a collector's item to rival Northern paintings

Figs. 61 and 62 ANTONIO DEL POLLAIUOLO, *Hercules and the Hydra*, panel, 17.5 × 21 cm, and *Hercules and Antaeus*, panel, 16 × 10.5 cm, both 1470s. Florence, Galleria degli Uffizi.

Fig. 63 ANTONIO DEL POLLAIUOLO, *Portrait of a Woman*, 1467–70. Panel, 47.6 × 34.5 cm. Milan, Museo Poldi-Pezzoli.

was able to call on his brother, and presumably on *ad hoc* assistants, when necessary. However, it was his goldsmith business that was his mainstay.

Related as they were to his goldsmith activity, Antonio's skills as a sculptor seem to have resided in modelling and casting rather than carving, though some art historians have wanted to attribute to him works in marble and wood. He never won any large-scale sculpture commissions in Florence and it was only in the 1480s, when he was chosen to make the bronze tomb of Pope Sixtus IV, that this aspect of his career took off. The early proof of Pollaiuolo's skills as a sculptor came rather in his contribution to the developing genre of the bronze statuette (fig. 64 and cat. no. 58), in his work in terracotta – the bust of a young warrior for example (fig. 97) – and as a specialist in relief-moulded and cast sculpture. Though the works themselves are small-scale, his approach to sculpture was consistently monumental and experimental. The *Hercules and Antaeus* statuette, probably the sculpture of the same subject mentioned in the Medici palace inventory of 1492, breaks new ground in exploiting the formal and spatial complexities afforded by a two-figure group. Taking its structural cues from the triangular, chamfered form of the base, the group is constructed so that the tensed limbs of the combatants fall into geometric formations that satisfy the eye in both three and two dimensions. It is a connoisseur's object by virtue of its mythological subject and its status as a revival of an antique type, but also in the formal pleasure it affords the owner who can easily revolve the figures manually.[39] Ingenious spatial effects of a quite different kind characterise the large pageant shield now in the Louvre (fig. 65). Here the strong curvature of the wood allows for the gesso relief of the muscle-bound Milos of Croton (a mythical athlete who

Fig. 64   ANTONIO DEL POLLAIUOLO, *Hercules and Antaeus*, 1470s. Bronze, height 45 cm. Florence, Museo Nazionale del Bargello.

overstretched himself) to gain a temporal and dynamic dimension as the modelled and painted limbs emerge from, and appear to pull against, their support. Vasari records another relief project, now lost – a metal (presumably bronze) sculpture by Antonio showing battling nude figures, which was apparently sent to Spain. Though Vasari mentions gesso impressions rather than clay replicas, cat. no. 54 is perhaps one of the many copies that he says were owned by Florentine workshops. It may well have been this lost bronze which encouraged the sculptor Bertoldo to cast his own battle relief, based on a Roman sarcophagus in Pisa, once placed above the fireplace in the Medici palace (fig. 20).

Antonio's lost relief can be compared in both its subject and its influence with his highly original design project of the *Battle of nude men* engraving (cat. no. 53). Such a large-scale excursus in the new medium has a deliberately demonstrative quality that appealed to contemporary artists interested in the problem of depicting the human figure in movement, as well as to patrons. Though Antonio apparently never made another engraving, his *Battle* was reproducible, highly marketable and, by circulating both his name and artistic capabilities, served to perpetuate his fame more than any other object he produced. By contrast, his most monumental commission as a Florentine *maestro di disegno* is not often discussed. This is partly because, unlike the engraving, which marks a turning point for a new genre, his extended cycle of designs on the life of Saint John the Baptist (see cat. no. 48) was executed in the form of liturgical embroideries, a tradition of luxury manufacture neglected by art history. Pollaiuolo's drawing ability can be seen as a legacy of his Florentine goldsmith training. His ability both to visualise and invent subjects clothed in an *all'antica* mantle was an aspect of *disegno* that he

Fig. 65 ANTONIO DEL POLLAIUOLO, *Shield with Milos of Croton*, 1470s. Wood and painted and gilt gesso, height 47 cm. Paris, Musée du Louvre.

Mercanzia, the cupola ball for the Opera del Duomo). In the documents regarding the Duomo choir project in 1471, he is named as an expert, as a 'huomo intendente'.[40] His expertise extended from a knowledge of the techniques necessary to work with silver, bronze, marble, terracotta, stucco, wood, tempera and oil to a command of spatial design, narrative expression and a curiosity about the useful applications of the legacy of ancient art. It made him one of the most influential teachers of his time as well as one of the most important masters.

Inventiveness is the defining, and unifying, feature of Verrocchio's works. The *David* and the *Putto with a Dolphin* are among the first statues in the Renaissance to succeed as sculptures in the round (figs. 17 and 66). The *Lady with Flowers* is the first three-quarter-length sculpted portrait produced in modern times (fig. 67). Whether called upon for an unprecedented task, like

made very much his own and which, in the absence of painter followers, was his most potent legacy to the art of central and northern Italy. In Florence, Antonio's keen representational and technical abilities, his imaginative response to antique art, especially its qualities of animation, and an obvious flare for self-marketing, ensured he was in demand for everything from portraiture to pageant armour.

ANDREA DEL VERROCCHIO
Andrea del Verrocchio (*c.*1435–88) was the Pollaiuolo brothers' chief rival. Around 35 years old at the opening of the 1470s, the decade marks his artistic maturity. By 1470 he had become Donatello's successor as the Medici's favoured sculptor and had been awarded commissions by the city government (the Signoria candlestick, cat. no. 12) and other major civic bodies (the *Christ and Saint Thomas* for the

Fig. 66 ANDREA DEL VERROCCHIO, *Putto with a Dolphin*, early 1470s. Bronze, height 67 cm. Florence, Palazzo Vecchio.

Fig. 67 ANDREA DEL VERROCCHIO, *Portrait bust of a Lady with Flowers*, mid-1470s. Marble, height 67 cm. Florence, Museo Nazionale del Bargello.

the Medici tomb, or addressing routine compositions of the Virgin and Child, Verrocchio seems to have studied the meaning of the subject and reflected on how best to give it form. He shrewdly exploited prestigious sources. He referred to Bernardo Rossellino's Virgin and Child roundel above the tomb of Leonardo Bruni in S. Croce and to the infant Saviour on Desiderio da Settignano's sacrament tabernacle in S. Lorenzo (fig. 95) for the positions taken by mother and infant in domestic devotional images (figs. 68 and 69). Posing them frontally, he represented their relation to each other and to the onlooker with a monumentality and formality that asserted the sacredness of the Holy Child, without sacrificing sentiment or liveliness.

Verrocchio was acutely sensitive to the properties and potential of his materials, which he worked in novel ways and to great decorative and dramatic effect.

The bronze of the Medici tomb represents coarsely twined rope, lush acanthus, hard and woody acorns, tortoise shells and lion's paws: an abundance of visual sensations that parallels the eternal abundance promised by the Medici diamond emblem crowning the sarcophagus (fig. 16). In the Christ of the Mercanzia group, bronze becomes the heavy cloth of Christ's robe, the smooth surface of his chest and the horrible torn flesh of his open wound (fig. 29). As a founder and metalworker Verrocchio was second to none. The Christ and the Saint Thomas were cast as single pieces – a technological challenge.[41] In the silver panel of the *Beheading of the Baptist* (fig. 32) for the Baptistery he took the opposite path, looking at the fourteenth-century reliefs on the altar, which assembled separately wrought elements. Rather than shaping the story as one cast or wrought panel, he composed his scene by fixing individual figures, one of

Fig. 68 Workshop of ANDREA DEL VERROCCHIO, *Virgin and Child*, c.1475–80. Marble, 84 x 57.5 cm. Florence, Museo Nazionale del Bargello.

Fig. 69 ANDREA DEL VERROCCHIO, *Virgin and Child*, c.1475. Painted terracotta, 86 x 66 cm. Florence, Museo Nazionale del Bargello.

them cast, the rest of beaten silver, to the background. Light falls around and between the figures, making the viewer experience the moment as dynamic. The separation of parts reinforces the diversity of the action. This is enhanced by meticulous finish. Careful chasing defines the details and heightens the impact of each element in expressing violence and compassion and the contrasting strengths of brute force and unquestioning faith.[42]

Vasari significantly remarks that in his youth Verrocchio 'studied the sciences, especially geometry'.[43] This study is evident not only in his explicitly measured perspectives, in the pavements of the *Beheading of the Baptist*, the altarpiece for Pistoia cathedral and the *Virgin and Child* now in Edinburgh (figs. 32, 70 and cat. no. 25), but also in his constant attention to nuances of space, to the implicit

geometries of viewing angles and distance points. He also applied himself to the study of the human body, in nature and from antique statues. Between *c*.1453 and 1456 he was a student of the goldsmith Antonio di Giovanni Dei; he then worked with the goldsmith Francesco di Luca Verrocchio; but who trained him in painting, sculpting and bronze-casting is not known. On stylistic grounds the painter Fra Filippo Lippi and the sculptor Antonio Rossellino have been considered the most likely masters. He manifestly took inspiration from a wide variety of sources, ancient and modern, and he never ceased seeking new ideas. His quest was in part to arrive at the perfected forms that could become canonical – such as the beautiful heads, three-quarter views and upturned faces that exist in finished drawings (fig. 71 and cat. nos. 31 and 32). In his chapters on famous sculptors

Fig. 70 ANDREA DEL VERROCCHIO AND LORENZO DI CREDI, *The Virgin and Child with Saints John the Baptist and Zenobius ('The Pistoia Altarpiece')*, *c*.1476 to after 1485. Oil and tempera on panel, 189 × 191 cm. Pistoia, Duomo, Chapel of the Sacrament.

four terracotta infants, three being models for statues that were blocked out. As the draft for the Forteguerri monument indicates (cat. no. 13), Verrocchio used terracotta as a sketching material for works in marble as well as bronze. Working with a pliable substance gave him the freedom to think about the complicated poses and delicately defined textures that give his statues their astonishing vivacity. Vasari describes in some detail how Verrocchio enjoyed making plaster casts and how, in addition to whole figures, he would make parts – hands, feet, knees, legs, arms and torsos – so as to be able to study them with ease.[47] Such models were useful teaching tools, as the drawings by Francesco di Simone prove (cat. no. 42). Verrocchio referred to them for themes and variations in figure studies, as did Leonardo (cat. nos. 26 and 39). They provided motifs for paintings. They also provided a means to examine and to master the effects of light in order to translate three dimensions into two. In his Life of Leonardo da Vinci, Vasari also describes studies made after clay models draped with rags dipped in clay or plaster and drawn on 'fine cambric or used linen working in black and white with the point of the brush'(cat. no. 26; fig. 79). The results, as he says, were 'marvellous', but the technique of making studies after stiffened cloth was not itself original.[48] The novelty was in using brush on linen. The fabric support and the brushstrokes enhance the descriptive and evocative nature of such studies in their ability to convey the texture and weight of folded cloth. The method might have evolved in Verrocchio's shop during the design phase of the Mercanzia group when full-scale draped models were being prepared. A by-product of sculptural activity, these drawings are concerned with the way that light controls the experience of form as well as with researching expressive fold vocabularies, issues involved in both painting and sculpture.

and painters, the Roman writer Pliny the Elder celebrated their specific contributions to their arts and their creation of new standards. The humanist poet Ugolino Verino compared Verrocchio to Phidias.[44] Even though their works did not survive, the enduring reputations of the artists of antiquity might have inspired Verrocchio to make such comparisons for himself.

No complete suite of drawings or set of models exist to demonstrate how Verrocchio arrived at his finished works, but there is some record of his workshop properties and procedures. An inventory of his shop includes both paintings and sculptures, so he must have worked on both in one studio space.[45] Leonardo's contempt for the physical effort, perspiration, grit, noise and dirt of sculpting doubtless recalls his days in Verrocchio's shop watching the marble dust fly.[46] The inventory includes

Fig. 71 ANDREA DEL VERROCCHIO, *Head*, *c*.1470s. Metalpoint, grey ink and wash, white heightening on orange-red prepared paper, 26.7 × 22.5 cm. Paris, Musée du Louvre, Cabinet des dessins, inv. 18.965.

One of Vasari's most revealing remarks about Verrocchio's working habits is that because he always had some painting or sculpture in progress, he would often leave one kind of work for another, to avoid boredom.[49] He might also have been prompted by the need to meet the demands of the most pressing, or most profitable, patron. Whatever the reason, this behaviour meant that there was inevitably a creative crossover between projects in different media and in different phases of completion. The fact that he was so busy on so many things also meant that Verrocchio relied on his trusted assistants. He often delegated the completion of his paintings. This is hardly surprising, given the calibre of his chief pupils.

LEONARDO DA VINCI

According to Renaissance educational theory it was a father's duty to observe his son's natural talent – his *ingegno* – and then to nurture it by placing him with the best possible master. Exactly how Ser Piero da Vinci determined his son's gifts is a mystery, but by selecting Verrocchio's shop he happily placed Leonardo with a master whose investigations into the nature of nature and its description would stimulate his own enquiring mind. Verrocchio was apparently not threatened by his remarkable apprentice, instead he fostered Leonardo's genius to the advantage of his shop.

It is not known when Leonardo (1452–1519) was apprenticed to Verrocchio.[50] But by 1472, when he was inscribed in the confraternity of Saint Luke, he must have been qualified to be regarded as an independent painter. Leonardo did not matriculate in any guild as a sculptor, but he later wrote that he had equal experience of painting and sculpture.[51] In a letter to Duke Ludovico Sforza, which can be dated to 1482, he

Fig. 72 LEONARDO DA VINCI, *Annunciation*, 1472–5. Oil and tempera on panel, 98 × 217 cm. Florence, Galleria degli Uffizi.

presented himself primarily as a military engineer, but he also noted that 'in times of peace' he was able to work as well as anyone in architecture and in marble, bronze and clay sculpture.[52] Although the combination of professions might seem peculiar now, other sculptor-bronzecasters like Michelozzo (1396–1472) had become architect-engineers. The diverse activities of Verrocchio's shop undoubtedly encouraged his versatile student to develop multiple skills and to move freely between work in two and three dimensions.[53]

The Uffizi *Annunciation* (fig. 72) is an accomplished statement of Leonardo's mastery of the forms and motifs available in Verrocchio's studio in the early 1470s. The Virgin's marble reading-stand is an obvious tribute to the Medici tomb (fig. 16). The gracefully posed hands of the angel and Mary, their geometrically massed draperies, and the complicated

spatial patterns of the setting are also verrocchiesque features. They are not repeated from Verrocchio's repertoire, however; they are reconsidered, with attention given to each shape and texture – the feathers and bones of the angel's wings and the flutter of its drapery, the parchment and leather of Mary's book, the soft curls of her hair – thereby rendering the moment of the miraculous greeting both impossibly beautiful and palpably real.

A landscape drawing that Leonardo dated to the feast day of Holy Mary of the Snow, 5 August, shows the young artist engaging with nature through art (fig. 73). The panoramic viewpoint and the staging of the scene are taken from landscape conventions developed by Northern artists and followed by Florentines, first by Alesso Baldovinetti at SS. Annunziata and then by the Pollaiuolo brothers.[54] Leonardo used them to structure his perceptions of the passage of light over the near hills and distant valleys and to record the qualities of atmosphere on a sunny summer's day. He also tried out various pen strokes – short, long, curved, crossing and parallel – to arrive at a descriptive graphic. This kind of notational exercise must have been encouraged in Verrocchio's shop. Verrocchio's own drawings range from deft pen and ink sketches to highly polished black chalk drawings and were part of his imaginative process and his archive of serviceable types (cat. nos. 36 and 31). In his notebooks, Leonardo says that 'the artist ought first to exercise his hand by copying drawings from the hand of a good master. And having acquired that practice, under the criticism of his master, he should next practise drawing objects in relief.'[55] Leonardo's fluent and varied pen line resulted from such exercise and criticism. His ability to describe relief is exemplified by his minutely observed and vividly rendered metalpoint profile of a warrior in the British

Fig. 73 LEONARDO DA VINCI, *Landscape*, 1473. Pen and brown ink on paper, 19.4 × 28.6 cm. Florence, Galleria degli Uffizi, Gabinetto Disegni e Stampe, inv. 8P recto.

Fig. 74 ANDREA DEL VERROCCHIO AND WORKSHOP,
Baptism of Christ, 1468 and 1471 to *c*.1476. Tempera and oil
on panel, 177 × 150 cm. Florence, Galleria degli Uffizi.

Museum (cat. no. 63). Drawing not only trained Leonardo's hand, it furnished his memory. The contrasting types of attractive youth and hardened age based on Verrocchio's *David* and his *Darius* became reflexive and recur throughout Leonardo's career, as do spiralling curls and pudgy infants.

Leonardo's conspicuous participation in painting the *Baptism* now in the Uffizi demonstrates Verrocchio's recognition of Leonardo's special skills (fig. 74). The circumstances of the commission are not known, but the painting was probably made as an altarpiece for the Vallombrosan abbey of S. Salvi just outside Florence, where Verrocchio's older brother Simone was abbot in 1468, and again from 1471 to 1473 and 1475 to 1478. The painting was produced in at least two phases: the first when the composition was laid out and begun in tempera, and the second when the foreground angel and the body of Christ were

painted using oil and the landscape was repainted, also using oil. In both phases Verrocchio undoubtedly and characteristically relied on his assistants, with Leonardo being given extensive responsibilities in the second stage, notably in painting the left-hand angel and in revising the landscape. The break in painting is likely to have coincided with a break in payments, as was later the case with the Pistoia altarpiece. The interruption may well have been connected with Simone's terms as abbot, dating the conception of the painting to either 1468 or 1471 and its completion to about 1476.[56] The painting is an example of the ensemble work characteristic of Verrocchio's production. It is also, as completed, a summary of what Leonardo had learnt, and what he now had to teach. He demonstrated how the medium of oil made it possible to achieve softly luminous surfaces and unified tonal gradations. With this he also showed

Fig. 75 LEONARDO DA VINCI, *Ginevra de' Benci*, c.1480. Oil and tempera on panel, 38.8 × 36.7 cm. Washington, National Gallery of Art, Ailsa Mellon Bruce Fund.

Fig. 76 LEONARDO DA VINCI, *Studies of heads and machinery*, 1478. Pen and brown ink on paper, 20.2 × 26.7. Florence, Galleria degli Uffizi, Gabinetto Disegni e Stampe, inv. 446E recto.

how distance and nearness were part of an atmospheric and emotional continuum: that painting not only recorded states of being, but could influence the viewer's mood.

Leonardo achieved a similar immediacy in the portrait of *Ginevra de' Benci* (fig. 75). The painting has been cut down. Originally Ginevra was probably three-quarter length, and in terms of painted portraits, the picture was as revolutionary as its sculpted prototype, Verrocchio's *Lady with Flowers* (fig. 67).[57] Having exposed Ginevra's physical charms so thoroughly to the viewer, Leonardo distanced her psychologically through her stillness, her sober dress and her meditative gaze.

Leonardo left Verrocchio's shop sometime before the beginning of 1478, when he received the commission from the Signoria for an altarpiece for their chapel (which he never completed). In that year, while drawing various mechanical devices, he doodled two heads and practised his penmanship, noting with a flourish that in 'D[ecem]ber I started the two Virgin Marys' (fig. 76). A list of his works, probably made when he moved to Milan in 1482, included one finished picture of 'Our Lady' and another in profile. There are two completed paintings of the Virgin and Child that can be dated to this period, one in Munich and one in St Petersburg (fig. 77), and there are drawings of the Virgin and Child with a cat (cat. no. 38), studies for a Virgin in profile and for the Virgin and Child with Saint John (cat. no. 9).[58] There are many more projects than finished paintings, and the possibilities seemed to multiply as Leonardo studied them. Domestic devotional panels of the Virgin and Child would ordinarily have been a workshop staple. Leonardo's temperamental inability to settle on a stock formula would inevitably sabotage any such steady production. The machine drawings on the

Fig. 77 LEONARDO DA VINCI, *Virgin and Child ('The Benois Madonna')*, 1478–80. Oil on panel, transferred to canvas, 48 × 31 cm. St Petersburg, Hermitage.

Fig. 78 LEONARDO DA VINCI, *Adoration of the Magi*, 1481–2.
Panel, 243 × 246 cm. Florence, Galleria degli Uffizi.

dated sheet (fig. 76) are also symptomatic of the problem. They demonstrate Leonardo's investigative turn of mind, which inevitably challenged the confines of the artisan status of the painter or painter/sculptor.

In March 1481 Leonardo was given the commission for the high altarpiece of S. Donato a Scopeto, a monastery just outside the city's southern gate. His father was the monastery's *procuratore*, or agent, and he might have used his influence to secure the job for his son. It gave Leonardo an opportunity to muse on a dramatic and solemn subject, the *Adoration of the Kings*. He thought extensively about how to convey the moment when doubt is converted to faith and the high become humble. He even began painting (fig. 78). But he did not get very far before payments ceased, in September, and he was soon fixing his sights on wider horizons. In 1482 he left for Milan, to be employed at the court of Ludovico Sforza. This transfer might have been aided or even engineered by Lorenzo de' Medici – Leonardo was one of the artists who studied the antiquities in Lorenzo's sculpture garden.[59] Lorenzo not only fostered the talents of Florentine artists, but used them as as part of his diplomatic manoeuvres. Leonardo's preparation for his part in the exportation of Florentine excellence owed much to the creative flexibility as well as the knowledge he acquired during his years in Verrocchio's shop.

LORENZO DI CREDI

If Leonardo was Verrocchio's most talented assistant, Lorenzo di Credi (*c*.1457–1537) was his most trusted. In 1486 when Verrocchio went to Venice to work on the equestrian monument of Bartolommeo Colleoni, he left Credi in charge of his Florentine business and two years later named him as chief heir and executor of

his will. One document identifies him as a 'painter in Verrocchio's shop' and even though Andrea tried to bequeath him his sculpture commissions (the completion of the Colleoni monument in Venice and the Forteguerri monument in Pistoia), painting seems to have been Credi's specialisation.[60] He probably entered Verrocchio's employ in the mid-1470s, when oil was becoming the predominant medium in the shop and when the master, for whatever reason, was increasingly inclined to hand his brushes over to his students. He seems to have been given a substantial part in painting the Pistoia altarpiece, which was possibly begun around 1476, and was definitely commissioned sometime before 1478–9 (fig. 70). A document from November 1485 notes that it was almost completed, and would have been finished more than six years before had payment been forthcoming. This document also gives a price of sixty florins for the panel and says that it was executed following a drawing by Verrocchio. Verrocchio clearly pondered the design of this important altarpiece, but he also relied on Credi to develop ideas in more detailed drawings, such as those in Edinburgh and Paris (cat. nos. 19 and 20). The underdrawing on the panel shows that adjustments were made in the outlines of the Baptist, the Child and, crucially, the Virgin's head, directing her gaze downward toward the infant Christ. The painting is a result of a dialogue between Verrocchio and Credi, with Verrocchio as inventor and Credi as principal executant.[61] Vasari, who might have met Credi and who certainly knew his students, comments on his fastidious and laborious technique, saying that he used pigments that were ground extremely fine which he blended to minute gradations, up to twenty-five or thirty for a colour.[62] This painstaking procedure, resulting in intense local colour and delicate, soft changes of tone, is a feature of Lorenzo's style and is a painterly response to the problems of illumination and texture set by Verrocchio. Totally lacking Leonardo's restless curiosity, he was instead content to rehearse the shop's repertoire in polished variations on successful themes.

VERROCCHIO'S ASSISTANTS AND FOLLOWERS
Leonardo da Vinci and Lorenzo di Credi were Verrocchio's two most established (and best documented) assistants, but a number of other painters and sculptors were also influenced by Verrocchio. Vasari says, for example, that along with Leonardo, the Umbrian painter Pietro Perugino (c.1450–1523) was one of Credi's 'companions and friends' in Verrocchio's shop, 'even if they were competitors.'[63] Perugino is listed in the 1472 register of the Company of Saint Luke, so he was in Florence and active as a painter and a likely competitor to the other young painters of the town. His sensitivity to volumetric modelling and his famously sweet-faced and pensive figures show a lasting debt to Verrocchio. His composition for the *Assumption of the Virgin* fresco for the altar of the Sistine chapel (destroyed, but known from a copy drawing in Vienna) was based on Verrocchio's composition for the Forteguerri monument – the figure displayed in a mandorla subsequently became a signature motif of his altarpieces. Perugino was an influential channel for diffusing and propagating beyond Florence the patterns that had been developed in Verrocchio's shop. He is an instance of a painter who entered the shop after being trained elsewhere. This meant that he could be assigned significant tasks, as could other experienced assistants. It was an effective way for Verrocchio to maintain a high standard of steady production. Whoever the executant, Verrocchio was, however, ultimately responsible for the final work. For

this reason, Perugino's exact production in Verrocchio's workshop is impossible to determine with any certainty, despite persistent, if conflicting, attempts.[64]

Other artists whom scholars have named as students or assistants of Verrocchio include Sandro Botticelli (c.1445–1510), Francesco Botticini (c.1446–98), Domenico Ghirlandaio (1449–94) and Biagio di Antonio (1446–1516).[65] Of the same generation, all were independent masters by the 1470s. Botticini, the son of a painter of playing cards, is documented as a painter and assistant to Neri di Bicci in 1469; in May 1470 Botticelli was commissioned to paint one of the Mercanzia *Virtues* (fig. 30), in competition with Verrocchio; in the early 1470s Ghirlandaio was operating a firm with his brother, and in 1472 Biagio di Antonio was in partnership with Jacopo del Sellaio.[66] It is widely, if not universally, agreed that Biagio painted a substantial portion of an altarpiece now in Budapest, which Vasari says that Verrocchio made for the nuns of S. Domenico del Maglio in Florence. If Biagio was granted such a prominent role on a major work, then for a brief time he might have acted as a principal assistant to Verrocchio, like Leonardo and Lorenzo di Credi.[67] By analogy with the practices documented in Neri di Bicci's records, these young men (or others) could have been contracted for different periods, or even subcontracted from other shops. There is no doubt that they were strongly and variously influenced by Verrocchio, but there is no consensus and no absolute proof as to their participation in his studio. It is clear, however, that certain shop properties (such as terracotta models of wriggling infants) were widely copied, as were modes of study that allowed for the convincing three-dimensional representation of figures in equally convincingly constructed space.

DOMENICO GHIRLANDAIO

One study, now in the Louvre (fig. 79), relates closely to the composition of the drapery of the Virgin in the panel that Domenico Ghirlandaio painted as the high altarpiece of the church of S. Giusto in the early 1480s (fig. 80). The tubby-bellied child with legs akimbo and left arm bent and supported is a type that can also be traced to Verrocchio's studio, variants occurring in drawings by Leonardo da Vinci and Lorenzo Credi.[68] The conspicuously elegant display of gently angled hands, such as the Virgin's right hand or the Archangel Raphael's left, is a recurrent feature of Verrocchio's compositions, found, for instance, in the National Gallery *Tobias and the Angel* (cat. no. 21). Parallels can also be found for the careful depiction of details such as lilies and jewels. The overall composition, with the Virgin seated on an open-air throne with an oriental carpet covering the stairs and pavement before her, follows that of the Pistoia altarpiece. It reveals, in sum, a very knowing or knowledgeable assimilation of forms and formulas from Verrocchio's shop, and also shows how such formulas provided a vocabulary for other painters to create richly articulated, luminous and solidly modelled displays of the heavenly hierarchy. It also shows Ghirlandaio's own careful observation of the way that reflected light could illuminate and shape surfaces – one of the chief lessons to be learned from making studies such as that in the Louvre, which, though similar to Ghirlandaio's painting, is not the same. As painted, the drapery is simpler, insisting on essential structural forms. It lacks the animation and dramatic cascades of the drawing, which accord far better with Leonardo's perceptions than Ghirlandaio's compositional aims. The drawing is also lit dramatically from above, and would hardly have suited as a study for the painting. It should be taken not as a

Fig. 79 LEONARDO DA VINCI, *Drapery study*, c.1470s. Brush and grey and white wash on grey prepared linen, 26.5 × 25.3 cm. Paris, Musée du Louvre, Cabinet des dessins, inv. 2255.

Fig. 80 DOMENICO GHIRLANDAIO, *Virgin and Child enthroned with Angels and Saints Michael, Justus, Zenobius and Raphael*, early 1480s. Panel, 200 × 191 cm. Florence, Galleria degli Uffizi.

drawing done by Ghirlandaio, but as a type of study known to him as he gained his mastery of painting in the course of the 1470s.[69]

When he registered in the confraternity of San Paolo in May 1470, Domenico is noted as being with a goldsmith, and his father's 1480 tax return states that his three sons had all been placed with a goldsmith.[70] This training not only influenced Ghirlandaio's taste for ornament, but seems to have given him an introduction to pen and ink, which became his preferred drawing tool and a powerful and precise means for recording and transmitting visual information. However tempting it may be to assume that the goldsmith in question was Verrocchio, it should be remembered that by 1470 Verrocchio referred to himself as a painter and sculptor or carver, not as a goldsmith. In any event, early sources indicate that it was Alesso Baldovinetti, not Verrocchio, who taught Ghirlandaio how to paint. Ghirlandaio remained largely faithful to tempera, often applied in very complex layers to achieve deep colours and crystalline surfaces in a manner that can be compared to Baldovinetti. His systematic graphic notation in pen drawing, relying on careful cross-hatching and delineation of planes, is a suitable preparatory style for this type of modelling. Even when taking up verrocchiesque forms and using black chalk, as in a three-quarter-profile cartoon for the head of the Baptist in the *Pietà* frescoed in the Vespucci chapel, he did not smudge and blend the chalk, but relied on areas of hatching to study the fall of light over the figure.[71] This mural is also a reminder that the Ghirlandaio family firm was receiving commissions from the early 1470s. With his younger brother David, Domenico seems to have found a market niche in mural painting, which he could not have learned from Verrocchio, who did not work on walls. His father's

statement in his 1480 tax return that the brothers did not have a workshop, but painted here and there, records their success, not their failure. By that date, in addition to the Vespucci chapel, the brothers had painted frescoes for chapels in the churches of S. Andrea in Cercina and S. Andrea a Brozzi in San Donnino, the *Last Supper* for the refectory of the Vallombrosan Badia at Passignano (all on the outskirts of Florence), and, farther afield, had taken on the highly prestigious commissions of the S. Fina chapel at S. Gimignano (fig. 54) and decorations for one of Pope Sixtus IV's library rooms (the *bibliotheca latina*) in the Vatican. They also painted (now lost) frescoes in the funerary chapel of Francesca Tornabuoni in S. Maria sopra Minerva in Rome, whose sculpted tomb Vasari attributed to Verrocchio. All of the surviving works demonstrate careful study of the monumental cycles by esteemed past masters, such as Giotto and Masaccio, and an up-to-date interest in Northern painting and command of narrative detail, graceful ornamentation and perspectival play.

SANDRO BOTTICELLI

Acquisitive as he was of Verrocchio shop practices and props, Ghirlandaio's career strategy – taking up mural painting and working largely outside the city in the 1470s – removed him as a direct competitor. Instead Sandro Botticelli was emerging as an important master in Florence during that decade, seeking support from the same patrons as Verrocchio and even vying for the same commissions. He was sponsored by Tommaso Soderini as an alternative to both Verrocchio and Piero del Pollaiuolo in the Mercanzia commission and painted the figure of *Fortitude* for the tribunal in 1470 (fig. 30). The fantastic opulence that characterises the throne and the armour, baton, dress and headdress of the figure not only pays shrewd homage to the ornamental styles of both older masters, but could owe something to Sandro's own early training with a goldsmith. The solid oval of the face, with deep eye-sockets and fetching cupid-bow mouth, as well as her gracefully positioned hands, also show Botticelli's debt to the attractive types fashioned in Verrocchio's studio. He seems to have studied the sculptor's methods for achieving volume and solidity in painted figures, in the depth given to single features and in the play of light over varied surfaces.

The construction of Fortitude herself, with her impossibly long torso and overlapping layers of differently textured fabrics, betrays instead Botticelli's training with Fra Filippo Lippi (*c*.1406–69). In the commentary to his 1481 edition of Dante's *Divine Comedy* (partly illustrated with woodcuts after Botticelli's designs), the humanist Cristoforo Landino praised Lippi for being 'graceful and ornate and exceedingly skilful … very good at compositions and at variety, at colouring and relief, and … at ornaments of every kind, whether imitated after the real or invented'.[72] Botticelli was probably well aware of such terms of praise, and these are the very qualities that he took from Lippi. His affinity with Verrocchio might owe something to their shared background with Lippi. Like Verrocchio, Botticelli appreciated and adapted Lippi's idealised type of female head, with headdresses made up of intricate and subtly overlapping veils, curls and jewels (figs. 81 and 123). Again, like Verrocchio he admired the wistful downcast glances of Lippi's Virgins and the eager emotional urgency he could give to dramatic figures. Whereas Verrocchio then gave them the solid appearance of three-dimensional forms, Botticelli pursued Lippi's love for dense surface patterns and

spatial complexity; he found beauty in exaggeration and elongation. The horizontal *Adoration of the Magi* in the National Gallery (cat. no. 68), painted in conjunction with Filippino Lippi, relies on this profusion and complexity of design to suggest the wondrous confusion of the arrival of the kings and the contrasting solemnity of the recognition of the infant saviour. Such subtle spatial editing – or artful composition – learned from Lippi, became a defining feature of Botticelli's works.

His training with Lippi prepared Botticelli to supply the whole range of the painter's stock, from monumental wall paintings to intimate domestic Virgins and subjects sacred and profane. In the course of the 1470s and 1480s Botticelli expanded that range. A preferred painter among the leading men of the city, he seems to have been nurtured by their cultural aspirations and nurtured, in turn, the desire to give

Fig. 81 FRA FILIPPO LIPPI, *Virgin and Child with Angels, c.* 1465. Tempera on panel, 92 × 63.5 cm. Florence, Galleria degli Uffizi.

them exquisite form. This could be in the jewel-like rendering of sacred history, as in the paired panels showing the story of Judith (cat. no. 85) or in life-size or near life-size renderings of subjects from classical myth and poetry, like the *Venus and Mars* and the *Primavera* (cat. no. 86; fig. 15). Fra Filippo Lippi had been among the first to produce large-scale painted tondi, glamorous descendants of the decorated birth trays (*deschi da parto*) produced as good augur for childbirth; Botticelli promoted this new form to a position of sustained popularity. These paintings could be artistically demanding and materially lavish: the National Gallery *Adoration* tondo (cat. no. 7) represents the upper end of this market and may well have cost as much as the 40 florins that Benedetto Salutati paid for a tondo sent as a gift to Cardinal Francesco Gonzaga.[73]

In works like the *Primavera* and the *Pallas* standard for Giuliano de' Medici's joust, Botticelli fashioned himself as the major visual interpreter of the poetic and intellectual aspirations of the Medici circle. The same inventive concerns are also evident in the work of Antonio del Pollaiuolo (as in the Lanfredini *Dancing Nudes*, fig. 46) and Verrocchio (fig. 14). Although by no means all his patrons were associated with the regime, Botticelli had already firmly positioned himself as a Medici client by 1478, when he was asked to paint the lifelike defamatory images of the Pazzi conspirators.[74] This commission is indicative not only of Botticelli's skills as a mural painter, but also, since the effigies had to be convincing, of his abilities as a portraitist. Proof of his success in this field is amply provided by his surviving portraits, which engage with the commemorative problems of truth to life and mortality, as in the portraits of Giuliano de' Medici and Smeralda Bandinelli (cat. nos. 1 and 83) or the ingeniously contrived *Man holding a Medal of Cosimo de'*

Medici (fig. 82). The latter brings together the honorific form of the medallic profile, produced after Cosimo's death, with the dramatised immediacy of the sitter painted in three-quarter view. Contrasting attractive youth and wise old age, it expresses a relationship of faithful allegiance operating beyond the grave. It leaves no doubt as to the reasons for Botticelli's appeal to those who saw the potential of art to articulate (or indeed, dissimulate) their position in Florentine society.

FILIPPINO LIPPI

In the 1472 membership list of the painters' confraternity of Saint Luke, Fra Filippo's son, Filippino Lippi, is listed as being 'with Sandro Botticelli'. Filippino (1457–1504) was only twelve when his father died in Spoleto in 1469. Although by the end of the 1470s he was receiving independent

Fig. 82 SANDRO BOTTICELLI, *Portrait of a Man with a Medal of Cosimo de' Medici*, c.1475. Tempera on panel, 57.5 × 44 cm. Florence, Galleria degli Uffizi.

Fig. 83 FILIPPINO LIPPI, *Head of a young woman*, 1470s. Metalpoint, heightened with white, on paper rubbed with reddish chalk, 21.4 × 17.3 cm. Florence, Galleria degli Uffizi, Gabinetto Disegni e Stampe, inv. 1156E.

commissions, Filippino seems to have kept close working ties with Botticelli throughout the decade. He therefore shared in Botticelli's refining of Lippi's style, pursuing its graceful distortions to a new ideal of abstracted and perfected beauty. He studied and adapted his father's veiled ladies, like Lippi making metalpoint drawings that were serviceable as models for Virgins and dreamy female saints (fig. 83). Even more than Botticelli, Filippino explored the possibilities of drapery – billowing or bunched up, gossamer or heavily layered – to express motion and emotion. In paintings like the National Gallery *Adoration* (cat. no. 69) he displays a compositional talent learned, if not inherited, from his father, using the landscape both to punctuate the devotional narrative and to create a luxuriant overall surface. Painter son of a painter, he exploited colour as an animating force. His painterly sensibility is evident in his lifelong preference for metalpoint and white heightening on prepared paper for making studies and finished drawings. This combination allowed him to think of light in terms of colour and colour in terms of light.[75] By the early 1480s he was receiving important commissions for monumental frescoes and altar panels from civic bodies and private citizens in Florence, Lucca and San Gimignano. His versatility and virtuosity made him one of the most highly praised painters of his generation.

ANTONIO ROSSELLINO

The situation for sculpture was just as competitive and varied as that for painting. Verrocchio's stature and position as a sculptor for the Medici gave him a predominance but not a monopoly on the statuary produced for Florentines in this decade. His shop faced high-level competition from other marble workers. Antonio Rossellino (1426–78?), from

Fig. 84 ANTONIO ROSSELLINO, *Virgin and Child*, c.1465.
Terracotta, height 48.3 cm. London, Victoria and Albert Museum.

Settignano, was the universally admired author of the
tomb of the Cardinal of Portugal (fig. 56). After the
death of his sculptor/architect brother in 1464, his
shop in the via del Proconsolo continued to produce
marble portrait busts, tombs and Madonna reliefs
that rival those of Verrocchio in their delicacy of
handling and evocation of physical and psychological
movement. The terracotta Virgin with the laughing
Christ Child (fig. 84), perhaps a model for a marble
sculpture, is also a model in terms of its formal and
expressive subtlety.

Even before the death of Francesco Nori,
murdered in the Pazzi conspiracy in 1478, Rossellino
had been commissioned to make Nori's tomb with its
fictive marble curtain and Virgin and Child relief, to
be placed against a pier in Santa Croce. By the time of
his own death, Rossellino's reputation had spread well
beyond the city and he is recorded at the early stages
of major projects that had to be completed by others
– the extravagant marble tombs of Maria of Aragon
in Naples and of Bishop Lorenzo Roverella in San
Giorgio, Ferrara.

MINO DA FIESOLE

The sculptor Mino da Fiesole (1429–84), a pupil of
Desiderio da Settignano, supplied much the same
market in Florence as Antonio Rossellino. Unlike
Rossellino, however, Mino was not destined to be a
favourite of Vasari, though evidence suggests that he
was every bit as successful, with a career that took him
to Naples, and to the curial court in Rome. In early
commissions from the Medici in the 1450s he revived
the marble portrait bust (fig. 85), a type that would
later be shown as a characteristic product of the
sculptor in the Mercury engraving (fig. 50). Mino is
now also believed to have restored an ancient Marsyas
statue in Lorenzo's collection.[76] In Florence, he rented

Fig. 85 MINO DA FIESOLE, *Piero de' Medici*, 1453.
Marble, height 55 cm. Florence, Museo Nazionale del Bargello.

Fig. 86 MINO DA FIESOLE, Tomb of Count Ugo of Tuscany,
completed 1481. Marble, 359 x 208 cm. Florence, Badia.

a house from the Benedictines of the Badia, for whom he made several of his most important works. His tomb of Bernardo Giugni in their church seems to have inspired the commission for the monument to the Badia's ancient benefactor Count Ugo of Tuscany (fig. 86). Mino began the tomb in 1471, and completed it ten years later.[77] The recumbent effigy of the count is surmounted by a somewhat austere, arched tabernacle with plain marble revetments and it is in the upper figures that Desiderio's legacy in the treatment of relief comes to the fore. The dynamic central figure of Charity with her suckling babies looks down benignly on her devotee, testifying to his patronal virtue, while the Virgin and Child of the tondo serve as his intercessors.

FRANCESCO DI SIMONE FERRUCCI

If we set aside the vexed question of Leonardo's sculptural production, the best-known sculptor to be associated with Verrocchio was Francesco di Simone Ferrucci (b. 1440). The son of the stonecarver Simone Ferrucci from Fiesole, Francesco had already set up his own Florentine workshop by 1466 and his earlier work was much influenced by Desiderio. He travelled to Northern Italy in the later 1470s and early 80s but in 1490 we find him back in Florence working in the via dei Servi.[78] A number of marble tombs and reliefs (fig. 87) as well as terracotta Virgin and Child images (such as cat. no. 28) can be attributed to him.[79] He also undertook large-scale major commissions locally (for example the tomb of Lemmo Balducci of 1472, once in SS. Annunziata) as well as in other cities, such as Prato, Venice and Bologna (the verrocchiesque tomb of Alessandro Tartagni [d. 1477] in S. Domenico).[80] Ferrucci was an able practitioner rather than an inventor. The many sheets of workshop sketches surviving from a drawing book of the 1480s,

Fig. 87 FRANCESCO DI SIMONE FERRUCCI, *Virgin and Child*, 1470s. Marble relief, 113 × 77 cm. Cambridge, Harvard University Art Museums, Fogg Art Museum, Gift of Landon T. Clay.

as well as his highly finished designs for sculpted altars and tabernacles, reveal Ferrucci's magpie-like rapacity in collecting and adapting a whole range of motifs from predecessors in the profession such as Desiderio and Rossellino, but especially from his contemporary Verrocchio for whom he probably also worked.[81] On any one sheet, ideas for pollaiuolesque heroes or heavily mantled saints jostle with profile heads or the standing babies beloved of Desiderio and Verrocchio. These were Ferrucci's stock-in-trade – a supply of motifs useful for the elaborate and ornate relief-sculpted altarpieces with sacrament tabernacles which became increasingly popular from the 1470s, especially outside Florence.

GIULIANO AND BENEDETTO DA MAIANO

The fraternal partners Giuliano and Benedetto da Maiano were the youngest of this remarkable group

of carvers. As masters of perspective and architects, as well as sculptors in wood and stone, they were also the most versatile. In 1469 they had a woodworking workshop in the via dei Servi and by 1480 they also had a stoneworking shop in the via del Castellaccio. Benedetto, a master of inventive architectural ornament and narrative relief, had long been a maker of large-scale wood furnishings and tabernacles. According to one contemporary source, after completing a large day bed (*lettuccio*) for Filippo Strozzi, Benedetto went to Rome in 1473 to learn to carve in marble, but this is the year he matriculated in the Stone and Woodworkers' Guild in Florence and there seems to be no reason why he should not have acquired his stonecarving skills closer to home.[82] In the 1470s he completed the inventive sculpted relief altar and tomb of S. Fina in San Gimignano and the *all'antica* architecture, reliefs and figures of the door between the audience hall and the Sala dei Gigli in the Palazzo della Signoria (figs. 54 and 9). Despite Vasari's eulogy of Benedetto, payments suggest it was his brother Giuliano who, together with Francione and two other woodworkers, worked on the massive wooden ceilings for the palace of government, completed in the second half of the decade. Giuliano, Benedetto and another brother, Giovanni, were also involved with work on the Pazzi family palace and country property, work for which they remained creditors after Jacopo Pazzi's involvement in the failed conspiracy of 1478. Such blows of fate highlight the advantages of the artistic diversification practised by the brothers. Like Rossellino, Mino and Verrocchio, Benedetto provided portrait busts (fig. 23) and he also developed the possibilities of life-size bust portraits of saints. Confronted by the expressive 'speaking' head of his youthful bust-length Saint John the Baptist, now in Washington, it is difficult to imagine

Fig. 88 BENEDETTO DA MAIANO, *Saint John the Baptist, c.*1480. Painted terracotta, height 48.9 cm. Washington, National Gallery of Art, Andrew W. Mellon Collection.

an object with a more direct appeal to a Florentine market (fig. 88).

When the seemingly indefatigable list-maker Benedetto Dei summarised the glories of his city, he noted that it had achieved 'every perfection in handicraft' and he inventoried the painters and sculptors ('of bronze, marble and stone') in Florence in 1470.[83] There are over fifty names, and although some could be subtracted – as already dead – others could be added. But more important than rehearsing or revising the list is recognising that by the 1470s artistic production had become inseparable from civic pride. The artists chosen for discussion here amply justify that pride. It is difficult to generalise about the great diversity of practice and production found in Florentine workshops of the 1470s, but some characteristic features can be discerned. Variety is one. Experimentation is another. Physical immediacy and, almost paradoxically, idealisation are others. The search for forms that were both expressive and beautiful – in ornament, in draperies, in settings, gestures and facial types – was pursued with calculating curiosity as artists found inspiration in things both foreign and familiar: Northern paintings and prints, antique cameos and sculptures, and chubby babies chasing cats (cat. no. 37).

The cosmopolitan and mercantile nature of Florence played its part in defining the subjects and modes of representation in this period. The influx of men and merchandise from the east and from Northern Europe seems to have captured artists' imaginations. Just as to own a Turkish carpet or gorgeously striped cloths was a sign of status, the depiction of such luxury items in painting enhanced the value of the picture. Netherlandish art was greatly appreciated throughout Italy, especially at the courts of Naples and Ferrara. While some of the Netherlandish works of various types mentioned in the Medici inventories had been acquired in the 1450s and 1460s, the taste for them continued to develop. Florentine merchants resident in the Netherlands provided an impetus; Tommaso Portinari and Angelo Tani, for example, commissioned altarpieces from Hugo van der Goes and Memling respectively.[84]

Features such as the landscape glimpsed through an elevated window or objects closely observed from the domestic interior appealed to patrons and were imitated by Florentine painters (fig. 89). But Netherlandish paintings not only supplied motifs, they also provided examples of the use of oil technique. In Florence, experimentation with the use of oil, long known but not regularly used in Italy, where tempera was favoured, seems to have occurred in response to the mimetic effects in the depiction of texture and focused light seen in Netherlandish paintings. Antonio del Pollaiuolo, for example, shows his debt to Northern art in his use of oil medium and choice of colours, as well as in his abandonment of gilding and his facility in imitating luxury materials and reflective surfaces. Even though the adoption of oil brought new technical problems, in his case its flexible covering power and slower drying time compared to egg tempera seem to have encouraged an unprecedented freedom in paint handling. It was this gestural boldness that allowed him to depict ephemeral effects in nature entirely new in Florentine art, such as rushing water and shifting mists over a landscape (cat. nos. 46 and 88).

Landscape was itself a highly developed element in Netherlandish painting which appealed to the naturalistic interests of Florentine artists in the 1470s. Antonio and Piero del Pollaiuolo translated Northern panoramas to the Arno river valley and Leonardo da Vinci meditated on the creation of distant horizons (fig. 73). Northern paintings supplied landscape features that were taken up in order to create backgrounds at once believable and yet special and distant, like the holy figures set against them. Given their own strong tradition of drawing, it is not surprising that Florentine artists were also responsive to graphic qualities found in Netherlandish work. The decorative, angular crumpling of heavy drapery was exploited for its expressive possibilities. Some artists, like the Pollaiuolo brothers and Verrocchio, seem to have had Northern prints among their studio properties. The marked geometric quality of their fold vocabularies is indebted to such prints (cat. no. 8 and fig. 93). The relation of drapery to underlying body structure remained a fundamental concern, however. Intensely studied as it was in Verrocchio's shop, the complex, ornamental fall of cloth was but part of the overall composition of a figure's pose and its meaning.

It has been argued that the emotive qualities of Northern paintings and prints, with their devotional intensity, stimulated Florentine artists to depict similarly heightened pathos in their works. Ghirlandaio's Vespucci *Pietà* (fig. 40), for example, appears to draw some of its emotive force from the mourners in the small *Presentation of Christ before the Tomb* attributed to Rogier van der Weyden now in the Uffizi.[85] But Ghirlandaio was also attentive to the physical expressiveness of ancient sculpture. So too were Verrocchio and Antonio del Pollaiuolo. Their fascination with depicting states of joy and anguish drew inspiration from the art of antiquity, as well as from the sculpture of Donatello. The roots of such interest were deeply grounded. For the aggressive snarl of the warrior on horseback or the wild abandon of

Fig. 89 Attributed to DOMENICO GHIRLANDAIO, *Virgin and Child*, c.1470s. Oil on panel, 79 × 56 cm. Paris, Musée du Louvre.

the Bacchic dancer (fig. 46) admired in ancient art were seen as the physical manifestation of a particular state of mind. A command of the psychology of the physical was one of Donatello's greatest legacies to subsequent generations. Antonio del Pollaiuolo, Verrocchio, and others like Leonardo da Vinci and Botticelli, explored this idea in different ways in the 1470s, one of them being an investigation of anatomy (fig. 90). The concern with movement was by no means restricted to emotional extremes or muscular exertion. Indeed, psychological subtlety is a distinguishing feature of the art of Verrocchio and Leonardo in this decade. The charm of Verrocchio's *David* (fig. 17) resides in great measure in the fact that his expression seems to change as one looks at the head from different angles – teetering between cocky self-satisfaction and contemplative anxiety.

The expressive range of the human subject was further extended through the repertoire of gesture and comportment that became ever more elegant and stylish – literally mannered – in this decade. This fashion can be explained both by the diffusion of ideas taken from ancient texts on rhetoric, notably Cicero's writings, and by an interest in courtly etiquette. The former supplied a critical vocabulary, valuing charm and grace as persuasive forces. The latter presented actual models of dress and behaviour. Beauty and elegance could be appropriately applied to figures in art who were supposed to be exemplary and to behave in ways deserving admiration. The Virgin was, after all, queen of heaven and her heavenly company the court of heaven, who might be expected to display courtly style both in dress and manners – denoted, for example, by a slight turn of the head or the show of a long-fingered hand. The imitation of courts, discouraged in civic life, was not suppressed in the private life of the Florentine patriciate. It was,

Fig. 90 ANTONIO DEL POLLAIUOLO, *Studies of Saint John the Baptist, hands and feet*. Black chalk, pen and ink on paper, 27.9 × 19.4 cm. Florence, Galleria degli Uffizi, Gabinetto Disegni e Stampe, inv. 699E.

rather, strengthened by events such as the visit of the Duke of Milan or Giuliano de' Medici's joust.[86] In Angelo Poliziano's poetic account of the joust, the reader is made aware of what amounts to a cult of beauty encouraged by the philosophical grounding of Neoplatonism. While the belief that beauty was a sign of virtue and ugliness of evil was already deep-seated in all levels of society, Poliziano claimed that the spiritual virtue signified by the beauty of the beloved could be an inspiration to virtue in the yearning lover. The superabundance of beautiful effects in the work of Botticelli, Verrocchio and others who served the cultural élite can be understood as a signifier of worth, even when the subject of the work is apparently, like Verrocchio's *Sleeping Youth* (cat. no. 18), morally neutral or merely desirable. The proliferation of imaginative forms – not just fantastic beasts such as sphinxes and centaurs, but forms found in nature, such as knotted rope, rippling and curling ribbons, curling and plaited hair – appealed to a love of decorative beauty addressing a taste for *fantasia*. Such imaginative abundance was the proof of the parity of the visual arts with poetry. This claim also sanctioned the invention of new and often learned subjects that elude decoding in relation to a specific text, but that operate as allegories or as a form of visual poetry (cat. no. 57 and fig. 15).

The premium attached to novelty and difficulty – both by knowledgeable patrons and by artists – and the attendant experimentation in forms and objects cannot be divorced from the process of drawing. Beginning within the workshop, drawing involved the imitation and assimilation of motifs developed by the master as useful formulas for regular tasks. It was also the means to approach new problems of representation. Learning to draw and learning by drawing took place by copying drawings and by the direct study of the male nude, of dressed or draped models and from sculptures of whole or partial figures. These exercises provided the basic building blocks of mastery: a command of postures and poses and their description through line and the placement of light and shadow. Mastery also involved the cultivation of a personal style and the ability to develop and repeat from memory figures and motifs that could be adapted to a variety of contexts. Antonio del Pollaiuolo's success in drawing and composing active figures made him a *maestro di disegno*. The dynamic nature of the design process is apparent in the fertile invention of Leonardo's pen. It is equally apparent in the facility shown by Antonio del Pollaiuolo and Verrocchio in translating their ideas into a variety of media. The concern with what have been called painterly values in sculpture and sculptural values in painting results from a common set of problems and observations relating to among other things, the structure of the human body and its movements, the play of light over surfaces and the creation of relief. These could and did manifest themselves in both two- and three-dimensional forms.

Artists' shops in the 1470s produced an extraordinary volume of remarkable and beautiful works. They also provided essential tools and a sophisticated range of drawing and design techniques. Above all, they fostered and encouraged the experimental turn of mind that would inspire new forms of artistry for generations to come.

NOTES CHAPTER 3

1 *Giovanni Rucellai ed il suo Zibaldone*, vol. 1, ed. A. Perosa, London 1960, pp. 60-1

2 For this relation see D.L. Bemporad, 'Il rapporto abito gioiello nel costume del Rinascimento', *Il costume nell'età del rinascimento*, Florence 1988, pp. 60–1.

3 *Zibaldone*, vol. 1, ed. Perosa, 1960, pp. 23–4.

4 Ibid., p. 61.

5 In 1489, for example, when Luigi di Ugolino Martelli bought a tondo from Botticelli, the costs included payment to his brother Antonio di Mariano *battiloro*, see J.K. Lydecker, *The Domestic Setting of the Arts in Renaissance Florence*, PhD thesis, The Johns Hopkins University, Baltimore 1987, pp. 289–90.

6 *Le opere di Giorgio Vasari*, G. Milanesi, ed., Florence 1878–85, vol. 3, p. 310. Vasari's account is confused and lacks confirmation in early sources or documents, however. For a discussion of this see H.P. Horne, *Alessandro Filipepi, Commonly called Sandro Botticelli Painter of Florence*, London 1908, pp. 4–5.

7 For the interpretation of documents concerning the matriculation of painters see I. Hueck, 'Le matricole dei pittori fiorentini prima e dopo il 1320', *Bollettino d'Arte*, 5th series, anno LVII, 1972, 2, pp. 114–21, and M. Haines, 'Una ricostruzione dei perduti libri di matricole dei Medici e Speziale a Firenze dal 1353 al 1408', *Rivista d'Arte*, 4th series, 5, 1989, pp. 173–207.

8 U. Dorini, *Statuti dell'Arte di Por Santa Maria del tempo della Repubblica*, Florence 1934. For the guild statutes for the goldsmith's trade see also M.G. Ciardi Dupré dal Poggetto, ed., *L'Oreficeria nella Firenze del Quattrocento*, exh. cat. Florence 1977, pp. 164–7. The statutes were regularly re-enacted, see D.L. Bemporad, ed., *Argenti fiorentini dal XV al XIX secolo. Tipologie e marchi*, Florence 1992, I, pp. 4–25.

9 R. Ciasca, *Statuti dell'arte dei Medici e Speziali*, Florence 1922, 'Statuto del Membro dei Pittori del 1315', no. 9, p. 81.

10 Neri di Bicci, *Le Ricordanze (10 marzo 1453 – 24 aprile 1475)*, ed. B. Santi, Pisa 1976.

11 G. Passavant, *Andrea del Verrocchio als Maler*, Düsseldorf 1959, p. 219, Docs VI (1472, St Luke) and VII (1478, Arte dei Maestri di Pietra e Legname).

12 D.L. Bemporad, ed., 1992, p. 25.

13 Lorenzo Ghiberti, *I commentarii*, ed. L. Bartoli, Florence 1998, Book I, p. 47, the sculptor should be 'perfectissimo disegnatore, conciò sia cosa lo scultore e 'l pictore, el disegno è il fondamento e teorica di queste due arti'. Cennino Cennini, *The Craftsman's Handbook: The Italian 'il Libro dell'arte'*, ed. and trans. D.V. Thompson, New York 1954, chapters II, V, VIII–XV, XXVII–XXXIV.

14 C. Fiorilli, 'I dipintori a Firenze nell'Arte dei Medici Speziale e Merciai', *Archivio storico italiano*, 78, 1920, 2, p. 67.

15 *Zibaldone*, ed. Perosa, 1960, p. 24. Benedetto Dei gives a fuller list of such masters in his *Memorie*, Biblioteca Riccardiana, Cod. 1853, f. 90r, published in G. Romby, *Descrizioni e rappresentazioni della citta di Firenze nel XV secolo*, Florence 1976, p. 73.

16 Florence, Biblioteca Riccardiana, MSS Moreni 103 (*Ricordanze*), f. 99.

17 Spoleto, Archivio, *Libro dell'Opera del Duomo di Spoleto*, Entrate e Uscite, 1465–1505, fol. 133, published by L. Fausti, 'Le pitture di Fra Filippo Lippi nel Duomo di Spoleto', *Archivio per la storia ecclesiastica dell'Umbria*, 2, 1915, p. 14, note 2.

18 For contracts see H. Glasser, *Artists' Contracts of the Early Renaissance*, PhD thesis, Columbia University, New York 1965. More generally see A. Thomas, *The Painter's Practice in Renaissance Tuscany*, Cambridge and New York 1995, chapter 5, 'Doing Business', pp. 101–48. M. O'Malley, 'Late fifteenth and early sixteenth-century painting contracts and the stipulated use of the painter's hand' in E. Marchand and A. Wright eds., *With and Without the Medici. Studies in Tuscan Art and Patronage, 1434–1530*, Aldershot 1998, p. 153–78.

19 Fiorilli 1920, pp. 67–8.

20 M. Wackernagel, *The World of the Florentine Renaissance Artist*, trans. A. Luchs, Princeton 1991, pp. 338–44, on 'Price Formation and Forms of Payment'.

21 For Piero's rivalry with Verrocchio over this commission, see above, pp. 35–6. Verrocchio asked for 350 florins at a time when only 300 florins had been allowed for the project by the council of Pistoia. Before choosing Piero del Pollaiuolo's design, the *operai* had been authorised to spend up to 380 florins. For a synopsis of the documents from 1476–1477, see A. Butterfield, *The Sculptures of Andrea del Verrocchio*, New Haven and London 1997, p. 224

22 Vasari/Milanesi, vol. 3, p. 302.

23 For these partnerships, see U. Procacci, 'Di Jacopo di Antonio e delle compagnie di pittori del Corso degli Adimari nel XV secolo', *Rivista d'Arte*, 3rd series, 35, 1960, pp. 370. More generally for workshop structures and practices in late fifteenth-century Florence see M. Gregori, A. Paolucci, C. Acidini Luchinat, eds., *Maestri e botteghe. Pittura a Firenze alla fine del Quattrocento*, exh. cat. Palazzo Strozzi, Florence 1992.

24 For the market for luxury goods and its relation to artistic production in Italy, see R. Goldthwaite, *Wealth and the Demand for Art in Italy 1300–1600*, Baltimore 1993.

25 For the Signoria commission, which Leonardo never executed, see N. Rubinstein, *The Palazzo Vecchio 1298–1532*, Oxford 1995, p. 59. The work was reassigned to Domenico Ghirlandaio on 20 May 1483; he also failed to complete it. Although it is often said that the *Virgin and Child with Saints* by Filippino Lippi in the Uffizi was the painting finally delivered to the Signoria chapel, this is not the case. The Lippi, painted in 1486, was painted for the council hall, the Sala dei Dugento (see Rubinstein, pp. 59, 66). For Ser Piero da Vinci's possible interventions in Leonardo's career, see A. Cecchi, 'Una predella e altri contributi per l'Adorazione dei Magi di Filippino', in *Gli Uffizi. Studi e Ricerche*, 5, *I pittori della Brancacci agli Uffizi*, L. Berti and A. Petrioli Tofani, eds., Florence 1984, p. 59.

26 D. Covi, 'Nuovi Documenti per Antonio del Pollaiuolo e Antonio Rossellino', *Prospettiva*, 12, 1978, pp. 61–71.

27 For an overview of the commission and the related documents, see F. Hartt, G. Corti and C. Kennedy, *The Chapel of the Cardinal of Portugal*, Philadelphia 1964.

28 See D. Carl, 'Zur Goldschmiede Familie Dei mit neuen Dokumenten zu Antonio Pollaiuolo und Andrea Verrocchio', *Mitteilungen des Kunsthistorischen Institutes in Florenz*, 26, 1982, pp. 128–66 and esp. p. 162, docs XXII and XXIII.

29 R. Krautheimer, *Lorenzo Ghiberti*, Princeton 1970, I, p. 14. 'Mi fu data licentia io la conducessi in quel modo ch'io credessi tornasse più perfettamente e più ornata e più richa . . . mi ingegnai con ogni misura osservare in esse cercare imitare la natura quanto a me fosse possibile, e con tutti i linimenti . . . con egregii conpanomenti e dovitiosi con moltissime figure' (*I commentarii*, ed. Bartoli, Book 2, p. 95).

30 Archivio di Stato, Florence, Carte Strozziane, II, 51.1, f. 126 reprinted by M. Cruttwell, *Antonio Pollaiuolo*, London and New York, 1907, p. 258.

31 The matriculation is Archivio di Stato, Florence, Arte della Seta, VIII, 105, f. 13.

32 See A. Angelini, *Disegni italiani del tempo di Donatello*, exh. cat., Gabinetto Disegni e Stampe degli Uffizi, Florence 1986, cat. no. 161, pp. 118–19.

33 For the helmet, see above p. 18. For the silverware see D. Carl, 'Addenda zu Antonio Pollaiuolo und seiner Werkstatt', *Mitteilungen der Kunsthistorischen Institutes in Florenz*, 28, 1983, pp. 285–301. For an excellent source for the range of goods, from knife handles to silver crosses, produced by a goldsmith with similar skills, see the 1472 inventories of Bartolommeo di Piero published by G. Cantini Guidotti, *Orafi in Toscana tra XV e XVIII secolo: storie di uomini, di cose e di parole*, vol. 2, Florence 1994, pp. 51–5.

34 For this weighty tome, see Archivio dell' Opera del Duomo, Entrate e Uscite 1477, f. 171, published by G. Poggi, *Il Duomo di Firenze: documenti sulla decorazione della chiesa e del campanile tratti dall'archivio dell'opera*, Florence 1909, vol. 2, doc. 1723, p. 57; for its recycling, see doc. 1933, p. 98

35 For the application of this term in the work of Antonio del Pollaiuolo see A. Wright, 'Antonio Pollaiuolo, "maestro di disegno"' in E. Cropper, ed., *Florentine Drawing at the Time of Lorenzo the Magnificent*, Villa Spelman Colloquia, vol. 4, Bologna and Baltimore 1994, pp. 131–46.

36 Vasari/Milanesi, vol. 3, pp. 290–1.

37 Archivio del Comune di Pistoia, Registro di Provvisioni 1482–1492, vol. 68, no. 676, published by A. Chiti, 'Di una tavola ignota di Piero del Pollaiuolo', *Bullettino storico Pistoiese*, 2, 1900, p. 47.

38 Published in Cruttwell 1907, pp. 245–6.

39 Ancient statuettes were certainly being collected by Lorenzo de' Medici at this time. A small antique figure of Hercules excavated near Luni was offered to Lorenzo de' Medici by Antonio Ivani and Donato Acciaiuoli in 1473. See L. Beschi, 'Le antichità di Lorenzo il Magnifico' in P. Barocchi and G. Ragionieri, eds., *Gli Uffizi. Quattro secoli di una galleria. Atti del Convegno Internazionale di Studi*, Firenze 1982, 1, Florence 1983, p. 166, note 23.

40 Poggi 1909, vol. 1, doc. 1206, p. 243.

41 For this, see the essays on 'The Technique of Execution', in L. Dolcini, ed., *Verrocchio's Christ and St. Thomas. A Masterpiece of Sculpture from Renaissance Florence*, exh. cat., Palazzo Vecchio, Florence, and the Metropolitan Museum of Art, New York, 1992–3, New York 1992. See also S. Butters, *The Triumph of Vulcan. Sculptors' Tools, Porphyry, and the Prince in Ducal Florence*, Florence 1996, vol. 1, pp. 204–5, regarding Verrocchio's metallurgical skills, which probably helped him to develop tools to work the porphyry for the Medici tombs.

42 See Butterfield 1997, pp. 106–24, for an enlightening account of Verrocchio's technique and compositional strategies in this panel.

43 Vasari/Milanesi, vol. 3, p. 358.

44 In his poem in praise of Florence (*De Illustratione Urbis Florentiae*); for an English translation of the verses on artists, see C. Gilbert, *Italian Art 1400–1500. Sources and Documents*, Englewood Cliffs, NJ, 1980, pp. 192–3.

45 Dated 5 November 1490, two years after Verrocchio's death, the inventory was taken as part of a legal dispute concerning his estate; it is published by D. Covi, 'Four New Documents Concerning Andrea del Verrocchio', *Art Bulletin*, 48, 1966, p. 103.

46 J.P. Richter, *The Literary Works of Leonardo da Vinci*, London 1970, vol. 1, p. 91.

47 Vasari/Milanesi, vol. 3, p. 543.

48 Vasari/Milanesi, vol. 4, p. 20. Fixed drapery studies were described in the early 1460s by Filarete in his *Treatise on Architecture*, J.R. Spencer, ed., New Haven and London 1956, vol. 1, p. 314. For the group of drawings associated with Verrocchio and his followers, see D.A. Brown, *Leonardo da Vinci. Origins of a genius*, New Haven and London 1998, pp. 79–82.

49 Vasari/Milanesi, vol. 3, p. 365: 'E perchè Andrea mai non si stava, e sempre o di pittura o di scultura lavorava qualche cosa; e qualche volta tramezzava l'un'opera con l'altra; perchè meno, come molti fanno, gli venisse una stessa cosa a fastidio.'

50 The proposed dates vary between 1466, when Leonardo was fourteen, a usual age for apprenticeship, and 1469 when his father rented a house from the Mercanzia, so is known to have been in Florence. For a discussion of this see Brown 1998, p. 7.

51 Richter 1970, vol. 1, p. 369: 'Adoperandomi io non meno in iscultura che in pittura e faciendo l'una e l'altra in un medesimo grado.'

52 Ibid. p. 326.

53 For discussions of Leonardo's involvement with sculptural projects in Verrocchio's shop see W.R. Valentiner, 'Leonardo as Verrocchio's Coworker', *Art Bulletin*, 12, 1930, pp. 74–89, and Brown 1998, pp. 58–73. For a summary of the documents regarding Leonardo and sculpture, see M.V. Brugnoli, 'Documenti, notizie e ipotesi sulla scultura di Leonardo', in A. Marazza, ed., *Leonardo. Saggi e ricerche*, Rome 1954, pp. 359–89.

54 For Leonardo and landscape conventions, see E.H. Gombrich, 'Light, Form and Texture in Fifteenth-Century Painting North and South of the Alps', in *The Heritage of Apelles*, Oxford 1976, pp. 33–5.

55 Richter 1970, vol. 1, p. 303.

56 The dates of Simone's tenure as abbot are discussed in A. Natali, ed., *Lo Sguardo degli Angeli. Verrocchio, Leonardo e il 'Battesimo di Cristo'*, Milan 1998, p. 94, note 62. The techniques and stages of painting are discussed in essays by Natali (pp. 61–94) and the restorer A. del Serra (pp. 95–118). There are no documents regarding the commission. The painting was first noted as being at S. Salvi in F. Albertini's guidebook, *Memoriale di molte statue et picture sono nella inclyta cipta di Florentia*, Florence 1510 (unpaginated, in the concluding section 'Nelli ingiesuati & altri lochi': 'in sancto Salui tauole bellissime & uno Angelo di Leonardo Vinci').

57 For a detailed analysis of the portrait of Ginevra de' Benci, see Brown 1998, pp. 101–22.

58 See M. Kemp, *Leonardo da Vinci. The Marvellous Works of Nature and Man*, Cambridge, Mass, 1981, pp. 53–8, who counts at least five Madonna projects in drawings and extant paintings from between *c.*1478 and 1482.

59 A manuscript source dating from the late 1530s or early 1540s, known as the Anonimo Gaddiano or Codice Magliabecchiano, describes Leonardo as a form of artistic protégé of Lorenzo, sent by Lorenzo to the Duke to present him with a lyre ('Stette da giovane col Magnifico Lorenzo de Medicj; et dandolj prouisione per se il faceua lauorare nel giardino sulla piaza di San Marcho dj Firenze ... che'l dal detto Magnifico Lorenzo fu mandato al duca di Milano ... a presentarlj una lira'); published by C. Frey, *Il Codice Magliabecchiano*, Berlin 1892, p. 110. For Lorenzo's garden, and confirmation of the statement about Leonardo's presence there, see C. Elam, 'Lorenzo de' Medici's Sculpture Garden', *Mitteilungen des Kunsthistorischen Institutes in Florenz*, 36, 1992, pp. 41–83, p. 58 for Leonardo.

60 He is identified as a 'dipintore in bottega d'Andrea del Verrocchio' when he rented lodging from S. Maria Nuova in August 1486, and in her 1480 tax declaration, Credi's mother lists 'Lorenzo mio figliuolo d'anni 21, istà chon Andrea de' Verochio e è a dipingnere, per salaro di fiorini 12 l'anno', see G. dalli Regoli, *Lorenzo di Credi*, Pisa 1966, pp. 91–2. For Verrocchio's will see Passavant 1959, pp. 219–20.

61 For this painting and its technique, see the essays by A. Padoa Rizzo and F. Falletti in F. Falletti ed., *I Medici, Il Verrocchio e Pistoia. Storia e restauro di due capolavori nella cattedrale di S. Zeno*, Livorno 1996, and the article by M. Kemp, 'Verrocchio's "San Donato" and the Chiesina della Vergine in Piazza in Pistoia', *Pantheon*, 56, 1998, pp. 25–34.

62 Vasari/Milanesi, vol. 4, p. 571.

63 Ibid., p. 564: 'avendo per compagni e per amici, sebbene erano concorrenti, Pietro Perugino e Lionardo da Vinci.'

64 See, for example, the attributions made by F. Zeri, 'Il Maestro dell'Annunciazione Gardner', *Bollettino d'Arte*, 4th series, 38, 1953, pp. 131–6 (which include the National Gallery *Virgin and Child with Two Angels* and the *Tobias and the Archangel Raphael*, cat. nos 23 and 21) and, for further discussion and references, Brown 1998, pp. 40–5, 186–7.

65 See Brown 1998, pp. 34–40, 183–6, for some of the possibilities and problems regarding the presence of these painters in Verrocchio's shop, with a discussion of the related literature. See also G. Passavant, *Verrocchio: Sculptures, Paintings and Drawings. Complete Edition*, London 1969, pp. 202–13, and R. Bartoli, 'La palestra del Verrocchio', in Natali 1998, pp. 11–37.

66 Botticini's career is outlined by A. Padoa Rizzo in *The Dictionary of Art*, 4, London 1996, pp. 505–7. For Botticelli and the Mercanzia commission, see above pp. 53 and 106. Ghirlandaio's early career is discussed above, pp. 104–6. For Biagio and Jacopo del Sellaio, see cat. nos. 78 and 79.

67 Vasari/Milanesi, vol. 4, pp. 365–6. For the attribution of the painting, see Brown 1998, pp. 183–4. Its dating varies from the late 1450s (which precludes Biagio's participation or authorship) to the mid-1470s. The figure of Saint James from this altarpiece might have been the basis for a Saint Peter in an altarpiece attributed to Francesco Botticini, now in the Musée Jacquemart-André in Paris, which is dated 1471 (illustrated and discussed by Bartoli in Natali, ed., 1998, p. 20). J. Eisler, 'Dans l'atelier de Verrocchio', *Bulletin du Musée Hongrois des Beaux-Arts*, 80–81, 1994, pp. 77–90, discusses the recent restoration, and dates the painting to 1468, arguing for Biagio's participation. In her forthcoming book on Biagio d'Antonio, R. Bartoli suggests, instead, a date in the mid-1470s.

68 For Leonardo see, for example, A.E. Popham and P. Pouncey, *Italian Drawings in the Department of Prints and Drawings in the British Museum: the fourteenth and fifteenth centuries*, London 1950, cat. 100r, p. 60, pl XCIV. For Lorenzo di Credi, see dalli Regoli 1966, cat. no. 4, p.102, fig. 5 (Cambridge, Fitzwilliam Museum, inv. 2260, attributed to Fra Bartolomeo).

69 There is a version of the Louvre drapery composition, by Lorenzo di Credi in the British Museum, 1895-9-15-459 (Popham and Pouncey 1950, no. 115, p. 71, pl. CIX, as a copy after Leonardo da Vinci). See also dalli Regoli 1966, no. 20, pp. 108–9, fig. 33. A better candidate for a linen drapery study by Ghirlandaio is Berlin 5039, which in pose, attributes and lighting can be associated with the Saint Matthew on the vault of the S. Fina chapel, see J. Cadogan, 'Linen drapery studies by Verrocchio, Leonardo and Ghirlandaio', *Zeitschrift für Kunstgeschichte*, 46, 1983, pp. 33–6. K. Christiansen, 'Leonardo's drapery studies', *Burlington Magazine*, 132, 1990, pp. 572–3, summarises the attributional problems concerning these drawings, and divides them into three groups, as by Verrocchio, Leonardo and Ghirlandaio. He, too, attributes the Louvre drawing to Leonardo.

70 These documents are quoted and discussed by L. Venturini in her brief, but very useful, discussion of the Ghirlandaio family business, in M. Gregori, ed., *Maestri e botteghe. Pittura a Firenze alla fine del Quattrocento*, exh. cat., Palazzo Strozzi, Florence 1992, p. 109 ('sta all'orafo' and 'non istettono mai al dipintore, stavano all'orafo').

71 See J. Cadogan, 'Reconsidering Some Aspects of Ghirlandaio's Drawings', *Art Bulletin*, 65, 1983, p. 275, fig. 1, for a detailed discussion of the techniques used in this drawing (Uffizi 2635).

72 For this passage and a gloss of its terms, see M. Baxandall, *Painting and Experience in Fifteenth-Century Italy*, Oxford 1972, pp. 118, 128–39.

73 D. Covi, 'A documented tondo by Botticelli', in M.G. Ciardi Duprè dal Poggetto and P. dal Poggetto, eds., *Scritti di storia dell'arte in onore di Ugo Procacci*, Milan 1977, vol. 1, pp. 270–2.

74 On 21 July 1478, the Otto di Guardia paid Botticelli 40 florins for the painting. See M.A. Morelli Timpanaro, R. Manno Tolu and P. Viti eds., *Consortorie politiche e mutamenti istituzionali in età laurenziana*, exh. cat., Archivio di Stato, Florence 1992, pp. 159–61, for an excellent account of what was probably shown and the eventual fate of the paintings.

75 For discussions of Filippino's career and his drawings, see G.R. Goldner and C. Bambach, eds., *The Drawings of Filippino Lippi and His Circle*, exh. cat., Metropolitan Museum of Art, New York 1997.

76 F. Caglioti, 'Due restauratori per le antichità dei primi Medici: Mino da Fiesole, Andrea del Verrocchio e il "Marsia rosso" degli Uffizi. I', *Prospettiva*, 72, 1993, pp. 17–42.

77 G. Poggi, 'Mino da Fiesole e la Badia Fiorentina', *Miscellanea d'arte*, 2, 1903, pp. 98–103, and *La Chiesa e la Città a Firenze nel XV secolo*, exh. cat., San Lorenzo, Florence 1992, section 6, cat. no. 6.12 p. 116. See also S.E. Zuraw, 'The Public Commemorative Monument: Mino da Fiesole's Tombs in the Florentine Badia', *Art Bulletin*, 80, 1998, pp. 452–77 esp. p. 452.

78 He is recorded as living in via dei Servi in 1490 when he contributed a drawn design for the façade of the Duomo, F. Borsi. ed.,'*Per bellezza, per studio, per piacere', Lorenzo e gli spazi dell'arti*, Florence 1991, p. 83. The street was home to many dyers' shops as well as to the wax workers of SS. Annunziata.

79 The attribution of the Bargello relief in the style of Verrocchio to Ferrucci has recently been argued convincingly by Francesco Caglioti in *Eredità del Magnifico*, exh. cat. Museo Nazionale del Bargello, Florence 1992, cat. no. 24, pp. 54–6.

80 For a recent discussion of his 1470s altarpiece for a Venetian merchant see S.S. Wolohojian, 'Francesco di Simone Ferrucci's Fogg "Virgin and Child" and the Martini Chapel in S. Giobbe, Venice', *Burlington Magazine*, 139, 1997, pp. 867–9.

81 For the finished designs see especially O. Kurz, 'A Group of Florentine Drawings for an Altar', *Journal of the Warburg and Courtauld Institutes*, 18, 1955, pp. 35–53. For Francesco di Simone's probable presence in Verrocchio's shop see Butterfield 1997, pp. 153–4 and 238.

82 E. Marrese, ed., *Marco Parenti, Lettere*, Florence 1996, p. 237. For the *lettuccio* see E. Borsook, 'Documenti relativi alle cappelle di Lecceto e delle Selve di F. Strozzi', *Antichità Viva*, 9, no.3, 1970, pp. 3–20.

83 See C. Gilbert, *Italian Art 1400–1500. Sources and Documents*, Englewood Cliffs, NJ, 1980, pp. 182–4, from the *Memorie istoriche*.

84 For a concise summary of what is known about Florentine ownership of Netherlandish paintings and the Portinari and Tani commissions, see M. Rohlmann, *Auftragskunst und Sammlerbild. Altniederländische Tafelmalerei im Florenz des Quattrocento*, Alfter 1994.

85 See M. Rohlmann, 'Ein Flämisches Vorbild für Ghirlandaios "prime pitture"', *Mitteilungen des Kunsthistorischen Institutes in Florenz*, 36, 1992, pp. 388–96.

86 Cosimo Bartoli declared that the dress of the young people at the wedding of Lorenzo de' Medici and Clarice Orsini was richer than anything to be found in the courts of great lords (letter published in *Parenti*, ed. M. Marrese, p. 250).

Catalogue

I The Art of the 1470s

Florentine art of the 1470s can be understood as the product of many skilled masters and their workshops. We can examine the practices of those who designed and made the paintings and statuettes, the palaces and parade armour that were admired all over Italy during their lifetimes. Their works can also be understood as products of the needs and interests of the people who commissioned them. While prestigious objects such as altarpieces might even be ordered by Florentines of no more than artisan status, the patronage of the most spectacular, and often the most innovative, works reflects the priorities of the influential families, the merchants and bankers, at the top of the Florentine social and political hierarchy.

In 1469, on the death of his father Piero, the young Lorenzo de' Medici stepped to the top of this hierarchy. The position he inherited was precarious. The city and state of Florence was one of the few remaining republics in Italy and proud of its resistance to the tyranny of an individual ruler. Yet the familial or clan interests of its wealthiest citizens were as strong as their civic ones. Constantly vulnerable to rival factions, the long-term prosperity of the Medici family could be served only by asserting its position of authority in government (as Lorenzo put it: 'it goes ill for the rich if they do not have control of the state'). To maintain and strengthen his privileges Lorenzo had to strike a difficult course: he had to appear able and magnificent – and therefore worthy of respect – while avoiding the appearance of despotism. Works of architecture, sculpture and painting played a subtle part in negotiating this course and Lorenzo 'il Magnifico', acting alone or with his brother Giuliano, proved remarkably sensitive to the potential of monuments and of art to help etablish his position, whether in relation to his fellow citizens or to foreign powers.

The commission to Andrea del Verrocchio for the tomb of Lorenzo's father and uncle can be taken as a case in point. An honourable burial site was considered a spiritual advantage in the period. It could also fulfil the social imperatives of the living, especially if it was part of a family burial chapel. The tomb of Piero and Giovanni di Cosimo de' Medici stands within a wall opening that looks, in one direction, into the sacristy of the parish church of San Lorenzo (fig. 16). The sacristy was built by Brunelleschi at the behest of Giovanni di Bicci de' Medici, the founder of the

family's fortunes, who lies buried with his wife directly below its dome. In the other direction, the tomb was open to the admiring gaze of lay people in the Medici family's transept chapel. The casket-like form of the sarcophagus, which recalls that of reliquaries, is unprecedently sumptuous in the choice and treatment of materials – 'imperial' porphyry, serpentine (green porphyry) and bronze. But unlike the tombs of contemporary rulers, there are no portrait effigies. In Florence effigies were an honour reserved for knights and high-ranking churchmen, or those celebrated by the state, and the Medici could not be seen to appropriate this privilege. Instead the identification of the family is carefully marked by inscriptions in beautiful Roman letters and by the crowning bronze diamond, a device signifying eternity used by Piero de' Medici.

Like the Medici tomb itself, the vast majority of objects and images commissioned by Florentines – chapel decoration, altarpieces, chests, vestments and devotional paintings – were functional before they were ornamental. But the levels of intellectual investment (*ingegno*) and technical or decorative finesse expended in making such objects in this decade tends to heighten the perception of these works, especially those made for the domestic chamber, in independent terms. But apparently 'private' panel paintings, like the great tondo of the *Adoration of the Magi* (cat. no. 7), also served the needs of social representation and they did so partly through their very beauty. Though individual political interests might also be reflected in civic patronage, the production of works that were both worthy and beautiful was also a central concern to citizens of Florence, who periodically served on the special committees charged with seeing through corporate projects involving artists. Expensive commissions such as the silver reliefs to complete the altar of the Baptistery, overseen by the guild of international merchants, were complex and lengthy undertakings. Guild committee members, to whom questions of quality control were part of everyday business, needed to allocate work to ensure efficient completion, but they also needed to exercise their judgement, including their artistic judgement, when hiring and rewarding the various goldsmith workshops involved.

Judgement and expense were also at issue in the private sphere of collecting, a practice restricted to the wealthiest and most cultivated individuals, particularly those with an interest in the inheritance of antiquity. The Medici were again protagonists in this field. In 1471, Lorenzo de' Medici augmented his collection of antiquities – especially the engraved gems – begun by his father and grandfather, when he bought most of Pope Paul II's spectacular collection sold off by Sixtus IV. Lorenzo was constantly on the look out for beautiful and prestigious pieces, which were valued for their historical significance as well as their intrinsic beauty. Many works were reset and 'restored' by contemporary goldsmiths and sculptors (cat. no. 5). The inscribing of ancient gems and hardstones with Lorenzo's name seems to modern eyes like an extraordinary act of arrogation. It testifies to Lorenzo's awareness of the politics of possession.

Enormous sums were expended – or rather, invested – in acquiring antiquities and, if to a much lesser extent, on collectable Netherlandish paintings. But just as native Florentine artists' competition with one another encouraged novelty, contemporaries seem to have used such ancient and foreign 'rivals' productively. Andrea del Verrocchio and Antonio del Pollaiuolo both produced designs, reliefs and sculpture in the round that were inspired by forms and subjects found in antique art and that appealed to the taste of knowledgeable or aspiring patrons, but which were also distinctively modern. Verrocchio in particular was favoured with a number of commissions of this kind from the Medici, ranging from the restoration of an antique marble sculpture of Marsyas to the production of a bronze statue of David. With typical diplomatic flair, Lorenzo and Giuliano sold the latter to the Florentine government in 1476 at a knock-down price. The goldsmith/sculptor Bertoldo, who became a member of the Medici household, was also involved in a commission which demonstrated Medici interest in antique commemorative forms when he designed an ingenious medal which simultaneously commemorated Giuliano de' Medici's death in the Pazzi conspiracy in 1478 and celebrated Lorenzo's survival at the helm of state (cat. no. 2). Antonio and Piero del Pollaiuolo also benefited from Medici patronage directed to similar ends. The former is thought to have produced his bronze statuette of *Hercules and Antaeus* for Lorenzo (fig. 64), while the latter painted a commemorative portrait of an ally, the Duke of Milan (fig. 19), that hung in a ground-floor room of the Medici palace. Both Antonio del Pollaiuolo and the young Botticelli also provided paintings for families of the pro-Medici faction, profiting from a climate of taste that was the result, in part, of a perceived need to emulate and flatter the city's political masters.

The shops of Verrocchio and the Pollaiuolo brothers were active in goldsmith work, small-scale and monumental sculpture and painting. Each of these activities required particular, and sometimes highly specialised, technical skills. Some of them, like bronze casting or painting using an oil medium, were, in their hands, subject to experiment and change. All of them depended to a greater or lesser degree on the capacity to draw and to design. By looking at surviving designs by artists of the period we can see the processes and patterns of thought that lay behind finished works. Drapery studies like cat. no. 8 show how the fall of cloth, made in preparation for a devotional figure, could take on an expressive power that affirms the gesture's meaning, but also reveals a fascination with the material itself. In the study of human subjects (e.g. cat. no. 10) the skills of an observing eye and controlling hand are brought to bear on both physical surface and inner animation. Drawing was also a means of communication. In his chalk and pen design for a sculpted wall tomb (cat. no. 11) Verrocchio perfected his composition and displayed his sophisticated invention. The result is a drawing of great intrinsic beauty. As the monument was never built, it is also the only record of a commission which combines so many of the qualities developed in Florentine art of the 1470s, uniting pictorial fluidity with sculptural relief, the ornamental with the experimental. This commission of the early 1480s also shows how, in the following decade, ideas and abilities nurtured in Florentine workshops became available for export. Responding to new opportunities for patronage, as well as new artistic challenges, Verrocchio took his talents to Venice and Leonardo departed for Milan. Others, including Ghirlandaio, Botticelli and the Pollaiuolo brothers, became the cultural ambassadors of Florence in papal Rome.

A W

I

SANDRO BOTTICELLI

Portrait of
Giuliano de' Medici

Tempera on panel,
75.6 × 52.6 cm
Washington, DC, National Gallery of Art,
Samuel H. Kress Collection 1952.5.56, no. 1135

Friedmann 1959, pp. 116–19; Rochon 1963, pp. 26–9,
pp. 55–8 (for Giuliano); Lightbown 1978, vol. 1,
pp. 40, 44, and vol. 2, cat. B20, pp. 29–32;
Shapley 1979, vol. 1, pp. 83-4; Langedijk 1982, vol. 1,
pp. 32–4, vol. 2, p. 1065 and pp. 1067–8 (for the
portrait in the *Marriage Feast of Nastagio degli Onesti*,
now in a private collection).

I would like to thank Rolf Bagemihl for sending
me a draft copy of his entry on this painting for
the new edition of the Washington National Gallery
of Art catalogue of Italian paintings.

PLR

This portrait or a related drawing is a possible source for the head of Giuliano in Bertoldo's Pazzi conspiracy medal (cat. no. 2). Whereas the medal urges 'public mourning', this painting has a more private mood. In the medal, Giuliano seems to look forward in a bold and forthright manner. Here, instead, he looks downward, in a melancholic fashion. The turtledove on the window sill is a symbol of mourning. It was held that the turtledove who lost its mate never took another one and would perch only on lifeless branches. Poliziano invoked the turtledove as a measure of grief in his ode on Lorenzo's death. Some have connected the portrait to Giuliano's sorrow at the death of the ideal lady-love of his joust, Simonetta Vespucci, and dated it to about 1476; but this seems an unlikely purpose for such a monumental work. The panel is about one-third larger than usual for Botticelli's portraits. Three workshop variants of this portrait (in Berlin, Bergamo and Milan), for example, measure approximately 54 x 36 cm each. The complex setting, which is not copied in the other versions, is incised on the panel. Giuliano is shown through a window, with a window behind him. The task of commemoration here seems to be that of fixing Giuliano's presence in the mind of the viewer, who can both consider the transience of the moment (as conveyed by the passage of light over the figure) and the permanence and sadness of the loss, as symbolised by the turtledove. The broken branch is perhaps a poignant reference to Giuliano's life, cut short so violently when he was but twenty-five years old.

A tall broad-chested youth, Giuliano had been a keen hunter and passionate horseman. He was well-schooled in Latin and adept at chess. Correspondence regarding the joust of 1475 suggests that he cared at least as much about the horses, sought zealously all over Italy, as about Simonetta (who is never mentioned). Occasionally resentful that his older brother did not give him more opportunities to increase his reputation, he was sent on diplomatic missions and he was also subject to the attentions of literary and learned men, who included him in their dedications and in their dialogues. During the 1470s, Lorenzo tried to engineer his creation as a cardinal, a hope foiled by the deteriorating relations with Pope Sixtus IV that culminated in the Pazzi conspiracy and Giuliano's death. Rather than becoming an actual prince of the church, therefore, he remained in memory as the 'prince of youth'. He is celebrated as such in Poliziano's *Stanze* on the joust, where he is a figure of chivalric love. He is included in the company at the wedding feast that concludes the tale of Nastagio degli Onesti, painted by Botticelli in 1483 for the Pucci family to celebrate the marriage of one of Antonio Pucci's sons, which had been arranged by Lorenzo. Giuliano's memory was purposefully kept alive in poetry, painting and medals done by and for Medici supporters. This stately portrait, which was so important in establishing Giuliano's posthumous image, is not recorded in the inventory of Lorenzo's palace. It may be the one referred to in the inventory of the palace of his cousins Lorenzo and Giovanni di Pierfrancesco, who owned other important and inventive paintings by Botticelli such as the *Pallas and the Centaur* and the *Primavera* (fig. 15).

2

BERTOLDO DI GIOVANNI

Medal commemorating
the Pazzi Conspiracy

Cast bronze,
6.4–6.6 cm
Obverse: London, British Museum, Department of
Coins and Medals
Reverse: Collection of Jonathan Kagan

Obverse: Choir of Florence Cathedral with mass
being said at the high altar (right). In the foreground
the attack on Lorenzo de' Medici (cloaked and
holding a sword) and his escape (to the right and
in the centre of the choir). The whole surmounted
by three-quarter-view head of Lorenzo with the
inscription LAURENTIUS MEDICES and at centre
SALUS PUBLICA. To the left a lion beneath a tree
(the Florentine *Marzocco* under the laurel's,
i.e. Lorenzo's, protection); to the right a
female allegory holding aloft a garland.
Reverse: Choir of Florence Cathedral with capture
and murder of Giuliano de' Medici taking place in
the foreground. The whole surmounted by head
of Giuliano with the inscription IULIANUS MEDICES
and at centre LUCTUS PUBLICA. To the left and right
ancient warriors turn away from the main scene
with their hands clasped in sorrow.

Hill 1930, vol. I. pp. 240–1; Draper in *Donatello e i suoi*,
exh. cat., Florence 1986, cat. no. 110, pp. 262–3;
Caglioti in *Eredità del Magnifico*, exh. cat., Florence
1992, p. 58; Draper 1992, pp. 86–95; Scher, ed.,
New York 1994, pp. 15–16 and 129–32;
Rubinstein 1995, p. 72.

A W

The extraordinary character of this medal can only be understood as a response to an extraordinary event. Though medals were sometimes cast to commemorate particular occasions, such as the foundation of a new building, Bertoldo's image responds to a moment of crisis in Florentine politics, the 1478 assassination attempt on Lorenzo and his brother Giuliano that nearly succeeded in toppling the Medici family from their position of dominance. Commissioned by Lorenzo, who survived the attack of the Pazzi conspirators, the medal seems to have been designed as a reproducible image that would in some way help to absorb or even deflect the blow to his regime.

The medal, a relatively new type of object developed in the Italian courts, usually reflected roman coinage by supporting a profile portrait on one side and a symbolic image or scene on the reverse. Here both sides are given equal weight, each side supporting a portrait, a narrative scene with flanking allegorical figures, and inscriptions. Instead of including the date of the Pazzi attack, 26 April 1478, the event itself is visualised, giving the medal a type of documentary value, as though to impress the viewer with the horror and sacrilege of the assault that took place in Florence cathedral. The theatre of the attack is the octagonal choir screen. As the communion of priests takes place before the high altar, a group of Florentines run in to kill Lorenzo and Giuliano. The attackers are shown here without civic garb and, arguably, naked in imitation of the antique. On one side of the medal the attack on Lorenzo, his successful defence and initial escape into the choir are depicted below his portrait and the inscription SALUS PUBLICA, public safety. On the other, the choir is viewed from the north. Giuliano is shown being accosted and then brought to the ground, where he is stabbed to death; his portrait is accompanied by the inscription LUCTUS PUBLICA, public mourning. The combination of a portrait with a narrative and an inscription that conveys a political and ethical message is a formula invented in the earliest humanist cycle of historical Famous Men devised by Petrarch, whose ideas influenced the development of the commemorative medal. The formulation SALUS PUBLICA reuses that devised by Lorenzo's father for the patriotic inscription on the base of Donatello's *Judith* sculpture.

Lorenzo entrusted the invention of this medal to an artist who became a member of his intimate circle, a loyal member of the household who was able to take advice concerning the details of the event. As we are told in a letter to Lorenzo of 11 September 1478 that accompanied some examples of the medal, Bertoldo's model was cast by the goldsmith Andrea Guacialoti. The many surviving copies vary in condition but the generally rubbed appearance of the surface may have been deliberately intended to imitate the patina acquired by antique *medaglie* which were avidly collected by Lorenzo and others at this time. The medal is certainly related in function to other portrait images produced in the aftermath of the Pazzi conspiracy. While the extent of the medal's circulation is not known, the imagery makes clear that it had two purposes: the commemoration of the murder of Giuliano de' Medici and the simultaneous celebration of Lorenzo's own survival. By presenting his survival as necessary to the safety and health of the republic, Lorenzo both affirmed Medici supremacy and rebuffed his opponents' claim that his family's position undermined republican liberty. On both sides of the medal the Medici appear literally and metaphorically to rise above their enemies as they face, devoutly, towards the high altar of Florence cathedral.

This magnificent illustrated copy of works by the Florentine poets Petrarch and Dante, bound with their biographies, was written in 1476 and belonged to Lorenzo de' Medici. The specific collection of texts is patriotic and includes the life of Dante written by the famous humanist chancellor of Florence, Leonardo Bruni. It testifies to Lorenzo's promotion of the Tuscan vernacular and of Florence's poets, especially Petrarch, whom he emulated in his own lyric poetry. The book is the type of luxury item that, although ostensibly made for an individual to read and contemplate, was also intended to communicate the owner's wealth, cultural aspirations and exquisite taste. It is everywhere stamped with Lorenzo's identity and it may be assumed that he commissioned the work himself, employing a favourite illuminator for its decoration. The unusually elaborate cover has a central roundel showing the youthful Apollo Musagetes (leader of the Muses), sun god and god of music. Seated upon a golden bow and radiating light he plays his viol while ranged around him, on the front and back cover, a band of the nine Muses (one is now lost) play a variety of instruments. While this imagery would have been appropriate to adorn a book of poetry, the depiction of Apollo playing the viol harmonised with Lorenzo de' Medici's own musical accomplishments. Indeed the philosopher Marsilio Ficino likened Lorenzo's playing to that of Apollo among the Muses and Poliziano evoked the same Apollo-Lorenzo theme in his poetic lament, 'Quis dabit capiti meo', that described the Muses mourning at Lorenzo's death. Unusually, the figures of the engraved plates are freely incised into the silver without any modelling, a somewhat crude technique that nonetheless serves to highlight the boldness of the draughtsmanship. The figures are characterised by dynamic poses with limbs akimbo that exploit the tondo form. Some of them – the maenad-like Muse playing cymbals, or Euterpe – can be directly related to figures found on ancient sarcophagi. Their dramatic presence, and their heavy, angular drapery, often bunched up to display powerful limbs, are strongly reminiscent of the work of Antonio del Pollaiuolo, especially of the angels in the Cardinal of Portugal's chapel of the late 1460s (fig. 57). The attribution of the cover to Pollaiuolo, first proposed by Garzelli, is obviously strengthened by the artist's close relations with the Medici family, which would have made him a likely candidate for such a commission.

The motif of the Laurentian laurel found around the foot stud on the cover is developed in a highly original way on the first illuminated page of the manuscript (fig. 91). Not only does it appear in the roundels of the border, protecting the earth from scorching flames, alongside the traditional Medici emblem of the diamond ring (framing the *bas-de-page*), but it is also found in the allegorical episode taking place in the central picture field. Here a ship is blown against a rocky shoreline, apparently symbolising the wreck of the fortune of the figure in the water, perhaps, as Trapp has suggested, caused by love. This young man is saved from disaster only by grasping the branches of the laurel tree. At the bottom of the page the same figure is shown in contemplation seated beneath a laurel. It has sometimes been suggested that the youth is meant to represent Lorenzo himself, saved by love. In this interpretation the laurel, evoking Petrarch's Laura in the sonnets, represents his beloved. However, in the medallic image by Niccolò Fiorentino, the laurel tree appears as a symbol of Lorenzo himself who lends his protecting shade to the state. Following this reading the main scene could be understood as the salvation offered *by*, rather than *to* Lorenzo, an interpretation strengthened by Lorenzo's association with SALUS on the Pazzi conspiracy medal (cat. no. 2). While this claim might appear overweening, it should be remembered that

3

FRANCESCO D'ANTONIO DEL CHIERICO
(illuminator)
ANTONIO DEL POLLAIUOLO
(cover attributed to)

Manuscript of Francesco Petrarch's *Triumphs* and *Sonnets* (XXVII-CCCLVII), Life of Petrarch, the *Canzonieri* and *Sonnets* of Dante and Leonardo Bruni's Life of Dante

27.1 × 17.5 cm
Paris, Bibliothèque Nationale, MS italien 548, f. 10 verso, the *Triumph of Love*; f. 11 recto, first text page of the *Trionfi*.

Cover: gilded silver frame with cloisonné enamels and separate silver roundels containing remains of translucent enamel. The fragmentary gilded inscriptions and their traces on the central enamels permit the identification of Apollo and the nine Muses. The roundel top right on the front cover is missing. The cloisonné enamels show rose garlands, swans and crows. One stud for supporting the book survives on the back cover.
The silk covers and satin spine are modern.

Inscribed: on front cover roundels:
top left THALIA, bottom right EU/TERPE;
on back cover roundels: at centre CALLI/OPE,
top left POLI[HYMNIA], top right URA [NIA],
bottom left [ERA] TO

Della Torre, ed., 1902, p. 792 citing Ficino *Opera*, vol. I, p. 917; Dionisotti 1974, pp. 61–113; Garzelli 1984, no. 2, pp. 690–95; Garzelli 1985, pp. 101-70; Lafitter, ed. Lenzuni 1992, pp. 161–65; Trapp 1992-3, esp. pp. 29–30 and 39–65; Ventrone 1996, p. 109.

AW

Fig. 91 F.I verso of cat. no. 3.

Fig. 92 F.II recto of cat. no. 3.

this illumination would only have been seen by Lorenzo himself and favoured individuals likely to support his assumption of the role of patron and protector.

The first text page of Petrarch's *Triumphs* (fig. 92) faces an illustration of the Triumph of Love and its victims, which begins the cycle (opposite). A project that extended from an earlier poem on the Triumph of Love (1340s), the *Trionfi* (completed later 1360s) constituted vivid allegorical presentations of the forces of life (Love, Chastity, Death, Fame, Time, Eternity) and their workings in human history. The first printed edition appeared in 1470 and Jacopo Bracciolini also wrote a commentary on the *Triumph of Fame* for Lorenzo at this time. In these facing pages the pictorial brilliance and thematic inventiveness of the shipwreck scene are sustained, along with the more familiar iconography of the Triumph. Cupid's cart leads pairs of courtly lovers on horseback and is preceded by the historical lovers Samson and Delilah and Aristotle and Phyllis, examples of strength and wisdom enfeebled by love. The cart recalls the appearance of the Triumph of Love included in an equestrian parade devised for the young Galeazzo Maria Sforza's entertainment on his visit to Florence in 1459. The illuminator Francesco d'Antonio del Chierico (d. 1484) uses a dramatic head-on depiction of the carriage, which seems to trundle towards the spectator from the depths of a translucent landscape panorama. Working in the tradition of goldsmith/draughtsmen such as Maso Finiguerra, Francesco demonstrates his command of the most fashionable decorative and pictorial vocabulary of the 1470s, including that of Pollaiuolo and Verrocchio. Here Cupid's cart with its sphinxes and *all'antica* mouldings suggests a magnificent piece of gilded bronze work, bringing to mind Verrocchio's candelabrum (cat. no. 12) or his gilded copper ball for the Duomo lantern. In the roundels bordering the page are narratives of famous lovers and their unhappy fates, some of them referred to in the poem – Paolo and Francesca (top centre), Danae and Jupiter (top right); they continue in the facing page – Hercules, domesticated by Omphale, shown spinning (top left), Pyramus and Thisbe. The *bas-de-page* of the Triumph ties Petrarch's amatory theme into Lorenzo's own imagery by depicting a young fair-haired woman, apparently Petrarch's beloved Laura, plucking laurel branches which will then form the poet's laurel crown. This roundel would originally have formed a companion to the Medici arms of the opposite *bas-de-page* (which now has French royal arms superimposed by its subsequent owners). Petrarch himself appears in the letter N, reclining in the melancholy pose of the dreaming poet, who in the opening verses recalls the beginnings of his love and subsequent unhappiness. The famous opening line 'Nel tempo che rinuova i miei sospiri' ('In time which renews my sighs') would have reminded the contemporary reader of Lorenzo's own motto 'le tems revient' which set the tone of golden age optimism for his joust in 1469. It also appears with his device in the borders of the Shipwreck page (fig. 91).

The manuscript leaves no doubt as to why Francesco d'Antonio, whose work was often commissioned by the famous Florentine bookseller and biographer Vespasiano da Bisticci, was a favourite with the most important manuscript collectors of the period. Along with his liturgical works for the Florentine Duomo, Francesco was one of the great visual interpretors of ancient texts such as Pliny's *Natural History* and those of the humanists, including Cristoforo Landino and the founding father of the *studia humanitatis*, Francesco Petrarch. For a modern viewer, his illuminations also offer a remarkable insight into the way such texts were used and reinterpreted by Florence's élite as a subtle tool of social and political image-making.

4

FRANCESCO D'ANTONIO DEL CHIERICO

(illuminator)

Manuscript Book of Hours

15.4 × 11.4 cm cover, 14.5 × 10 cm folios
Library of the Earl of Leicester, Holkham Hall,
Ms 41, f. 44 recto

Wieck 1997; Garzelli 1980; Garzelli 1985,
pp. 93–5, 108.

AW

The imagery of the Holkham Book of Hours, strewn with Lorenzo de' Medici's emblems and with the bear (*orso*) of the Orsini family, testifies to its commemorative purpose as a gift from Lorenzo to his Roman bride Clarice Orsini, probably on the occasion of their marriage in 1469. Illuminated with minute care by Francesco d'Antonio del Chierico, the book's tiny scale reflects its function as a devotional aid for lay people. Books of Hours, produced in larger numbers than any other book in the early Renaissance, contained a cycle of prayers and readings prescribed for different times of the day, including certain ecclesiastical Offices. They were commonly owned by patrician women and often formed part of the dower goods that they brought with them into marriage.

Following, for the most part, the orthodox structure of Books of Hours, the Holkham Hours includes a calendar of church feasts, the Hours of the Virgin (a sequence of Latin prayers to the Mother of God, here following the Roman rite), the Passion Cycle, Penitential Psalms, the Office of the Dead, and ends with the Office of the Cross. The Hours of the Virgin focus on her role as prime intercessor with Christ for the salvation of souls as well as her role as an exemplar for the female reader. It is here also that most of the imagery referring to the Medici-Orsini alliance appears. Cat. no. 4 shows the opening of Prime in the Hours of the Virgin (f. 44 recto, marked later as 43). The page is dominated by an illuminated scene from the apocryphal story of the Virgin's parents in which Joachim is expelled from the temple because of his childlessness. The temple itself is Brunelleschian, with Corinthian columns and a blue and gold coffered ceiling receding in perspective, a picture of order disrupted by the ejection of Joachim. The patronage and ownership of the book are directly marked by the inclusion of the Medici arms flanked by those of the Orsini over the temple front, but they are also referred to in a variety of more coded and personal ways. The border itself is structured around a pruned branch (a Medici emblem) that sprouts rosehips and roses, a device of Clarice Orsini. The *bas-de-page*, one of several in this section showing astrological spheres and ringed with Lorenzo's motto 'le ten revient', is thought to refer to the position of the heavens at an important moment in Clarice and Lorenzo's life – here the sun is shown in Capricorn. But the most charmingly inventive references appear in the border vignettes where, to the top right for example, a laurel tree (Lorenzo) is shown leaning down to embrace a bear (Clarice). The manuscript is equally unusual in its choice of scenes to accompany specific texts as well as in its visualisation of the mystical and the abstract – especially in the numerous marginal depictions of the heavens, the celestial Virgin and the City of God. It has been pointed out that the iconography is particularly rich in themes of penitential piety (occasionally so unorthodox as to leave their precise meaning unclear). Such images were intended to encourage the type of interior, meditative devotion and personal responsibility for the state of one's soul preached by fifteenth-century religious reformers. The humanist desire to reconcile astrological and Christian views of the cosmos found here may also be traced in sites such as the Medici Old Sacristy in San Lorenzo as well as in Matteo Palmieri's theological poem, the *Città di Vita*. Thus, like the Petrarch manuscript (cat. no. 3), the Medici-Orsini Hours must be seen as a sophisticated and carefully customised product, one which testifies to the collaboration between the intellectual circle of the patron and the interpretative skill of the illuminator.

Ad primam. m. Versus.

Eus i ad
iutorum
meum in
tende. Et
Domine
ad adiuu
dum me
festina. t

Gloria pri t. Sicut. hymnuc
Emento salutis auctor. quod
nostri quoniam corporis. t
ex illibata uirgine. nascero formam
sumpsens Maria mater gratie. o
mater misericordie. tu nos ab hoste p
tege. t in hora mortis suscipe Glo

5

UNKNOWN CRAFTSMAN

Two-handled cup and cover

Jasper with foot of silver gilt and rims of cup and
cover of silver gilt with red, green and white enamels,
27 cm height,
Florence, Palazzo Pitti, Museo degli Argenti,
inv. no. 638 (1921)

Inscribed: LAV. MED

Heikamp and Grote 1974, vol. 2, pp. 127–8,
cat. no. 26, pp. 165–6 (docs.), figs. 49 and 50.

NP

Hardstone vessels of this kind had been greatly prized for centuries but the
important medieval collections had been kept in ecclesiastical treasuries, such as
that which survives in St Mark's in Venice, where they were often adapted as reliquaries
or as chalices. The fifteenth-century Medici collected such vessels and remounted them
simply as beautiful objects. This one was to be donated in the sixteenth century by Pope
Clement VII (Giulio de' Medici) to San Lorenzo to serve as a reliquary for the hand
and skin of Saint Sabina.

Some Medici hardstone vessels were made in Roman Alexandria, others were
Sassanian of the seventh century or Byzantine of the tenth. This piece may have
originated in Venice or in Fatimid Egypt. The beautiful classical letters LAV. MED
inscribed on the body of the cup not only testify to Lorenzo de' Medici's ownership
(see also the cameo, cat. no. 6) but also show that he too sponsored the rare art
of working in hardstone.

The cover is missing a finial which is recorded in an early drawing. It featured the
Medici armorial *palle* – five red balls and one blue one indicating a date after 1465.
However, the vessel was already mounted in silver ('leghata in ariento') in an inventory
of Piero de' Medici's possessions in 1465. The mounts have been attributed to the
goldsmith Giusto da Firenze. The boldly embossed lobes of the foot are gothic forms,
but the miniature fluting and beads in the rim and the consoles joining vase and foot
reflect the *all'antica* taste increasingly dominant in fifteenth-century architecture.

This is perhaps the finest hardstone sculpture to survive from the thirteenth-century court workshop of the Emperor Frederick II of Hohenstaufen (d.1250), who is thought to have recruited Arab or Byzantine craftsmen to make such works. Noah stands to the left attentive to an angel. His sons Shem, Ham and Japheth, their wives and Noah's wife stand beside the ark, as do pairs of horses, lions, dogs, goats and sheep. Numerous fowls perch above and flutter about it. Cattle already lurk within. The holes of the miniature drill, especially conspicuous in beards and hair, are used also to indicate features and thus determine the character of expression. The management of the strata to suggest different planes is very ingenious – especially the preservation of a fine translucent layer for the distant ark. The gold mount, fitted with a suspension ring, is pounced on the reverse with exquisite floral motifs of a style associated with French or Burgundian fifteenth-century goldsmiths.

LAV./R. and MED (for Lorenzo de' Medici) is inscribed on the gothic doors of the ark. Lorenzo inherited this cameo from Piero de' Medici in whose inventory of 1465 it was valued at 300 florins – more than any other of the thirty cameos and intaglios listed as *Greche* (i.e. ancient Graeco-Roman). It was then clearly regarded as an ancient work of art. Precious antiquities of this kind were soaring in value. In Lorenzo's inventory of 1492 this cameo was estimated as worth 2000 florins. It was again the most valued work of its kind and equal to the most highly valued hardstone vessel. No painting in the Medici collection approached this – the most highly prized was a tondo by Fra Angelico at 100 florins. Few cameos had such ambitious narratives scenes, but the crowding and animal life shown here are reminiscent of the retinues of the kings in Florentine paintings of the Adoration.

6

UNKNOWN CRAFTSMAN *c.*1250

Noah and his family

Oval cameo of brown and white onyx
of three strata in a gold mount,
5.1 cm width,
London, British Museum, 1890, 9-1, 15.

Inscribed: LAV.R/R and MED

Dalton 1914, p. 4, no. 18; Panofsky 1960, p. 67; Dacos, Giuliano and Pannuti 1972, no. 37, p. 64 and pp. 119, 121, figs. 33–4; Alsop 1982, pp. 385–420; Tait 1986, p.218, fig. 541 (including reverse).

NP

As noted above (cat. no. 6) the most highly valued painting in the 1492 inventory of the Medici palace was a large tondo by Fra Angelico in a gilt frame with 'our Lady and our Lord and the Magi that are coming with gifts'. Its value of one hundred florins, was equivalent to the highest amounts paid for altarpieces. The tondo was a deluxe category of picture, often lavishly framed. The luxury was enhanced when, as in the Medici tondo and here, the subject was the *Adoration of the Kings*.

Botticelli painted the subject no fewer than six times, including the altarpiece for Guasparre del Lama (fig. 38), a *spalliera* or private devotional panel (with Filippino Lippi, cat. no. 68), and a fresco at the head of the staircase leading to the Sala dei Gigli in the Palazzo della Signoria (destroyed in the sixteenth century). Botticelli's talent and business acumen partly account for this frequency, but it is also explained by the importance of the feast of the Magi in the ritual, and to a certain extent, the political life of the city. The Epiphany processions left a distinctive imprint on the Florentine iconography of the Adoration, which often rejoices in teeming crowds and all the trappings of court life as they are shown here: animals both domestic and exotic, horses and grooms, a dwarf, trumpeters and courtiers of all ages. Until the 1470s a horizontal, or processional, format like that of cat. no. 68 was common. Then, coincidental with the last of the Magi parades, centralised compositions became the norm.

Here Botticelli has exploited the force of the centre, making the Holy Family the pivot of the painting. Following the rules of perspective, the Virgin and Child are smaller in scale than the foreground figures. But they are not diminished. The steeply receding lines established by the walls of the crumbling classical temple place the onlooker well below them – a suitably humble position humorously reinforced by the foreshortened view of the horse's rump which more or less marks the location of the viewer's imagined, and invited, approach. The grandiose, but decaying, Roman temple provides spatial logic and symbolic order, as the old order is shown giving way to the new. The manger roof rests solidly below the arch, whose slipping keystone foretells its ruin. The faithful are the living architecture of the church. The peacock, a symbol of the resurrection, elegantly juxtaposes the surety of the eternal life of the soul against the vanity of worldly hopes.

Such an ingeniously devised and sumptuously composed painting would seem to contradict its own other-worldly message. But one function of devotional art was to be like the offerings of the kings, acting as a form of gift made out of reverence and intended to bestow honour. Here the tribute may nonetheless have been tinged by worldly resonance. Vasari saw a tondo of the Epiphany by Botticelli in the 'house of the Pucci' in the mid-sixteenth century, presumably made for Antonio Pucci (patron of the *Martyrdom of Saint Sebastian*, cat. no. 43), who was head of that branch of the family in the 1470s. The Pucci's ownership of a glamorous painting of this subject may well have been a form of homage to the Medici, who were strongly identified with the imagery of the Magi and who had two *Adoration* tondi in their palace (the 1492 inventory lists one by Pesellino in addition to the one attributed to Fra Angelico). The National Gallery tondo belonged to the Guicciardini family in the early nineteenth century, and can probably be identified as having come from the Pucci through marriage. There is, however, no absolute proof that this is the picture seen by Vasari. What can be said with certainty is that this picture shows how affluent Florentines welcomed the magnificence of kings and stimulated the excellence of artists through their ownership of brilliantly produced devotional paintings.

7

SANDRO BOTTICELLI

Adoration of the Kings

Tempera on poplar,
diameter of painted area 130.8 cm
and of panel 138.5 cm
London, National Gallery, NG 1033

Vasari/Milanesi, vol. 3, pp. 312–13; Horne 1908, pp. 37–8; Davies 1961, pp. 101-2; Lightbown 1978, vol. 1, pp. 33–5, vol. 2, B11, pp. 25–6; Dunkerton et al. 1991, pp. 312–13; Spallanzani and Bertelà 1992, p. 12 (Medici inventory, Fra Angelico).

PLR

8

LEONARDO DA VINCI

Kneeling figure

Metalpoint, brown wash, white
heightening on red prepared paper,
25.7 × 19 cm
Rome, Istituto Nazionale per la Grafica, Gabinetto
Nazionale delle Stampe,
FC 125770

Quattrocchi, exh. cat., Rome 1979, cat. no. 19,
pp. 37–8; *Léonard de Vinci. Les études de draperie*,
exh. cat. 1989, cat. no. 17, pp. 76–7; Popham,
ed. Kemp 1994, pp. 12–13; Brown 1998, pp. 76–9.

PLR

Fig. 93 MASTER E.S., *Annunciation*, 1460s. Engraving,
17.5 × 12.2 cm. Berlin, Staatliche Museen Preussischer
Kulturbesitz, Kupferstichkabinett.

The late fourteenth-century manual by Cennino Cennini instructs painters on the method for making a drawing in metalpoint, fixing its accents with ink and shading with wash. This combination remained standard for much of the fifteenth century, particularly for drapery studies, because it enabled a controlled and nuanced description of fold structures. This drawing is both greatly indebted to traditional methods and characteristically innovative.

The shimmering luminosity of Leonardo's drawing is anticipated in drapery studies by Fra Filippo Lippi. The complicated, bulky and overlapping layers of cloth dressing the figure as well as the fanned-out folds that form its base are also found in Lippi's later works. The parallels are probably due to the fact that Leonardo's teacher, Verrocchio, was strongly influenced – if not actually instructed – by Lippi. There are significant differences, however, and they are defining differences of the 1470s, of Verrocchio's shop and of Leonardo's creative personality.

The drapery composition is representative of the period in its reference to fashionable models found in Northern art, probably studied through engravings such as those by the German artist known as Master E.S. (fig. 93). The angular bunching of folds into independent decorative patterns is very similar to the Northern engraver's style. Leonardo's technique of using white hatching in extremely fine lines which follow the direction of the forms they describe may well have been observed from the sophisticated and rich linear modelling systems recently developed by accomplished Northern printmakers.

Leonardo's close observation of both surface texture and relief – the passage of light over clearly defined volumes – is a product of his training with the goldsmith/sculptor/painter Verrocchio. The extraordinary intellect behind those powers of observation is, of course, Leonardo's own. Here he applied light and shade in subtle gradations: metalpoint and wash create degrees of shadow, and different densities of white express the varied intensity of the light. Typically, the fabric is far from inert; it is almost disconcertingly charged with life. Typical as well is the way that Leonardo's mind was as mobile as the light he was studying. His first concern was to achieve a convincing modelling system for the drapery composition. The choice of red as the colour for the ground accords with this aim because it complements the blended dark tones of shade and accentuates the contrast of the highlights. Having resolved one area, Leonardo then began to consider, or reconsider, the underlying pose, effectively calling the whole image into question. He sketched alternatives for the position of the head and shoulders. Two versions of the face are clearly resolved: one in profile and one in three-quarters view. There is even a hint, in an oval slanted to the right, that Leonardo flirted with the notion of turning the face in the opposite direction – a sort of dramatic reversal which would later be almost reflexive in his design process. Here Leonardo remained faithful to the original conception of the pose, which is reverent and humbly accepting. The study can be interpreted as an idea for an annunciate Virgin, and it has been considered as an early solution for the Virgin in the Uffizi *Annunciation* (fig. 72). Abandoned for one painting, it was not forgotten. Very similar drapery is arranged on the angel, in reverse, in an Annunciation predella panel in the Louvre attributed to Lorenzo di Credi. This derivation is not the only instance of Leonardo's drawings supplying ideas for other artists. It is even possible that Leonardo's study became Verrocchio studio property (as with cat. no. 24). In this way the young artist's uncommon gift for learning became part of a common stock of knowledge.

This sheet demonstrates the way that Leonardo exercised his pen and his imagination in drawing. Both sides have profiles, pairing and contrasting male and female, old age and youth: a repertory of types derived from contemporary sculpture, engravings and ancient coins which became recurrent, even haunting, motifs in his drawings (fig. 94). His mind and his pen moved between motifs and between human and animal with a creative freedom that he compared to poetic invention. Although slightly trimmed and damaged by a fold and a cut, this sheet is a rare survival because it is probably close to its original size. It shows how Leonardo filled the available paper: first using its expanse as a surface for the associative series of profiles and then using its edges as a notional frame for the composition of the holy group.

This drawing also shows how Leonardo was trained to use the pen in a precise and descriptive fashion, with careful, close hatching to produce the effect of relief (as in the youthful and aged faces in the centre), and in fluent, but expressive, annotation with different weights and lengths of stroke to capture and describe contour and volume. However spontaneous, the pen work – in its curves, twists and turns – is extremely purposeful, and as a shorthand owes much to Verrocchio's example (see cat. no. 36). Characteristic of Leonardo, however, is the left-handed hatching, which goes from top left to bottom right.

The drawing is dominated by the large compositional group of the Virgin with the nursing Child. The young Saint John the Baptist approaches them with an adoring gaze. A landscape is indicated behind and to the right. Leonardo seems to have been concerned to achieve both spatial and emotional balance; his aim was to arrive at figures whose actions expressed the spirit which animated them.

Typical here is Leonardo's own restlessness at achieving this aim. The Virgin has several heads. Leonardo tried out different angles for her face, and with them different moods. The first alternative had the Virgin looking towards the Infant Christ and depicted the attentive intimacy of the mother nursing her child. Leonardo then decided to turn the Virgin's head to the right, drafting schematic possibilities, ultimately fixing her face in a meditative downward gaze. Physically the change in the Virgin's position counterbalances the weight of the wriggling child. Other drawings show Leonardo contending with the problem of matching a graceful sitting position for Mary with adequate support for her lively child (cat. no. 38). Here he proposes a totally new solution by combining the currently popular format of the Virgin who kneels to adore the Infant Christ with the more traditional domestic type of a seated, nursing mother. This hybrid is not totally happy, and the arrival of Saint John (drawn over the Virgin's hip and leg) serves to complete a compositional triangle and to anchor the Virgin's awkward and somewhat unstable position. These ideas, which can be dated to about 1478, were not directly developed in any painting by Leonardo, but they later became extremely influential. They were taken up by Raphael in the early sixteenth century. The Virgin and Child in a painting attributed to Andrea da Salerno in the Capodimonte Museum in Naples are also based on this composition. These derivations are not only proof of Leonardo's willingness to share his inventions, but of the fact that he kept inventive drawings such as this one in order to return to the lessons and the inspiration which they offered.

9

LEONARDO DA VINCI

Studies of the Virgin and Child and Saint John and other figures

Pen and brown ink on paper,
40.4 × 29.1 cm
Windsor, Royal Library, The Royal Collection, 12276 recto

Suida 1929, p. 53, pl. 26, figs. 38–9 (for the painting by Andrea da Salerno); Clark 1969, vol. 1, pp. 3–4, vol. 2 (pls.); *Leonardo da Vinci*, exh. cat., Hayward Gallery 1989, cat. no. 5, pp. 52–3; Popham, ed. Kemp 1994, pp. 16–17, 108, no. 23.

PLR

Fig. 94 Verso of cat. no. 9.

10

CIRCLE OF VERROCCHIO

Portrait of a man

Metalpoint, pen and red-brown ink and
white heightening on paper, grey-brown
background wash (probably added later),
19.2 × 17.5 cm
Florence, Galleria degli Uffizi,
Gabinetto Disegni e Stampe, inv. 250E recto

Jacobsen 1904, p. 195; Van Marle 1928, vol. 10, p. 374;
Degenhart in Degenhart and Schmitt 1968,
cat. no. 497; Meller 1974, esp. pp. 266–72;
Horster 1980, p. 184; Bellosi 1987, pp. 401–17;
Caneva in *Il Disegno fiorentino*, exh. cat. Florence 1992,
no. 4.4, pp. 96–7; Griswold 1994, pp. 151–4
(for the Botticini drapery study); Venturini 1994,
cat. nos. 23 and 38, figs. 26 and 66.

AW

The compelling character of this portrait drawing derives both from formal features – the bold, lively treatment of the hair, the broad but individualised facial features – and from the psychological effect of the direct gaze. While the head is turned to the left in three-quarter view, positioning the near eye in the centre of the sheet, the subject looks back towards the viewer from the corner of his eye. This is a dramatic device familiar in the portraits of Andrea del Castagno (d. 1457), to whom this sheet has frequently been attributed. Yet the elaborate curls of the hair, the attention to surface effects and indeed the whole complex technique, are much more characteristic of Florentine art of the 1470s than of the mid-century. The low viewing angle and the fixed intensity of the gaze might be cited in favour of the argument that this is a self portrait. At the beginning of this century it was already claimed that the sitter might be Andrea del Verrocchio, on the basis of the engraving that illustrates Vasari's Life of the artist. The resemblance is inconclusive though and Vasari's portrait itself may not be reliable. Therefore, setting aside the question of whether Verrocchio is represented, an attribution to Verrocchio would need to rest on style and technique. In fact no drawings of a comparably individualised subject survive by him and the technique of tonal modelling using a brush is somewhat less delicate than we find in other drawings considered autograph.

The draughtsman/painter has outlined the major features and preliminary tonal values with metalpoint, adjusting the line of the hat and the far cheek. Taking up a brush he stroked in the curling hair and then, using meticulous touches of a smaller brush, carefully moulded the surface of the face following the contours of the features. The darkest areas were reinforced with a broader brush or pen, while the white highlights complete the totally systematic depiction of light, which is shown as though falling from above and to the left, leaving the near side of the nose in shadow. This technique is strictly comparable with the practice of tempera painting, using tiny hatching strokes to build up a powerful effect of volume and nuanced surface forms. Whether or not this carefully observed drawing was ever used for a painting, it functioned as practice for the eye and hand of a painter. The concern with relief and with surface, as well as the intended use of the drawing, relate it most closely to the Verrocchio workshop. Portrait-like features and the sidelong glance occur in many verrocchiesque paintings of the 1470s, including the Saint Michael of the Uffizi *Three Archangels* altarpiece, and other works of Botticini. Though Botticini's miniature pen portrait of Matteo Palmieri illustrating his *Città di Vita* employs a freer technique, a drapery study in the Biblioteca Reale, Turin, recently attributed to him uses the same tonal system of brushwork. Meller has pointed out similarities to the head of the older Saint Vincent Ferrer in the altarpiece from the Verrocchio shop for San Domenico del Maglio (now in Budapest), usually attributed to the young Biagio di Antonio. The treatment of fleshy skin and the system of modelling light on the face using a restricted amount of white highlight are common to both. An attribution to a younger contemporary of Verrocchio seems convincing in these respects, though this would mean that the drawing, which depicts a mature sitter, could not be a self portrait.

145

The lion of Saint Mark in the central oval and the faint, but discernible, Vendramin arms on the shields held by the putti identify this drawing as a project for the tomb of the wealthy Venetian patrician Andrea Vendramin. Vendramin was elected doge in 1476 – an honour which qualified him for a grandiose funerary monument. But even before this, when he made his will on 24 March 1472 (having reached the venerable age of 79 and the high office of procurator of St Mark's), he ordered his heirs to construct a large and 'well adorned' tomb above an extant family monument near the Vendramin chapel in the Venetian church of Santa Maria dei Servi. Some time after Vendramin's death in 1478 and before his own in 1488, Verrocchio proposed this novel design (which was not executed; Vendramin's tomb, completed 1493-4, was sculpted by Tullio Lombardo). Verrocchio's official involvement with the Venetian state began sometime before July 1481 when a document mentions one of the models being submitted in competition for the equestrian monument to Bartolommeo Colleoni, a commission won by Verrocchio.

The drawing probably dates from the 1480s and it certainly relates to a Venetian project. It is, however, proudly Florentine in character and completely characteristic of Verrocchio's imaginative approach to sculptural design. In this case he transformed the traditional Venetian console tomb into a theatrical representation of Justice with allegorical figures floating on cloudlets to each side. The one to the right, Fame, offers a laurel wreath, that to the left holds symbols of plenty and peace – a cornucopia and an olive branch. The Cardinal of Portugal tomb (fig. 56) probably gave Verrocchio the idea of composing a monument with opened curtains. But the actual composition is closer to a festival float. There is no effigy. Andrea Vendramin, and his successors in the Vendramin family, are instead celebrated as upholders of justice, the supreme virtue of the Venetian republic.

The shapes and ornament of the tomb chest come from the repertory of goldsmith's work. Sculptures by Donatello and Desiderio da Settignano inspired other aspects of the design. The garland-bearing putti precariously positioned on the consoles or cornice in front of the arch recall those on top of the frame of Donatello's Cavalcanti *Annunciation* in Santa Croce. The crowning placement of Justice resembles the position of the eucharistic Infant Christ standing above a chalice on the sacrament tabernacle by Desiderio in San Lorenzo (fig. 95). An unusual thought for a tomb, it might have occurred to Verrocchio when he considered the intended location of this monument near the Vendramin chapel, which was a sacrament chapel. In any event, the perspective composition, ornamental vocabulary and the formal contrast suggested between filigree carving and solidly sculpted figures are all found in Desiderio's tabernacle as well. Verrocchio employed different techniques in this drawing in order to study the different aspects of his design. He first used black chalk to sketch speculatively the basic composition and consider its elements. There are numerous adjustments, particularly in the outline of the tomb chest. Once the overall structure was resolved in relation to the frame, Verrocchio focused on modelling the central sculptures and defining the fleshy shapes of the putti, which he did with different combinations of chalk, ink and wash. He used the pen diagrammatically to outline the ornament and to make each motif clearly legible. This shift in attention changed the perspective: description not illusion was the primary concern in this section of the study. His adaptation of drawing style to drawing purpose and the consequent changes of focus give the whole a disjointed effect. This should not be seen as a failure, but recognised as the result of Verrocchio's systematic approach to problem solving and related to the complexity and the brilliance of his contrivance.

II

ANDREA DEL VERROCCHIO

Design for a funerary monument

Black chalk, pen and ink, brown wash on paper,
27.1 × 17.5 cm
London, Victoria and Albert Museum, 2314

Möller 1935, pp. 193–5; Stedman Sheard 1979,
pp. 115–56; Ward-Jackson 1979, cat. no. 18, pp. 24–6;
Stedman Sheard 1992, pp. 78–85.

PLR

Fig. 95 DESIDERIO DA SETTIGNANO, *Sacrament tabernacle*, *c.*1460–1. Marble, *c.*350 cm high. Florence, San Lorenzo.

II   Verrocchio's Workshop and its Projects

IN HIS 1457 tax declaration Verrocchio states that he had abandoned the goldsmith's art for lack of work. Forced into other crafts, within ten years his talents were finding ample recognition. The first payment from the Mercanzia for work on the statues of Saint Thomas and Christ for the corporation's niche at Orsanmichele dates from 15 January 1467. He had probably already started work on the Signoria candlestick (cat. no. 12); he received eight florins as partial payment on 29 June 1468. In 1468 he also sat on the board deliberating the commission of a ball to crown the lantern of the Duomo – a job given to him that year. Lorenzo de' Medici's joust and Piero de' Medici's death in 1469 brought further work: Lorenzo's pennant and Piero's tomb. Although he failed to take part in painting the Virtues for the Mercanzia's tribunal (he was paid eight *lire* for a drawing of Faith, but Piero del Pollaiuolo won the job), this setback in December 1469 did not seem to discourage him unduly with respect to his potential in that field. He registered in the confraternity of Saint Luke as a painter and sculptor in 1472.

A summary of the principal dated or datable projects from the 1470s proves the volume, the versatility and the complexity of Verrocchio's output in the decade. It also amply demonstrates the necessary interweaving of creative endeavours, as circumstances required tasks to be started, suspended, renewed or revised.

In 1470 the bronze for one of the Mercanzia group – the figure of Christ – was reweighed. A model must have been prepared for casting, but the statue was only completed nine years later. Work on the model for Saint Thomas probably dates from between 1476 and 1479; the figure was cast that year. A dispute about payments delayed the finishing touches and installation of the group. It was unveiled on 21 June 1483. A contemporary, the apothecary Luca Landucci, noted in his diary that it was 'the most beautiful thing imaginable, and the finest head of the Saviour that has as yet been made'. Luca was not the only one to feel this way about Verrocchio's portrait of Christ: it was the basis for the production of a number of terracotta busts presumably sold as private devotional objects.

In 1474 Verrocchio is documented as casting a (now lost) bronze bell for the Vallombrosan monastery at Monte Scalari, where his brother Simone was abbot. 1474 is also the year of Donato de' Medici's death, marked on his tomb slab in the former oratory of the Virgin of the Piazza in Pistoia cathedral. Donato, the bishop of Pistoia, had earlier (in about 1440) founded the oratory to honour a miracle-working image of the Virgin and Child which was on one of the cathedral's exterior walls. Through his testamentary bequests the oratory was transformed to become his funerary chapel as well (in the late sixteenth century it was transformed once again into a chapel devoted to the Holy Sacrament). The ornamental vocabulary of the tomb marker is Verrocchio's, but it is not known if he was commissioned to make the slab, or the portrait bust of the chapel's benefactor dated 1475. He was, however, called upon to paint the panel for the altar, and its composition took into account the commemorative ensemble, with Donato's name saint, Donatus, oriented to look towards the memorial bust. Preliminary work on the composition can be dated to around 1476. An agreement of November 1485 made between Verrocchio and the town councillors on behalf of the executors of Donato's will says that it would have been finished six years earlier (1479) had the executors fully paid the sum due. Three years is a normal time span for an altarpiece of this scale, and *c.*1476–9 might have been the years when the painting was designed and worked on until payments halted. In the 1485 document it is described as a 'most beautiful thing and brought to that finish which it has with great skill'. The painting was completed and delivered by 1486. Vasari attributed it to Lorenzo di Credi, who was probably given primary responsibilty for its execution. But Verrocchio determined its form and the composition, which would bring 'honour and ornament' to Pistoia, became an influential pattern for altarpieces designed in the later 1470s and the 1480s.

Verrocchio's professional interest as painter and sculptor coincided in July 1475 when he was paid, through the office of works of the Florentine cathedral, for painting a (now lost) banner for the quarry city of Carrara. It was as a sculptor that Verrocchio next became involved with the (famously contentious) Pistoians. His model for the monument to Cardinal Niccolò Forteguerri was selected in May 1476, but when the board of works started to negotiate the cost they found that Verrocchio's asking price of 350 florins exceeded their allowed price of 300. It was not until March 1477 that matters were settled with Lorenzo de' Medici's intervention and the commission was definitively given to Verrocchio. Documents from 1483 describe the sculpture as finished 'in good part', but the project was dogged by dissent and by serious, and possibly scandalous, complications in funding. Only seven of the nine promised figures had been sculpted by Verrocchio's death in 1488, when Lorenzo di Credi agreed to have the work finished within fifteen months. Although ready by November 1489, problems with the costly business of transporting the sculptures delayed their installation until the spring of 1493. Even then it seems to have been a makeshift and unsatisfactory solution, revised at least three times in the coming centuries. The current appearance of the cenotaph (fig. 96) is the result of remodelling undertaken in the mid-eighteenth century. Fortunately Verrocchio's bold and theatrical conception is preserved in the sketch model dating from the original deliberations in 1476 (cat. no. 13).

It is likely that it was sometime around 1476 that work on the San Salvi *Baptism* (fig. 74), apparently suspended earlier in the decade, was resumed. Verrocchio's brother Simone had returned to that monastery as abbot in 1475, so had both the institutional and fraternal power to insist upon its completion. By this date Leonardo da Vinci was an experienced assistant in Verrocchio's workshop and Verrocchio could and did rely upon his demonstrated skills. Leonardo's intervention in the *Baptism*, most famously in painting the foreground angel, was already regarded as noteworthy in the early sixteenth century when it was recorded in the first published guidebook to Florence, Francesco Albertini's 1510 *Memoriale*. It was sealed into art-historical mythology by Vasari in his Life of Leonardo, where he said that the quality of Leonardo's angel was the reason that Verrocchio never touched colours again. The many different ways of handling colour – both tempera and oil – in paintings from Verrocchio's shop and the way that compositions are assembled indicate that delegation was standard practice, even if in this case the results were exceptional.

As the master of the shop Verrocchio provided the inventions or compositional designs for projects (as documented in the Pistoia altarpiece). He also made studies from life and from sculpted models, which could both serve specific purposes and become general stencils or formulas for repeated or replicated types. He handled colours well enough to attract and teach able pupils. He certainly had to be satisfied with their work, which would be regarded as a product of his hand or 'mastery'.

But he was equally willing to devolve responsibilty to assistants and allow them some degree of freedom in both sculpting and painting. The decision to deputise might have depended upon the prominence or challenge of a commission, the expertise of a particular assistant or the amount of work in hand.

Overlapping tasks were the rule, not the exception for Verrocchio. In the summer of 1477, just a few months after he was awarded the Forteguerri commission, for example, he was busy making models for the silver altar for the Baptistery. The competition was announced on 24 July; he submitted two models by 2 August. He was allotted the scene of the Beheading of the Baptist on 13 January 1478, and the relief was completed within the year (30 December). In 1477 Verrocchio was also engaged to provide two gilt bronze reliefs to adorn a marble tabernacle by Luca della Robbia in the hospital church of Santa Maria Nuova: a *Christ the Redeemer* (now in the Bargello Museum, Florence) and a *Dove of the Holy Spirit* (stolen in 1919 and still missing). In September Giovanni Tornabuoni's wife Francesca died in Rome in childbirth. According to Vasari, Verrocchio made a tomb for Francesca in Santa Maria sopra Minerva in Rome, which had a relief showing the sorrowful scene of her death.

The documented, or partly documented, works are only a portion of the surviving or recorded sculptures and paintings from the decade, and the rhythm of work must have been constant. The pace of each commission was decided by the nature of the project and the frequency of payments. Some tasks, like the pennants for Lorenzo's and Giuliano's jousts and the decorations for Galeazzo Maria Sforza's visit in March 1471, needed to be done rapidly in order to be ready for the occasion. Some permanent and technically involved works, like the tomb of Piero and Giovanni de' Medici or the *Beheading of the Baptist* for the silver altar, were also executed with relative dispatch. Others – the *Christ and Saint Thomas*, the Forteguerri cenotaph and the Pistoia altarpiece – dragged on over many years. The documents for all three commissions suggest that it was a matter of money. Verrocchio could not afford to continue work without regular payments. Whatever the financial drawbacks, the delays brought benefits to his shop in the form of creative interaction between different projects.

PLR

12

ANDREA DEL VERROCCHIO

Candelabrum

'Bell Metal' bronze (with a high proportion of
tin, lead and zinc), cast in at least three sections,
156 cm high
Rijksmuseum, Amsterdam
Inscribed on the plinth:
MAGGIO/E GIUGNO/ MCCCCLXVIII
(May and June 1468)

Rubinstein 1995, pp. 58–59, 106; for technique
see also Scholton 1996, pp. 123-9; Butterfield 1997,
cat. no. 10, pp. 212–13, and pp. 81–2.

NP

The candelabrum was commissioned for the chapel of the Sala dell'Udienza (Audience Chamber) in the Palazzo della Signoria in Florence in 1468. Payments suggest that it was modelled in that year and cast by September 1469. It was an expensive work. Verrocchio received eight florins in 1468, probably for the model, and forty florins when the casting was complete or underway in the following year. There is also a payment of three large florins for *saldatura* (soldering) in April 1470, perhaps for assembling the completed works or for fixing some separate component such as a drip pan.

Candles were offerings to God; candleholders or candelabra were more durable offerings. The date on this bronze is that when the offering was agreed upon. It commemorates the conclusion of the 'Colleoni War' which left the Florentine Republic in a powerful position in the Italian peninsula and confirmed the control of the Medici family. The initiative must be associated with Carlo di Niccola de' Medici who was Gonfaloniere in May and June, the months named in the inscription.

The cast itself seems to have been nearly perfect except for a few cracks, one of which may explain the loss of a scroll on the plinth. Many bronze statuettes of the period are much rougher. The different sections (there may have been as many as six) would have been modelled in wax over a clay core and cut with the soft rippling leaves and crisp letters before being encased in a mould. The wax would have been melted out of this mould and molten bronze poured in. The cast would then have been joined, polished, sharpened and textured (notably in the punched ground around the letters).

No ancient Roman candelabrum of exactly this form has survived, but Verrocchio was inspired by the candelabra carved in low relief in ancient pilasters. Also, one of the documents mentions that the candelabrum was 'lavorato a similitudine di certo vaso' – which may mean that an antique urn served as a model. In any case, the type of low-relief leaf decoration on the vase section of the candelabrum is found in many Roman marble funerary urns. The lions' feet with acanthus curling into scrolls on the plinth are also derived from an antique model, probably an altar. Similar ornaments are found in the lectern and supporting chest painted by Leonardo probably a year or two after the completion of the candelabrum (fig. 72). Here, however, the acanthus is far richer. The object Leonardo depicts appears to have been carved out of marble, but not even Desiderio da Settignano (whose work it recalls) could have undercut the overlapping leaves or the threads by which the swag is suspended (Leonardo has included a shadow to show that these are detached). There would be a far better chance of executing such a work in metal, and indeed something no less richly undercut was achieved by Verrocchio in the bronze feet and acanthus scrolls he devised for the tomb of Giovanni and Piero de' Medici (fig. 16) of the same date.

The copper alloy 'bell metal' used in the casting of this bronze reminds us that Verrocchio was responsible for bell-casting. Bells and cannons were the staple business of major foundries at this date.

The competition for the marble monument (strictly, a cenotaph) to Cardinal Niccolò Forteguerri in the Duomo of Pistoia commissioned by the city's town council is discussed on page 150. It is not clear how commonly sculptors in the fifteenth century made three-dimensional *modelli* – small-scale clay models – as distinct from drawings, for presentation or competition. In any case this work, which must be the *modello* submitted by Verrocchio in 1476, is one of very few works of its kind to survive from this period. Perhaps such works were not usually fired and were thus vulnerable to damage. The conception of the monument is highly original, especially for the treatment of the effigy of the deceased – animated and kneeling rather than recumbent and in repose. Butterfield speculates that conventions may have been more easily ignored in a cenotaph than in a tomb, and in Pistoia as distinct from Florence. It is surely also the case that the sculpture is radically influenced by pictorial conventions. Below the four angels supporting Christ's mandorla the three Theological Virtues, Faith, Charity and Hope (in that order), accompany Forteguerri as he prays, as if they too were spiritual supporters. Such a vivid embodiment of virtues was unprecedented in sculpture: allegorical elements of this kind had previously been confined to a separate zone, usually below a tomb chest.

The marble sculpture (fig. 96) was not complete at the time of Verrocchio's death and, as is discussed in the introduction to this section, his heir Lorenzo di Credi took over responsibility for the work, renegotiating the contract in 1488 and supplying the completed work in 1493 (it was, however, further modified in 1514 and again in the eighteenth century). The marble figure of Christ is widely accepted as by Verrocchio. The head is certainly of very high quality, but the rest of the figure is both less impressive and less characteristic, although well carved. The strong and simple design of the drapery in the clay model, with clear folds between the legs of Christ, is replaced in the marble with a complex but somehow puffy and inarticulate pattern (a development of Verrocchio's style much favoured by Lorenzo di Credi). Faith has a far more urgent motion in the clay model. Her rigid pose in the marble is concealed by more elaborate drapery. In the clay model, figure and drapery respond to each other. The marble angels are poorly carved with none of the lively movement seen in the clay. Furthermore, there is a drama in the relationships of every part which is absent from the finished work. There is some connection between the angels in this *modello* and those in the two finished terracotta reliefs in the Louvre (see cat. nos. 14 and 15 here). The walnut frame may date from the later sixteenth century and the large cherub (in fact modelled in wax) supporting the plinth upon which the Cardinal kneels was perhaps made at the same time.

13

ANDREA DEL VERROCCHIO

Modello for the monument to Cardinal Forteguerri

Terracotta with some repairs in wax
(notably the Cardinal's hands) and plaster
(e.g. the heads of Faith, Hope and the Cardinal),
39.4 × 26.7 cm
London, Victoria and Albert Museum, 7599–1861

Passavant 1969, cat. no. 9, pp. 179–80; Butterfield 1997, pp. 137–54, 233–8.

NP

Fig. 96 ANDREA DEL VERROCCHIO AND WORKSHOP, *Monument to Cardinal Niccolò Forteguerri*, 1478–93. Marble. Pistoia, Cathedral of San Jacopo.

14 and 15

WORKSHOP OF ANDREA DEL VERROCCHIO

Two angels

Reliefs of ruddy orange-coloured terracotta (irregular shapes), minor losses at corners, 36.5 × 32.8 (angel facing right) and 37 × 34 cm
Paris, Musée du Louvre, Département des Arts Graphiques, Inv. Th. 33 and 34

Passavant 1969, pp. 184–5, cat. no. 14; Seymour 1971, pp. 125, 169; Gaborit in *Léonard de Vinci* 1989, pp. 104; Butterfield 1997, pp. 228–9.

NP

Relief sculpture in fifteenth-century Florence is often assembled from separately fired pieces of irregular shape (this is true of Verrocchio's *Resurrection* relief in the Bargello, Florence (fig. 18), also of numerous works by Luca della Robbia). These two angels, which are among the most beautiful and perfectly finished terracottas of the fifteenth century, must be parts of the same relief. They are unmistakably close to Verrocchio in style and they have been associated for over a century with the Forteguerri monument (cat. no. 13). But it is hard to see why anything so finished would have been required in the preparations for that sculpture and as Gaborit has observed, 'the only certain thing would seem to be that in the complete composition these two angels surrounded a central figure (Christ? Virgin? Magdalen?) placed in a mandorla or circle.' In a forthcoming article he argues for the Magdalen, interpreting the lines by the angels' hands as her long hair.

The undercutting of the nearer arms is remarkable; so too is the deep cutting of the folds of drapery behind the legs of the second angel (with raised right arm). The second angel's near wing may have been separately modelled and applied before firing. If the meticulous virtuosity of the second angel is more remarkable, then the first is bolder in modelling, clearer in outline and articulation, and has more plasticity in the handling of the hair. Many scholars have felt that the angels are the work of different artists. The second one may have been modelled by a talented pupil with more experience in two-dimensional work: Leonardo has, not absurdly, been proposed as this artist.

157

16

LORENZO DI CREDI

Angel and other studies

Metalpoint, pen and brown ink and white
heightening on pink prepared paper,
24.3 × 18.2 cm
London, British Museum, Department of Prints
and Drawings, 1860-6-16-29

Popham and Pouncey 1950, cat. no. 45, pp. 28–9,
vol. 2, pl. XLI; Dalli Regoli 1966, cat. no. 4, p. 101,
figs. 1–2 (figs. 50, 51 for the paintings in the
Huntington Art Gallery and at Esztergom);
Butterfield 1997, p. 150.

PLR

By the time of Verrocchio's death in June 1488 seven of the statues for the Forteguerri cenotaph had been completed in the workshop: Christ, four angels, and the figures of Faith and Hope. Five years earlier the monument had been described to the authorities, probably optimistically, as in good part finished. Work on this commission, still unfinished at his death, dated from 1476 when Verrocchio submitted his model, and spanned the last twelve years of his career. The prolonged process of execution, most likely caused by delays in payment and doubtless frustrating to both Verrocchio and his patrons, was apparently fruitful in the creative life of the shop. The Louvre terracotta angels develop ideas from the design into finished works (cat. nos. 14 and 15). Here, Lorenzo di Credi examined the pose of the angel holding the mandorla at the top right (fig. 96). The study is based on the sculpted figure, not the draft version (cat. no. 13). Like the statue, it has a downturned glance and extended left arm. In a manner similar to the Louvre terracottas, Credi has shown the windblown drapery in greater detail than in the sketch model, bringing out the swirling patterns which both describe the force of the movement and decorate the form. He has used white heightening to imitate the glistening reflections of light hitting the surface of marble. The effect in the drawing is to evoke both a substantial presence and the splendour of the heavenly being.

The study is not a simple copy. Credi referred to two sources as he worked on the drawing – the sculpted prototype and a model. The statue supplied all of the basic elements of the pose, but Credi made some adjustments to the position as he placed the figure on the page. The angel in the drawing lacks wings, and the tunic over the torso looks more like a shirt with rolled sleeves than the fancy costume of the sculpture. This part of the figure may have been studied from life. The task for Credi, as for Verrocchio, was to make an effortful gesture (supporting the mandorla) look convincing and effortless. The pose also presented the problem of showing a figure who turns downward while rising upward, with a torsion typical of Verrocchio's spatial sensibility. As Credi concentrated on the components of the pose – legs, waist, torso – the whole became awkwardly distorted. To the right he drew the underlying body from a model. The drapery study resembles the swag of fabric across Christ's lap in the monument, but is not exactly the same as any drapery passage in the sketch or the cenotaph. It may record an intermediate phase of design, or, like the Louvre angels, it may be an interpretative study rather than a faithful copy. Variants of the Forteguerri angels occur in later paintings by Credi: a *Saint in Glory* in the Huntington Art Gallery in Pasadena, California, and the *Elevation of Mary Magdalene* in the museum at Esztergom in Hungary. One aspect of the novelty of Verrocchio's design was its pictorial quality. This drawing demonstrates how the exchange between painting and sculpture was continuous in his shop.

17

ANDREA DEL VERROCCHIO

Bust of Giuliano de' Medici

Terracotta covered with red-brown pigment and wax,
61 cm high, 66 cm wide at bottom of arms,
28.3 cm deep
Washington, DC, National Gallery of Art,
Andrew W. Mellon Collection 1937.1.127

Seymour 1949, p. 179; Pope-Hennessy 1958, p. 62;
Pliny the Elder, trans. Rackham 1968, Book 35,
chapter 2, lines 6-8, pp. 264–5; Passavant 1969,
pp. 40 and 119; Seymour 1971, pp. 123 and 167;
Adorno 1991, pp. 137–9; Butterfield 1997,
pp. 239–40.

I should like to thank Alison Luchs of the
National Gallery of Art, Washington, for sharing
her knowledge of the sculpture with us.

AW

Fig. 97 ANTONIO DEL POLLAIUOLO, *Bust of a warrior*,
*c.*1470. Painted terracotta, height 50 cm. Florence,
Museo Nazionale del Bargello.

This impressive, over-life-size portrait bust is highly worked at the front and sides but largely unmodelled on top of the head and at the back. Part of the decorative detailing of the armour is incomplete. To some this has suggested that the bust was a model for a work to be completed in marble. But it might equally imply that it was designed for a position where closer views were restricted, perhaps above an architectural feature. In his *Natural History* Pliny praised the ancient custom of setting up three-dimensional portrait images, sometimes made of clay and wax, above doors in domestic settings in order that worthy ancestors should be remembered and made to serve as virtuous examples to future generations. The use of terracotta could thus have carried an appropriately antique association and had the advantage of allowing for the forms to be moulded and altered. Indeed it is possible that Verrocchio as head of the workshop added refinements to an object that was seen through its early stages by assistants. There are areas of damage on the face and bust, though nothing as radical as the loss of the arms suffered by Antonio del Pollaiuolo's comparable bust of a young warrior in the Bargello (fig. 97). The armour may have been gilded or silvered and drill holes at the base of the arms suggest lost metal attachments.

The identity of the sitter has been established by comparison with other portraits of Giuliano, such as that by Botticelli (cat. no. 1). The subject looks younger and fuller featured in the sculpture and it is usually presumed that the bust was made during Giuliano's lifetime. Since he is shown wearing a type of decorative non-functional armour related to those worn at pageants, the bust could have been made around the time of his joust in 1475, when Giuliano was 22 years old. The bust is not mentioned in the list of Medici commissions for which Verrocchio had never been fully recompensed, but he is recorded there as having made the standard for Giuliano's joust. The stylistic arguments for an attribution to Verrocchio are compelling. Giuliano's curly hair provided an opportunity to work the clay into heaps of heavy locks, like those lovingly described in the bronze figure of Saint Thomas for Orsanmichele (fig. 29). The cuirass, perhaps a response to the use of *all'antica* armour for Mino da Fiesole's bust of Giuliano's uncle, Giovanni de' Medici, supports a wealth of relief-modelled detail of a kind found elsewhere in Verrocchio's oeuvre. In particular, the magnificent screaming head at its centre can be compared to the howling warrior in the terracotta relief of the *Resurrection* from the Medici villa at Careggi (fig. 18). Like the head of Medusa that appeared on Giuliano's pageant shield, the winged head, which is apparently a Fury, is meant to arrest the viewer's gaze. The animation of the sitter himself is necessarily restrained. He appears nobly upright in bearing and decorously detached, perhaps smiling slightly as he looks out beyond the spectator. The screaming head thus forms a deliberately enlivening counterpoint and makes the claim that this serene youth has the fierce spirit of a formidable warrior. Such a juxtaposition of beautiful youth and ferocious maturity, beloved of Leonardo, was a theme explored in Verrocchio's relief heads of Darius and Alexander given to Matthias Corvinus. In making this bust of Lorenzo de' Medici's younger brother, Verrocchio brings together his knowledge of ancient busts, like those in Lorenzo's collection that he apparently helped to prepare for display, with a sense for decorative naturalism and invention that recalls Pollaiuolo's work in the same genre. This special category of portrait, evoking antique and chivalric ideals of behaviour, can be associated with the ethos of patrician jousts. Like the 1475 *giostra* which gave Giuliano his public face, the commissioning of such a bust serves to remind us of his important representative value within a family in which he wielded little real power.

Sculptures of nude figures had seldom been fashioned since antiquity and this high relief in terracotta of a sleeping youth seems to be breaking new ground. The reclining figure is recurrent in images from the Verrocchio shop, where sculptural models for studying the limb formations of, for example, the reclining baby were used as workshop tools. The Berlin sculpture seems too large, too highly finished from the front and too incomplete from the back to have served as an ideal model. But its exemplary qualities are undeniable. The insistent modelling of the clay shows Verrocchio as a master of the medium, contrasting effects of pliant flesh and resistant bone and catching subtle nuances of light upon its surface. The treatment of the repertoire of beautiful forms in the reclining head is closely comparable to that of female heads produced in the Verrocchio shop (cat. nos. 29 and 31), playing on the graceful curves of the lips and eyelids and the fall of ringlets over the neck. Here the male body is displayed both as an anatomical and as an aesthetic *tour de force*, focusing attention on the smooth surfaces of the skin, the heavy musculature of the torso and limbs, and the poised articulation of the wrists and ankles. Indeed a strong tension is set up between the figure's ostensible passivity and vulnerability as a nude youth sleeping, totally off guard, and the innate vitality and virility of the pose. The muscles and joints are treated as though the figure were strained in movement (seen from the feet the pose is comparable to one of Pollaiuolo's dancing figures from the Lanfredini villa; fig. 46). Renaissance art theory required that movements of the body reflected those of the mind, but Verrocchio's figure presents a disjunction between the unconsciousness of the dormant features and the consciousness of the body. It is perhaps not so much the figure's state of mind that is at issue in this work, as that of the viewing subject. The poetic conceit of this sculpture, as also in Verrocchio's drawing of a sleeping nymph surprised by Cupid (fig. 14), seems to be that the youth, in his sleeping state, is unaware of the viewer's gaze. This fact renders the act of viewing illicit, sensual and hence, as the Cupid in the nymph drawing makes clear, erotically charged. The figure may represent Endymion, condemned to sleep by Jupiter in return for perpetual youth, or even a figure from contemporary lyric poetry, but the lack of attributes makes any precise identification speculative. In practice, the total nakedness of a figure appearing outside an explanatory narrative could only be sanctioned at this early period by the emergent notion of the object as 'art' and the illustrious precedent of antique figures. Statuettes and reliefs which exalted the heroic male nude were eagerly collected and Verrocchio's sculpture seems to be catering to this connoisseurial taste, using a material that also had antique connotations. Descendants of this type of figure include an antique-style bronze ink stand of a sleeping nymph reclining on rocks (private collection, ex Daniel Katz Ltd) and a late fifteenth-century marble sculpture by Adriano Fiorentino. In the latter a male nude sleeping figure is juxtaposed with *vanitas* and bacchic symbols (a skull, a goat, a vine) that suggest a meditation on sleep, drunkenness and death and allow the work to be read didactically. The success of terracotta sculptures for the domestic setting can be gauged from the number of high reliefs on subjects such as the Penitent Saint Jerome and the Magdalen attributed to Verrocchio and his shop, which probably post-date the Berlin example. However the character of these ascetic subjects as exemplars could have made them appropriate decoration for more public *camere*. The specialised appeal of Verrocchio's sleeping youth may rather suggest a one-off commission from one of Verrocchio's admirers. If Verrocchio's sculpture was intended for a collector's study, the nude youth's viewer would inevitably be construed as male.

18

ANDREA DEL VERROCCHIO

Sleeping youth

Terracotta,
36 × 58 cm
Berlin, Staatliche Museen Preussischer Kulturbesitz-Skulpturensammlung, no. 112

The sculpture is not hollowed out at the back and is too solid to have required an armature. Cracks are visible in the base to either side of the knee, in the figure's left arm above the elbow and through the top of the testicles.

Leithe-Jasper 1981, p. 3190, Draper 1992, pp. 50–1 and fig. 17 (for the Adriano Fiorentino sculpture); Butterfield 1997, p. 151; Thornton 1997, fig. 95, p. 151 (for the sleeping nymph).

A W

Like the Louvre *Saint John the Baptist* (cat. no. 20), this is a working drawing which can be situated at the heart of Verrocchio's workshop and its activities. The side shown here is prepared, and was drawn in the first instance, in metalpoint. The central subject is the figure of Saint Donatus, seen much as he appears in the Pistoia altarpiece (the fingers of his right hand are more open and the top of his crosier, added faintly, is lower and closer to his head than in the painting; fig. 70). Surrounding him are four studies of a youth and one of an old man, all in metalpoint. Contrasting ages and characters also occur on the other side of the sheet, drawn in pen and ink (fig. 98). The reverse has some fragmentary verses and notes in a handwriting that can be compared with Verrocchio's as known from his tax return and from notes on a drawing of a horse in the Metropolitan Museum, New York. The deft and spirited use of pen on this sheet also compares with that seen on the Louvre drawing of infants (cat. no. 36). As in the Louvre drawing, Verrocchio used his paper economically and efficiently, turning the sheet as he changed his subject. In this case it allowed him to consider pairs of strolling couples, a Darius-type warrior, and a gaunt head reminiscent of a Roman portrait bust. The latter also recalls the ascetic features of Saint Jerome, of a sort popular in Florence at the time, as well as the aged faces of Donato de' Medici, the patron of the altarpiece, and of his name saint Donatus. Verrocchio seems to have been reflecting on how to render age with dignity and character, and how to mediate between portraiture (as of Donato de' Medici) and type (as in Saint Donatus).

Whereas delineation is the concern of the pen and ink studies, description of form is the issue on the prepared side of the sheet. Saint Donatus has been delicately and fully drawn in stylus to confirm the pose (which must have been studied previously) and the composition and structure of the drapery. Once these were established, pen and ink and wash and white heightening were used to study the range of tones and textures that would occur in the painting. The saint, at this stage, has the softened features and rather flaccid hands of Saint Donatus in the altarpiece and in the predella scene of *Saint Donatus and the Tax Collector* (in the Worcester Art Museum, Worcester, Mass.), both attributed to Lorenzo di Credi, which suggests that he was responsible for this painterly phase of the design process.

19

ANDREA DEL VERROCCHIO AND
LORENZO DI CREDI

Saint Donatus and studies of heads

Metalpoint with white heightening (partly oxidised), pen and brown ink, brown wash, on pink prepared paper,
28.5 × 20.1 cm
Edinburgh, National Gallery of Scotland,
inv. D642 recto

Dalli Regoli 1966, cat. no. 14, p. 106 (as retouched and difficult to judge, probably a copy); Andrews 1968, vol. 1, pp. 43–4 (Saint Donatus by Credi, gone over in a later hand); Ames-Lewis and Wright, exh. cat., Nottingham and London 1983, cat. no. 6, pp. 66–9 (Verrocchio workshop); Cadogan 1983, pp. 383–8 (as by Verrocchio); MacAndrew, exh. cat., Washington 1990, cat. no. 3, pp. 26–7 (as by Verrocchio, reworked in pen and ink by a later hand); Padoa Rizzo, in ed. Falletti 1996, p. 71 (as from the shop of Agnolo di Donnino del Mazziere); Kemp 1998, p. 25 and p. 34, note 6 (metalpoint underdrawing possibly by Verrocchio).

PLR

Fig. 98 Verso of cat. no. 19.

166

This drawing of Saint John the Baptist for the Pistoia altarpiece (fig. 70) shows how Lorenzo di Credi, entrusted with the execution of the painting, also participated in its planning. A documented drawing for the altar by Verrocchio is now lost. As the commissioned artist Verrocchio was responsible for the design of the painting, the guarantee of its quality and its recognisable character as a Verrocchio product. The early stages of invention must have been his. This elaborate drawing indicates that Andrea was able to delegate parts of the later preparatory phases to his assistant.

The *Saint John*, awkward and even unappealing if viewed as a work of art, is actually an excellent example of a working drawing where both problems and solutions are evident. It is also a laboured drawing, built up in layers of different media, pondered and painterly in a fashion typical of Credi.

There are three major areas of concern here: the definition of the Baptist's drapery, the general modelling of the form in light, and the position of the Baptist's legs. His pose fits into the overall scheme, or drama, of the altarpiece and the chapel in its original arrangement. In the painting the Baptist moves forward towards the viewer, Saint Donatus (the intercessor and name saint of the oratory's patron) has a meditative gaze directed to meet that of the supplicant funerary bust of Donato de' Medici, which was placed on an adjacent wall. The infant Christ leans towards the cross held by the Baptist, innocently and poignantly yearning for the sign of his sacrifice. Saint John's body is angled to point at once inwards towards Christ and outwards to the chapel with an expressively sculptural possession of space characteristic of Verrocchio. Credi must have had a separate drawing by Verrocchio which he consulted as he lightly sketched in the basic forms in metalpoint on this sheet. The disjointed result of such copying is similar to that seen in the angel based on the Forteguerri monument (cat. no. 16). The underdrawing lacks unity and anatomical force, but composing the figure was not the primary task here. Instead Credi concentrated on studying the modelling of the drapery in detail, which he did by laying in areas of shadow with fine metalpoint hatching and then brushing in white highlights, finishing with pen and ink and wash to add the deepest and largest areas of shadow.

Credi also corrected his first draft of the legs better to suggest forward movement and to provide a more stable base for that motion. Drawings of this sort allowed both Verrocchio and Credi to gauge the effect of the figure as it would be painted and to make adjustments accordingly. The illumination of the Baptist in the painting is similar to the drawing, but the drapery was simplified to emphasise his prophetic gesture.

20

LORENZO DI CREDI

Saint John the Baptist

Metalpoint with white heightening, pen and brown ink and grey wash on pink prepared paper; laid down,
27.5 × 13 cm (entire sheet),
26 × 10 cm (original surface)
Paris, Musée du Louvre, Département des Arts Graphiques, inv. 455

Dalli Regoli 1966, pp. 15–16, cat. no. 13, pp. 105–6 (as by Credi); Passavant 1969, pp. 57–8 (as sketched in by Verrocchio and finished by Credi); *Léonard de Vinci. Les études de draperie*, exh. cat. 1989, cat. no. 22, pp. 88–9 (as by Credi); Bartoli in *Il Disegno fiorentino*, exh. cat., Florence 1992, cat. no. 2.30, pp. 74–5 (as by Credi); Brown 1998, pp. 153–4 (discussed with relation to a drawing of the Baptist by Leonardo da Vinci in Windsor); Kemp 1998, p. 33, note 6 (as wholly by Verrocchio).

PLR

21

WORKSHOP OF VERROCCHIO

Tobias and the Angel

Egg tempera on poplar,
84.4 × 66.2 cm
London, National Gallery, NG 781

The panel appears to have been cut, or at least
shaved, on both sides, but the original painted
surface stops with a broken line within all the edges
and approximately 3.5 cm short of either side.
The strips of old repainting reproduce the original
composition.

Suida 1954, pp. 317–18; Davies 1961, pp. 555–7;
Passavant 1969, p. 188, cat. no. 19; Brown 1998,
pp. 47–56.

NP

The subject of Tobias and the Angel enjoyed great popularity in Florentine painting, presumably because of the cult of the Archangel Raphael (venerated as Saint Raphael), which was promoted by the confraternities dedicated to him. In addition to altarpieces, in which he was included with the other archangels or saints, by Piero del Pollaiuolo, Botticini and Neri di Bicci, there are numerous separate panels of approximately this format including, for example, one by Filippino Lippi in the National Gallery of Art, Washington, but also many by lesser artists. Raphael and Tobias also appear in the background of Florentine paintings of the Virgin and Child (for example the panel attributed to Botticini in the Cleveland Museum of Art and Lorenzo di Credi's *Virgin and Child* in the National Gallery; NG 593).

Some of the separate panels of Tobias and Raphael may have hung as votive offerings in churches but others were presumably used for domestic devotion. They always show Raphael escorting Tobias, who was sent by his father to collect a debt (*Ricordo* is written here on the small scroll in the boy's hand) – the sort of errand with which many young Florentine apprentices were familiar. The fish held by the boy was the one he caught in the river Tigris on Raphael's bidding and from which the heart, liver and gall were extracted at the angel's instruction to heal the boy's father's blindness (a red line here shows that the fish has been gutted). Raphael was invoked as a protector of travellers and as a healer.

This painting is one of the most puzzling as well as one of the most engaging productions of Verrocchio's workshop. The invention seems as unequal as the execution. The movement and torsion of Raphael are sophisticated, whereas the pose of Tobias is entirely conventional. The heads are worthy of the sculptor of the bronze *David* but the hands are stock, each one repeated, and none originally designed to perform the task given to it. The landscape with its cylindrical towers and bun-like rocks is naive in conception as well as perfunctory in execution, but the dog has a spring in its step and a ripple in its coat found in no other canine of the period and the fish appears from the beautiful observation of light on the scales to be painted, rather than merely drawn, from life. Both dog and fish were added relatively late and the painting below now shows through (especially in the case of the dog). The claim first made by Suida that parts of the painting are the work of the very young Leonardo is attractive and plausible – more so than the idea that the rest of the picture or even most of it was painted by Verrocchio – but it can only remain hypothesis. The claim has recently been revived and elaborated by Brown with minute analysis of the dog, the fish and certain passages in the hair and fabric. As Brown notes, the rendering of light on the sleeves and hair of Tobias is different from that on the equivalent parts of the angel. This is true too of the boy's face where white is used not only for the eye but for the light around it.

Some incised lines can be seen indicating the angel's legs below the drapery and the boy's cloak (the folds of which are not all followed at the painting stage).

22

ANDREA DEL VERROCCHIO

Head of an angel

Black chalk, pen and brown ink
on paper, pricked, laid down,
21 × 18.1 cm
Florence, Galleria degli Uffizi,
Gabinetto Disegni e Stampe, inv. 130E

Cruttwell 1904, pp. 46–7, 230; Berenson 1938, vol. 1,
p. 47, vol. 2, cat. no. 2781, p. 359, vol. 3, fig. 124;
Passavant 1969, pp. 56–7, cat. no. D7, p. 191;
Petrioli Tofani in Tempesti 1973, cat. no. 14; Petrioli
Tofani 1991, p. 95 (for an illustration of the verso
of cat. no. 35, Uffizi 212FV); Brown 1998, pp. 30–1,
p. 182, notes 33-5.

PLR

This drawing has been associated with the boyish angel in the San Salvi *Baptism* who gazes raptly at the angel painted by Leonardo (fig. 74). The shapes in black chalk at the lower right and rising above the head at the top left in the drawing are probably part of wings (that at the top is pricked along its right edge) and identify the figure as an angel. The face in the drawing has the same overall broad shape as the face in the painting and they have similar features: deep, round eye-sockets, a snub nose, bow-shaped lips, a narrow chin and tightly curled hair. The volumetric three-quarter turn of the head is the same in both, as is the way that the curve of the figure's right eyebrow forms a continuous contour with the outline of the forehead and cheek. In both painting and drawing the surface of the skin is luminous. But the angel in the drawing looks resolutely downwards in meditation. Its glance is the opposite of that of the angel in the painting (who has no wings). The head is also larger. While these factors exclude it from having been a cartoon for the figure as painted, the drawing can still be included in its development either as a rejected, but influential, early stage or as a model for the facial type. The pricked outlines could as easily have been used to transfer the drawing to another sheet for study and adaptation as to the panel.

The study has a comparable, indirect, relation to the angel in the painting of *Tobias and the Angel* in the National Gallery (cat. no. 21). In this case the expression and position of the heads are alike, but they are shown in reversed directions. The angel's neck in the painting is proportionally longer, its curly hair more compact and its features more pinched. The head in the drawing is nearly life-size and about one-third larger than the angel's head in the painting. It was not a cartoon for this composition, but it could have provided the starting point in its design.

The drawing's long life in the studio helps to explain its battered condition. There is a weak copy of this head, in metalpoint, on the recto of cat. no. 35, which looks like a student's exercise undertaken to memorise the type and demonstrates another function of such patterns.

The drawing is multi-layered, with black chalk applied in different stages, followed by pen and ink. Verrocchio fully exploited the tonal range of the chalk. He worked lightly on the preliminary design and then pressed down to strengthen some of the outlines (the chin and neck, for example). He also employed a heavier line to describe the full locks of hair, enhancing both their decorative and volumetric effect. He smudged and stumped the chalk to make smooth surfaces of flesh on the angel's face. Whether applied in the first drawing session or somewhat later to reinforce areas worn down by rubbing, the subsequent pen lines became integral to the modelling system, adding depth to the shadows. Verrocchio let the untouched paper act as the lit or highlighted form, rather than adding lights by applying white. He used the ink hatching to strengthen the shading of the cheek and neck and deepen the contrasts that shape the brow, nose and jaw. The description of light through juxtaposed areas of colour (rather than blended tones) was the traditional way of modelling in tempera painting, and it seems to be adapted to drawing here. This is compatible with dating the drawing to the same period as the first phase of work on the San Salvi *Baptism*. The concern for the way that the passage of light modulated the appearance of the surface relates instead to Verrocchio's sensibilities as a sculptor and is a constant and characteristic feature of his paintings and drawings.

171

This painting is, with the exception of the San Salvi *Baptism*, the most finely executed of all the devotional paintings associated with Verrocchio's workshop – and probably the best preserved (although some old repaints on the cheek of the Virgin have discoloured). In it, rare and beautiful parts and possessions – fine golden hair, cloth of gold, perfectly curved lips and turned hands, intricate jewels – are rendered with dazzling skill. Only the conventional parted curtains are less well painted – the borders seem not to have been studied from real fur and the brocade pattern (identical on each side and so taken from the same cartoon) is not really distorted by the folds. The fact that (unusually for a work of this kind) the light falls from the right may suggest that it was painted for a specific location or that it was executed by a left-handed artist. Charles Holmes noted that 'the handling of the landscape has a very close resemblance to Leonardo's first dated drawing. It is permissible to think therefore that Leonardo may have helped, not only with this background, but also with the exquisite finish of the figures.' Holmes presumably had in mind the brisk segmental curves with which the trees are rendered, as well as the rock forms and aerial perspective on the right (fig. 73) The hill on the left and the rock on the right seem devised to mask the sudden transition between foreground and distance and the upper part of the rock was clearly an afterthought painted on top of the landscape behind.

The painting has also been attributed to the youthful Perugino. This would seem possible only if Perugino employed drawings by others, for it has none of the idiosyncratic physiognomy and formal preferences which we find in all his documented paintings. It is of interest that the heads, hands and lily (see cat. no. 24) are the same size as that favoured for the most finished drawings made by Verrocchio and his workshop. That separate drawings were utilised for different parts seems likely given the disjointed composition: the angel on the right has no real place in space and the Child is inadequately supported, his head is awkwardly close to that of one angel and his feet oddly close to the other angel's elbow. It is clear from Verrocchio's own drawings (see cat. no. 34) and from his bust sculpture (for example fig. 67) that he had a fine grasp of the structure of the body such as is absent in the Virgin here, and obvious from his terracotta relief of the Virgin and Child (in the Bargello Museum, Florence; fig. 69) that he had a feeling for organic composition which this compilation lacks. Although it has been said that the panel has been cut down this seems not to be the case, but the cropping of the angel on the right especially is uncomfortable. This angel is in not integrated in a narrative sense. It may be argued that Verrocchio, whose sculpture exhibits a more sophisticated interest in narrative than any other artist of his time, neglected this interest here, but it is surely easier to question whether he did make this painting – although it is impossible to doubt that he authorised it and assisted in its preparation.

23
WORKSHOP OF VERROCCHIO

The Virgin and Child with Two Angels

Egg tempera on wood,
97 × 71 cm
London, National Gallery, NG 296

Holmes 1923, pp. 60–1; Ragghianti 1935, p. 196, note 1; Davies 1961, pp. 554–5; Camesasca 1969, p. 86; Passavant 1969, pp. 209–10 (App. 38).

NP

24

LEONARDO DA VINCI

Lily

Metalpoint, black and yellow chalk, pen and
brown ink on paper, two shades of ochre wash,
white heightening, pricked,
31.4 × 17.7 cm
Windsor, Royal Library, The Royal Collection, 12418

Clark 1969, vol. 1, p. 65, vol. 2 (pl.); Kemp 1981, p. 53
(for the 1482 inventory); *Leonardo da Vinci*, exh. cat.,
Hayward Gallery, London 1989, cat. no. 42, p. 101;
Tongiorgi Tomasi in *Il Disegno fiorentino*, exh. cat.,
Florence 1992, cat. no. 9.3, pp. 182–3; Popham,
ed. Kemp 1994, pp. 74–5, 153, no. 254; Brown 1998,
p. 88.

PLR

Fig. 99 Detail of cat. no. 23.

The lily is a spectacular flower. It is also a powerful symbol, standing for purity and for the Virgin. As held by the angel to the left in the National Gallery *Virgin and Child with Two Angels* (cat. no. 23) it is a reminder of her special virtue and its heavenly source. The lily is never incidental in Renaissance religious painting. 'Many flowers copied from nature' are the first items in Leonardo's 1482 note of his works. Although this flower is based on close observation, the purpose of the drawing was not to represent a botanical specimen but to give a pictured lily a pleasing composition and a convincing physical presence. Numerous changes in the black chalk underdrawing show that Leonardo designed the lily even as he copied its natural traits. The most conspicuous change is the fully detailed bud at the right which Leonardo covered over with the yellow ground when he began to model the rest. But there are many other shifts and alterations throughout as Leonardo moved the flowers and leaves up and down the stem in his preliminary sketching in black chalk. The pictorial aims of the drawing are confirmed by the use of coloured washes and white for modelling; its functional aspect is indicated by the fact that it is both squared for enlargement and mostly pricked for transfer (the closed buds at the top are not pricked).

This lily can be compared to the one in cat. no. 23, and it could have been its model, but not its cartoon. They are close in size, but the position and number of flowers and buds is different and they are turned at different angles. The drawing is lit from the left, whereas the painting is lit from the top right. Nor was it the cartoon for the lily in Leonardo's *Annunciation* (fig. 72). It is different in form, position and size, and in the general approach to describing the flower, which in the painting looks as though it has been ruffled by the wind of the angel's eager arrival. The lily in the drawing has, by contrast, a fleshy solidity. The moving and varied pen and ink outline gives the flower a vivid sense of energy, while simultaneously enhancing its decorative effect. This combination of solidity and ornament corresponds to Verrocchio's sensibility. The perspective exercises, done in stylus with the sheet turned on its side, also correspond to Verrocchio's as much as Leonardo's interests. As a workshop product the study represents how well the young assistant's talents could serve his master's aims. As a preparatory drawing it may have been made for a now lost composition, but like other finished drawings from Verrocchio's studio, it could also have had recurrent use as a reference sheet. In this case, the drawing offered detailed information about how to depict the reality and evoke the divinity of a highly charged symbolic form.

175

The image of the kneeling Virgin had been familiar in devotional painting in Florence for nearly a century before 1470, but the ruined architectural setting here is more ambitious than usual and it has been suggested that it represents the Temple of Peace in Rome (the great structure we now identify as the Basilica of Maxentius) which, according to legend, crumbled when Christ was born. Ruins are of course often included in paintings of the Nativity – the stable itself commonly being constructed out of one. But sometimes the emphasis on rubble does suggest that this legend was in the artist's mind – a *Nativity* by Botticini in the Museum of Fine Art, Montreal (1956.1154), is one example in which the Holy Family resemble earthquake survivors. In the Edinburgh painting an actual topographical reference to this Temple has been proposed. There is a resemblance in plan and elevation but not detail; collapse was not recent since weeds have already grown up in the rubble. Some symbolism may rather be intended by the conjunction of Christ and a cornerstone of the building.

The painting, which has been associated with Verrocchio since its acquisition by John Ruskin more than a century ago, is distinguished among the half-dozen paintings of high quality widely acknowledged as products of his workshop both by its attention to pictorial space (linear and aerial perspective) and by its coherence of composition (the receding diagonals of the architecture are cleverly related to the tilt of the Virgin's head and the lines of her wrists). There is some resemblance to Verrocchio's altarpiece for the Duomo of Pistoia, largely executed by Lorenzo di Credi (fig. 70). In both the Virgin is framed by fluted Corinthian pilasters of similar size, but in the Edinburgh picture they are much farther behind and the paving (representing about ten feet in depth in the altarpiece) recedes far into the distance. The depiction of the foreshortened walls is a virtuoso *tour de force* comparable with that in Leonardo da Vinci's *Adoration* (fig. 53); such exercises are not otherwise typical of Verrocchio's workshop.

The Virgin and Child are close in type and handling to those in the panel in Berlin (fig. 101) where the Child has a similarly tilted nose and bright blue eyes. The Virgin has finer features and tighter lips than Verrocchio preferred (to judge from his drawings). The young Domenico Ghirlandaio has been proposed as the artist by several distinguished scholars but no certain work by him has such intricacy of design or delicacy of detail.

The painting has been extensively retouched in losses along the original vertical joins in the wood. The legs of the Child and the drapery lower right are much damaged. The original texture of the painting was flattened by the process of transfer. The greens of the plants and the lining of the Virgin's cloak have darkened.

25

WORKSHOP OF VERROCCHIO

Virgin adoring the Infant Christ ('The Ruskin Madonna')

Egg tempera on canvas, transferred from wood, 106.7 × 76.3 cm
Edinburgh, National Gallery of Scotland, 2338

Brigstocke 1993, pp. 201–3, citing (for Ghirlandaio) Zeri and Fahy.

NP

26

LEONARDO DA VINCI

Drapery study for
a kneeling figure

Brush and grey brown ink,
white heightening, on linen,
28.3 × 19.3 cm
London, British Museum, Department of
Prints and Drawings, 1895-9-15-489

Berenson 1938, vol. 1, p. 60, vol. 2, cat. no. 1037A,
p. 114, vol. 3, fig. 561; Popham and Pouncey 1950, no.
95, pp. 56–7; Richter 1970, vol. 1, no. 132, p. 172 (for
the definitions of light and lustre); Cadogan 1983,
pp. 43–4 (attributed to Verrocchio); Popham, ed.
Kemp 1994, p. 12, p. 105, cat. no. 5; Royalton-Kisch
et al., exh. cat., London 1996, cat. no. 8, pp. 32–3.

PLR

Since the time of Giotto, Florentine painters had studied and depicted forms in terms of relief. Structure was analysed according to light and shadow. The resulting sense of solidity was inherently sculptural. The word, 'relief' or *rilievo*, is taken from the vocabulary of sculpture. Its use by Florentine artists (like Cennino Cennini in his manual on painting or Leonardo in his notebooks) is a sign of the interaction between the arts which was characteristic of Florence and which made the sculptor-painter a plausible figure there. Verrocchio's paintings add a further dimension to the observation of light. In his 'books on light and shade' Leonardo wrote 'of the difference between light and lustre', that is, between the illumination which shapes form and the gleaming light which is reflected from its surface. He learned this difference in Verrocchio's shop, where it was mastered through studies like this one.

By setting up plaster– or clay-dipped cloths and placing the fixed model in strong, but controlled, light, the problem of rendering fugitive effects could be carefully considered. The novel choice of brush on linen rather than metalpoint on prepared paper made it easier to create gradations in areas of shadow and to approximate the effects of painting. Although draughtsmen could achieve subtle shading by dense hatching using metalpoint, as in cat. nos. 8 and 40, this was probably more laborious than applying the dark tones with a brush. Wash is often used in addition to metalpoint in such studies, indicating that a non-linear medium was thought to have advantages in this context. Preparing the linen with a grey wash automatically increased the contrast with the white applied as highlight. The impression of depth is also increased because of the dark middle tone, which intensifies the illusion of recess. With this technique, employing grey and white, the draughtsman literally worked with dark and light. The dark areas were brushed in first, establishing volume through shadow, then dilute white was employed to describe the highest areas of relief and the sheen of the fabric. The edges of the turning folds were indicated with the point of the brush, charged with white. The sharply glimmering creases are like facets of a cut gem, seeming to reflect the light as it hits the protruding angles of the drapery.

The study was not done as an exercise in optics; it was a problem set for practical purposes. Like most of the meticulous drawings from Verrocchio's shop, it does not match a single extant painting, but it could have provided useful information for a number of them. The drapery is composed for a kneeling figure, presumably a Virgin adoring the infant Christ or an annunciate Virgin. And like so many of the works from Verrocchio's shop, its attribution has been debated. The sketched-in figure has her head turned against the central axis of the pose – a physical and psychological twist characteristic of Leonardo. The pronounced accents of the crooks and turns of the highlight can also be compared to the treatment of light in cat. no. 39. Yet the whole lacks the intensity of focus and the forceful sense of structure of that study. It is both more decorative and more even in the attention given to describing fold patterns. In this way it is more practical. Whether by Verrocchio, the young Leonardo or another assistant, this is a case where the individual hand was guided by the workshop's mentality – by Verrocchio's aims as he worked to make it possible to translate the three-dimensional forms he could fashion as a sculptor into the two dimensions of painting. It was by means of such studies (technical innovations in themselves) that stable forms and moving light were combined in a depicted subject, arriving at a fusion of the monumental with the momentary that is one of the defining features of Verrocchio's works in all media.

27

ATTRIBUTED TO
PIERMATTEO D'AMELIA

Virgin and Child

Original panel transferred to board,
84.7 × 64.5 cm
Frankfurt, Städelsches Kunstinstitut und Städtische
Gallerie, inv. 702

The painting surface has been enlarged by about
3.2 cm on all sides. The original surface measures
c.78 × 57.8 cm. The additions continue the incisions
of the architecture. They were probably made
when the original frame was removed at the time
the painting was prepared for sale in the early
nineteenth century.

I would like to thank Bodo Brinkmann and Rudolph
Hiller von Gaertringen for making available the
technical data regarding this painting.

Zeri 1953, pp. 136–7 (attributed to Piermatteo
d'Amelia – the Master of the Gardner
Annunciation); Passavant 1969, p. 208, App. no. 31
(attributed to Cosimo Rosselli); Grossman 1979,
pp. 101–25 (attributed to Ghirlandaio); *Italian
Renaissance Sculpture in the Time of Donatello*, exh. cat.
Detroit 1985, cat. no. 70, pp. 206–7, (for relief
sculptures); Gardner 1996, pp. 679–80; Holland
1997 (attributed to Piermatteo d'Amelia), p.
40, pl. 39.

PLR

The Virgin and Child at a parapet was one of Verrocchio's most popular compositions. In addition to painted variants, such as this one, there are versions in marble, stucco and terracotta (figs. 68 and 69). Copy drawings show that his workshop equipment included at least one statuette of the Christ Child standing with his right hand raised in blessing (cat. no. 42), which was probably itself in demand and replicated. The model for the figure was the Christ made by Desiderio da Settignano to crown the sacrament tabernacle at San Lorenzo (fig. 95). One reason for the success of Verrocchio's version might have been its reference to such a powerful, and charming, prototype. The Desiderio Christ, designed to be seen from below, stands on top of a eucharistic chalice and has his arm raised to shoulder level. In adapting the figure to his repertory, Verrocchio gave the Child a cushion as his perch and lowered the arm so that the gesture became more direct. The changes of pose and position created greater immediacy, which was suited to the likely function of most of these Virgin and Child images as domestic devotional works.

Among the unifying features of these compositions is the sculptural solidity of their parts, which appear as though assembled from studies and pattern drawings of hands, heads and drapery, as occurs here. Even the modelling of the Virgin's face in this example looks as if it were based on an established scheme and is comparable to the blocking out of light and shade in finished studies such as the angel's head from the Uffizi (cat. no. 22). Reliance on formulas is evident in inconsistencies of the depicted light, which sharply illuminates separate elements but lacks overall unity: the painter has not coped with the two implied light sources in a systematic fashion.

Although derived from a common model – probably a relief sculpture like that in the Bargello (fig. 68) – the surviving paintings are different in details and in essentials, such as their settings, size and style of execution. The Virgin's drapery here follows incised lines which mark out the sharp folds, but a number of changes in the underdrawing (visible in infra-red reflectographs) prove that it was not simply worked up from a standard stencil or cartoon. The Child's head was placed higher and towards the right: there are an eye and a nose drawn above the present eyes and nose. The right leg was also originally further to the right. X-rays show that the Virgin's left hand was once higher up and that it also had longer fingers. A base planned for the column or pilaster at left was abandoned, probably because it would have cluttered the ledge and crowded the cushion.

Like so many verrocchiesque works the authorship of this painting is an open question. It is presently attributed to Piermatteo d'Amelia (c.1450–1500), an Umbrian painter documented as a *garzone* or assistant of Fra Filippo Lippi at Spoleto between 1467 and 1469. It is possible, though not proven, that he came to Florence some time after Lippi died in October 1469 and did a stint in Verrocchio's shop. An altarpiece showing the *Annunciation*, now in the Isabella Stewart Gardner Museum in Boston and once the high altar of the Franciscan church of Amelia, has features in common with this painting which tend to confirm Piermatteo as its painter. There are resemblances in the facial type chosen for the Virgin, the pyramidal form containing her figure and the deliberate gestures and angular, heavy draperies. The Frankfurt *Virgin and Child* – a representative Verrocchio shop product – is equally representative as a project: the master allowed a reliable assistant, possibly Piermatteo, to get on with the job, which in this case was to reproduce a winning formula for a receptive market.

A substantial number of high-relief sculptures of the Virgin and Child have been connected with Verrocchio's workshop. Like the Madonna paintings, to which they are a three-dimensional counterpart, they are made by a number of different hands. They appear to represent a distinctive shop product that, in its range of materials — and thus, presumably, in its range of prices — responded flexibly to the thriving market for Madonna images. But in fact some of the reliefs in cheaper materials may have been produced outside the Verrocchio circle in imitation of his style. The example here seems to have been made by modelling the clay against a wooden board placed at an angle, with a narrow ledge at the bottom to support the weight of the clay. The carefully worked surface rivals the effect of marble in its smoothness of finish.

The relief has been attributed to Francesco di Simone on the basis of its stylistic similarity to figures on his tomb of Alessandro Tartagni in Bologna (1481–2). In his earlier career Francesco had adopted the sculptural style of Desiderio da Settignano, whose Virgin and Child compositions were important in establishing the rapport between mother and baby found in Verrocchio's designs but had less corporeal presence and plasticity. Comparing the Victoria and Albert relief with the remarkable painted terracotta *Virgin and Child* from Santa Maria Nuova (now Bargello, fig. 69) that is thought to be by Verrocchio's own hand, both this spatial boldness and the repertoire of compositional elements characteristic of the shop style can be recognised. The nearly free-standing Christ Child is presented to the devotee in an easy but authoritative pose with his hand raised in blessing, a pose that Francesco di Simone studied in many variations in his drawings (see cat. no. 42). The solicitous Virgin turns towards her son and steadies him with long, elegantly turned fingers. The protective mantle held around Christ's hips draws attention to the sacred character of his body while a second heavy swathe of drapery performs a more decorative function, falling in complex, crumpled patterns from the shoulder. The logic of this drapery, which in the Santa Maria Nuova relief spills out over the frame and stabilises a triangular composition, is not obvious in the London terracotta where the mantle seems to shift upwards before falling over the arm of the Virgin's stool. The apparent ambiguity results from the sculptor combining motifs designed for a standing Virgin who supports the Christ Child on a ledge (figs. 68 and 69 and cat. no. 27) with a seated Virgin of the type found in Verrocchio's paintings (fig. 101). The bunching of the cloth over the upper arm is especially reminiscent of Leonardo. The sculptor shows a command of the difficult three-quarter view of the Virgin's head beloved of Verrocchio, but the veil falling back over her ear is comparatively lifeless. Both conception and detail suggest that this is a relief designed, as well as executed, by a member of the shop.

28

ATTRIBUTED TO
FRANCESCO DI SIMONE

Virgin and Child

Terracotta relief,
81.9 × 62.6 cm
London, Victoria and Albert Museum, 7576-181

There are extensive losses to the original background, including the entire upper right and lower left corners, as well as to the right of the Virgin to just below her shoulder; these have been made up with a pink-tinted cement and the whole is backed on slate. The Virgin's right knee, Christ's feet and some of the Virgin's fingers supporting the feet have been replaced with painted plaster. There are numerous smaller restorations.

Cruttwell 1904, pp. 123–4; Pope-Hennessy 1964, I, pp. 172–3; Passavant 1969, p. 204 (as workshop of Antonio Rossellino).

A W

29

ANDREA DEL VERROCCHIO

Studies of a female head

Black and white chalk (recto), black chalk (verso),
31.8 × 26.5 cm
London, British Museum, Department of Prints
and Drawings, 1895-9-15-785, recto and verso

Popham and Pouncey 1950, cat. no. 258, pp. 160–1;
Pliny the Elder, trans. Rackham 1968, Book 35,
chaper 36, line 79, pp. 318–19; Passavant 1969, pp. 58,
192, cat. no. D5; Richter 1970, vol. 1, no. 583, p. 341;
Seymour 1971, cat. no. 5, pp. 28, 172, ; Royalton-Kisch
et al., exh. cat., London 1996, cat. no. 7, pp. 30–1;
Brown 1998, pp. 126–7.

PLR

Fig. 100 Detail of fig. no. 14.

In his precepts on painting, Leonardo wrote that 'women must be represented in modest attitudes … their heads inclined and somewhat on one side.' That such a demure tilt also expressed essential femininity for Verrocchio is demonstrated by the studies on this sheet.

The verso shows that Verrocchio was certain of the position of the head even in the preliminary stages of working on the drawing. On the basis of a light, schematic sketch, he blocked in dark areas for the eye-sockets, cheeks, lips and edge of the nose with broad hatching and smudging. He marked the features with stylised notation and confirmed major features with seemingly quick, heavy strokes, largely avoiding confining lines. Mass, not design, was his interest. He analysed the face in terms of shading in order to give the head convincing volume. The economy and apparent rapidity of the drawing in defining the shaded surfaces suggest that he was looking at a model, possibly sculpted. In any event, the way that shadow is roughed in betrays a sculptor's touch, as though Verrocchio approached the blank sheet like a solid surface. A slight sketch of a hand against the head is a key to the subject; it links the drawing to the study of the sleeping nymph in the Uffizi (fig. 100) and to the decorations for Giuliano de' Medici's 1475 joust.

The study on the recto confirms that this head was mythological or poetic in conception. The hairstyle of flowing locks and coiled braids fastened by a jewel was derived from the fantastic wigs of festive and festival figures. Leonardo made a note about the similarly elaborate braided hairstyle he designed for one of the descendants of this nymph, his figure of Leda (Windsor, Royal Library, 12515): 'this kind can be taken off and put on again without damaging it.' One purpose of Verrocchio's study was to

define the ornamental arrangement of the hair, at times working strand by curling strand, and in general rendering its weight, texture and substance with changing pressure on his chalk or chalks. Another was to resolve the all-important downcast gaze in an appropriately dreamy fashion, a matter requiring some attention. Whereas he marked the angle of the head with a cross, still visible from the forehead to the mouth and over the brows – without hesitation or change – he worked and reworked the eyes. The completion, or perfection, of the face was achieved by modelling its surface with extraordinary precision, combining fine, closely spaced lines and smudged black chalk with touches of white highlight to create the impression of skin both soft and pearly – one item in the list of the attributes of an ideal beauty. The others, all present here, are a high and serene forehead, arched eyebrows, a small mouth, a rounded chin and a sweetly wistful smile.

Devised for Giuliano's joust, this type of beautiful head had a successful career in various guises in Verrocchio's works. The face resembles that of the Virgin in the Bargello marble (fig. 68) – though precedence is impossible to determine because the marble is not dated. The drawing has been discussed as a study for the Virgin in the Pistoia altarpiece (fig. 70), and it can be considered as such if viewed as a prototype or pattern rather than as directly preparatory. Verrocchio did not spare his efforts, nor did he waste them. In this case he had fashioned a face from the canons of courtly love. Gracious and sweet, it must have seemed both hauntingly familiar and delightfully fresh to contemporary viewers. As a description of beauty it was designed to find favour. It did so in a way that made Verrocchio's work comparable to that of the most famous painter of antiquity, Apelles, whose art was described by Pliny as 'unrivalled for graceful charm'.

210.

'Her hands were beautiful beyond all others that nature ever made.' So wrote Lorenzo de' Medici in the catalogue of his beloved's charms. He dedicated sonnets to them – white, delicate, lovely, noble, soft and charming – capable of drawing his heart from his breast and binding it with knots of love. In another context, that of civic morality, Matteo Palmieri wondered at the expressive power of hands and advised his readers to pay attention to decorum, contrasting 'feminine repose' (*riposo femminile*) with male readiness. The beauty and repose of a woman's hands are salient features of this study, which has been connected with Leonardo's portrait of Ginevra de' Benci. A truncated emblem on the painting's reverse proves that it has been cut down and the whole has been reasonably reconstructed as a three-quarter view including Ginevra's hands. As such it would have been similar to Verrocchio's sculpted *Lady with Flowers* (fig. 67). The portrait and these hands adopt many aspects of the feminine ideal of the bust – an ideal which responds to the conventions of beauty and behaviour sung and sighed over by Lorenzo and his friends in their sonnets. Ginevra herself became the subject of poetic exchange. The portrait is a visual counterpart to this literature of loveliness, with its parts fashioned to give the sitter enduring life as beautiful, noble and virtuous.

More prosaically, or perhaps more practically, Vasari said that Verrocchio would copy plaster casts of hands taken from life. Leonardo's inventory of goods that he brought to Milan in 1482 included many arms, legs and feet. The practice of studying parts, from nature and from plaster casts, was habitual in Verrocchio's shop. In this study Leonardo concentrated on the hands, possibly from life. Their position is related to the entire pose and the drawings at the top and bottom of the page represent alternatives. The hands below are placed as though folded over the sitter's lap, with the figure turned in a three-quarters view (like Ginevra in the portrait). The foreground left hand is dominant and more closely studied. The raised thumb of the right hand seems to have intrigued Leonardo, who developed it as the focus of the hand above. In this second drawing, the arm is at a steeper angle and apparently moved up the body, holding a sprig or the stem of a flower. The light source, a strong but diffuse light from the top right, is the same for both of the studies – a consistency which gives them a deceptive unity, so that the hand holding the flower is often interpreted as a detailed study of the hand below instead of being seen as a variant. In both cases there are two main concerns: to delineate the graceful shape of the hands and to articulate their shape in light. A swift but searching compositional sketch in light black chalk underlies the metalpoint hatching which models the hands. The choice of a soft tone as a ground for this study perhaps depended upon the delicate modelling Leonardo wished to use to suggest the flesh of a young woman. At the top left of the drawing looms the familiar profile of a clamped-faced old man, one of Leonardo's reflexive doodles – in this case possibly a form of marginal comment on the fragility and transience of the beauty to be created and commemorated in the portrait.

30

LEONARDO DA VINCI

Hands

Black chalk underdrawing, metalpoint, wash and white heightening, on pinkish-buff prepared paper,
21.4 × 15 cm
Windsor, Royal Library, The Royal Collection, 12558

Clark 1969, vol. 1, pp. 104–5 (dates the drawing to 1478–80, the period of the Ginevra portrait, but notes its technical similarity to metalpoint drawings of *c*.1490); Kemp in *Leonardo da Vinci*, exh. cat., Hayward Gallery 1989, cat. no. 4, p. 51, states that the drawing has been related to the portrait of Ginevra, which he dates to 1474, but adds that its technique is 'almost identical to that in studies for the Sforza monument' of *c*.1490–3; Palmieri, ed. Belloni 1982, p. 96; Popham, ed. Kemp 1994, pp. 17, 187, cat. no. 18; *Lorenzo de' Medici*, ed. Cook 1995, pp. 78-9, 118–21; Clayton, exh. cat., London 1996, cat. no. 1, pp. 14–15; Brown 1998, pp. 106-9.

PLR

III Verrocchio and his Workshop: Teaching and Transmission

In the early sixteenth century the humanist poet Ugolino Verino celebrated Verrocchio as a 'fountain from whom painters imbibed whatever [skills] they have'. Vasari made Verrocchio's own application – his endless study – a subject of his qualified praise for the artist and it is notable just how many aspects of study are recorded in his biography. He tells of the plaster casts of 'hands, feet, knees, legs, arms and torsos' which Verrocchio would copy, and of the drawings of beautiful heads and other things which he did with patience and intelligence. He mentions his study of geometry and perspective, and, in the Preface to the third section of *The Lives*, of the ancient statue of Marsyas that he restored. The extent of Verrocchio's influence owed much to the intensity of his study and the diversity of his techniques. His own exploration of compositional problems led him to develop a range of design practices, with a creative crossover between two and three dimensions.

The large group of surviving pen and ink drawings by the goldsmith Maso Finiguerra suggests that Verrocchio's training as a goldsmith accustomed him both to the use of pen and to making life drawings. In his case the command of line, which was an aspect of the goldsmith's/graver's art, was enriched by his training both in painting and sculpting.

As a sculptor Verrocchio carefully observed the actions of light over various surfaces. He found ways to record those actions in his drawings and was particularly adept at exploiting the gradations of tone possible with black chalk. But he was also skilled in using white, applied highlight or the exposed surface of paper, to create volume and to represent reflected light. This sensitivity to the effects of light – essentially the problem of how things are seen – had a profound effect on Leonardo. It is also registered in drawings by Lorenzo di Credi. Learning how to transcribe those effects must have been an insistent aspect of their training.

Before picking up his pen, Verrocchio almost invariably used black chalk to place or to lightly sketch his subject. Sometimes the preliminary drawing was meant to remain hidden once the form was determined and given a definitive contour in pen. At other times Verrocchio worked the chalk into the modelling of the figure. The habit of making nearly invisible or disappearing chalk underdrawings is one he passed to Leonardo. Both assimilated chalk and blended chalk are found in Fra Filippo Lippi's drawings, and – as Verrocchio's likely master in the art of painting – it might be a habit Verrocchio learned from Lippi. As a draughtsman Lippi was acutely aware of the relation between the description of reflected light and modelled form, using different combinations of prepared papers, chalk, pen and white heightening to represent the veiled textures he wished to render in paint. This concern was sympathetic to Verrocchio, who took up the problem in drawing. Even the limited number of surviving drawings by Verrocchio demonstrate the ways that his solutions expanded the range of techniques: from the nuanced use of traditional media like black chalk to the invention of new drawing types like the brush drawings on linen (cat. nos. 26, 39 and 40).

Verrocchio's activities as a sculptor had the direct and useful by-product for his work as a painter and teacher in the models and casts that he made as he prepared and produced statues and reliefs. Such casts became studio properties, ready for replication, for reference and for study. The inventory of Verrocchio's shop documents the existence of these models as do drawings by his assistants such as Lorenzo di Credi, Leonardo da Vinci and Francesco di Simone. Sheets from the sketchbook attributed to Francesco di Simone show how the casts or statues were examined from all angles and in all particulars until they were memorised. A note on the back of one of those sheets (now in Hamburg) records that Lorenzo di Credi had loaned Francesco the figure of a baby by Verrocchio, which he used to make two copies for a client. The persistence of Verrocchio inventions in the 1480s and beyond shows not only how well his students had mastered those forms, but how they were circulated and made available to a wider group of artists who could borrow, buy and copy them. Such an exchange is documented by Francesco di Simone's memorandum. It can be inferred from Ghirlandaio's paintings dating from the 1480s, for example, where the imprint of Verrocchio is as strong, if not stronger than in the 1470s. Verrocchio's research towards perfected ideas and his record of them in drawn or sculpted patterns meant that they could be widely diffused, even when not directly taught.

Like other successful craftsmen, Verrocchio had to maintain a reputable and recognisable standard of production. He did this in part by encouraging a regime of careful copying among his pupils and assistants. There are, for example, four drawings – all by different hands – of the kneeling drapery shown here (cat. no. 41). First in the 'order of learning to draw', according to Leonardo, was to 'draw from drawings by good masters done from works of art and from nature … then from plastic work, with the guidance of the drawing done from it; and then from natural models'. The next stage was to practise drawing after things in relief.

This order of study seems to have been the one set down in Verrocchio's shop. Cat. no. 41, for example, is a drawing of drapery whose prototype was a drawing by Verrocchio. Verrocchio himself made copies of other artists' works, both ancient and modern, to extend his repertoire and to literally profit from the past. The differently posed infants on cat. no. 36 include some that are his recollection of other works of art. The drawing could have then been used by his students to copy both the poses and the penwork. Having learned the schematic structures of 'plastic work' as transcribed in drawings such as this, his students could then proceed to make their own studies from statuettes or casts (as cat. no. 42). Lorenzo di Credi's adaptation of the angels from the Forteguerri relief model, with its correction from a posed model in cat. no. 16, illustrates that Verrocchio's assistants were in the habit of making drawings from his reliefs. Relief was itself one of the defining preoccupations of all of Verrocchio's works, and the means of depicting it convincingly was an object of constant study.

His temperament and talents as a sculptor imbue his drawings with remarkable presence. They are often life-size or nearly so. He seems to have enjoyed this close contact with the physical reality of the subjects which he intended to transform and make his own through his art. The keenly analytical process of transcription and transformation is one that he transmitted in various ways to his students and through them to the following generation of artists.

PLR

31

ANDREA DEL VERROCCHIO

Head of a young woman

Black chalk (recto and verso), grey wash,
pen and brown ink (recto) on paper, pricked,
40.8. × 32.7 cm
Oxford, Christ Church, inv. 0005

The vertical line at the right side of the drawing
marks a later damage and repair. The matching chain
lines of the paper prove that the drawing was done
on one sheet, not two joined together.

Vasari/Milanesi, vol. 3, pp. 363–4; Berenson 1938,
vol. 1, p. 59, vol. 2, p. 359, cat. no. 2782A, vol. 3,
fig. 127; Byam Shaw 1976, vol. 1, p. 36, cat. no. 15,
vol. 2, pl. 8; Ames-Lewis and Wright, exh. cat.,
Nottingham and London 1983, cat. no. 72,
pp. 310–13; Bambach 1988, p. 465, cat. no. 338;
Caneva in *Il Disegno fiorentino*, exh. cat., Florence 1992,
cat. no. 4.13, pp. 110–11, (see also cat. no. 4.14,
pp. 112–13, [Verrocchio, Louvre, inv. 18.965] and
cat. no. 4.15, pp. 114–15, [Leonardo, Uffizi, inv. 428E]
for examples of ideal heads); Viatte, in ed. Cropper
[n.d., 1994?], p. 48.

I would like to thank Christopher Baker for
information about the drawing's condition.

PLR

Among Vasari's treasured collection of drawings were 'a number of female heads [by Verrocchio] with lovely expressions and hair which Leonardo da Vinci used to imitate for their beauty'. The provenance of this breathtaking drawing cannot be directly traced to Vasari, but as a type it can be directly related to Vasari's remark and to Leonardo's appreciation. Other elaborately coiffed and highly idealised heads survive by Verrocchio and his students, attesting to their importance in his shop as preparatory drawings and as patterns to consult and to study so that hand, eye and memory might become well-versed in perfected forms.

This drawing has been carefully and comprehensively pricked, which means that its main elements could be transferred to another surface by tapping along the lines with a bag of fine black dust (chalk, charcoal or ashes, for example). Both sides are displayed here. The dotted lines visible on the verso show the schematic drawing that would result. The principal features are legible, including the costume and hairstyle, which were not considered to be incidental details but integral features of the image. If transferred to a painting surface the resulting drawing would be a spare, diagrammatic underdrawing and the original sheet could be used as reference for the details and subtleties of modelling. If transferred to another piece of paper, the outlines could become the basis for a close copy or an inventive variation.

No extant painting exactly follows this drawing. There are some, however, that are influenced by its ideas. The demurely thoughtful Virgin in the Berlin *Virgin and Child* (fig. 101) is similar in conception. The pattern of strongly reflected light and equally strong shadow which models the face and neck is almost identical. But the head in the drawing is nearly a profile, while that in the painting is a three-quarter view.

Fig. 101 ANDREA DEL VERROCCHIO, *Virgin and Child*,
early 1470s. Egg tempera on panel, 72 × 53 cm.
Berlin, Staatliche Museen Preussischer
Kulturbesitz, Gemäldegalerie.

VERSO

Verrocchio had experimented with a profile Virgin in the altarpiece that he supplied to the convent of San Domenico del Maglio (now in the Fine Art Museum, Budapest): her face, but not her dress, is comparable to this drawing. Drawings by Verrocchio's assistants Biagio di Antonio and Leonardo da Vinci respectively take up the profile model (Uffizi 1254E and 428E). The fluttering veil, the turning of the head away from the main axis of the body and the lifted right arm suggest motion. The fancy dress and braided hair suggest a secular subject. This mysterious lady is more likely to have been drawn first as a poetic nymph (related to Verrocchio's work on Lorenzo's and Giuliano's jousts, for example) rather than as a nobly attired Virgin. It is possible that this drawing served as a cartoon for a lost work, but it is certain that it provided a stencil of elegant femininity. It embodies the desired parts (high arched forehead, small lips, long neck) and the desired behaviour – grace and modesty – of virtuous womanhood as construed in the fifteenth century. These could be applied to an idealised lady-love or to the Virgin Mary.

Verrocchio was indebted to Fra Filippo Lippi in finding his formula for the beautiful woman. The facial type, pose and intricate veil are like those in Lippi's Uffizi *Virgin and Child* (fig. 81). He imitated Lippi's interplay of textures – wispy veil, soft hair, smooth skin – and the sinuous, sensuous play of line that decorates and enlivens the form. But he made the whole more substantial. Verrocchio used black chalk with the utmost refinement and delicacy in order to achieve this illusion of sculptural solidity. Although there are some adjustments to the outline of the face and neck, Verrocchio's aim from the outset was not to find the idea but to define a finished ideal. The first stage of drawing was done lightly and Verrocchio blended some of these lines into subsequent layers. He used soft, heavy lines for the hair and robe and minute, meticulous hatching to lay in the shadow that forms the surfaces of the flesh. He then rubbed over the hatching to give those surfaces a subtly inflected and polished tone. As in the Uffizi *Angel* (cat. no. 22), pen and ink were used to reinforce shadow as well as some outlines. The outcome was exemplary both as a beautiful head and as a beautiful drawing.

32

ANDREA DEL VERROCCHIO

Head of a youth looking upwards

Black chalk on paper with white
heightening, pricked,
18.4 × 15.7 cm
Berlin, Staatliche Museen Preussischer Kulturbesitz,
Kupferstichkabinett, inv. 5095 recto

Berenson 1938, vol. 1, pp. 48, 59, vol. 2, cat. no. 2780E,
p. 359; Pouncey and Gere 1962, vol. 1, pp. 5–6, cat. no.
5, vol. 2, p. 6 (for Raphael); Passavant 1969, p. 59, cat.
no. D7, pp. 192–3; Cadogan 1983, pp. 374–5;
Bambach 1988, cat. no. 336, pp. 463–4; Schulze
Altcappenberg 1995, pp. 141–3.

PLR

Fig. 102 Verso of cat. no. 32.

Lifted to the light, the physical illumination of this face also describes its spiritual expression. Now cut so that only the head remains, it is probable that originally the shoulders were also included in a manner similar to cat. no. 31. The whole body is implied as the impetus behind the dramatic pose and the figure's right shoulder has been studied and modified. Further evidence that more was once shown comes from the verso, now reduced to a coyly peering face cut off just below the nose, which must have been drawn as a complete head (fig. 102). Here as in cat. no. 29 the drawings on either side of the paper are similar in subject but different in function. The verso is a wiry sketch in black chalk, where the principal lines of the features are sought and noted. It is a free adaptation of the angel in Fra Filippo Lippi's Uffizi *Madonna and Child* (fig. 81) who turns and smiles at the onlooker as he lifts the Christ Child towards the Virgin. In this drawing we see how Verrocchio not only studied a motif but engaged with the lessons to be learned from Lippi regarding the disconcerting relationship between distortion and beauty and the psychological power of striking and unsettling poses.

These lessons also inform the drawing on the recto, which takes a potentially ungainly view and renders it beautiful. Although the features are foreshortened, they are not cramped. Their articulation is pronounced. The composition is harmonised by overall balance. The open mouth, expressing wonder, offsets the ample hollow of the eye-socket, for example. Verrocchio has characteristically employed black chalk to varied effect. Individual lines create a pattern of swirling curls which frame the head. Rubbed black chalk builds the strong forms of the jaw, cheek and edge of the nose against the white of the paper. Highlights represent the dramatic light shining down from above.

The task here was to arrive at a finished model of this rapt pose. Resolved and ready for transfer as it is, this head does not occur in a known painting or sculpture. It has sometimes been associated with the angel at the left of the National Gallery *Virgin and Child* (cat. no. 23), but both the direction and the angle of the gaze are different. The response to divine splendour is more active and exultant. Within Verrocchio's works it is closer to the draft for the figure of Hope on the Forteguerri monument (cat. no. 13). It is not a direct study because the allegory is female and this head is male. Similar spiritual elation was conveyed by Luca della Robbia in the upturned faces of the jubilant musicians he carved for the singing gallery of Florence cathedral, and those sculptures might have been one source for Verrocchio. The mood of spiritual uplift, suitable for an angel could also have been handy as a prototype for other inspired figures. Among Verrocchio's students Perugino made the upward foreshortened gaze a standard element of his devotional compositions. A black chalk study (now in the British Museum) by Perugino's pupil Raphael for the head of Saint James in his 1503 *Coronation of the Virgin* is a descendant of this drawing. Not only was the pose transmitted from master to pupil over two generations, but dotted outlines in Raphael's drawing show that he relied on the method of transferring studies from one sheet to another that must have been standard practice in Verrocchio's shop and that accounts for the survival and diffusion of his ideas.

da vinci

33

ANDREA DEL VERROCCHIO

Studies of the Virgin with the Child on her lap

Charcoal and black chalk on paper, laid down,
28.3 × 19.3 cm
Florence, Galleria degli Uffizi,
Gabinetto Disegni e Stampe, inv. 444E

Gombrich 1966, p. 59 (for the quote from Leonardo);
Passavant 1969, p. 57, cat. no. D2, p. 191;
Adorno 1991, pp. 194, 266–7; De Marchi in
Il Disegno fiorentino, exh. cat. Florence 1992, cat. no. 7.4,
pp. 148–9; Kemp 1998, p. 33, note 5.

PLR

Two positions for the Virgin and (at least) three for the Child can be discerned through what is now a misty realm of possibilities on this sheet. Verrocchio used black chalk and charcoal to ponder the composition of this group. Abrasion is in part responsible for making it difficult to read his thoughts at first glance, but Verrocchio also intentionally smudged the chalk as he transformed and formed his alternatives. This material metamorphosis of figures can obviously be compared to sculptural design. Verrocchio effectively sketch-modelled in a way that paralleled making drafts in clay. Here chalk and charcoal are the malleable substances that accommodate changes of mind. They were also used to work on forms through gradations of tone – imitating surfaces as well as defining boundaries.

Verrocchio started here by lightly sketching in the group to establish its position, which is turned towards the viewer's left. In the first draft the Virgin looked outwards, majestic and melancholy as she pointed to the child lying across her lap. Verrocchio was apparently not satisfied with this first idea. He reconsidered the relationship between the mother and child. He made the Virgin more responsive to the infant, bending her face towards him. Under the artist's restless chalk, the child began to squirm as Verrocchio adjusted the position of his legs and arms. In a subsequent dramatic move, Verrocchio repositioned the child to sit on the Virgin's knee, looking outwards and towards another focus, possibly blessing an approaching figure (as in an Adoration) or pointing towards something (as the Christ Child gestures towards the Baptist's cross in the Pistoia altarpiece). Though decisive, the change took some definition and Verrocchio tried out different placements for the baby's arms and legs before confirming a position with dark accents. He went over some of the scribbles and smudges of the first child to turn them into a cushion for the second and to suggest the fabric of the Virgin's dress. He did not entirely abandon the child turned towards its mother, however; he returned to it with charcoal to trace the alternate pose.

Verrocchio also used charcoal to articulate the anchoring structure formed by the Virgin's legs and the folds of her robe. The essential geometry of the group is pyramidal. The stabilising, yet decorative, motif of drapery swagged over the Virgin's knees and gathered in over her feet was one favoured by Verrocchio and is often found in his paintings and those influenced by his ideas. Variants occur in the Pistoia altarpiece and in Leonardo's *Annunciation*, for example (figs. 70 and 72). Cat. no. 40, the drapery study by Lorenzo di Credi, shows how this motif was studied and recorded.

The composition with the child facing outwards in some ways resembles the Virgin and Child of the Pistoia altarpiece and this drawing has been associated with that project. The differences, above all in the orientation of the Virgin, outweigh the similarities. Cat. no. 34 proves that Verrocchio's shop had other occasions to study Virgin and Child groups of this sort. This drawing might have been a reference or a starting point in the genesis of the Pistoia altarpiece rather than a direct preparatory study. It demonstrates Verrocchio's mental agility in developing his ideas. Leonardo is often quoted as advising artists to be like poets in composing verse and to rough out their ideas rather than 'trace beautiful letters'. The present drawing shows that his notion of drawing as a generative process was one taught by Verrocchio.

34

ANDREA DEL VERROCCHIO

Study of a seated Virgin and Child

Charcoal on paper, laid down,
22.2 × 15.2 cm
Florence, Galleria degli Uffizi,
Gabinetto Disegni e Stampe, inv. 443E

Petrioli Tofani 1986, p. 198; De Marchi, in *Il Disegno fiorentino*, exh. cat. Florence 1992, pp. 148–9 (citing E. Fahy's attribution of the drawing to the young Lorenzo di Credi).

PLR

Many elements of this Virgin and Child refer to stock Verrocchio shop motifs: the 'beautiful head' of the Virgin shown looking downwards in three-quarter view, her gracefully displayed hand, the weighty cascade of drapery over and around her knees and the fetching pot-bellied Child. The composition is not, however, a tired assembly of well-tried formulas. It is, instead, a demonstration of the way that the intense and varied study of parts undertaken in the studio created an assured vocabulary and fluency in approaching new tasks.

The result was also a standard of production where the inventive authority remained Verrocchio's, even if the actual author was one of his assistants. In this case, the Virgin's broad face and the generally rounded, even puffy, forms, are characteristic of Lorenzo di Credi. The energetic baby, however, is equally characteristic of Verrocchio. This compositional draft may be an instance where the student made a drawing while closely following the master's instruction.

One of the problems being addressed here is the crucial one of the nature of the contact between the mother and child, which would determine the emotional as well as the symbolic narrative of the final image. The first possibility seems to have been to show the child looking outwards and reaching for its mother in a way that would have been similar to Leonardo da Vinci's *Virgin and Child* now in the Alte Pinakothek, Munich. As the design progressed it became more intimate, and abstraction was replaced by satisfaction as the Child grasps the Virgin's outstretched fingers with one hand and puts his other hand in his mouth. This literally touching piece of infantile behaviour expresses the humanity of the Christ Child.

The choice of charcoal for a compositional study such as this allowed the draughtsman to consider the textures as well as the shapes and outlines of the figures. Forms appear in broadly defined areas of light, which emphasise mass and volume. The softness achieved by the manipulation of the medium here, as in cat. no. 33, parallels the blended tonality of oil painting. The use of charcoal for sketching might have developed in Verrocchio's shop alongside experiments with oil as a medium for painting. It is, in any case, an example of the technical experimentation typical of its procedures.

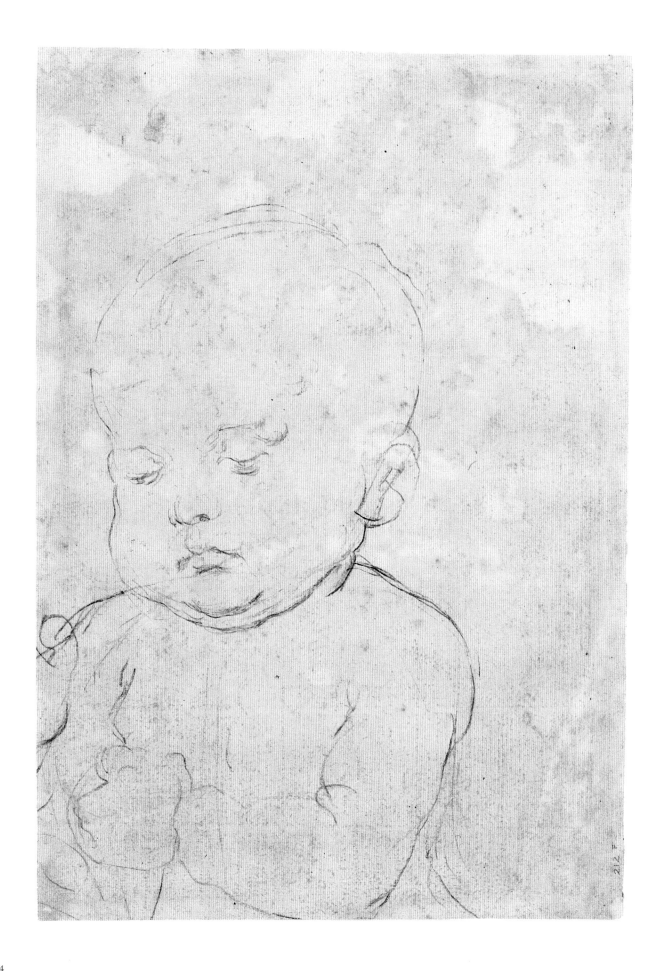

Even though it is a fragment, this drawing has an almost startling physical immediacy. Originally it probably showed an infant seated in a position similar to one of those on the recto of cat. no. 36. In this case, however, rather than record a generically useful pose, Verrocchio studied a specific gesture. The child is shown clutching a piece of cloth in his left hand while raising his right hand, presumably in blessing. This seems to have been a second thought. Faint lines trace an arm bent downwards. Verrocchio also changed the position of the ear and reinforced the fleshy compression of the chin and neck. He managed to give the child a concentrated and pensive expression suitable for an infant Christ and still maintain the awkward tenderness of an actual child.

The drawing may be related to the Pistoia altarpiece. It seems to be evolving a position for the child comparable to that of the Christ Child in the painting (fig. 70). The downcast eyes of the infant on this sheet give it a more contained expression than the outward glance of the Christ as painted, however. In its emotional tenor and as a physical type it is also similar to the Christ Child in Leonardo's *Benois Madonna* in St Petersburg (fig. 77), which suggests a date in the later 1470s. Whether for the Pistoia altarpiece or another Virgin and Child composition, the large scale of the drawing indicates that it was made as part of the preparation for a painting. The sheet has not only been cut down, but it has been cut out of what must have been an extensive design procedure, which unfortunately has but few precious survivors to act as reminders of its various stages.

The extraordinary economy of this drawing shows just how practised Verrocchio was as a draughtsman and how much he could teach about drawing. Here he relied on the tonal range of black chalk in order to lightly and tentatively make a preliminary sketch. Pressing harder on the chalk he confirmed his decided forms with swift and sure strokes. He did no shading; the baby nonetheless emerges fully shaped on the page. Verrocchio was able to see the paper's surface sculpturally and to use lines to model as well as to delineate. The lines are disconnected and they arch, loop and hook in different lengths around the fleshy contours Verrocchio wanted to evoke. The child is completely convincing, and was possibly studied from life. Graphically, it is totally schematic. Typical of Verrocchio's touch are the quickly drawn lines that form the baby's right eyebrow and create the downward turn of its cheek, the dashes that make the bow mouth and the mitten-like shapes that are the hands. Such systematic notation was as important a lesson for Verrocchio's students as the sculptural qualities of form that it transcribed and depicted.

35
ANDREA DEL VERROCCHIO

Study of a baby

Black chalk on paper,
28.3 × 20 cm
Florence, Galleria degli Uffizi,
Gabinetto Disegni e Stampe, inv. 212FV verso

Passavant 1969, p. 57, cat. no. D3, p. 191;
Adorno 1991, p. 267.

PLR

36

ANDREA DEL VERROCCHIO

Studies of infants

Pen and brown ink on paper, with faint traces
of black chalk underdrawing,
15.7 × 20.9 cm
Paris, Musée du Louvre, Département des Arts
Graphiques, RF 2, recto and verso
Inscribed (on recto):
Viderunt equum mirandaque arte confectum / Quem nobiles
veneti tibi dedere facturum / Florentiae decus crasse mihi crede
Varochie / Qui te plus oculis amant diliguntque coluntque /
Atque cum Jupiter animas infuderit ipsi / Hoc tibi dominus
rogat Salmonicus idem / Vale et bene qui legis.

Berenson 1938, vol. 1, pp. 46–7, vol. 2, p. 359,
cat. no. 2783, vol. 3, figs. 122, 123; Cadogan 1983, p. 373;
Adorno 1991, pp. 269–70; Natali in *Il Disegno*
fiorentino, exh. cat. Florence 1992, cat. no. 6.5,
pp. 132–3; Brown 1998, pp. 37–8.

PLR

The drawings on this sheet form a set of variations on the theme of infancy. Linked by subject, the sketches are mainly separate as concepts. Only two on the verso are progressive variants of a pose (one running, one lying down), where the child's head is turned in the opposite direction from its torso. Otherwise Verrocchio seems to have intentionally avoided comparisons by turning the sheet around as he added figures. Exactly how many figures, and of what sort, is impossible to know. The size of the paper and the fact that the foot of the baby leaning over at the lower right edge of the verso has been trimmed suggest that this is part of what was once a larger sheet, which was probably cut down when it became a collector's item. This might have been early: the Latin inscription on the recto in praise of Verrocchio's Colleoni monument dates from the late fifteenth or early sixteenth century.

As a studio property, the drawing provided a valuable stock of motifs, mostly for devotional compositions of the Virgin and Infant Christ. The baby poised on one foot (on the verso) could have served a profane purpose, however; its pose resembles that of a terracotta putto in the National Gallery in Washington and can also be related to the putto with a dolphin from Careggi (fig. 66). Verrocchio carefully maintained the legibility of the individual figures, generally avoiding overlaps, as though aware of their reference potential. But reference was the consequence and probably not the purpose of the exercise. Verrocchio seems to have been concerned with somewhat different questions as he sketched each child. So, for example, on the recto, the child resting on its arm is mainly a contour study. Verrocchio positioned it with a few light pen marks and then concentrated on defining the turn of the child's shoulders, the angle of its face and the bend of its left arm. This was the most complicated portion of the composition, because it gave the pose a dynamic balance – stable, yet turning in space – and it determined the direction of the child's expression. The infant to its left, posed as though cuddling up to its mother, is an even more schematic draft, whereas the two other seated children are modelled with rounded hatching. They are defined by light, and given volume and weight. The child on the top of the sheet is fully formed. The baby flanked by the inscription is more tentative. There is black chalk underdrawing visible in the faintly sketched left leg. Here the chubby torso is clearly defined, as is the child's left side. Its right side is in play – the gesture is resolved with the right arm raised in blessing, but at one point Verrocchio thought that he might depict the child putting his fingers in his mouth. The drawings on the verso range from the diagrammatic sketch of the child bending over – a trial of a foreshortened pose – to the volumetrically studied seated child. The standing child at the left was a setpiece, a familiar form in paintings, sculptures and drawings from the shop, which Verrocchio kept fresh by reviewing and redrafting as here.

All the sketches demonstrate Verrocchio's ready command of a figurative repertoire. They are most likely based on sculpted models or are variants made from memory. Many can be related to prototypes in Verrocchio's works and those of the Rossellino brothers. The adaptation from sculptural to pictorial might have been one of their purposes. Within a two-dimensional format the figures are composed to give the impression of occupying space. Verrocchio's narrative sensibility is also manifest here. The infants are expressively composed, each one responds to an external stimulus: their poses require completion or explanation by the presence of another figure (the Virgin) or the viewer. The infants are also united by the descriptive powers of Verrocchio's fluent pen. He traced the swelling of their pudgy limbs with deft strokes and with short

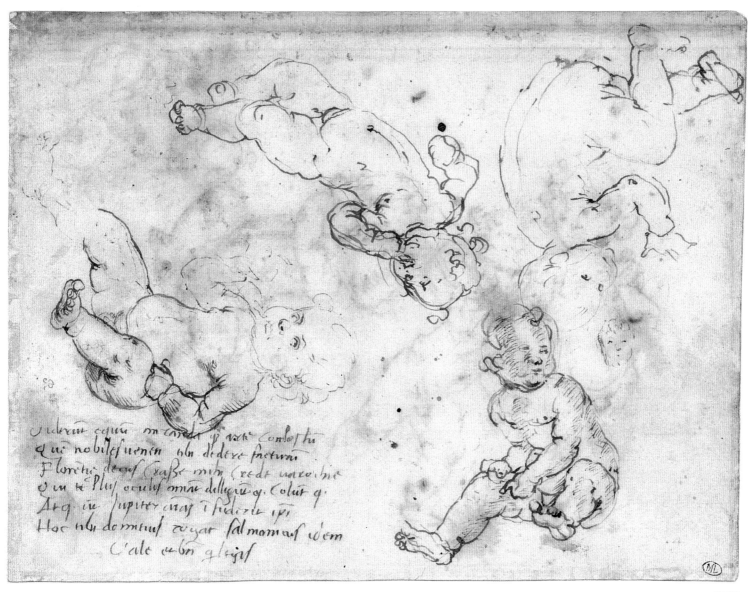

VERSO

hooks and curves he captured the creasing of their soft flesh. The drawings mediate between observed reality and pictorial artifice.

As completed the sheet must have been useful both as a stock of ideas and as an example of how to draw them. This is a kind of drawing that could be copied by students or assistants to master its graphic vocabulary as well as the varied positions of the children. Some, like Francesco di Simone, approached such drawings as glossaries, and diligently made copybook studies (cat. no. 42). Leonardo learned his shorthand from pen drawings of this sort and fully understood the emotional intensity of Verrocchio's figures. He adapted both the actual inventions and the general principle of thematically linked studies to his compositional method, but he transformed the effectively complete narrative units to elements in a continuous creative sequence (cat. no. 37).

37

LEONARDO DA VINCI

Studies of a child and cat

Metalpoint underdrawing, pen and brown ink
and brown wash on paper,
20.6 × 14.3 cm
London, British Museum, Department of Prints and
Drawings, 1857-1-10-1 recto

Popham and Pouncey 1950, no. 99, pp. 59–60;
Richter 1970, vol. 1, pp. 303, 308 (nos. 483, 498);
Kemp 1981, p. 54; Popham, ed. Kemp 1994,
nos. 12,13, pp. 14, 106–7.

PLR

Fig. 103 Verso of cat. no. 37.

In his notes for a treatise on painting Leonardo observed that it was 'a poor pupil who does not surpass his master'. The way to do this was first to copy 'drawings from the hand of a good master' and then from nature. This drawing demonstrates that his advice was born of practice.

Both sides of the sheet have sketches of a child and a cat. Leonardo began each of the studies on the verso, which may well have been the first side, by making nearly invisible drafts with a stylus (fig. 103). The group at the top right actually includes a mother supporting the child, smiling as she watches him clutch the cat. When Leonardo took up the pen to clarify and continue his study, his interest was focused only on the interplay of baby and cat. The play, however, is not between a real baby and a real cat, but between familiar motifs and their fantasised combinations. The child's pose was based on stock forms from the Verrocchio shop repertoire. As he began thinking about this subject, Leonardo summoned up appropriate shapes and drew them in a serial fashion reminiscent of the drawings of babies by the hand of his 'good master' (see cat. no. 36). Indeed the improbably seated cat at the lower right of the drawing is basically a variant of a seated child.

In the sketches at the top and in the middle of the recto, Leonardo pursued his subject with an eager fascination that parallels the child's attraction to the cat. In these two drawings both infant and feline behaviour seem very natural, as though observed or remembered from observation. At the top the cat crawls towards the child's cuddle, and Leonardo has used sinuous lines to convey their mutual affectionate twisting. Below, the cat walks away, sensuously arching its back as it glides beneath the child's arm – its tail stroking the baby's neck. At this point, narrative and nature had taken Leonardo from the study of an unusual theme for a devotional painting to a totally unusable situation. The drawing beneath it, which has some metalpoint underdrawing, reverts to possibilities considered in the sketch at the top right of the other side of the sheet. It also reverts to motifs which Leonardo had learned from his master. The intertwined spiral of forms is similar to Verrocchio's *Putto with a Dolphin* (fig. 66). In this sketch, Leonardo emphasised the lines that defined the intricate figure group and then used hatching and wash to describe its volume. The dynamic poise of this invention is undermined by the subsequent sketch, which shows the cat – still in the child's grasp – fallen backwards, as though the artful contrivance of the group could not resist the very real pull of gravity.

The sculptural qualities of the drawings on this sheet prove the profound influence of Verrocchio on Leonardo's conception of form. For Leonardo light and shade were the primary components of painting. In Verrocchio's shop he was taught to understand how surfaces responded to light and therefore how they could be described in terms of illumination and shadow. The purpose of the drawings on both sides of the sheet is to examine the composition and the mass of the figure group, whose separate elements had been studied in previous drawings, such as cat. no. 37.

This was not a matter of simply assembling pre-conceived parts; at no point in Leonardo's works or working process is form divorced from meaning. He began here, on what is now the verso, lightly sketching in metalpoint in order to position the figures (fig. 104). The central episode of fond mother, clutching child and uncomfortable cat was quickly confirmed in pen, and hatched lines bind the trio together, solidly shaping them through contrasts of light and shade. The principal questions became those of stability, projection and scale, which depended on the position of the Virgin's legs and the placement of the frame. Because there began to be a danger that the solution would be dissolved among the alternatives, Leonardo turned over the sheet. He returned to metalpoint to unobtrusively fix the seemingly decided poses of the Virgin and Child from the other side, which meant they were in the reverse direction. He then used pen to describe their shapes, not enclosing them in outline, but defining principal contours. Both the change of direction and the emphatic diagonal of the Virgin's raised legs altered the balance of the composition enough for Leonardo to begin to reconsider the position of the Virgin's head, and with that the emotional content of the whole picture; having tried both left and right, he opted for a downcast gaze. He then modelled the group with brush and wash, not only setting it into relief, but suggesting the movement of light that enhances the impression of immediacy.

Leonardo's ideas for Virgin and Child projects from the period after he left Verrocchio's shop all stress the momentary, exploring the dynamics of affection, poignancy, joyful innocence and wistful knowledge that could bind the mother and child emotionally as well as physically. Although in many ways reliant on Verrocchio's figural vocabulary, Leonardo used the design process to articulate his independence.

There are six sheets with drawings relating to the subject of the Virgin and Child with a cat, this one is the most resolved and the only one where Leonardo sketched in a frame as though seeing the picture. There is, however, no completed painting and the studies here demonstrate mobility rather than finality of thought. As they show, drawing was as much an inspirational as a functional process for Leonardo.

38

LEONARDO DA VINCI

Virgin and Child with a cat

Metalpoint underdrawing, pen and brown ink and brown wash on paper,
13.2 × 9.5 cm
London, British Museum, Department of Prints and Drawings, 1856-6-21-1 recto

Popham and Pouncey 1950, no. 97r, pp. 58–60; Marani 1989, no. 5A, pp. 128–9; Kemp, exh. cat., Edinburgh 1992, no. 8, pp. 52–3; Popham, ed. Kemp 1994, nos. 9A,B, pp. 13–14, 106; Kemp 1981, pp. 53–4; Wiemers 1996, pp. 269–76 (for the most extended discussion of the Virgin and Child and cat drawings, the other drawings in the group are: Uffizi 421E recto and verso; British Museum, Popham and Pouncey nos. 98 recto and verso, 99 recto and verso; Bayonne, Musée Bonnat inv. 152; formerly Pollen collection, London).

PLR

Fig. 104 Verso of cat. no. 38.

39

LEONARDO DA VINCI

Drapery study for
a kneeling figure

Brush and grey-brown tempera with
white heightening, on grey prepared linen,
16.4 × 17 cm
Florence, Galleria degli Uffizi,
Gabinetto Disegni e Stampe, inv. 420

Vasari/Milanesi, vol. 4, p. 20; Richter 1970, vol. 1,
p. 270, no. 391; Cadogan 1983, pp. 48–54; *Léonard
de Vinci. Les études de draperie*, exh. cat. 1989, cat. no. 2,
pp. 46–7 (cat. no. 1, pp. 44–5, for the Louvre study,
inv. 2256); Brown 1998, p. 82, p. 196, n. 26.

PLR

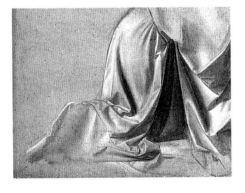

Fig. 105 LEONARDO DA VINCI, *Drapery study*, 1470.
Grey tempera with white highlights on grey
prepared canvas, 18.2 × 23.4 cm. Paris, Musée du Louvre.
Département des Arts Graphiques, inv. 2256.

Leonardo's method for making this sort of drawing is described in detail by Vasari, who owned some examples. He tells how Leonardo sometimes fashioned 'models of clay figures, which he covered with soft rags dipped in plaster and then patiently copied them upon fine cambric or used linen, working in black and white with the point of the brush – marvellous things.' Leonardo later criticised the drapery style which resulted from this concentrated form of study, saying that the artist 'ought not to give to drapery a great confusion of many folds, but rather only introduce them where they are held by the hands or arms.' Draperies, he said, should be drawn from nature and observe the nature of different cloths. His later drawings confirm his change in practice. The crystalline abstraction of this study – an object of beauty in itself – was replaced by the soft rendering of fabrics shaped by underlying forms.

At no point in his career did Leonardo deny the importance of drapery as a key aspect of composition. In this case the bend and angle of the folds compare with the pose of the angel in his early *Annunciation* (fig. 72). The care lavished upon the drawing suggests that it had a purpose beyond a training exercise. There is a related drawing in the Louvre which shows more of the body and includes a light sketch of an extended arm. Neither drawing has exactly the same drapery as the angel, but combined they indicate the intense study of separate parts that Leonardo had been taught to make as guarantees of the physical conviction and charm of the whole. Some details of the fold structure as well as the overall crisp clarity of its articulation are similar to the robe of the left-hand angel in the *Baptism* (fig. 74). Once made, this drawing had its place in Leonardo's portfolio, usable as long as his aesthetic aims matched his master's.

Rigorous and systematic analysis of light and the means to translate its operations into pictorial terms were abiding lessons learned by Leonardo in Verrocchio's shop. The intricate and angular patterning of folds, later rejected by Leonardo, also hints at the geometry of optics – the scientific study of vision – and the fundamental geometries of creation that came to preoccupy him. In making such studies he was absorbing a way of thinking as well as a way of drawing. Characteristic of his own approach is the way that the plaster– or clay-dipped fabric before him became a territory to survey with hand and eye. Bunched folds have the presence and elemental force of steep cliffs and gorges, peaks and valleys seen in sharp light and deep shadow. Using the grey preparation as mid-tone, Leonardo drew in the underlying scheme and then made the dark recesses, shaping the relief with his brush. He then applied white, first in diffuse and dilute strokes, afterwards he took a charged brush and patiently, as Vasari says, used its tip to represent the bright reflected light that picks out and illuminates the creases and ridges. He both described the effects of light and, through the interaction of tones and highlight, the dynamic of its passage over the surface of the drapery. Although in leaving Verrocchio's shop Leonardo left behind this particular sort of fabric fetishism, he never renounced the fascination with light which accompanied it.

215

In his biography of Lorenzo di Credi, Vasari describes how Credi 'took extraordinary pleasure in Leonardo's style and knew how to imitate it so well that no one came nearer to it than he did in the high finish and thorough perfection of his works.' Vasari cited as proof 'the many drawings' that he had collected, 'executed in metalpoint, in pen or in wash, among which are some drawings made from models of clay covered with waxed linen cloths and with liquid clay, imitated with such diligence, and finished with such patience, as it is scarcely possible to conceive, much less to equal.' Vasari included these among the reasons Credi was beloved by his master.

The present drawing illustrates Vasari's words in its patient execution, its perfection and its assimilation of lessons from Leonardo as well as from Verrocchio. The drapery structure, with a prominent v-shaped fall of fabric in the centre of a triangle formed by legs and lap and with a generous fanning out of folds around and over the feet, was a standard Verrocchio shop solution. The composition of this study, and the clay model Credi probably had before him, can be compared to drapery of the Virgin's robe in the Pistoia altarpiece, for example (fig. 70). As a formula, it neatly and pleasingly combined compositional values of balance and decorative display. Credi did not forget its lessons in his later works.

Credi undoubtedly owed his habit of studying from three-dimensional models to Verrocchio's teaching, and it accounts for the sense of solidity and depth achieved in this drawing. But the soft moulding of the form through shadow is the mark of Leonardo's abiding influence on Credi and, through Credi's contribution to Verrocchio's paintings, on Verrocchio himself. As Vasari says, Credi took great care to achieve his desired result. Extremely fine hatching follows the ridges and caverns of the folds. With stroke by meticulous stroke Credi laid in dark areas, following and shaping the forms taken by the fabric he was drawing. He then alternated between applying white and returning to metalpoint lines, finishing by adding white highlights and by sharpening up the splayed-out folds with pen. The evenness, smoothness and laboriousness of metalpoint seem to have suited Credi, who used it often and to great effect. With his combination of stylus, pen and brush he was able to translate light into subtle luminosity, quite possibly the transformation of nature by art which he so admired in Leonardo and which he sought to imitate.

40

LORENZO DI CREDI

Drapery study for a seated figure

Metalpoint, pen and ink, white heightening on pale pink prepared paper,
21.9 × 17.7 cm
Paris, Institut Néerlandais, Collection Frits Lugt, inv. 2491

Vasari/Milanesi, vol. 4, p. 564; Berenson 1933, pp. 253–4; Dalli Regoli 1966, cat. no. 15, p. 106, fig. 28; Dalli Regoli 1976, pp. 44–6; Byam Shaw 1983, vol. 1, cat. no. 10, pp. 15–16; *Léonard de Vinci. Les études de draperie*, exh. cat. 1989, cat. no. 21, pp. 86–7.

PLR

41

WORKSHOP OF VERROCCHIO

Kneeling Virgin and Christ Child

Stylus underdrawing, black chalk, ink wash?
and white heightening (with incidental red chalk)
on paper, laid down,
19.7 × 16.9 cm
London, British Museum, Department of Prints
and Drawings, 1963-11-9-23

Grossman 1971, pp. 15–18; Petrioli Tofani in Abbate,
ed., 1995, pp. 88–9 (Biagio di Antonio);
Nathan 1996, p. 712.

PLR

The British Museum sheet is one of four surviving drawings that record the same figure of the Virgin kneeling in prayer, in three-quarter view, her drapery falling in an elaborate series of swags and billows before splaying out upon the ground. Two of these drawings (New York and Chantilly), showing only the Virgin, appear on sheets of studies that have been convincingly attributed to Francesco di Simone Ferrucci, who is thought to have worked in Verrocchio's shop (see cat. no. 42). The most accomplished of the four drawings, now in Palermo, is executed in subtly worked black chalk with white heightening and traces of brown wash, and includes a delicate chalk sketch of the seated Christ Child stretching his arms towards his mother. The drawings have been discussed as products of Verrocchio's workshop and the Palermo drawing has recently been suggested as the work of Verrocchio himself. The rather literal repetition of the unworked areas around the Virgin's right shoulder and arm in these studies confirms that, whatever the status of the Palermo drawing, the model used for the figures was certainly another drawing, rather than a similarly posed model or a completed painting.

The inclusion of the Christ Child in the British Museum sheet explains the Virgin's devotional pose. While the child is larger in scale than the child in the Palermo drawing, the study is close in technical terms. Stylus marks underlie the more complicated folds around the Virgin's foot and knees while fine black chalk is used for underdrawing. This was followed by firmer strokes, parallel hatching and smudgy chalk shading to confirm the outlines of folds and build up the pattern of relief. The more intense accents of light on the folds were described with lead white, now oxidised, applied with a brush.

The drawing has three principal elements that are typical of Verrocchio's design in terms of both subject and treatment. The first is the seated baby whose pudgy limbs have been adjusted several times to establish a stable but animated pose. The second is the gracefully lowered head of the Virgin, combining a delicately turned contour with repeated curves to describe the eyes and mouth (compare cat. no. 29). The third is the relief pattern of the drapery, which is peculiarly complex and contrived. The Virgin is apparently wrapped in a long mantle which turns back along its upper edge and puffs out over her belly, while draped ends fall from a knot behind her left arm. Further curls of drapery drop in front of the near leg, repeating the angle of her knee and closing the profile of the body to the right. The drapery with its soft secondary folds shares the slightly inflated quality found in Verrocchio's *Saint Thomas* sculpture (fig. 29). Like the statue it was also intended to reveal the position of the body beneath. In the bowed head, the draughtsman has copied the careful modelling of the face and cork-screw curl of the hair without fully grasping their underlying form. But his failure to understand the figure's three-dimensional structure is more apparent in the drapery, with its busy effect of minor folds. To some extent, the drawing merely exaggerates unresolved qualities in the model itself, for example in the Virgin's left knee, which seems to hover above the right one. But the Virgin's garments are also flattened into a decorative schema of v-shapes and curves. Copied variants like this show how drawn designs were used as models to learn from in Verrocchio's workshop, in this case providing a formula for the adoring Virgin that could be easily repeated in painting or relief. In their tendency to create superficial pattern, such copy drawings also illustrate the hazard of using two-dimensional models to study from rather than three-dimensional ones.

42

FRANCESCO DI SIMONE FERRUCCI

Sheet of studies with the standing Christ Child

Pen and brown ink and wash on paper,
27.1 × 19.1 cm
Paris, Musée du Louvre, Département
des Arts Graphiques, 446 recto
Inscribed: *traluciente / fiere a dite*

Gronau 1896, pp. 65–72; Cruttwell 1904, pp. 201–5;
Van Marle 1923–39, pp. 571–6; ; Ames-Lewis and
Wright, exh. cat., Nottingham and London 1983,
pp. 140–3.

AW

Fig. 106 Verso of cat. no. 42.

This sheet of studies once formed part of a book of drawings attributed to the sculptor Francesco di Simone Ferrucci da Fiesole. Sheets from the book contain a wealth of motifs that depend on ideas developed in Verrocchio's workshop where Francesco probably once worked and to which he remained indebted in his independent sculptures. On the verso (fig. 106) Francesco also copied the outlines of Antonio del Pollaiuolo's *Hercules and the Hydra* composition (fig. 61), which he may have known in the form of a print. Suppressing Hercules' leonine expression, Francesco is chiefly concerned with absorbing the system of contour lines used to describe the limbs and their muscles. A record with the date 1487 on another sheet from the sketchbook suggests that Pollaiuolo's composition was well over twenty years old when Francesco still found it exemplary.

Like both Antonio del Pollaiuolo and Verrocchio, Francesco favoured pen and ink for rapid studies and, though he does not revolve the page, he also follows Verrocchio's method of rethinking poses on the same sheet of paper, apparently with more than one task in mind. There are frequent changes or *pentimenti* to individual figures as he struggled to resolve details of pose on top of a basic schema. To the top left a running baby is shown balanced on the head of a dolphin, a dynamic variant of a type of fountain figure developed by Verrocchio (fig. 66). The motif of the standing blessing Christ Child, the main object of study on the present sheet and one which recurs on several others by Francesco, was a popular theme in both sculpture and painting. Its applications ranged from the isolated figure in the round, of which Desiderio da Settignano had produced the most widely admired example to crown a sacrament tabernacle (fig. 95), to Virgin and Child reliefs like those produced by Verrocchio and his workshop (figs. 68 and 69 and cat. no. 28). The sequence of studies on the present sheet appears to begin on the verso where an upright child, like Desiderio's, may have been studied from a sculptural model, using neat parallel hatching to create relief. To the right the figure is adjusted to create greater flexion in the resting leg and bring in the arms closer to the body. On the recto Francesco then explores the different positions for the blessing gesture and shifts the weighting of the body and angle of the head. The first in the sequence on this side seems to be that to the left, followed by the small central figure who looks down as though positioned at a height. In the swaddled figure at the top, the weight of the *contrapposto* is shifted to the other leg and it is a variation of this figure, standing on a cushion and looking directly at the viewer, that is integrated into the Virgin and Child group at the bottom right. The tender pose of the Virgin and the treatment of the drapery, which reveals the line of the legs and falls in v shapes next to the thigh, can be found in studies from the Verrocchio shop (see cat. no. 34). What is unusual here is the way Francesco combines within a single drawing a Virgin and Child composition and a study of the fall of light on drapery, tasks more often approached separately by Verrocchio.

In studying the subject of the animated baby, Francesco adopted a range of pen notations, including the bracketing curves that describe folds of chubby flesh, and parallel hatching that allow a rapid and readable language for the investigation of problems of pose and relief. Comparison with Verrocchio's studies of babies (cat. no. 36), however, highlights Francesco's distance from the live model, his much weaker grasp of form and complete lack of interest in the psychological implications of movement.

IV   The Pollaiuolo Brothers

Makers of mural and panel paintings, sculptures, goldsmith-ware and designs for work in many media, Antonio and Piero del Pollaiuolo were, with Andrea del Verrocchio, the most inventive and versatile artists established in Florence in the decade of the 1470s. The nature of the brothers' workshop meant that their influence operated in ways quite distinct from that of Verrocchio. As brothers they were able to support one another's careers and collaborate on major projects while also cultivating their own areas of specialisation. Indeed it is better to speak of their having workshops, rather than seeing them as a centralised firm in which an apprentice could potentially be taught both painting and sculpture. Antonio del Pollaiuolo (1431–1498), the elder of the brothers by ten years, was also the more able and wide-ranging, taking the initiative in all the main areas of production in which they engaged. He is first documented in the goldsmith workshop of Miliano Dei in 1457 and, working under Miliano's aegis, he won the major commission to make the lower half of the reliquary cross for the Baptistery in the same year. By the 1470s he was running a thriving goldsmith business, renting his own workshop between the Palazzo Vecchio and the Mercato Nuovo. The Pollaiuolo brothers' work is permeated by a sense for the dramatic and ornamental effects of rich materials that must have been sharpened by constant contact with precious metals and enamels.

In a competitive market, Antonio's success was based on refined technical skills and, above all, on his exceptional talent as a draughtsman and designer which earned him the epithet *maestro di disegno* from a patron, Giovanni Rucellai. This mastery developed from his training as a goldsmith that demanded not only sculptural and architectural sensibilities (fig. 59) but ability in figure design. In goldsmith work the production of engraved plaques depicting saintly or secular episodes encouraged study from the life of the male figure in the linear medium of pen. The drawings of Maso Finiguerra, an older influence on Antonio, demonstrate this phenomenon (fig. 52). In the work of Antonio the same preference for pen and ink as a vehicle for exploring figure contour was made to serve new aesthetic and functional ends. In highly finished designs which were potentially usable in more than one

Fig. 107 Hadrianic sarcophagus relief showing the *Rape of the Daughters of Leucippus*. Marble. Florence, Galleria degli Uffizi.

context, Antonio took antique relief sculpture as a source of compositional and figurative inspiration as well as an ideal with which to compete (cat. no. 57). His *Battle of nude men* engraving, an isolated project (cat. no. 53) that would help to change the status of prints, demonstrates the range of his interests. The male body is anatomised into a convincing bone and muscle structure in a way that simultaneously develops the possibilities of depicting human animation as a principle of good narrative design. Antonio significantly favoured moralising inventions as much as any specific mythological or historical episode as a subject for the composition of battling men.

In compositions of the 1470s, like the monumental *Martyrdom of Saint Sebastian* and the stylistically comparable drawing of *A man seen from three angles* (cat. nos. 43 and 51), Antonio refined the depiction of the male figure tensed for action using highly developed and reusable formulae for the drafting of limbs in variously virile and elegant poses. His solutions exercised a considerable appeal for patrons keen to demonstrate their advanced taste. One of the most remarkable products of Antonio's experiment with the dynamic nude figure is the ruined mural of dancing nudes discovered at the end of the nineteenth century in a villa once belonging to the Lanfredini family (fig. 46). Giovanni and Jacopo Lanfredini were, like Antonio Pucci, the patron of the *Martyrdom*, loyal supporters of the Medici family who had also employed the Pollaiuolo brothers. In the domestic setting of their ground-floor hall, they appear to have allowed Antonio free rein to develop a subject in which the wild, sensual joy of bacchic dancers is expressed in a flamboyant but rhythmic progress across a perspectivally conceived stage. The painting represents, in part, an inventive meditation on the dancing putti of Donatello and the aesthetic of small-scale antique reliefs. Such figures were undoubtedly also informed by Antonio del Pollaiuolo's own activity as a sculptor in this decade. As well as treating his favourite battle theme as a relief, cast in the 'antique' medium of bronze (see cat. no. 54), Pollaiuolo used his ability to conceptualise the male nude figure in the round. His *Hercules and Antaeus* now in the Bargello (fig. 64) is a connoisseur's piece, the most complex and compelling bronze statuette of the early Renaissance.

Antonio del Pollaiuolo found a wider market for his design skills in commissions for objects to be executed by others. In the 1460s Antonio had been engaged to provide a large series of drawings (probably made in ink and wash) showing scenes from the life of Saint John the Baptist. These were translated into embroideries that decorated a set of vestments for the Baptistery (cat. no. 48). The project continued throughout the 1470s and constituted one of the most important narrative cycles to be produced in the decade. Surviving copies after individual scenes as well as figure motifs illustrate the value of Antonio's draughtsmanship as a model for other artists (cat. no. 49).

The distinct qualities of Antonio and Piero del Pollaiuolo's handling of painting on panel – in portraits, altarpieces, *spalliere* and independent small-scale panels – were perhaps more difficult to assimilate. With the notable exception of Leonardo da Vinci, who evidently admired their treatment of landscape and attention to precious surfaces, these were hardly imitated at the time. Inspired by the mimetic brilliance of painters such as Jan van Eyck, the brothers adopted an oil medium which could be applied in glazes in order to evoke transitory and spectacular effects. Ambitious illusions such as the reflective gleam of a brocaded velvet robe or the progressively veiled depths of a landscape receding in perspective had never been captured so successfully by Florentine artists. What is especially striking is the brothers' flexibility of method. The highlights of the foaming torrent in the *Hercules, Nessus and Deianeira* are dashed down with an impetuous speed that leaves the process of painting exposed, while the minutiae of man-made objects are described with extraordinary control. It is only occasionally in Piero del Pollaiuolo's independent work, for example in the Virtues painted for the Mercanzia in the 1470s, that such brush control is sometimes lost. However, as the Mercanzia commission progressed Piero also appears to have adopted a more verrocchiesque approach to the depiction of drapery viewed under a specific light. This was an intelligent response to the task of depicting the seated female figure (fig. 11), a subject of little interest to Antonio, whose preferences lay with figures of Herculean or primitive energy. That Antonio was able to indulge these preferences is indicative of the economic security offered by his work as a goldsmith and of the many benefits of fraternal collaboration.

AW

43

ANTONIO AND PIERO
DEL POLLAIUOLO

The Martyrdom of Saint Sebastian

Walnut oil (where analysed) on poplar,
291.5 × 202.6 cm
London, National Gallery, NG 292

Vasari/Milanesi, vol. 3, pp. 292–3; Davies 1961,
pp. 443–6; Ettlinger 1978, pp. 36–51 and 139–40;
Dunkerton et al. 1991, pp. 201–3 and 316; Wright
1992, pp. 188–218; Wiemers 1996, pp. 121–4 and 129.

We should like to thank Rolf Bagemihl for allowing
us to cite the 1474 documents in anticipation of
his forthcoming article in *Prospettiva*.

AW

Fig. 108. PIERO DEL POLLAIUOLO, Study of the head
of *'Faith'* for the Mercanzia *'Virtues'* cycle, 1470.
Black and red chalk on paper, pricked, 10 × 17 cm.
Florence, Galleria degli Uffizi, Gabinetto Disegni e
Stampe, inv. 14506.

The very large scale and pictorial complexity of the National Gallery altarpiece make it one of the most ambitious paintings to have been produced in 1470s Florence. According to Vasari, the painting was completed in 1475 and more than fulfilled the expectations of its patron, the merchant and banker Antonio Pucci, who was prepared to pay the improbably large sum of 300 scudi (about 300 florins) for it. Two payments by Pucci to Piero del Pollaiuolo in 1474 recently discovered by Rolf Bagemihl support Vasari's dating for the altarpiece. Its size can be explained by its original position dominating the east end of Antonio Pucci's large family oratory dedicated to Saint Sebastian at SS. Annunziata, under construction from the 1450s. The original frame, removed during a seventeenth-century refurbishment, was presumably of the *all'antica* type with flanking pilasters supporting an entablature. By building and endowing the St Sebastian oratory at a church whose miraculous shrine was being adorned by Piero de' Medici, Antonio Pucci (whose armorial device of the Moor's head is incorporated into the triumphal arch within the painting) would have hoped to gain spiritual benefits. The chapel also gave permanent expression to his family's triumph on the Florentine social and political scene, a triumph engineered by their unswerving loyalty to the Medici family (see Chapter 2). The alignment of the Pucci with the Medici is arguably inscribed in the very style of the altarpiece. By commissioning such a monumental work on a quasi heroic subject Antonio Pucci provided the Pollaiuolo brothers with the chance to display the command of the male figure in movement, conceived in an antique idiom, which had been the chief characteristic of their ground-breaking and admired *Labours of Hercules* canvases painted for the Medici palace over a decade earlier (figs. 61 and 62). The immediate function of the altarpiece as a focus for devotion to Saint Sebastian was quite different from that of mythological canvas paintings, but the Pollaiuolo made its representational skill equally apparent. Certainly the many derivations of Pollaiuolo's muscular archers in later paintings show that the altarpiece was received by other artists as exemplary. To cite just one example, the figure of Saint Thomas in Matteo di Giovanni's *Assumption of the Virgin* in the National Gallery seems to represent a very early response to the painting.

The altarpiece shows the (failed) martyrdom of the Roman centurion Sebastian, condemned to death by the emperor Diocletian for his profession of Christianity. Sebastian was not a name saint in the Pucci family, nor did the making of the altarpiece coincide with one of the many bouts of plague for which Saint Sebastian's protection was fervently sought. Instead Antonio Pucci adopted a devotion already established at SS. Annunziata, gaining the right to house a relic of Saint Sebastian's arm bone in the chapel.

The altarpiece has a semi-narrative emphasis and the dominance given to Sebastian's persecutors may have been surprising to the saint's devotees. With its prominent geometry and fascination with muscular masculinity the design is characteristic of Antonio's, rather than Piero's invention. The composition contrives to place Saint Sebastian at the apex of a human triangle grounded in two ranks of archers and crossbowmen arranged on a foreground knoll before an expansive landscape. Yet the stagey complexity of the executioners' poses and their anatomical sophistication tend to draw the eye away from the saint, encouraging appreciation of a visual rhetoric that deliberately compares and contrasts pairs of figures in poses that are approximate mirror images or pivoted variants of one another. Vasari devoted one of his most eloquent passages in the *Lives* to the pictorial achievement of the two foreground

crossbowmen loading their bows, with their difficult, foreshortened poses and appearance of breathless, bodily tension. These muscle men, who can be compared with Antonio del Pollaiuolo's study of a *Man seen from three angles* (cat. no. 50), are arranged parallel to the picture plane like figures on an antique sarcophagus (fig. 107). Indeed the depiction of fictive relief scenes in the triumphal arch referring to Sebastian's life as a soldier and his judgement under Diocletian reinforces an implied competition with ancient sculpted reliefs (fig. 110). Sebastian himself seems less compelling in terms of draughtsmanship, but it is worth remembering that the 'vulgar' types of the bowmen would have diminished their status for any contemporary viewer, while the saint's effete physical type and smooth features would have been read as signs of noble distinction. An early source, repeated by Vasari, has it that Saint Sebastian's features were those of Gino di Ludovico Capponi, who was considered to be one of the most beautiful youths of his age. The physiognomy of the saint, apparently drafted by Piero del Pollaiuolo (compare fig. 108), seems more generic than portrait-like, but the depiction of an admired contemporary 'type' – the youthful and glamorous patrician male – could have served to capture the viewer's attention and inspire devotion for the saint.

The displayed body of Saint Sebastian is framed by dramatic rock formations and raised above a deep panoramic landscape which must have seemed exceptionally naturalistic to a contemporary observer familiar with the misty Arno valley on which it is based. Comparable depictions of rocks and landscape could only be found in Netherlandish paintings, much admired in Florence at this date. However, close examination shows that the achievement of such spatial and atmospheric depth also depends, in the National Gallery painting, on a much looser, more experimental technique than that found in the work of Northern painters such as Jan van Eyck. Liquid paint has been applied with great freedom using glazes, now turned brown, sometimes employing the splayed hairs of the brush. Numerous flecks of blue and impastoed white, and other broken, scumbled effects, are used to conjure up features like trees and houses that register convincingly from a distance (fig. 109). Such effects could only have been achieved with a malleable oil medium and, in those areas where paint samples have been taken, this has been shown to be walnut oil. Complex and extensive incisions using a ruler and compasses suggest that the triumphal arch was constructed directly on the prepared surface of the panel, even though it was finally painted on top of the landscape. Underdrawing, which is visible to the naked eye in the figure of Sebastian, reveals how the figure poses were transferred to the panel in the form of linear contours; several figures, including Saint Sebastian and the second rank of archers, seem to have been drawn nude to establish the positions of their limbs and only 'dressed' at the painting stage, an approach to composition which is characteristic of Antonio del Pollaiuolo. Equally, quite significant changes, such as the enlargement of the front right archer's foot, took place at an advanced stage. That such changes are now visible to the naked eye, and that the paint surface has, in places, shrunk and cracked, is due to the brothers' adoption of a medium in which they apparently had no orthodox training. The painting as a whole also bears the strain of its monumental ambitions, notably in the sometimes uncomfortable disjunctions of viewpoint and the additive figure relations. But the extraordinary treatment of the landscape, the animation of the middle-ground soldiers, not to mention the superbly observed plants, weapons and figures of the foreground testify to the way this painting set new pictorial standards – standards against which the young Leonardo in particular would measure himself (see cat. no. 45 and fig. 73).

Figs. 109 (OPPOSITE) and 110. Details of cat. no. 43.

44

ANTONIO DEL POLLAIUOLO

Man taking aim with a bow

Brown ink and wash with black chalk
underdrawing on paper,
26 × 18 cm
Berlin, Staatliche Museen Preussischer Kulturbesitz,
Kupferstichkabinett, inv. 471

Fusco 1982, pp. 175–94; Schulze Altcappenberg 1995,
pp. 144–6; Wiemers 1996, pp. 128–9.

AW

Fig. 111. ANTONIO DEL POLLAIUOLO, *Study of a nude man*,
mid-1470s. Pen and brown ink and wash on paper,
26.8 × 8.8 cm. Bayonne, Musée Bonnat, 1269.

The poor condition of this drawing may have hindered its acceptance as an autograph work by Antonio del Pollaiuolo, but the approach to the figure as a physical and psychological unity and the vigorous pen technique are comparable with other studies usually attributed to him (fig. 111). The study of an archer taking aim with concentrated relish is conceived in relation to a narrative subject of the type of the *Martyrdom of Saint Sebastian* (cat. no. 43). Though the positioning of the Berlin archer's legs, with one leg in profile and the other extended in three-quarter view, is comparable to the archer to the front left of the National Gallery painting, this configuration is extremely common in Antonio del Pollaiuolo's designs in all media (compare especially cat. no. 50) and need not indicate a specific connection with the altarpiece, where the light falls from the opposite direction. Pollaiuolo is engaged here with his favourite subject, the vigorous male nude in action seen in isolation. As Laurie Fusco has shown, Antonio's compositional inventions in all media economically reuse active poses such as this one, freely adapting them in ways that reveal a flexibility in thinking about forms in both two- and three-dimensional terms. This practice also helps to account for the fact that Pollaiuolo seems to have been able to draft certain figural motifs from memory without recourse to a live model, as seems to be the case in the Berlin drawing. Close examination suggests that disjunctions between, for example, the position of the right arm and head compared to the left arm, which aims the arrow much higher than the head position presupposes, results from a treatment of the figure as a composite of individual limb motifs. While the penning of the archer is supremely confident and flexible, this sureness is partially grounded on faint preparatory drafting in black chalk, not always followed by the pen. The same black chalk is used to sketch horizontal lines between the legs, possibly as an aid to establishing the proportions and alignments of the limbs. The primacy of the linear medium of pen for realising figure contours is even more marked in Pollaiuolo's studies (the knees are left in black chalk and relief is indicated with wash alone) than in those of his fellow goldsmith Maso Finiguerra, whose practice he seems to have followed. Moreover, Antonio achieves a superior mastery of both form and medium by using variations in the width of the pen line to describe the varying swell of muscles as they wrap around the limbs. This minimalist technique encourages the viewer to admire the way that the position of muscles tensed for action can be clearly understood without their actually being described.

Panoramic views were as much a trademark of works by the Pollaiuolo shop as anatomical display. They were not a particularly noteworthy feature of paintings from the Verrocchio studio, however, until Leonardo reworked the background of the San Salvi *Baptism* in the mid-1470s: painting out formulaic trees, adding distant mountains and expanding and extending the river (fig. 74). With these changes the painting gained depth and a subtle sense of the moment as the water moves gently, but inexorably, forward through the landscape. This drawing includes many elements found in the *Baptism* – the craggy ledge, the rocky shore and the meandering water – and it may relate to Leonardo's recasting of the setting, not as preparatory study but as a form of exploration of its essential motifs.

Leonardo later deplored the 'cursory and simple investigations' of those 'who do not care for landscape'. His own investigations dated from at least 5 August 1473, when he made a note of that day on a drawing now in the Uffizi (fig. 73). In the Uffizi drawing he experimented with his pen, trying out different types of notation in order to render the textures as well as the topography of the view: at times precisely shaping, at others sketchily suggesting, its individual features. A similar combination of impressionistic strokes with convincing description is found in paintings by the Pollaiuolo brothers. The perspective of the Uffizi landscape also resembles the type of projection found in their works, which were probably a reference point for Leonardo. Even if the study was inspired by a specific place on a specific day, at this stage of his career Leonardo's way of rendering the landscape was conditioned by pictorial precedents. Like the Pollaiuolo brothers, Leonardo was also influenced by landscape conventions found in Northern painting and prints.

The craggy outcrop that is the focus of the present drawing is both a geological formation that occurs in Tuscany and a compositional formula, seen, for example, in prints by the German engraver known as Master E.S.; it is as though Leonardo sought to bring nature to art by examining a natural phenomenon that was also a serviceable motif. His graphic style is adapted to the subject. He used uneven and broken vertical lines of varying weight to capture the ragged and rugged face of the rocks. Sometimes he emphasised edges with darker lines, but he did not totally enclose the contours. Mass is created by diagonal hatching that shades the uneven surfaces of the cliff. Horizontal hatching, more densely drawn, describes the deep shadow of the gorge. The way that this shading carefully respects the edge of the rocks indicates that the drawing was composed around the massive group at the left. Those rocks were done first, with the responding ledge, the stream, the trees and the water birds added later to complete or create a picture. The development of the landscape, with the river or stream flowing between two ledges, demonstrates Leonardo's fascination with the elemental forces that operate in nature. Leonardo was convinced and moved by the traditional belief that the 'body of the earth' was similar to the 'body of man' and that the water that coursed through the veins of the earth was like the blood that gave life to men. It is this notion that made landscapes a vital component of his paintings and made their study a compelling part of his researches. This drawing shows how the subjects of his scientific curiosity originated in topics of concern in artists' shops in the 1470s.

45
LEONARDO DA VINCI

Ravine

Pen and ink on pink-tinged paper,
22 × 15.8 cm
Windsor, Royal Library, The Royal Collection, 12395

Clark 1969, vol. 1, p. 58, vol. 2 (pl.); Richter 1970, vol. 1, p. 84, for Leonardo on landscape; Gombrich 1976, pp. 33–4, for Leonardo's Uffizi landscape and Netherlandish conventions; *Leonardo da Vinci*, exh. cat., Hayward Gallery 1989, cat. no. 45, p. 107 and pp. 104–17 for the 'body of the earth'.

PLR

46

ANTONIO AND PIERO
DEL POLLAIUOLO

Hercules, Nessus
and Deianeira

Oil and tempera on canvas transferred
from cherry wood panel,
52.6 × 79.7 cm
New Haven, Yale University Art Gallery, University
purchase from James Jackson Jarves, 1871.42

Cruttwell 1907, pp. 78–81; Sirén 1916, pp. 112–17;
Philostratus the Younger, *Imagines*, trans. A Fairbanks
1931, Book 16, pp. 361–3; Seymour 1970, pp. 170–3;
Verdon in *Italian Primitives*, exh. cat., New Haven
1972, pp. 26–7; Owen Hughes 1988, pp. 12—15.

I should like to thank Ellen Callmann who
generously made her notes on the painting available
to us. I am most grateful to Dr Joachim Pissarro,
Dr Carl Strehlke, Andrea Rothe, Mark Leonard, and
above all to Mark Aronson, Chief Conservator at
Yale University Art Gallery, for supplying
information on the restoration of this painting.

A W

The painting exemplifies the Pollaiuolo shop's specialisation in the depiction of the hero Hercules. Transfered from panel to canvas in 1867, the picture surface is much abraded and there are areas of complete loss in Deianeira's body, Nessus' arm and Hercules' lower torso. Pentimenti at the painting stage, found in other paintings by the brothers, have become visible over time (for example, a second set of the centaur's rear hoofs). These problems have been readdressed in a recent cleaning and conservation campaign that has restored some sense of the painting's original spatial recession, which was compromised by the loss of glazes. The re-examination has also affirmed that it is a hazardous task to deduce which brother was responsible for the painting. Like the lost canvases of the *Labours of Hercules* for the Medici palace and the *Martyrdom of Saint Sebastian* (cat. no. 43) the painting may have involved both Antonio and Piero.

The Greek legend of Hercules, Nessus and Deianeira, recounted most accessibly in Ovid's *Metamorphoses*, illustrates Hercules' *virtù* in slaying the centaur, despite his adversary's superior speed, when Nessus had attempted to abduct his bride. Ovid relates that, wishing to cross the swollen river Evenus, Hercules entrusted Deianeira to Nessus who had offered himself as ferryman. Hearing the cry of the pallid and fearful Deianeira, the hero realised Nessus' intention to make off with her and slew him on the spot with a poisoned arrow. We do not know for whom the Pollaiuolo rendition was painted, nor its precise function, but the dimensions of the picture and its original cherry wood support suggest that it might have served as a *spalliera* painting set within, or above, a piece of furniture. Though the subject, characterised by one author as 'unflattering', was once thought to exclude it as a work commissioned for a patrician chamber, the depiction of rape was in fact increasingly popular in precisely this context in later fifteenth-century Florence, where it was used to reinforce the imperative of female chastity and submission to marriage bonds. Although Deianeira is a much more ambivalent figure in the Greek myth on which the painting is based, she is presented here as an appropriate example of marital continence, saved from the bestial attentions of the centaur by the heroic virtue of her husband.

The subject was rarely depicted in the early Renaissance, and the most vivid rendition of it appears rather in a description of a painting by the late Hellenistic writer Philostratus' in his *Imagines*. Similarities in evocative character, as well as in particular details, suggest that the antique text may have served as a source, or rather a word-picture to be competed with: 'Do not fear the river Evenus, my boy, though it rises in great waves and the water overflows its banks, for it is a painting; rather let us examine its details . . . Does not the divine Heracles attract your attention as he advances thus into the middle of the river, his eyes flashing fire and measuring off the distance to the mark, while he holds the bow in his outstretched left hand and still keeps his right hand in the attitude of one who has let fly the arrow? . . . Do you see the centaur giving his last leap? . . . Deianeira is painted in the attitude of one in danger, in the extremity of her fear stretching out her arms to Heracles.' In the Pollaiuolo painting, the impassable torrent, swollen with winter rain, seems to pour out of the picture towards the viewer, emphasising its pivotal role in the story. It also provides an equivalent in nature to the character of the narrative itself, evoking the lively movement of Nessus' escape and of Hercules' swift response. In the Yale painting the diagonal impulses and counter-impulses implied by the figures' movements in the Philostratus description extend through the whole design of the picture. Rocky outcrops, which serve as frames to the scene, restate the movement of Nessus and Hercules towards the centre of the picture.

The technique and appearance of the deeply receding panorama ringed by hills are closely comparable to the landscape in the *Martyrdom of Saint Sebastian* (cat. no. 43), with the valley based on specific observation of the Arno plain but combining different views. Deianeira's raised left arm and hand seem to place the diminutive view of Florence under its blessing, though examination has shown a now obliterated arm further to the left that may have represented a later change of mind. The impressively difficult tilted profile of Hercules' head also recalls that of the archer to the far left of the *Martyrdom*. Deianeira's body (considerably restored) is another object of representational *difficoltà* with her classicising, if not entirely successful, *contrapposto*. But it is the landscape, whose range of greens has now turned to brown, that really dominates, both in its structural importance to the narrative and in its naturalistic rendering. In particular the loose, layered handling of the river, only possible with an oil medium, is radically gestural, even unfinished looking, by the standards of the period. Layering glazes and scumbled highlights over the brown river bed, the painter exploits the potential of the new medium. It is almost as though the rapidity of the brushwork is claimed by the Pollaiuolo as a display of *virtù* to rival Hercules' swiftness.

47

ANTONIO DEL POLLAIUOLO

Hercules and the Hydra

Pen and ink on paper,
23.5 × 16.5 cm
London, British Museum, Department of Prints
and Drawings, 5210-8 recto
The drawing has been cut in half horizontally,
then reattached with a sliver missing, now replaced.

Popham and Pouncey 1950, cat. no. 225, pp. 138–9;
Ettlinger 1978, cat. no. 32, p. 160; Wright 1992,
pp. 99–102; Nathan 1996, pp. 88–9 and
Appendix pp. 97–9.

AW

Pollaiuolo has here used pen and ink to formulate a composition expressive of violent movement: the battle of the hero Hercules with the many-headed Hydra. Despite the summary rendering of the monster, the subject can be identified with reference to Antonio's project for three canvas paintings of Hercules' *Labours* (for the Medici palace). The mythological story in which Hercules destroys the Hydra that had poisoned the marshes of Lerna gave Antonio the opportunity to work out a motif – the lunging figure in battle – that was to become the most copied of all his inventions. The principal feature of the design is its forward impulse embodied in the combination of Hercules' supporting leg, shown bent and in profile, with his free leg extended behind him. Appropriately for the mythological theme, this motif derives from relief depictions of the battling male nude found in antique sculpture (fig. 107).

Comparing the Uffizi panel of the same subject with the pen drawing, the panel (fig. 61) seems further resolved in favour of Hercules' victory; the hero's head and torso fall into a continuous line with his extended leg, while the movement of grasping the Hydra's neck is completed. The drawing therefore probably represents an earlier and less developed stage than the paintings on canvas. Another variant in the drawing which appears in engraved copies is Hercules' flaming brand, a substitute for his usual club. This refers to the hero's ingenious cauterising of the severed necks to prevent them from resprouting two-fold. It has also been proposed as a contemporary allusion to the Medici device of the burning knotted staff or *broncone*, though it is not clear whether this device was used as early as 1460, when this drawing was probably made.

Anatomical shortcomings in the drawing, such as the connection of Hercules' right armpit to his bicep seem to have been adjusted in later versions. But it is in the pen study that the effect of movement is most strongly evoked. The Hydra and its serpentine coils are formed from no more than a few fluent and emphatic counter-strokes. The combination of sweeping curves and shorter broken lines in the figure of Hercules, executed without underdrawing and with few changes, indicates a new bravado and rapidity in handling the pen which rivals that of Verrocchio and inspired the young Leonardo. The possibility that the hero was studied from a live model is precluded by his almost floating movement, but the assurance in the depiction of the male nude speaks of the painter's continual practice of study from the life. Like Pollaiuolo's Louvre drawing (cat. no. 50), the *Hercules and the Hydra* traces a deliberate path between observation and schema. The tensed muscles are plotted in convincing relation to one another and to the substructure of the skeleton, but Antonio subordinates naturalism to the dynamic thrusts of the body. By bringing into view muscles not normally visible simultaneously, the body is legible in three dimensions as well as in two. Hercules' limbs form a matrix of diagonal, parallel lines of force that stand for a motion they cannot actually depict. This composition also demonstrates how such forces are specifically attached to the masculine virtues of Hercules. They are dramatically set against the mellifluous and clasping coils of the serpentine and essentially feminine Hydra. Thus the two-dimensional graphic effect of the work, with its contrasts of linear form, is both highly decorative and thematically appropriate.

48

DESIGNED BY ANTONIO DEL POLLAIUOLO

Saint John the Baptist at the court of Herod

Or nué embroidery,
30 × 51 cm
Florence, Museo dell' Opera del Duomo

Vasari/ Milanesi, vol. 3, pp. 299–300;
Schwabacher 1911, esp. pp. 89–90; Sabatini 1941,
pp. 72–98; Garzelli 1973, pp. 5–12; Ettlinger 1978,
cat. no. 26, pp. 156–19; Frank 1988, Part 1;
Newbigin 1996, pp. 121–2.

AW

The embroidery is one of 27 surviving panels cut down from a set of liturgical vestments commissioned by the Merchants' guild (Calimala) to be worn by the celebrant and his assistants on major feast days in the Florentine Baptistery. The scenes appeared as friezes (orphreys) and panels attached to a cope, a chasuble, a dalmatic and a tunicle worn by the officiating priest, his deacon and sub-deacon respectively, but no record was kept of their original positions before the white brocaded vestments woven in Florence were dismembered. Reconstructions have had to focus on the different formats of the panels and their subjects, as well as on supposed stylistic changes in Antonio's compositions as they were supplied to the embroiderers over many years. The spatial construction is more sophisticated in some scenes than in others, and especially in this example, but changes in approach from scene to scene were also dependent on the requirements of the narrative and the traditions of depiction that would help to make them legible and it is not possible to be categorical about the date of individual designs. Vasari pays eloquent tribute to the beauty of the finished vestments, and to the brilliance of the embroiderers, in his Life of the Pollaiuolo brothers, claiming they took 26 years to make. The documentation of the project in the records of the Calimala guild (known only through later, incomplete, transcriptions) suggest a time span little short of this, calculating from the election of the embroiders on 5 August 1466 to the final computation of expenses for the entire project, which cost many thousands of florins, in 1487. Some of Antonio del Pollaiuolo's designs presumably predate 1466 if the embroiders began work immediately, but the first documented payment to Pollaiuolo for designs is the sum of 90 florins recorded on 9 August 1469, while a second record, of a further 90 florins, is made in 1480, around the time the embroidered panels were being completed.

The Calimala was evidently prepared to spare no expense in honouring the cult of the Baptist and, indirectly, themselves as administrators of the Baptistery and as a powerful guild. Their investment was represented equally in ingenious design, quality of materials and the extraordinary executive skill of the weavers and embroiderers over a long period. The embroideries are executed in a technique devisded in the Netherlands known as *or nué*. The base canvas is given a horizontal foundation of silk thread wrapped in thin ribbons of beaten gold. It is then worked over vertically (couched) with coloured silks, allowing more gold to show through in the lighter areas. With this technique both line and tone are depicted with a subtlety that Vasari rightly compared to painting. The main contours of the setting and of elements of dress are outlined in gold-bound thread (many are restorations); the delicate modelling of the flesh and hair, which preserves Antonio's drawing style, is worked in panels of close stitching (*punto serrato*). Where the embroideries are damaged, traces of drawing fixed in black thread have become visible. Over the whole period the embroiderers employed numbered five from Italy (among whom one Paolo da Verona seems to have taken precedence) and six from the Netherlands, France and Spain, a team apparently headed by Coppino di Malines who was paid more than all the others for his work. Before the gold thread became tarnished the embroideries would have had an immensely rich effect comparable to the gold mosaics of the dome of the Baptistery; like the mosaics, they exploit a deliberately limited colour range which would give them legibility and coherence from a distance.

Counting the cycle in the dome, on the south doors and on the silver altar, Antonio del Pollaiuolo's was the fourth series of narratives on the life of Saint John for the

Baptistery, and his designs show an awareness of these illustrious precedents even though they are clearly conceived with the needs of their specific scale and eventual medium in mind. The vestment cycle, whose episodes are almost all biblical rather than apocryphal, is the most extensive of the four and, given the need to avoid repetition, it presented a considerable challenge to Antonio's powers of invention as a *maestro di disegno*. In fact the settings of the narrative, like the poses of many of the figures, provide variations on a theme: the rocky wilderness, the distant landscape, the arched arcades and regularly panelled and coffered spaces of Renaissance architectural interiors.

The large-scale horizontal format of the present panel (one of three surviving with the same dimensions) indicates that it must have been designed for one of four positions to the bottom of the front or the back of either the dalmatic or the tunicle. The scene illustrates Mark 6: 18 in which John declares to Herod that it was unlawful for him to have married Herodias who had been his brother's wife. Like other architectural interiors of the cycle, the space defined is a deep one but, more unusually, it is populated with figures from foreground to background. The staging of Herod's court is masterly, with a central perspective that sidelines the ruler's throne and frames the centrally positioned Baptist like a monumental sculpture. Saint John, in his camel hair garment, appears elevated on a podium with his accusatory gesture directed towards Herod and Herodias, while the former parries his speech with his pointing left hand. In the foreground Herodias' daughter Salome appears. Tellingly it is the latter, whose allure is the eventual vehicle of the Baptist's downfall, who directs the viewer back to the prophet with her engaging look and gesture. The simmering drama of the scene – the general stir caused by the Baptist's accusation – is registered in the highly animated gestures and postures of the gathered audience who, soldiers and sages alike, listen intently or dispute with one another. Characteristically for Antonio, the depiction of their hands is especially elegant and eloquent and, like their dress, is partly based on fashionable Northern court styles that he would have known in Netherlandish painting and Northern prints. By varying details such as the extravagant hats with their turbaned or curling rims, used almost indiscriminately by Pollaiuolo for exotic 'eastern' types whether Greeks, Turks or Jews (compare cat. no. 77), he introduces variety and establishes a distance in time and place from the contemporary viewer. The architecture is defined by three barrel-vaulted arches receding in perspective, a domesticated version of the great Roman vaults devised by Donatello as a backdrop for one of his bronze reliefs for the altar of the Santo in Padua. As elsewhere in the cycle (and in other Calimala commissions), the viewer is carefully reminded that the spectacle is brought to them by appointment of the guild by the inclusion of their device – the eagle carrying a parcel of cloth – within the architectural setting. The vividness of this scene, which was probably one of the later ones Antonio designed in the 1470s, recalls the events from the Baptist's life as they might have been staged in the sacred plays performed on feast days, involving, as they did, not just the main protagonists but hosts of bystanders. Though intended for luxurious vestments that were rarely on view, Antonio's designs for settings and for animated figures found their way back into common visual currency through copy drawings (cat. no. 49) as well as individual motifs introduced in engravings (cat. no. 67) and woodcuts illustrating printed texts of sacred plays.

241

49

AFTER ANTONIO DEL POLLAIUOLO

Saint John the Baptist questioned

Pen and grey-brown ink and brown wash
on paper (black line around edge of
sheet added later),
27.9 × 22.9 cm.
Berlin, Staatliche Museen Preussischer Kulturbesitz,
Kupferstichkabinett, inv. 5028

Inscribed: *Alessio Baldovinetti fiorentino* in
black chalk on the verso

Schwabacher 1911, pp. 36–8 and 66–7; Frank 1988.

AW

The drawing records Antonio del Pollaiuolo's design for one of the many embroidered scenes of the life of Saint John the Baptist (see cat. no. 48). Though the better preserved faces in the surviving embroidery panel have similarly small, slightly timid features, the handling of the feet, hands and faces in this drawing is feeble compared to pen and ink studies by Antonio's own hand (cat. no. 44). The main forms and contours, outlined in grey-brown ink, and the fine gradation of tone in the internal wash have, nonetheless, been handled with great care as though to ensure an accurate reflection of Pollaiuolo's intentions with regard to the design. The high degree of finish of this drawing and its resemblance in every detail to the embroidery indicate that it was made from Antonio's completed composition, but its precise relation is difficult to clarify, especially as there is no visible underdrawing. It is conceivable that Antonio himself commissioned an assistant to make a copy as a record before the original drawings left his hands but the dimensions are not identical to the embroidered design as one would expect if this were the case. Antonio's own designs may have been made directly onto the cloth to be embroidered or may have been damaged by their use as models for the embroiderers. No drawing by his hand now survives. Another possibility, suggested by the similarity in the facial types, is that this copy was made after the finished embroidery, in which the physiognomy is less robust than in works executed by Antonio himself. What is certain is that the Berlin drawing, like a more mechanical copy after another Baptistery composition (*Zachariah leaving the Temple*, now in the Uffizi inv. 98F), registers interest in preserving Antonio's figural compositions for the use of other artists. It is also feasible that the copy was made in anticipation of larger commercial exploitation of his designs in the form of prints after the Baptist cycle, though if such a project were planned it never materialised.

This episode corresponds broadly to Luke 3: 10-16 in which the Baptist is questioned by the people and he prophesies the coming of Christ. His interlocutors have been called tax collectors (Luke 3: 12–13) though they do not have any specific attributes; the Baptist's gesture towards his cross, indicating his secondary role to the Messiah, may refer to Luke 3: 16. The scene is the least dramatic of several from the Baptistery cycle that are staged against the rocky backdrop of the wilderness. In each, the diagonal emphasis of the stylised rocks gives a forward impetus to the narrative even though the panels were actually placed one above another on the vestments rather than juxtaposed. The Berlin drawing has an otherwise static composition, but the figural group would have provided a useful model for how to vary the postures of bystander figures. Equally, individual motifs are presented as exemplary. The angular treatment of cascading drapery folds in the central figure, which is indebted to Filippo Lippi, is similar to the type imitated by Leonardo in cat. no. 75, where he seems to have a pollaiuolesque 'exotic' figure in mind. Antonio himself reused this drapery motif, as well as the lower legs of the figure appearing to the right, in the scene of *Zachariah leaving the Temple*. This martial stance with the legs apart sprung to Antonio's pen with particular ease and he was able to exploit it in many contexts and on different scales: it can be compared here with the bottom right-hand archer of the *Martyrdom of Saint Sebastian* (cat. no. 43). His reuse of successful solutions for drafting human anatomy can also be demonstrated by comparing the Baptist's left leg, seen to our right in this drawing, with the identical formula used for this limb in the embroidery of *Saint John at the court of Herod* (cat. no. 48).

243

50

ANTONIO DEL POLLAIUOLO

Man seen from three angles

Stylus, pen and dark brown ink and light
wash on darkened paper, laid down,
26.5 cm (at highest point) × 36 cm
(at widest point)
Paris, Musée du Louvre, Département
des Arts Graphiques, 1486

The sheet is slightly cut down at either side
and along the base

Inscribed: *[A]ntonii Jaco[b]i excellentissimi ac eximii
florentini pictoris sculptorisque prestantissimi hoc opus est. /
Umquam hominum imaginem fecit / Vide quam mirum in
membra redegit*

Degenhart 1939, esp. pp. 125–35; Middeldorf 1958,
pp. 167–77, esp. p. 168; Richter 1970, vol. 1,
pp. 189–91; Fusco 1982, p. 186; Nathan 1995,
pp. 73–82.

A W

The Latin epigram inscribed on this drawing reads: 'This is the work of the
excellent and famous Florentine painter and outstanding sculptor Antonio di
Jacopo. When he depicts man look how marvellously he renders the limbs.' Providing
a prestigious gloss on the artist's powers of representation, the inscription was almost
certainly added to the drawing soon after it was made (the ink is the same colour as that
of the drawing, but it is in a neat humanist hand which is not Pollaiuolo's). Part of the
same inscription appears again on one of the several copies after the sheet (cat. no. 51).
The addition of this Latin verse, the existence of copies and the very form of the
drawing, with its neatly arranged figures and separate limb studies, suggest that the
sheet was always intended to demonstrate Antonio del Pollaiuolo's unique skills as
a draughtsman of human anatomy. Antonio is praised here as both painter and sculptor
and several scholars have argued that what the drawing represents is in fact views of
a sculpted figure by Pollaiuolo seen from three different angles. According to this
hypothesis, which appeals to our knowledge of Pollaiuolo as a maker of bronze
statuettes (see cat. no. 58), differences in the positions of the arms from one figure to
another would be accounted for by the use of a malleable sculpted model whose limbs
could be adjusted. Recently, however, it has been noted that the comparison between the
limb arrangements of the man seen from the front and that seen from behind suggests
a two-dimensional relationship as much as a three-dimensional one: the contours of the
two figures are substantially very similar and it is principally the interior modelling that
implies a single figure pivoted through 180 degrees. In this respect, the approach to
depiction of the figure in space is identical to that in the *Martyrdom of Saint Sebastian*
altarpiece (cat. no. 43), where not only do similar striding figures appear to be 'pivoted'
but the contours of the bending legs of the crossbowmen seen from the front and from
behind are virtually the same. Like the crossbowmen, however, the details of the
contours do not duplicate one another precisely. The figure to the right in the Louvre
drawing is slightly larger than its counterpart, the position of the shoulders is more
dynamic and the clenched right hand is positioned differently. While the relationship
between the figures (front, back and side) and the heads (three-quarter view, profile and
lost profile) is evidently a three-dimensional one, in which the form and muscle
structure of the parts are presented in three demonstration views avoiding any overlap,
the choice of pose and viewpoint and treatment of the contour suggests that Antonio
had in mind prototypes from antique sarcophagi as much as freestanding figures.

Antonio del Pollaiuolo's authorship of the Louvre drawing, which has sometimes
been questioned, is strongly implied by stylus incisions that are not followed in the final
pen lines, as well as by changes of mind (*pentimenti*) at the pen stage, such as the
readjustment of the arm to the far left. Emphasising unbroken contours, Antonio
skilfully manipulated the quill to vary the width of the pen stroke, defining the swell
of muscles as they fold around the figure, as he does in other pen studies such as that
of an archer (cat. no. 44). What is unusual in the present drawing is the way the muscles
themselves have been distinctly outlined to indicate their placement and interrelation,
as though Antonio was probing just below the surface of the skin. Restricting his
preferred wash technique, Antonio chose to employ a zig-zag hatching method rather
like that found in the *Battle of nude men* engraving (cat. no. 53) to bring out the relief
within the anatomy. It has been convincingly argued that Antonio del Pollaiuolo, who
was clearly unaware of certain muscles and tendons and misunderstood the forms and

interrelation of others, can never, as Vasari claimed, have undertaken the dissections of human cadavers that would have revealed those muscles. Leonardo, who later clearly did undertake dissections (*notomie*), would criticise anatomical renderings such as those of Pollaiuolo which show all visible muscles flexed simultaneously in a way that is physically impossible and disregards the requirements of a particular movement. Antonio appears to have based his observations in the Louvre drawing on the surface study of a live model with a distinct muscular development (perhaps even a professional fighter) and combined different muscle flexions within the same figure. Choosing postures and viewpoints that best display the main muscle groups and which encourage comparison between front, back and side views, he also demonstrates difficult effects of foreshortening, especially noticeable in the torso and far leg of the central figure. To anyone but a viewer with exceptional specialist knowledge, Antonio's figures would have appeared to be highly sophisticated from an anatomical point of view and convincingly imbued with vigorous life. Indeed the Latin inscription, urging the viewer to admire the depiction of the limbs (two arms are actually shown detached), literally inscribes an audience for the drawing that is educated, familiar with the tradition of the Latin epigram referring to works of art, capable of judging artistic value and whose interests centre on man and his works. In short, the inscription defines the drawing within the realm of humanist study. It is especially telling that the inscription refers to the rendering of the figure in terms of the division of the body into 'membra' – members, parts or limbs. This way of conceptualising the body follows an ancient model in which the harmony of the whole is constituted by the relation of parts, a model employed by the humanist Leon Battista Alberti in his treatises on the arts of painting, sculpture and architecture. But for all its programmatic quality the drawing never becomes a mere intellectual exercise. The figure, like so many that Pollaiuolo would have admired on antique reliefs, is tensed for action; indeed he can be imagined to be brandishing a weapon in his right hand. By suggesting a warrior, Pollaiuolo's favourite figure-type in both painting and sculpture, his invention could be freely adapted to the needs of his own art and, potentially, to that of other artists concerned with the active male figure, such as Luca Signorelli and Leonardo. In the work of the latter, a study such as his profile of an adult male leg that displays its proportions and musculature (Windsor, Royal Library, no. 12632, *c.* 1490–1500) pays obvious tribute to Pollaiuolo's design at the same time as it serves as a critique of the older master's work.

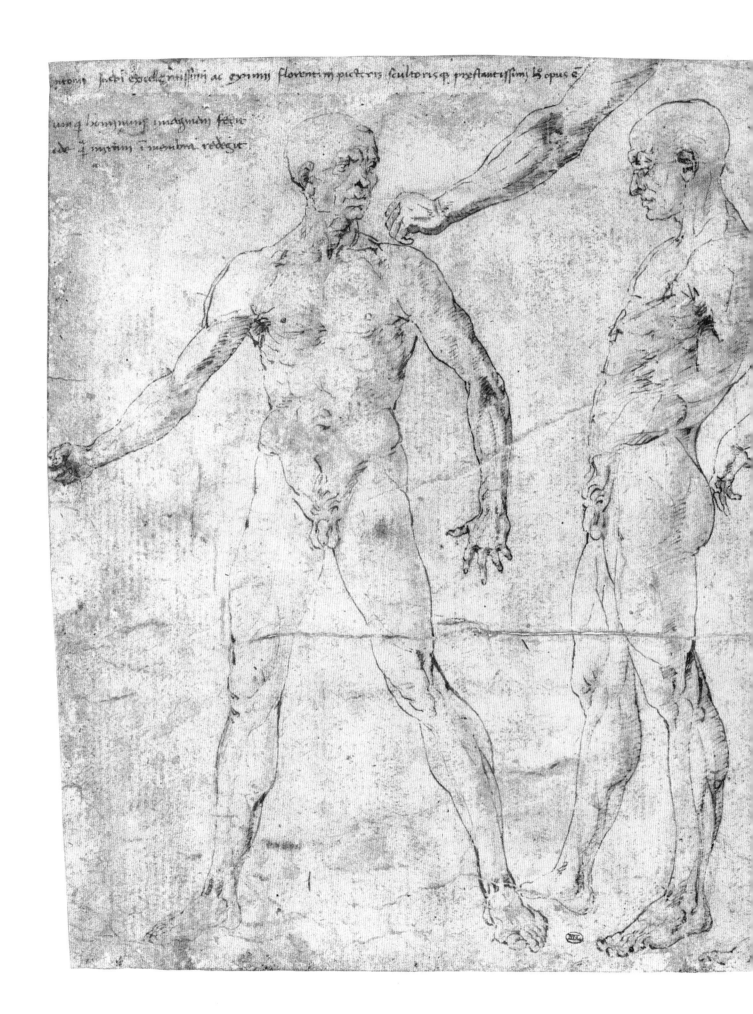

51

COPY AFTER

ANTONIO DEL POLLAIUOLO

Man seen from three angles

Pen and brown ink on parchment
(discoloured to yellow/orange), laid down,
25.5 × 28.1 cm
London, British Museum, Department of Prints
and Drawings, 1885-5-9-1614
Inscribed: [U]mquam hominum imaginem fecit / Vide quam
[...]rum in membra redegit

Popham and Pouncey 1950, cat. no. 226, pp. 139–40;
Ames-Lewis and Wright, exh. cat., Nottingham
and London 1983, pp. 196–9.

AW

This copy after Antonio del Pollaiuolo's drawing of a nude man seen from three angles has been cut down heavily along the right-hand edge but still provides evidence of having been based directly on the Louvre sheet showing a nude figure from three angles (cat. no. 50). The copyist has not only repeated *pentimenti* (such as the change of the arm position in the figure to the right) found in the Louvre drawing – but has clearly tried to imitate both the handwriting and positioning of the Latin inscription. The approximation of the earlier handwriting makes the British Museum sheet difficult to date, though the damage and discoloration to the parchment suggest that it is early. Certainly the existence of this type of copy proves what is already implicit in the presentation of the Louvre sheet: that Pollaiuolo's treatment of the anatomy of the active male nude held unprecedented authority and served as a model for other artists. Numerous copies and adaptations of individual figures from the Louvre sheet are known – a drawing now in the Fogg Art Museum (inv. no. 1932.0260) provides a basic tracing of the man seen from behind and the central, profile figure appears on another fifteenth-century sheet in the Uffizi (269E recto), to cite just two of the more literal copies. Undoubtedly many more have not survived. What is exceptional about the British Museum version is its completeness in every detail, and the choice of a durable parchment support suggests that it was thought important to preserve it as a model. Though the handling of the pen is much less flexible and assured than in Antonio del Pollaiuolo's drawing, the copyist has gone to considerable lengths to keep figures to the same scale as those in the Louvre sheet and has even, if somewhat unconvincingly, imitated the loose pen shading. Significantly, the first lines on the Louvre drawing, which refer to Antonio del Pollaiuolo as author of the design, have been omitted, perhaps to avoid the possibility of mistaking the sheet as autograph. Rather than passing itself off as an 'original' this drawing presupposes the superiority of Pollaiuolo's *disegno* and it seems likely that the model was so famous within Florentine workshops as to require no explicit acknowledgement of his invention.

52

ANTONIO DEL POLLAIUOLO

Profile portrait
of a young man

Black chalk on paper, traces of brown ink and stylus,
39.1 × 24.7 cm (at widest point)
Dublin, National Gallery of Ireland, 2233 recto
Inscribed on the verso: *Antº del pollaiuolo*
The sheet has been cut along the profile of the entire
bust and head on the recto and subsequently inlaid.

Sutton 1967, p. 5 (attributed to Francesco Pesellino);
Master European Drawings, Washington 1983, pp. 6–7;
Angelini in Bellosi ed. *Pittura di Luce*, exh cat.,
Florence 1990, p. 156.

A W

Fig. 112. Verso of cat. no 52.

Examination of this sheet, with its early attribution to Antonio del Pollaiuolo, yields clues to its different functions for the artist and to its later history. The main subject, on the recto, is the under-lifesize portrait head of a boy. Brown ink lines and traces of wash that follow the contours of the portrait indicate that this once had a dark background, probably not original, which was subsequently cut away. The great delicacy of the profile head, the barrel-chested stance, the lighting of the face from the front, and the careful positioning of the viewpoint to look down on the shoulder are characteristic of other portraits attributed to Antonio del Pollaiuolo (see fig. 63). The alert characterisation also recalls portrait-like drawings, probably of workshop assistants, made by Antonio's goldsmith colleague Maso Finiguerra. While Maso consistently used pen and wash, Pollaiuolo, like Verrocchio, can be seen here developing the possibilities of black chalk, a medium not extensively used before this date, to create the subtle nuances of tone and delicate textural affects that are so typical of his art in the 1470s. In this case Antonio seems to have used a soft, friable chalk for the facial features and for shading in the neck and hat before working over the drawing with a darker, greasier chalk that could be sharpened to a point, in order to give definition and depth to the swinging curls of the hair and the crumpled folds of the neckscarf. The profile, traditionally favoured for donor portraits on altarpieces, was a portrait view associated with the virtue and worth of the sitter, and its popularity in Florence was also sustained by association with the commemorative form taken by famous figures on ancient coins. Antonio del Pollaiuolo was one of the most talented exponents of the profile portrait, and his depictions of patrician sitters compensate for the lack of direct communication with the viewer by their extraordinary veristic immediacy and liveliness of contour. The sitter here is wearing a rather unusual soft hat worn forward on the head and turned up at the back, but there is nothing otherwise distinctive about his dress and it is difficult to judge his social status. It is possible that in this drawing Pollaiuolo was practising his skills of observation and of portrait composition employing someone available in the workshop rather than preparing for a painting of this sitter.

The use of a soft black chalk that registers any indentations in the paper has served to reveal the incised contours of a small figure drawn with a stylus. The outlines of the legs and outstretched arm of a nude youth in a *contrapposto* pose suggest a workshop study of a *garzone*, which preceded the use of the sheet to draw the head. The stylus lines of the legs, drawn against the current orientation of the sheet, are just visible across the boy's neckscarf. The verso of the sheet (fig. 112) shows part of an accomplished black chalk study of a right foot, which examines the articulation of the bones and the veins beneath the skin, brought dramatically into relief by strong side lighting. This type of foreshortened bare foot is extremely common in the paintings of both Antonio and Piero del Pollaiuolo; the treatment and direction of light here suggests the possibility of a study in preparation for the *Martyrdom of Saint Sebastian* (cat. no. 43) (it can be compared to the foot of the archer to the bottom left of the altarpiece). The rapid chalk drawing below this foot, with its indications of mouldings, dangling rings and rosettes (?) appears to be a design for a piece of goldsmith's work.

V   The Heroic and the Antique

FOR FLORENTINE ARTISTS of the fifteenth century, antiquity was understood less as an historical period than as a fount of ideas and artistic models. Contemporary scholarship was dependent on written accounts rather than archaeological investigation; few knew any ancient Greek art at first hand and Roman art was not yet chronologically distinguished. But the rather vague and encompassing notion of 'the antique' did not stand in the way of its exemplary function and for many artists of the 1470s, the style all'antica (in the antique manner) was increasingly equated with good style, being considered both beautiful and worthy. Fascination and competition with classical models can be traced in the work of Florentine artists of the 1470s in numerous forms – in exemplary subjects, in stylistic debts, and in the revival of specific types of antique object.

Heroes and heroines of classical myth and history had begun to inhabit the domestic sphere of the patrician palace in the first half of the fifteenth century, appearing on domestic objects, especially marriage chests. In the 1470s, episodes from heroic lives also invaded other types of domestic decoration such as wall panelling and sculpted reliefs. The inspiration of antique sculpture, whether monumental (like the bronze equestrian monument) or miniature (the cameo and intaglio, cat. no. 6), exercised a powerful hold over artists working in many media. Opportunities for large-scale sculpted monuments were not always forthcoming in Florence and both Antonio del Pollaiuolo and Verrocchio had to wait for commissions elsewhere in Italy to produce their greatest works in an antique idiom (fig. 113). Within Florence, Verrocchio's tomb of Piero and Giovanni de' Medici makes use of materials and forms characteristic of Roman monuments to create a wholly original object (fig. 16). Antonio del Pollaiuolo made new contributions to the development of the bronze statuette, a revival of an antique type that had been pioneered by Donatello and which, like medals, now joined ancient examples as new collectors' objects. Antique forms and ornaments permeated almost all aspects of design from the decorative vocabulary of domestic and liturgical furniture produced in the workshop of Giuliano and Benedetto da Maiano to engraved prints (cat. nos. 53). But what also emerges in the period is that antique examples licensed an approach to artistic invention and could even represent a type of fantasy world that stimulated the creative imagination.

For a Florentine artist to make a work all'antica rarely presupposed a concern for archaeological authenticity.

This is even true of one of the artists most obviously fascinated by antiquity, Antonio del Pollaiuolo, whose work in the heroic genre provides a focus here. The triumphal arch that flanks the martyred Saint Sebastian of his Pucci altarpiece (fig. 110) is a case in point. While Antonio almost certainly knew Roman monuments such as the Arch of Constantine, he avoided close imitation of an actual source. He preferred to invent a decorative structure appropriate to the period of the martyrdom, carrying reliefs that may be understood to refer thematically to the saint's life.

Antique sculpted reliefs, whether on monuments or sarcophagi, were the major source for Antonio's figurative vocabulary and to a lesser exent for his approach to composition. He also drew on the subjects of such reliefs, showing a special interest in fierce battles that provided the opportunity to show the male figure in vigorous action (fig. 107). It is above all this theme of combat that seems to have underpinned a more vigorous and often explicitly violent ideal that predominates in the all'antica imagery of the 1470s. Verrocchio is said to have made a cartoon of battling nudes for a mural painting, but it is Pollaiuolo's inventive compositions, especially his engraving of a *Battle of nude men*, that are now better known and which were widely reproduced at the time. They seem to have been partly intended to provide a model for other artists in the same way that antique art itself was exemplary. Pollaiuolo's designs circulated as drawings and as prints. According to Vasari, copies of a cast relief of battling figures by Antonio were kept in a number of artists' workshops. It is likely that cat. no. 54 records this model.

But Antonio del Pollaiuolo cannot have produced such works for a market consisting entirely of other artists and indeed it is a feature of the 1470s that both an all'antica figurative style and classical and mythological themes were extremely fashionable among patrician patrons. The works discussed below highlight the popularity of images of the warrior as hero and show how both traditional objects and new forms were devised as bearers of this heroic imagery. The statuette, a revived antique form further developed in this decade by Antonio del Pollaiuolo and Verrocchio, was particularly suitable to this task because of its possibilities for formal invention. Its small scale suggests that it was

Fig. 113. ANDREA DEL VERROCCHIO, completed by ALESSANDRO LEOPARDI, *Equestrian monument to Bartolommeo Colleoni.* Bronze on marble and Istrian stone plinth with bronze relief. Venice, Campo SS. Giovanni e Paolo.

intended to cater to a restricted, connoisseurial taste rather than serve public ends. Intensified interest in warrior heroes is difficult to relate to specific moments in the city's politics. Instead, like the *giostre* or staged combats of Medicean Florence (see Chapter 1) ancient and biblical warriors could serve as legitimising imagery whose message was conveniently generalised and open to a variety of interpretations, including anachronistic chivalric ones.

The mythical hero Hercules had been used as an example of victory over tyranny from the earliest period of Florentine communal government. Then, in the first half of the fifteenth century, the biblical victors David and Judith joined Hercules as republican exemplars. In these cases the protagonist overcame physical weakness to vanquish the tyrannical foe by stealth and intellect and the support of God, qualities that could be made emblematic of Florentine vulnerability, virtue and prowess. The subjects of David and Goliath and Judith and Holofernes, first treated in sculpture by Donatello, were readdressed in a number of works by Antonio del Pollaiuolo and Verrocchio from the 1460s and 1470s. In these sculptures the old republican exemplars take on new guises, accentuating qualities of *prontezza* (readiness), confidence and animation. One of these is Pollaiuolo's bronze statuette of Judith (cat. no. 58) whose treatment can be compared with a number of prints in an antique idiom showing her victorious over the drunken general Holofernes (cat. no. 59). Another example is Verrocchio's bronze statue of the victorious David (fig. 17) made for the Medici, which was sold to the Florentine government in 1476 for whom it served as an exemplum of righteous rule.

A display of civic credentials can also be suggested as one reason for the Medici commission to Antonio del Pollaiuolo for three canvases of the Labours of Hercules for the large hall of the family palace. While these monumental works, showing the over-lifesize male nude, are lost, the appearance of the same designs on ceramics and in prints and marquetry also testify to the enormous popularity of the mythological subject and Pollaiuolo's treatment of it, with its agile combination of assimilable elements for depicting the muscular male nude in action (see cat. no. 47). An equivalent success was enjoyed by a design by Verrocchio. The pair of heroic heads, which, according to Vasari, represented Darius and Alexander, were originally made in the form of a metal relief

(probably bronze) sent as a diplomatic gift from Lorenzo de' Medici to Matthias Corvinus, King of Hungary. While the subject forms part of the exemplary genre of Famous Men it may also allude more specifically to current conflict between the East and West. Hungary was at war with the Turks from 1479 to 1483 and Corvinus was flatteringly compared to Alexander (victor over the oriental power of Persia) in contemporary panegyrics. Verrocchio's treatment, which may date to the period of the war, is overtly inventive, drawing attention to contrasts of youth and age and developing a vocabulary of fantastic ornament with explicitly decorative effect. Though Darius may have lost this Renaissance beauty contest with Alexander, the leonine physiognomy devised by Verrocchio for the older warrior could be adopted with positive intent. The fierceness of the warrior head, ultimately derived from an imperial coin portrait of Galba, was also adopted in Verrocchio's equestrian 'portrait' of Bartolommeo Colleoni where it reveals the fortitude appropriate to Colleoni's military profession (fig. 113).

In the imagery of the 1470s moral and military conflict, defeat or victory could be played out and resolved fictively in the mythic figure of the warrior making him an ambivalent figure. In Antonio del Pollaiuolo's *Battle of nude men* engraving the conflict has no heroes and the expressive force of the figures appears to reveal their base and irrational instincts. The 'heroic' nude could embody every masculine virtue, but the naked body could expose every human vice.

A W

Florence saw an enormous expansion in the market for prints in the second half of the fifteenth century and a significant part of that production focused on secular images. Nonetheless, Antonio del Pollaiuolo's engraving of *Battle of nude men* is in most respects exceptional. It seems to have been a one-off production in Pollaiuolo's oeuvre which, without requiring a patron, enabled him to broadcast his skills as a draughtsman and designer and to experiment with the possibilities of a reproductive medium that was still in its infancy. As a goldsmith Pollaiuolo would have been familiar with the techniques of engraving metal plates, and a number of prints from *nielli*, a form of silver engraving producing monochrome images, have sometimes been attributed to him. Prints imported from Northern Europe were clearly also important for the development of Antonio's figure style. But the exceptional size and ambition of the *Battle of nude men* engraving and its use of consistent parallel hatching, more familiar to the graphic oeuvre of Andrea Mantegna, suggests that Pollaiuolo may have taken up the burin in competition with Mantegna's early prints, datable to the 1460s. In certain respects, however, the engraving technique seems to approximate Antonio's own use of pen and wash. The contours are strongly delineated with a nuanced line that varies in thickness to describe swellings of the internal form while, by using strokes arranged in a zig-zag, a finer, more silvery, effect is achieved in the modelling of light and shade within the figure. Antonio's experiment was a success. The exceptionally large scale, choice of subject matter, technical quality and even the self-conscious pride in authorship (the full Latin signature common to paintings was a first in this engraving) proved immensely influential, including on Mantegna himself. The engraving survives in well over forty impressions though only one example, in Cleveland (fig. 114), preserves the fine first state, where the effect of the internal modelling is much more subtle. A woodcut version was made in Germany and reflections of figural and other motifs from the engraving appear in works of Renaissance art across Italy, the Mediterranean and Northern Europe, testifying to the print's wide circulation. However, there is no secure date for the design's production and it is not clear whether Pollaiuolo's original engraved plate was later exploited by others in response to demand. The stylistic characteristics of the design are those of the later 1460s and 1470s and the reflection of a pose from the engraving in the book of drawings known as the *Florentine Picture-Chronicle* made in this period and attributed to Baccio Baldini undermines a more recently proposed date of the late 1480s.

The impact of the engraving on other artists' work is mainly registered as a response to the dynamic poses, anatomical explicitness (if not accuracy) and expressive character of the fighting figures. There can be little doubt that Antonio del Pollaiuolo intended the print as a demonstration of his capacities as a draughtsman of the nude male in movement. He poses the ten figures from a variety of angles in a carefully contrived arrangement of superimposed ranks that, as in the *Martyrdom of Saint Sebastian* altarpiece, stimulates comparisons between pairs seen from front and back, and draws attention to the primacy of contour as a vehicle for realising forms in motion. From the choice and treatment of the subject it would have been evident to a contemporary audience that Antonio's own model for his engraving was the relief sculpture of antiquity. The frieze-like arrangement and lunging poses of the combatants recall battle scenes on sarcophagi that he could have seen in Rome or Tuscany and it is telling that Pollaiuolo also devised a sculpted relief, apparently cast in metal, that shows many of the same characteristics (see cat. no. 54). Well-known literary sources, such as Pliny, could have suggested the

53

ANTONIO DEL POLLAIUOLO

Battle of nude men

Engraving,
40.8 × 60.6 cm
Oxford, Ashmolean Museum
Inscribed: OPUS . ANTONII . POLLAIOLI . FLORENTTINI

Condition: the engraving, which has been laid down, is rubbed and abraded especially along the left-hand edge and at bottom right. There is a hole in the figure bending over at the bottom right and signs of restoration with pen and ink near the left-hand edge. The sheet has been folded down the centre.

Richards 1968, pp. 63–70; Fusco in eds. Levenson, Oberhuber and Sheehan, Washington 1973, pp. 66–8; Fusco 1984, vol. 1, pp. 196–9; Emison 1990, pp. 261–75; Angelini in *Il Giardino di San Marco*, exh. cat., Florence 1992, cat. no. 2, pp. 36–8.

A W

choice of what appears to be a gladiatorial subject (the chain, shield and dagger are all described as gladiators' weapons in ancient literature). The emphasis on contour and on the animated battling figure recalls descriptions of the work of the ancient painter Parrhasius whom Ghiberti, following Pliny, had cited admiringly for his paintings of running foot-soldiers (see also cat. no. 56). Significantly, no one has convincingly pinned down a literary source that would explain the precise subject of the work, and the lack of differentiation between heroes and villains suggests that Pollaiuolo did not intend to portray a specific historical or mythological battle. Comparisons with other pictorial inventions of the period, such as those by Mantegna and Botticelli, might indicate that Pollaiuolo's design operates rather on a level of imaginative allegory, aligned rather to poetry than to history. Patricia Emison has suggested that the corn and grapes of the background create a sacramental backdrop which throws the bestial behaviour of the combatants into relief. That the force animating their actions is viciousness rather than heroism is especially apparent from their undignified grimaces and complete nakedness, features usually reserved for lowly and irrational creatures such as satyrs or centaurs (see cat. no. 67). As an example of good *disegno* Pollaiuolo's invention caught the eye of painters, sculptors and designers of all sorts, but its coded moral and didactic character would have enhanced the appeal of this materially humble object to an educated or literary viewer. While more difficult to prove, the case for this second ideal public – one fascinated by antique art and capable of recognising Antonio's claim to rival its achievements – rests mainly on the fact that these spectators were also his best clientele.

Fig. 114. ANTONIO DEL POLLAIUOLO, *Battle of nude men*, c.1469–70. Engraving, w. 60.7 cm. Cleveland Museum of Art, purchased from the J.H. Wade Fund, 1967.127.

54

AFTER ANTONIO DEL POLLAIUOLO

Battle of nude men

Terracotta relief,
42 × 54.2 cm, 4.6 cm deep at lower edge.
London, Victoria and Albert Museum, 7598-1861

Condition: The relief has been broken into five pieces, and restored. The main break runs in a curve from top to bottom passing along the contour of the figure second from left and the legs of the left-hand figure seated in the foreground. There are traces of gilding along the projecting lip at the front of the composition.

Pope-Hennessy 1964, vol. 1, pp. 154–5; Radcliffe in *Italian Renaissance Sculpture in the Time of Donatello*, exh. cat. Detroit 1985, cat. no. 69, pp. 203–4; *Il Giardino di San Marco*, exh. cat., Florence 1992, p. 24.

AW

This design showing muscular, naked figures in combat is strictly comparable with that of Antonio del Pollaiuolo's signed engraving (cat. no. 53), but is developed in terms of differing degrees of sculpted relief. As in the engraving, the integrity of the figure contours is achieved by a two-tier arrangement of bodies on a striated 'stage' including fallen figures in the foreground, that extend here on to a projecting shelf. The composition is dominated by a pair of figures whose bodies, arranged along diagonals, are in the same pose pivoted through 180 degrees. The number of weapons designed for close hand-to-hand combat – short daggers, shields and chains – is greater than those in the engraving, but once again, the range of activities (including the tying of one victim to a tree) does not suggest a historicising reconstruction of an actual gladiatorial trial, but a study of the anatomy of brutal violence. The characterisation of the figures, their proportions and the general treatment of muscles are also comparable with Pollaiuolo's design, though the three-dimensionality of the medium allows for more subtle delineation of the musculature than in his engraving. Antonio del Pollaiuolo was an expert in modelled relief sculpture, and a specialist in battle subjects, but an attribution of the Victoria and Albert relief to Antonio has been resisted. Vasari claims that Antonio made a 'very beautiful' metal (presumably bronze) relief of battling nude figures which was sent to Spain, gesso copies of which were kept in many Florentine workshops. It has been thought that the London terracotta might be another copy of this sort, made to record the exemplary design by Antonio. But the fact that the clay was demonstrably modelled up from scratch rather than being pressed into a mould suggests that, although based on Pollaiuolo, this relief must also represent a trial of modelling skills by another sculptor. Impressions on the back of the terracotta reveal how the clay has been built up against a surface of boards covered with paper to ease its subsequent removal from the work surface. The clay was then worked with the hands and a variety of tools including a spatula and a graving tool, used, for example, in the decoration of the shields where a victorious female figure recalls Pollaiuolo's Detroit *Judith* (cat. no. 58). Before firing, the upper edge and sides were trimmed and the projection of the terracotta along the lower edge of the composition suggests that the relief was designed to be inserted into a deep frame. The least pollaiuoloesque features of the finished object are the treatment of the neck muscles and of the faces which, with their Attic noses, deep-set eyes and gaping mouths recalling antique masks, are more classicising and less expressive than those of Antonio. Stylistically these heads bear a close resemblance to those on the glazed terracotta relief frieze of Lorenzo de' Medici's villa at Poggio a Caiano executed in the 1490s, which is sometimes thought to have been designed by Bertoldo di Giovanni. It is conceivable that the executant of Bertoldo's design, rather than Bertoldo himself, also made a copy of Pollaiuolo's relief, basing his work either on Pollaiuolo's bronze or on a stucco copy, but lending the figures a more archaeological character. The Victoria and Albert relief may date as late as the end of the fifteenth or early sixteenth century. But Antonio's bronze original is more likely to have been a product of the 1470s, almost certainly anticipating Bertoldo's surviving bronze battle relief which was once installed above a fireplace in the Medici palace (fig. 20).

The print is an impression of the first state of this engraving in which the background is incomplete. The second state includes a Latin inscription identifying the subject, apparently arbitrarily, as Hercules' fight and victory against twelve giants (QUOMODO . HERCULES . PERCUSSIT. ET. VICIT. DUODECIM . GIGANTES), the figure wielding the axe being labelled HERCULES. The composition is clearly incomplete to the right where an archer aims his arrow and a suspended hand holding a dagger appears. The engraving apparently preserves the left half of a larger composition, known through a copy drawing in Turin.

The Fogg drawing fragment by Antonio del Pollaiuolo's own hand (cat. no. 56), which shows three figures also appearing at the right of the engraving, seems to have formed part of this larger work. The Fogg and Turin drawings suggest that Antonio's composition had no background and the figures in the former lack internal modelling, so that the engraver had to devise these himself for the purposes of the print. But his invention here is not independent of Pollaiuolo either since the screen of vegetation and vine refers to the background of the autograph *Battle of Nude Men* engraving (cat. no. 53). The internal modelling also imitates the exaggerated muscle definition of the earlier print but, without any understanding of the anatomy, the effect is schematic and implausible. The stylistic traits of the printmaker, such as the consistent parallel hatching used for the shading and the angular treatment of the broken, rocky foreground have encouraged an attribution to an unidentified North Italian artist working in the orbit of Mantegna, rather than to a Florentine. Mantegna was the chief producer of large-scale narrative prints in Italy and the antique style and subject matter of Antonio's composition were likely to have appealed to an engraver wishing to exploit a taste for 'antiquarian' subjects.

The naked figures, which are not as tidily orchestrated as those in Antonio's better known *Battle of nude men*, are composed in a way that deliberately emulates classical battle reliefs. The disjointed relations between figures reveals the primacy given to the study of individual figure motifs, some of which can be traced to specific ancient sarcophagus types: the half-fallen warrior seen from the front derives from an Amazon battle sarcophagus, while the lunging figure to the right with a curved sword adapts a figure in head-on combat found on a Hadrianic sarcophagus showing the Rape of the Leucippids (fig. 107). The inscription appearing on the completed engraving is apparently a stab in the dark by the engraver who did not know what the subject represented but wished to sell it as a particular mythological episode. This lack of recognition was hardly surprising since, like Antonio's *Battle of nude men*, the design lacks any differentiation between the sides taking part in the fight. The battle is rather a vicious mêlée that gives no moral superiority to any individual but was to be read, like the *Battle of nude men*, as an allegorical invention *all'antica* rather than as an illustration. The engraving, which probably postdates the 1470s, represents the most complete exploitation of Pollaiuolo's design. Individual motifs from Pollaiuolo's original composition were, however, taken as exemplary by a number of other artists. The young Carlo Crivelli, for example, adapted the axe-wielding warrior in profile for one of Christ's flagellators in the predella of his altarpiece in Massa Fermana of 1468.

55

Northern Italian (Paduan?) engraver

AFTER ANTONIO

DEL POLLAIUOLO

Battle of Hercules and the giants

Engraving,
c.40 × 59.5 cm (size of plate)
London, British Museum, Department of Prints and Drawings, D.1.2.1

Ullmann 1894, p. 242; Walker 1933, Part 1, pp. 229–37; Hind 1938, vol. 1, p. 192–4; Armstrong Anderson 1968, pp. 155–67; Fusco in eds. Levenson, Oberhuber and Sheehan 1973, pp. 259–61; Bober and Rubinstein 1986, no. 126, pp. 161–2 (for Rape of the Leucippids sarcophagi known in the Renaissance).

AW

56

ANTONIO DEL POLLAIUOLO

Fragment of a battle scene

Pen and brown ink and wash on paper,
27 × 18 cm
Cambridge, Mass., Harvard University Art
Museums, Fogg Art Museum 1940.9

Cruttwell 1907, pp. 76–7; Pliny the Elder, Book 35,
chapter 36, lines 67–9 (for English translation
quoted here see *The Elder Pliny's Chapter on the History of
Art*, ed. Jex-Blake, pp. 111–13); Mongan and Sachs
1940, vol. 1, no. 37 pp. 30–4; Ettlinger 1978, p. 161,
cat. no. 36.

AW

The sheet shows three nude warriors that were originally part of a larger composition. The left-hand section of this composition, comprising a vicious battle of nude men is known through a fifteenth-century engraving referred to as 'Hercules and the Giants' (cat. no. 55). The Fogg fragment may be compared to the figures on the right-hand side of this engraving. A copy drawing in Turin suggests that the composition extended well beyond these figures to the right so that the dimensions of the complete drawing must have been unusually large. The Fogg fragment is executed in the same technique as Antonio del Pollaiuolo's other large-scale 'finished' composition drawing, a *Prisoner led before a ruler* in the British Museum (cat. no. 57). The figures are outlined in pen and reserved against a brown ground, formed by a wash using the same ink. Although the sheet has been harshly restored (making it difficult to be totally certain as to its autograph status), there is no evidence that the figures have lost effects of relief and the viewer is instead encouraged to read the figures' internal anatomy and their movement exclusively by means of their contours. In dramatising contour as the prime vehicle of figure representation Antonio's drawing recalls Alberti's emphasis on the importance of 'circumscription' in defining figure forms within a composition. Both the subject and its treatment further suggest a deliberate rivalry with the achievements of ancient artists. While ancient battle scenes would have been best known to Pollaiuolo as sculpted reliefs, he also seems to be attempting to emulate the ancient painter Parrhasius whose work was praised by Pliny for its unrivalled subtlety in the depiction of contour 'to give assurance of the parts behind, thus clearly suggesting even what it conceals'. Parrhasius' other accomplishments, demonstrated in pictures of highly naturalistic running foot-soldiers, Hercules, and designs on parchment that were 'instructive to artists', all call to mind characteristic qualities of Antonio del Pollaiuolo's art.

It is not clear what the specific function of the battle drawing may have been and whether Pollaiuolo ever considered using it for an engraving by his own hand, like his *Battle of nude men* (cat. no. 53; see also cat. no. 57 concerning function). It was demonstrably used, however, as a model by other artists. The poses of various active figures in the work of painters and illuminators, mainly from Northern Italy, can be traced to Pollaiuolo's composition. It is possible that a drawing described as a '*cartonum* with various nudes by Pollaiuolo' that had belonged to the painter Squarcione's workshop in the early 1460s, where it was used as a teaching aid, showed the same composition.

265

Like the *Battle of nude men* engraving (cat. no. 53) and the Fogg fragment (cat. no. 56), to which it is also comparable in technique, Antonio del Pollaiuolo's figure drawing represents a large-scale design in which the actions of the male nude form the basic unit of the narrative. The composition is bracketed to the left by a vase, to the right by a figure in profile, while, between them the standing warrior is depicted from the back, the side, in three-quarter view, with the head looking up, looking down, and turned in 'lost' profiles. The scene shows a young prisoner being led before an enthroned ruler – a subject that was frequently found on Roman triumphal reliefs. In conceiving the design as a series of idealised nudes isolated against a dark ground, Antonio also seems to have had smaller-scale ancient reliefs in mind, namely sardonyx cameos of the type being acquired in increasingly large numbers by his Medici patrons in this decade (see fig. 21).

In sympathy with Alberti's precepts for good invention in painting, Pollaiuolo uses facial expression and bodily movement to convey the states of mind of his protagonists. The viewer is made aware of the threat to the prisoner by the violent impulse of the figure to the right, as well as by the ruler (a generic king holding a lily-crowned sceptre), whose indecorous nudity, flabby physique and disagreeable grimace suggest that he is to be viewed negatively. The image strongly implies that the prisoner is suffering a miscarriage of justice: a theme that appears especially appropriate to the nature of the drawing as an artistic invention. False accusation, upon which tyranny thrived, was the theme of a famous painting devised by the Greek painter Apelles that is described in ancient sources. Alberti used Apelles, whose painted narrative of *Calumny* described by Lucian united an ingenious subject with an ingenious composition, as the prime example of the artist as inventor. The display of the ability to design both figures *and* subject – in this case a moral-political allegory set in a timeless world *all'antica* – is central to the appeal of Pollaiuolo's design in 1470s Florence and its implicit claim for the intellectual status of its author. The drawing has a finished quality which may imply that it was intended to be appreciated in its own right but the design could also have served, for example, as a model for an architectural frieze.

57

ANTONIO DEL POLLAIUOLO

Prisoner led before a ruler

Pen and ink and wash on paper with
traces of black chalk,
36.9 × 69.3 cm
London, British Museum, Department of Prints
and Drawings, 1893-5-29-1

Cruttwell 1907, p. 124; Lucian, trans. Harman 1913,
pp. 363–7; Popham and Pouncey 1950, I, no. 224,
pp. 136–8; Ettlinger 1978, cat. no. 35, p. 161;
Fusco 1979, pp. 262–3.

AW

58

ANTONIO DEL POLLAIUOLO

Judith

Bronze (98 per cent copper with some lead) with sword, guard and blade of zinc leaded brass (broken and reattached),
42.9 cm
The Detroit Institute of Arts, gift of Eleanor Clay Ford, 37.147.

Valentiner 1938, cat. no. 52; Richardson 1959, pp. 205–15; Radcliffe in *Italian Renaissance Sculpture in the Time of Donatello*, exh. cat. Detroit 1985, pp. 199–201.

A W

The heroic female, a rare subject in early Renaissance art, is a particularly surprising find in the work of Antonio del Pollaiuolo, best known for his treatment of male heroes such as Hercules (cat. nos. 46 and 47). This may have been a factor in the rejection of this statuette in the Pollaiuolo literature until the reattribution of the work in the late 1970s, when, among other arguments, the characteristic broad, planar modelling of the surface, and the intimate relationship to figures by Pollaiuolo's goldsmith follower Antonio di Salvi, were pointed out. The repertoire of warrior women is so small that the identification of Pollaiuolo's statuette as the Old Testament heroine Judith may be justified solely on the grounds of her non-military dress, and her pose, which is used for Judith in contemporary prints. Unlike Donatello's monumental sculpture for the Medici garden that showed Judith in the act of severing the head of the drunken general Holofernes, Antonio del Pollaiuolo, like Botticelli (fig. 123) focuses attention on Judith's virtuous and resolute character. He was able to rely on Florentine familiarity with Judith (liberator of her people from an enemy tyrant) as a civic emblem and lent her a triumphant pose, often associated with military heroes. Pollaiuolo creates a figure of enormous vigour and dynamism, but one which is nonetheless controlled in its movements and imbued with a seemly *gravitas*, apparent in the upright bearing and serene profile. The side views that reveal this profile are less satisfactory from a sculptural point of view. As the disposition of the base clearly signals, the figure is ideally to be seen from the front. As we stand opposite the flattened face of the rocky knoll that supports her feet, Judith appears to gaze beyond us to our right, her curving sword drawn back and mirroring the arm resting on her hip in a gesture of military prowess. The fluid lower half of the figure opens up in a series of broad parallel curves and counter-curves that both reveal and repeat her classicising *contrapposto* stance. The ancestor of this figure type in which wind-blown drapery is used to create a sense of movement and disclose the female form is to be found on ancient reliefs, but her nearer relative was a lost statue of *Abundance* by Donatello that crowned a column in the old market place. This nymph type recurs in many guises in Florentine art from the 1460s onwards and was particularly popularised in the work of Florentine print makers (cat. no. 59) and the paintings of Botticelli, who also used her for his painting of Judith (fig. 123).

The statuette is a thick cast, typical of fifteenth-century practice, and has several air holes, indicative of Pollaiuolo's relative inexperience in bronze casting. The interior of the figure shows that the wax model was built around a small terracotta core with a wire armature, some of which is visible inside. The lack of the pedestal base characteristic of Antonio's other statuettes raises the question of whether the Judith bronze may not have been an offshoot of a design for a larger figure. The monumental conception of a small figure is, however, typical of Pollaiuolo's approach to design and need not imply an idea for a monumental statue. The small base, not to mention the triumphal characterisation with its energetic silhouette, may reflect Pollaiuolo's design of figures as helmet crests (*cimieri*). His mainstream activity as a goldsmith also involved casting small figures and the traces of gilding found within the folds of the drapery suggests that he conceived this statuette as sumptuous collector's piece. The statuette, which passed through several English collections in the last century, has not so far been identified in any Florentine inventories.

The print belongs to the group of engravings known as the 'Otto prints' after their eighteenth-century owner (see cat. nos. 89-93). Its circular format suggests a practical use, perhaps for the decoration of a cylindrical box. The same subject appears on a slightly larger scale in another of the Otto prints in which the Old Testament slayer of Holofernes is shown with her sword raised in triumph. The nymph type employed here can be compared to Antonio del Pollaiuolo's characterisation of Judith in his bronze statuette (cat. no. 58) whose pose is also comparable to the larger print. The immediate predecessors of the figure, however, seem to be found in the so-called *Florentine Picture-Chronicle*, an encyclopaedic world history in drawings attributed to Baccio Baldini. The dress and figure of Judith are adapted in reverse from the drawing of an Amazon while, significantly, the group is directly based on the formulation for David with the head of Goliath in the *Chronicle*. The prostrate Holofernes, who takes on the gigantic proportions of the Philistine champion Goliath, is shown dressed in armour in a landscape rather than, following the biblical account, slain while in a drunken stupor in his tent, as he appears in Botticelli's contemporary narrative panel (cat. no. 85). While Judith's wind-blown drapery and the plaited tresses that curl over her shoulders recall Botticellian beauties, the print gives her a semi-military appearance with her winged hat and shoulder pieces. By confounding the iconography of Judith with that of another tyrant slayer, the victorious David, these graphic designs of the 1470s rob the Old Testament heroine of her seductive and potentially subversive power as a female exemplar.

59
ATTRIBUTED TO
BACCIO BALDINI

Judith with the head of Holofernes

Engraving,
11.8 cm, diameter of paper
London, British Museum, Department of Prints
and Drawings, A.IV.2

Hind, 1938, vol. 1, p. 88; Radcliffe in *Italian Renaissance Sculpture in the Time of Donatello*, exh. cat., Detroit 1985, p. 201; Randolph 1995, pp. 224–8.

AW

60

LORENZO DI CREDI

David with the head of Goliath at his feet

Metalpoint, heightened with white,
on off-white prepared paper,
28 × 12.6 cm
Oxford, Christ Church, 0057

Dalli Regoli 1966, p. 109, cat. no. 23, fig. 35;
Byam Shaw 1976, vol. 1, no. 29, p. 40, vol. 2, pl. 23;
Ames-Lewis and Wright, exh. cat., Nottingham and
London 1983, pp. 200–1, cat. no. 40, pl. 1; Bober and
Rubinstein 1986, no. 31, pp. 74–5 (for the Medici
Apollo and Marsyas now in Naples, Museo Nazionale,
inv. 26501); Sisi in *Il Disegno fiorentino*, exh. cat.,
Florence 1992, cat. no. 2.7, p. 49, who noted the
reference to the Medici gem; Butterfield 1997, p. 26,
fig. 29, for the 'Verrocchio sketchbook' drawing
(Paris, Musée du Louvre, Cabinet des dessins) and
its place in Verrocchio's studies for the bronze *David*.

PLR

In fifteenth-century Florence David's victory over Goliath was interpreted as an example of righteous defence of the fatherland and of the defeat of tyranny. The posture of Credi's *David* in this drawing is similar to that of Verrocchio's bronze (fig. 17). In both David is shown as easy in his triumph, standing with his weight resting on his right leg and his left hand on his hip. There is also a substantial difference between the sculpture and the drawing, which has generally been dated to the 1480s. Credi studies David not as the lanky boy modelled by Verrocchio, but as a beautiful young man. The developed anatomy, elegant pose, and broad facial features of Credi's *David* can be related to the figure of Apollo in a gem showing Apollo and Marsyas, which belonged to the Medici, possibly since Cosimo's day and which is engraved with Lorenzo's mark, 'LAV.R.MED'. Its subject was not identified at the time and it was thought to represent the three ages of man. Like Antonio del Pollaiuolo's dancing figures at Arcetri (fig. 46), the drawing presents an instance of the influence of the Medici collections on forming and informing figural styles in the time of Lorenzo. A pen drawing in a sketchbook with copies after drawings and sculptures from the Verrocchio shop shows a nude in a pose similar to Verrocchio's statue, and it may record a preparatory study by Verrocchio. Like the figure in Credi's drawing (and another attributed to Perugino), the body, though youthful, is manly, not adolescent. This group of drawings shows both how the pose became a subject of repeated study – a canonical figure – in the shop, and how Verrocchio and his students used drawings to master and bring to life the perfected forms of ancient sculptures.

Beauty was one of David's attributes. He is described in the Old Testament as 'of a beautiful countenance and goodly to look to' (1 Samuel, 16:12). There is no painting by Credi that relates to this drawing, so it is uncertain whether this is a study for a nude David (like Donatello's, or later Michelangelo's) or whether it is a nude study for a David to be dressed (like Verrocchio's). In either case, it was made to understand the anatomy of the pose, probably from life. Credi has made adjustments to the body's contour, starting with very fine and faint lines, which he repeated and changed, before adding a defining heavier outline. He was concerned with the fall of light over the entire body, but the modelling is most concentrated on the figure's torso. The combination of hatched modelling with white highlight over the muted tone of the prepared paper effectively gives the impression of flesh. Credi's *David* is both human and ideal and the attention to anatomical description suggests that David's nudity is part of his characterisation as a hero. Here the exposed male body, seemingly undefended in its openness, evokes David's faith, fearlessness and bravery. The young hero David, who went into battle unarmed, provided the opportunity to refer to civic, chivalric and antique heroic ideals in the person of the beautiful, long-haired youth. In the present drawing, the anatomically perfected body of the hero is simultaneously over-developed and softened, formulating a powerful mix of vigour and vulnerable sensuality of a kind displayed as desirable in other images of the period (see cat. nos. 18, 86 and 92).

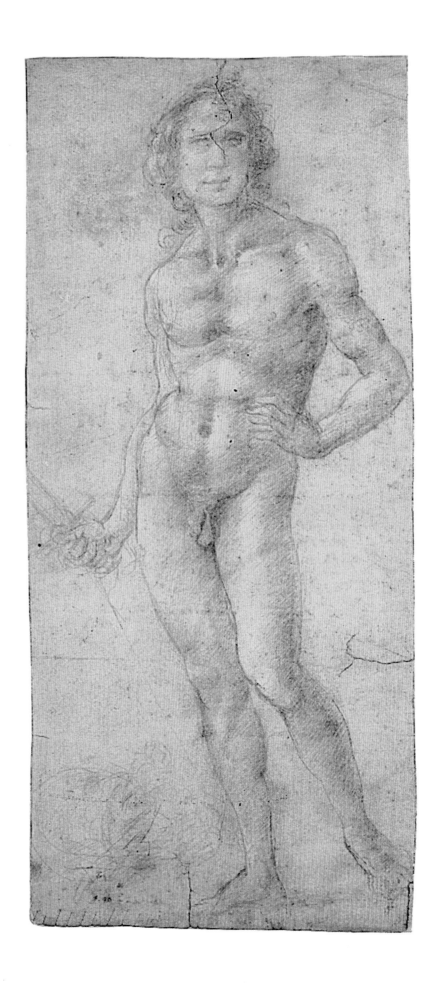

273

Of the many variants of Verrocchio's lost reliefs of the warrior emperors Darius and Alexander, referred to in the introduction to this section, the Washington marble of Alexander is the most powerful in its treatment of relief and wealth of ornament. It is stylistically related to the angels of the Forteguerri monument and was probably produced in Verrocchio's workshop. Lorenzo de' Medici may not have given Verrocchio's original reliefs to his ally Matthias Corvinus, King of Hungary, until the early 1480s, but Verrocchio had developed the warrior typology earlier (fig. 32) and similar portrait-head types appear in Leonardo's drawings of the later 1470s (see also cat. no. 63). Verrocchio's interest in antique heads would have been stimulated by his knowledge of Lorenzo de' Medici's collection of ancient portrait heads, and it is thought that he may have helped to restore some of the marble pieces on display above the doors of the Medici palace.

The profile format of *Alexander* and *Darius* derived principally from smaller scale ancient coinage and their imaginative quality also recalls relief heads, such as that of Hercules, found on cameos. Neo-antique relief heads rather like Verrocchio's had already been produced in the workshop of Desiderio da Settignano – the lost series of Caesars for the study of Giovanni de' Medici, Lorenzo's uncle, is, to judge from fifteenth-century copies, a major antecedent. Verrocchio's reliefs were given specific heroic connotations by being identified as the Greek and Persian empire builders Alexander and Darius, but neither the lost prototypes nor the Washington bust can be considered portraits in the sense of individualised likenesses. Indeed the fluid identity of such heads is highlighted by a marble relief in the Louvre of the 'Alexander' type inscribed 'Scipio', identifying a warrior hero of the Roman republic who was also visualised as a beardless young man with long hair. The representation in numismatic profile and the conspicuous beauty of the figure, contrasted with the screaming head on the breast plate (see also cat. no. 17), mark the subject as virtuous. But the relief does not insist on a specific historical reading and its popularity probably derived as much from its decorativeness and fashionable antique character as from specific moral implications. The 'Alexander' warrior head circulated not only as architectural decoration but in the form of prints (see cat. no. 65) and may be understood as a masculine equivalent to the better-known beautiful female heads popularised in this period in the type of the nymph (see cat. no. 29).

Serving as a counterpoint to the fleshy smoothness of the face, Alexander's headdress and armour amount to a treasury of animated natural forms (the shell carapace and wings), chivalric allusion (the dragon crest) and *all'antica* ornament (acanthus leaf fringes, ribbons and mythological relief figures). The cornucopia held by the reclining Nereid who is swept along by a Triton on the shoulder plate could be taken as emblematic of the abundance that characterises the whole work. Though individual components reflect the observation of natural forms, the excess of artifice is a manifestation of what Vasari chose to call Verrocchio's 'capriccio'. By using this term Vasari evaluated the relief as a product of the artist's fantasy and seen in this light the subject of the relief is as much the 'work of art' as it is Alexander.

61

CIRCLE OF VERROCCHIO

Head of a warrior, 'Alexander'

Marble,
55.9 × 36.7 cm
Washington, DC, National Gallery of Art,
gift of Therese K. Straus 1956.2.1
The relief has been broken diagonally in two places. The small holes, near Alexander's nose and on the screaming head of the breast plate, probably once served to attach restorations.

Vasari/Milanesi, vol. 3, p. 361; Möller, 1930-4, pp. 3–38; Passavant, 1969, pp. 42, 199; Middeldorf 1979, p. 29; Beschi in Barocchi and Ragionieri 1983, pp. 164–5; ed. Barocchi, *Il Giardino di San Marco* 1992, pp. 22 and 23; Fittschen 1996, 1, pp. 11–12; Butterfield 1997, pp. 156–7 and cat. no. 25, pp. 230–2; Brown 1998, pp. 68–72.

AW

62

DELLA ROBBIA WORKSHOP

Head of a warrior

Glazed terracotta relief,
76 cm diameter,
Lisbon, Museu Nacional de Arte Antiga

Möller 1930–4, pp. 33–35; Brown 1998, pp. 70–1.

AW

The Lisbon relief probably dates from considerably later than the production of Verrocchio's 'Darius' prototype (see above p. 256 and cat. no. 63), but, like the prints of warriors in fantastic armour, it bears witness to the success of Verrocchio's conception and its transformation into a number of media. Given the importance of imaginative variety in the aesthetic of Verrocchio's and Leonardo's warrior profiles, any attempt to trace a genealogy for the appearance of ornamental motifs may seem fruitless. But it is worth noting that the winged helmet, dolphin's crest, winged lion's head, circular shoulder piece or pauldron bearing a dragon relief and curling ribbons of the Lisbon relief all appear in different combinations in other variants and the fantasy of this version is apparently a borrowed one. The largest number of shared features are found in another glazed terracotta relief of the 'Darius' type once in the Kaiser-Friedrich museum in Berlin, which suggests the reuse of formulae within the della Robbia workshop that pioneered and monopolised this type of manufacture. The long curling forms of the winged helmet and the diminished breastplate register the sculptor's adaptation of the upright configuration of the profile to a circular or tondo format. He also emphasises the comparison of the lion's head with the warrior's features as studies in leonine expression by enlarging the former and bringing them closer together. The relief is modelled within the depth of a dish-like tondo framed by a rope pattern and a multicoloured fish-scale border dipped in clay slip and glazed before firing. Though we do not know where it came from, the frame of the relief recalls the roundels of Virtues made by Luca della Robbia for the ceiling of the Cardinal of Portugal's Chapel (fig. 55) and may have been intended to be plastered into a wall as a decorative, semi-architectural feature. Larger-scale tondo portraits were not known in this form in antiquity, but the della Robbia workshop devised a number of sculpted products that involved ancient portrait heads within tondi and in a sense the tondo form used here served to reinsert the profile within the tradition of coin portraits from which it derived. A work such as this, which was intended to evoke marble or cameo forms, but was much cheaper and easier to produce, would lend cultural cachet to the site in which it was inserted, while at the same time being colourful, decorative and, unlike marble or metal reliefs, legible from a distance.

63

LEONARDO DA VINCI

Head of a warrior

Metalpoint on prepared paper, laid down,
28.7 × 21.2 cm (bottom edge)
London, British Museum, Department of Prints
and Drawings, British Museum, 1895-9-15-474

Clark 1939, p. 71; Popham and Pouncey 1950,
cat. no. 96, pp. 57–8; Kemp 1991, p. 44;
Kwakkelstein 1994, chapter 1, esp. pp. 15–16; Popham,
ed. Kemp 1994, pp. 39–41; Brown 1998, pp. 68–73.

AW

One of the most highly finished drawings by Leonardo's hand, this profile of a warrior relates to the 'Darius' type in the pairing that Verrocchio devised for Lorenzo de' Medici's diplomatic gift to King Matthias Corvinus (cat. no. 62). A number of Leonardo's drawings reveal his fascination with the contrast between the smooth features of youth and the craggy profile of maturity or old age, a subject of rhetorical *varietas* proposed in Verrocchio's reliefs. While many of Leonardo's profiles of the fierce warrior appear as free pen and ink sketches, the finesse and control of the present drawing suggest a response to a finished work, presumably Verrocchio's *Darius*. It is presented as an exercise of the hand using an inflexible medium and as an object that could be appreciated in its own right. In comparing it with surviving works by Verrocchio we can see how Leonardo's study engages with a wide range of preoccupations current in his master's workshop of the 1470s. The choice of metalpoint, also found in Verrocchio's drawing of a *Nymph and Cupid* (fig. 14), enabled him to draft the contours of the head and bust and its ornamental details with absolute precision (though *pentimenti* are visible, for example, along the back of the arm), while at the same time manipulating the angle and pressure on the stylus to create refined effects of texture and relief. Leonardo used minute parallel hatching for modelling the face and other smooth surfaces whereas materials like feathers and fur are formed with freer curving strokes. Though apparently referring, like Verrocchio's bust of Giuliano de' Medici (cat. no. 17) to contemporary pageant armour, such textural qualities would be nearly impossible to imitate in actual armour. The response to the challenge of relief and the love of fluid ornament are, nonetheless, typical of Verrocchio's metal work (figs. 16 and 32) and indeed it is chiefly from recent goldsmith pieces that Leonardo derives the ornamental vocabulary of this drawing. The fanciful helmet and breastplate are edged with the curling flower forms used in antique acanthus borders and adapted in Verrocchio's and Antonio del Pollaiuolo's goldsmith work. The spotted wings of a dragon, the heavily projecting lion's head and rippling ribbons are also commonplaces (they appear together on the marble lavabo of the Old Sacristy of San Lorenzo, a work attributed to Verrocchio since the early sixteenth century). What is extraordinary in Leonardo's approach to this collection of recognisable elements is the tensile vigour invested in every form, bringing out analogies in shape between wind-blown ribbons and tightly coiled metallic decoration. The figure may be read as having two complementary profiles, dominated on the side of the face by powerful convex or protruding forms and on the right by concave ones. Unlike the Washington 'Alexander' (cat. no. 61), Leonardo chose a strict profile for the warrior's bust, avoiding the problematic three-quarter view and accentuating the extreme erectness of posture appropriate to the exemplary leader. In doing so he also succeeded in animating the warrior himself so that he can support the ornamental display without being overwhelmed by it. Crucially, the beautiful forms of the armour are presented as both a contrast to and a mirror of the man. By juxtaposing the profile of the snarling lion on the breastplate with the similarly jutting features, beetling brow and piercing eyes of the warrior he indicates the soldier's fearful leonine qualities – the unswerving fortitude and aggressive power that are reflected in his physiognomy.

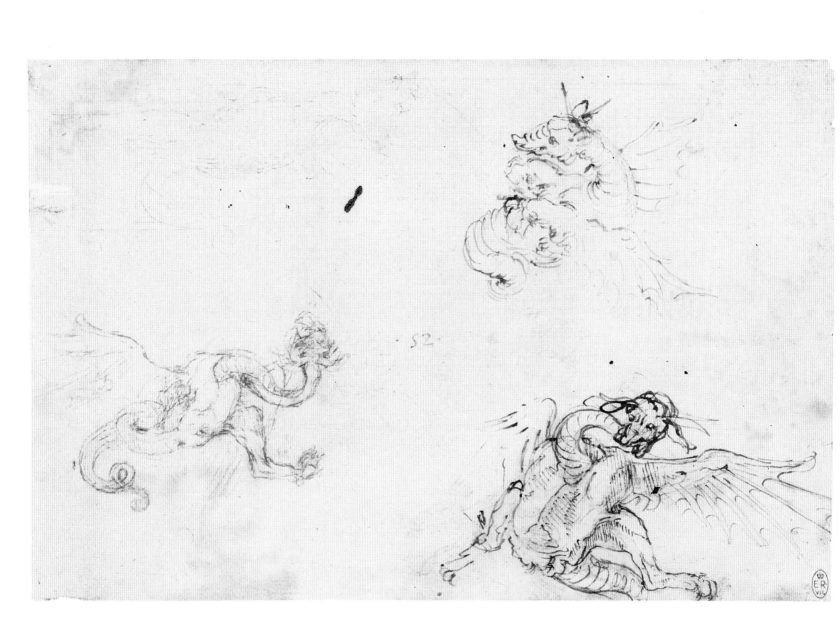

Dragon slaying ranked among the most heroic deeds in both Christian and chivalric tradition. Dragons represented the power of evil and Leonardo depicted them as coiling cyphers of fiendish energy.

Both sides of this drawing have martial associations: the verso has three studies of a breastplate (all in stylus, with one worked over in pen; fig. 115). Its design is principally foliate, but a lion glares out from the shoulder piece of the figure outlined in pen. Animals such as dragons and lions, which Leonardo associated both with the bravery and the bestiality of combat, were an integral part of the ornamental vocabulary of Verrocchio's shop.

The four sketches shown here relate to a series of studies of horsemen battling a dragon. The horsemen later appear fighting each other on the right side of the background of the Uffizi *Adoration of the Magi* in the shadowy realm of chaos and conflict that Leonardo juxtaposed with the central moment of the kings' submission to Christ (fig. 78). Even if not part of the resolved composition, these dragons can be connected with the evolution of Leonardo's *Adorations* in the late 1470s and early 1480s. They are part of his investigation of emotional forces and the ways they could be given physical form. In the animal world, they are a pendant to his close study of horses.

In his notes on the practice of painting Leonardo advised painters on how to 'make an imaginary animal look natural', giving as an example a dragon, which should be compounded of elements from real animals by taking 'for its head that of a mastiff or hound, with the eyes of a cat, the ears of a porcupine, the nose of a greyhound, the brow of a lion, the temples of an old cock, the neck of a water-tortoise.' Vasari tells the story of the young Leonardo doing just that in order to create a horrible and fearsome monster (a head of a Medusa) – assembling different parts from 'lizards, crickets, serpents, butterflies, locusts, bats and various strange creatures of this nature'. The studies on this page can be viewed literally as figments of Leonardo's imagination: fantastic creatures born from his memory of real and fabulous animals seen in nature and in art and given form by his stylus, chalk and pen. Because the metalpoint leaves only an imprint and no mark on the paper, Leonardo could choose which of the dragons would become fully visible by reinforcing the outlines with another medium. Using the stylus in this way also meant that he could first suggest a shape and then change it, bringing it to visibility, rather than obscuring it by a welter of conflicting lines. Clarity was also maintained by turning the sheet. The two recoiling dragons at the bottom right and left of the page as shown here are the most developed: the one at the left has been brought out in black chalk, and that at the left in chalk and then pen and ink. In both cases the positions were modified to intensify the sense of forceful reaction. At the top, in the opposite direction, is a defeated dragon, all puff gone, drawn splayed out. Rotating the page 90 degrees to the left reveals a dragon flying down in attack. Leonardo has predominantly used vigorous curving strokes to shape the dragons, a graphic device that conveys the force of their motion as well as describing their complicated positions in space. As with so many of the subjects that occur in this period, Leonardo's fascination with dragons continued and he later made their serpentine movements the object of scientific as well as dramatic study.

64
LEONARDO DA VINCI
Dragons

Metalpoint, black chalk and pen and brown ink, 15.9 × 24.3 cm
Windsor, Royal Library, The Royal Collection, 12370 recto

Vasari/ Milanesi, vol. 4, p. 24; Popham 1954, pp. 223–7; Clark 1969, vol. 1, p. 51; Richter 1970, vol. 1, p. 342, no. 585; Pedretti 1987, vol. 2, pp. 36–8.

PLR

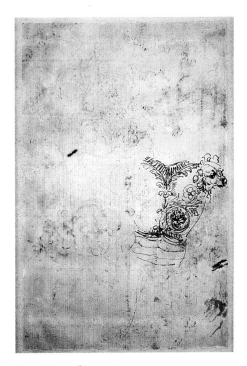

Fig. 115. Verso of cat. no. 64.

65

ANONYMOUS FLORENTINE

Bust of a warrior in fantastic armour

Engraving,
12.8 × 7.5 cm
Washington, DC, National Gallery of Art,
Rosenwald Collection 1943.3.9069 (Hind A.I.56)

Hind 1938, vol. 1, p. 47.

AW

The engraving has been cut down at the left- and right-hand edges, while the preservation of the lower edge shows that the bust is bounded by the border of the armour in imitation of ancient bust types. The treatment of the profile of the warrior adopts the genre influentially developed in the Verrocchio workshop (cat. nos. 61 and 63). The element of *horror vacui*, to some extent inherent in the prototype reliefs of Darius and Alexander, is pushed to the limits of fantastic effect for the purposes of this decorative engraving. The ill-proportioned profile preserves the essentials of the 'Alexander' type with its long Roman nose, whereas the armour becomes a support for a bizarre collection of motifs culled from a variety of contexts. The lions' heads (on the shoulder piece and just visible in profile on the distorted breastplate) and the eagle of the bust are distinctly medieval-looking, while the helmet brings together a jumble of fantastic elements that adapt ancient motifs such as the dolphin (given scales and legs) and winged infant into an entirely unarchaeological idiom. The putto, who appears to be about to slide down the dragon visor, relates to sculpted *cimieri* or decorative crowning figures on pageant helmets and is shown blowing a victory fanfare.

The print, which shows the decorative pairing of warrior heads in its most simplified and easily affordable form, also demonstrates the adaptablility of Verrocchio's Darius and Alexander idea (discussed above on page 256). This engraving, which lacks all sense of the relief so important in the images from the Verrocchio shop (cat. nos. 61 and 63), shows two youthful heads in profile wearing ornamental helmets within an honorary Roman frame – a ribbon-bound garland of the type found on Roman triumphal monuments. At the centre two small figures support a shield with the inscription SPQR, referring to the Senate and the People of Rome, and the letters RO and RU, evidently identifying the busts as those of the legendary founders of Rome, Romulus and Remus. By drawing on Florentine self-identification with the glories of the ancient Roman republic and a taste for pseudo-antique imagery of the sort developed in more illustrious workshops, the printmaker could probably guarantee a market for this engraving, despite its inferior quality.

66

FLORENTINE ENGRAVER

Busts of two warriors

Engraving,
10.2 × 16.7 cm
Paris, Bibliothèque Nationale (Hind A.I.57)

Hind 1938, vol. 1, p. 48

AW

67

FLORENTINE ENGRAVER

Fighting beasts regarded by soldiers

Engraving
19.7 × 30.8 cm
London, British Museum, Department of Prints
and Drawings, D.I.6
The circular marks scattered across the print, which
the engraver has sought to disguise, may result from
using a copper plate already worked on one side.

Mancini 1908, pp. 185–227; Hind 1938, vol. 1, p. 197;
Lucretius, *De rerum natura*, trans. W. H. D. Rose 1975,
Book 5, 878–924; Lightbown 1978, vol. 2,
cat. no. B43, pp. 57–60 (for *Pallas and the Centaur*).
Inaugural lecture by Alison Brown at Royal
Holloway and Bedford College, on 15 March 1999,
for Lucretius' influence in Florence in this period.

AW

The engraving, one of six known impressions, shows two half-human figures – to the left a centaur, to the right a beast half man and half lion – lunging at one another with ball and chain weapons while three young soldiers dressed in fantasy 'ancient' armour look on. The print has been associated with Antonio del Pollaiuolo on the basis of a number of motifs that derive from his designs, notably the two left-hand soldiers who are lifted directly from his design for the *Beheading of the Baptist* in the series of Baptistery embroideries (see cat. no. 48). The incoherent composition with its numerous spatial anomalies, the discontinuities in the landscape background, and the crude treatment of anatomy, exclude Pollaiuolo's authorship. But the printmaker was certainly dependent on Antonio for the conception of the engraving as a ferocious battle and for the treatment of the figures, registering the elegant articulation of his bystander types and the juxtaposing of similar heads and bodies seen from different angles (see also cat. no. 57). The torsos of the combatants appear to have been taken from the design which was the source for the Northern Italian *Battle of Hercules and the Giants* engraving (cat. no. 55), though the Florentine printmaker shows a better understanding of the musculature of the axe-wielding figure and his adversary than the Northern copyist. Given the derivative character of the engraving, the animal bodies probably also had a pre-existing design source, possibly in a print. The juxtaposition of soldiers in fanciful antique armour with battling beasts using savage weapons is presumably intended to provide a moralising contrast between the bestial and the rational aspects of man's nature. Beasts such as centaurs had been discussed (as impossible beings) in relation to the primitive ancestors of man in the writing of the ancient Epicurean Lucretius, whose poem *De rerum natura* appeared in print in the 1470s. They occur increasingly often in Florentine imagery from this decade onward, even making an appearance in the form of festive costume for the feast of Saint John the Baptist described by Pietro Cennini in 1475. The Florentine print follows medieval tradition by casting them as irrational creatures incapable of controlling their violent impulses. The soldiers in antique garb are presented, by contrast, as civilised and rational, completely human. The theme of the engraving thus anticipates that of Botticelli's allegorical painting of *Pallas and the Centaur* in which the goddess of wisdom controls the urges of the beast.

VI Sacred Beauty

In the city of merchants no account was more important than the account with God. The first pages of commercial and family record books invoked the glory and the protection of the Virgin, and the city's, the family's and the individual's patron saints. The records of Girolamo di Carlo di Marco Strozzi dating from the years 1471–2 include a list of his donations and devotional acts and are representative of the pious accounting habitual among Florentine citizens. The first item is a life-size wax votive image given to the church of SS. Annunziata, this is followed by another given to Saint Clement, 'but a small one', which he carried to the church dedicated to the saint above Fiesole, about six kilometres north of the city, 'on foot'. There are further donations of masses and candles to seven other churches and shrines in Florence and its environs, including the 'angel Raphael at Santo Spirito'. The devotional landscape in the background of Filippino Lippi's *Adoration* (cat. no. 69), with penitential saints dotted about the hillsides, was one traversed in reality as well as in prayer by Florentines in the 1470s.

The enthusiasms for pagan myth, Greek philosophy and Roman literature current at the time did not replace religious belief. Secular heroes exemplified Christian virtues and the forms of antiquity were adapted to the functions of Christianity. The compressed arrangement of Filippino Lippi's *Dead Christ Mourned* (cat. no. 72) uses the effects of relief sculpture to add to the intensity and dignity of the scene. The elongation of Filippino's figures follows proportions first found in the elegant figures of Ghiberti's second set of doors on the Baptistery, which were in turn probably suggested by Pliny's description of the slender bodies and the 'appearance of height' that the ancient sculptor Lysippus gave to his statues. Both the increased anatomical accuracy and the intentional distortions found in works by artists of this time can be related to the formal awareness which characterises the period and which, taken in the broadest terms, is a product of the revived interest in antiquity.

A great deal of intellectual energy was devoted to proving cultural continuities between the ancient world and the world of fifteenth-century Florence – in religious philosophy as well as in politics and poetry. In this regard Neoplatonic ideas about beauty are important to the perception and reception of the visual arts in the 1470s. The aesthetics of fashionable love literature provided a guide to the charms and the power of graceful gestures and appealing physical parts – particularly in the rapturous descriptions of the idealised ladies who were often the protagonists of such poetic endeavours. Beautiful women inspired love and devotion. No woman was more beautiful or more deserving of love than the Virgin Mary, who increasingly appears like a sort of Petrarchan fantasy. The traditions of decorum regarding religious imagery also required that it be beautiful in order to pay honourable tribute to the sacred mysteries it served. But the notion of beauty and love as spiritually elevating forces which could act as channels for divine grace was most fully expounded by Neoplatonists in Lorenzo de' Medici's circle, chief among them Marsilio Ficino. In his commentary on Plato's *Symposium*, for example, he wrote that love was a desire for beauty and through the contemplation of beauty the soul could rise towards divinity.

The function of religious art as a focus for contemplation gained force as its beauty could be seen to guide the inner eyes of its viewers to their true goal of spiritual enlightenment. This is not to mistake painters or sculptors for philosophers. Even if in the relatively small world of Florence they had seen Ficino or his learned friends, they most certainly had not read or discussed their writings. The heightened idealism of their works is a response to the value given to beauty in the philosophic theology and the poetry of the moment. It operates at the level of cultural commonplaces: ideas circulating among the influential men of the day, ideas which generated expectations and which could be simply formulated as 'beauty is goodness'.

Sacred images mediated between the reality of daily life and the awe-inspiring truths of eternal life. They made the mysteries of the faith visible, comprehensible and memorable. Girolamo Strozzi's casual reference to the 'angel Raphael at Santo Spirito' indicates how holy figures could be familiar. From large-scale altarpieces to more intimate domestic panels or sculptures of the Virgin and Child they reminded people of the true history of salvation and their true patrons, the intercessory saints and, most frequently, the Virgin. They also reminded people how to behave.

Religious art participated in what might be called the spectacle of devotion which was a characteristic part of the Florentine exercise of faith. Processions, pageants and holy theatre were integral features of the life of the city. Most were subsidised by the Commune with the express aim of promoting the city's fame, as well as for the 'consolation and joy' of its citizens. In addition to the magnificent show occasionally made for the feast of the Magi, which partly accounts for the popularity of the Adoration of the Kings as a subject for pictures (cat. nos. 7, 68 and 69), there were elaborate processions and festivals for other feasts, such as those of John the Baptist, patron of Florence, and Corpus Christi. The mysteries of the Annunciation, Ascension and the Descent of the Holy Spirit (Pentecost) were celebrated by holy plays mounted respectively in the churches of San Felice in Piazza, Santa Maria del Carmine and Santo Spirito. These plays were annual events involving lavish costumes, complicated stage machinery and beautiful little boys with curly hair dressed as angels. Not only do the latter sound much like the sort drawn and depicted by Verrocchio, but the staging of holy drama corresponds to the dramatic immediacy sought by Florentine artists in their work. There are connections between some of these spectacles and religious images. Vasari's description (in his Life of Brunelleschi) of the circling dome like a bowl or 'barber's basin turned upside-down' with ledges covered with cotton wool clouds for dancing angels – the heaven in the play of the Annunciation – sounds much like the heaven represented by Botticini in Matteo Palmieri's altarpiece (fig. 28). Christ raised aloft in his mandorla in the Forteguerri cenotaph would have been a familiar vision not only from previous sculptures but from actual experience; it was one repeated in the plays as holy figures were hoisted up and down in almond-shaped metal frames during the most dramatic moments. More generally the men and boys of the confraternities who acted out the gestures appropriate to the stories and the large audiences who witnessed them were practised in the choreography of the sacred. There was a diffused and popular understanding of the staging of the mysteries, not only as symbolically performed by the clergy, but as directly imitated by the laity. Religious representations were at once highly abstract and completely accessible. The artists of the 1470s addressed an audience well-versed in devotional performance and receptive to graceful variations of a shared language of sacred beauty.

PLR

68

FILIPPINO LIPPI WITH SANDRO BOTTICELLI

Adoration of the Kings

Egg tempera on poplar,
50.2 × 135.9 cm (painted surface)
58.6 × 148.5 (panel)
London, National Gallery, NG 592

Horne 1908, pp. 13–15; Davies 1946, p. VIII, pl. 8
(for the back); Davies 1961, pp. 97–8;
Lightbown 1978, vol. 1, pp. 22–5, vol. 2, pp. 20–1
(with bibliography); Rohlmann 1993, pp. 234–58
(for van Eyck); Zambrano in Zambrano and
Nelson (forthcoming).

This entry is indebted to a paper given by
Patrizia Zambrano at a National Gallery
research seminar.

NP

This painting resembles a predella panel in format but its intricacy makes that unlikely. The gilt leaf ornament attached to the panel, evidently original, suggests the framing employed for works incorporated into furniture and panelling. The painting is badly worn in parts especially at top left and around Joseph on the right. Botticelli may never have completed the painting: there are careful incisions for the masonry courses in the wall on the left but no traces of paint distinguishing the separate stones. Having little interest in landscape distance it was doubtless Botticelli who borrowed this part of the composition from a Netherlandish painting of the Stigmatisation of Saint Francis then believed to be by Jan van Eyck.

The young Filippino Lippi is first recorded as working with Botticelli. This painting has generally been given to Botticelli and those who have acknowledged it as the work of two artists have generally given the senior one the chief role. Zambrano, however, is right to claim for the younger artist the most important parts – Joseph, the Virgin, the king kissing Christ's foot, the king kneeling behind him and the four figures in the foreground to the left of this second king. Here we find the soft full drapery, transparent scarves and exquisite silhouettes beloved of Filippino. The shepherds breaking into the composition on the right and the crowd behind the wall on the left, also the dwarf, are typical of Botticelli – more vigorous in movement, more expressive in features and with elaborate costume rather than gracious drapery.

It is also clear that the youth in red and blue hose looking up (presumably at the star) near the centre of the composition and some at least of the heads behind him are by Botticelli and while this figure is a striking narrative device, he partly conceals the figure dressed in rose who may have been intended by Filippino as the third king. Botticelli was not only partial to crowds. He had less feeling for interval than the young Filippino. This then does not look like a work of collaboration. The *Adoration* must be an unfinished picture by Filippino taken over by Botticelli (who had perhaps delegated the commission to Filippino in the first place). It is noticeable that the Holy Family and the nearest king in Botticelli's *Adoration of the Kings* in the National Gallery of Art in Washington is very close to Filippino in style and that perhaps represents a real case of collaboration. The most notable example of collaboration between the artists can be seen in two panels of the sibyls in Christ Church, Oxford. Botticelli must have painted one of these and Filippino the other, so although Botticelli may have been the senior artist with a leading responsibility for design in this case, Filippino was clearly playing an equivalent role to Botticelli in the workshop. Nothing by him which can really be called immature survives and he may have come to Botticelli as a prodigy.

69

FILIPPINO LIPPI

Adoration of the Magi

Egg tempera on wood,
56.9 × 85.8 cm
London, National Gallery, NG 1124

Davies 1961, pp. 287–8; Mascalchi 1984, p. 272
(for provenance not in Davies); Burke 1999
(for Pugliese); Zambrano in Zambrano and Nelson
(forthcoming) (for dating and identification of
saints, and full bibliography).

NP

The Adoration of the Kings, as noted above, was a highly popular subject for paintings in fifteenth-century Florence. This is perhaps the most original treatment of the theme. It was long prized by great collectors and is now generally agreed to be one of the finest works by the young Filippino. It seems to have been acknowledged as by him in the seventeenth (although not in the nineteenth) century. The condition is generally good and the increased transparency of the paint, revealing fluent brush underdrawing in the hills, does nothing to distract from our pleasure in the painting.

All three kings are on their knees but not otherwise much distinguished from their entourage. The ox and ass are omitted as are the shepherds who are often included in the background in paintings of this subject (see cat. nos. 7 and 68). The group including the embracing figures on the left may allude to the legend that the kings came from three different directions and met shortly before they arrived at the stable. Other figures – notably the boy seated with a dog and the youth in blue with a sword – have a superfluous poetic elegance. The converging lines of the ashlar courses of the ruined building are designed so as not to create too strong a sense of recession. Instead we enter the landscape by winding paths, finding there not only the tail of the kings' retinue, but tiny episodes involving Saint Gregory (extreme right), Saint Ambrose baptising Saint Augustine, Saint Jerome, Saint Bernard receiving a vision of the Virgin, the archangel Raphael with Tobias and Saint Mary of Egypt. The idea of scattering subordinate sacred figures in the landscape must derive from traditional representations of hermits in the Theban desert. This particular scheme was imitated by Botticini in a square painting (possibly a small altarpiece) now in the Chrysler Museum, Norfolk, Virginia (55–10.3) and the general idea was adopted by other Florentine painters. It is tempting to relate this to hermetic religious practice, although not all of Filippino's saints were hermits.

The painting may date from the mid-1470s when Filippino was working with Botticelli, but his interest in landscape and rock forms derives from his father's work. It has recently been proposed that it was a Nativity with the Magi by 'Filippo di fra Filippo' bequeathed with a group of paintings to the chapel in his estate north of Florence, Sant' Andrea da Sommaia, at the end of the century by Francesco del Pugliese. Pugliese's painting is described as 'large' which seems odd even if it were slightly larger than the others, especially since the figures are small (probably smaller than in the others). But it is a possibility that this is the painting referred to. The document is a reminder that paintings of domestic scale could be transferred to chapels and even made to serve as altarpieces.

Christ holding a pomegranate (symbol of the Passion) converses with his cousin Saint John to whom the book (presumably of prophecy) belongs. John was popular with Florentines as a patron of their city and with artists because, depicted young, he provided a pretext for narrative, however minimal, and for tender sentiment, in devotional paintings of this format.

Although the painting was sometimes regarded as by Botticelli in the nineteenth century, Sir Charles Eastlake, the Gallery's first director, who acquired it for his private collection, considered it to be by Filippino. It is entirely typical of his early work and may date from the late 1470s. The somewhat vegetable spires on the horizon and the marble flowerpots with fluted necks are found in the *Christ adored by Angels* in St Petersburg; the roses occur in several of his paintings and both an eager, open-mouthed profile and a similarly weightless Child feature in his painting in Budapest (cat. no. 71). The rapid loose calligraphic painting of the trees contrasts with minutely careful treatment of other parts (most notably Christ's teeth).

The type of the Virgin and the Christ Child, the veil of the former and the curls of the latter, derive from revered models by Filippino's father, Filippo Lippi, but the broad curves and simple shape of the Virgin's robe are a novelty which may be related to Filippino's drawings as, for example, cat. no. 73. In these, rapidly brushed lines of white are often swept over more intricate work in metalpoint and there is sometimes a curious combination of the monumental and the delicate.

70

FILIPPINO LIPPI

The Virgin and Child with Saint John

Egg tempera on poplar,
59 × 43.5 cm
London, National Gallery, NG 1412

Scharf 1935, pp. 19–20, 108–109; Davies 1961, p. 288; Zambrano in Zambrano and Nelson (forthcoming).

NP

71

FILIPPINO LIPPI

The Virgin and Child with a Franciscan Friar commended by Saint Anthony of Padua

Egg tempera on wood,
57 × 41.5 cm
Budapest, Szépmüvészeti Múzeum, Inv. 1140 (52)

Scharf 1935, pp. 13–14, 19, 22, 109; Pigler 1967, p. 386; Boskovits 1969, pp. 45–6; Bartoli in *Maestri e botteghe*, Florence 1992, cat. no. 2.8, p. 76; Zambrano in Zambrano and Nelson (forthcoming).

NP

The disparity of scale between the group of the Virgin and Child and the group of the saint and friar is unusual in Florentine painting of the second half of the fifteenth century, although there are other cases, including Botticini's altarpiece from San Girolamo, Fiesole, painted at the end of the century (NG 227). The size and scale may have been stipulated by the friar for whose convent cell the picture was perhaps made – however he cannot have commissioned the work if he adhered strictly to his vows of poverty, and may rather have advised those of his family who had it made.

Christ, balanced on one foot, is supported only by the Virgin's fingertips. She herself seems to have little weight, which contributes to the idea that she is a vision. She is seated on the thin bar of cloud which hovers above the flowery meadow but her legs hardly seem to project and her feet are concealed beneath the horizontal fanned folds of her cloak. The clean oval outlines of her form are perhaps deliberately intended to suggest a mandorla. According to legend, Saint Anthony was privileged to hold the infant Christ in his arms and it is with Christ that he and the friar commune. The painting may date from the early 1480s. It is somewhat abraded (most apparent in the blues) and the greens have darkened.

The friar and perhaps also the saint are among the earliest portraits in Filippino's surviving paintings – the numerous highly expressive, as well as vividly idiosyncratic, portraits which he added to the frescoes in the Brancacci Chapel by Masaccio and Masolino probably date from soon afterwards.

This painting, formerly attributed to Filippo Lippi and to Botticelli, was first published as by Filippino by Zambrano in 1996: the rock forms (reminiscent of the landscape of the *Adoration of the Kings*, cat. no. 69), the transparent veils and the handling – the stippling of the haloes is especially exquisite – are highly characteristic of Filippino's work in the 1470s. The greater monumentality of style, as well as the larger format, suggests a date towards the end of the decade and there is also surely, as Zambrano proposes, a deliberate emphasis on his paternal legacy, as if the artist wished to remind us that he was 'son of the most outstanding master of his day' ('figliolo del più singolare maestro dei tempi suoi', in the words of the agent of the Duke of Milan in 1493). Perhaps a drawing by Filippo was used.

Some image of the dead Christ was usual in an altarpiece. In most parts of Italy this was found in the lunette, but in Florence, as elsewhere in Tuscany, such an image was normal in the central portion of the predella or was otherwise incorporated into the centre of the lower edge of the composition where its relationship with the Most Holy Sacrament placed on the altar would have been obvious. This painting may have been an altarpiece, perhaps in a domestic chapel, but it is perfectly possible that it was intended as a devotional image for a *camera*. The artist has, however, not permitted himself the licence found in his *Adoration of the Kings* and has been careful to ensure that the picture makes a strong impression from a distance. The figures are emphatically close to the front plane and our attention is not distracted by the distant hills or diverted by subordinate details. The figure composition is very clearly outlined but the effect is somewhat flat in consequence. The painting has been cleaned for this exhibition. The panel has been badly damaged by worm and there is a triangular insertion of canvas by the left cross. The drapery of the Virgin and of Mary Magdelene is severely abraded and has lost almost all of its original glazes. The flesh and the rocks are also worn. The crosses may not be original.

72

FILIPPINO LIPPI

The Dead Christ mourned by the Virgin, Mary Magdalene and Joseph of Arimathea

Egg tempera on wood,
95.5 × 65.5 cm
Cherbourg, Musée d'Art Thomas Henry, inv. 1912.12

Ruda 1993, pp. 488–9; Zambrano 1996; Zambrano in Zambrano and Nelson (forthcoming).

Jean-Luc Dufresne kindly showed us the report of Rosalia Motta, the conservator responsible for working on the painting this summer at Versailles. The reproduction here shows the painting before cleaning.

NP

73

FILIPPINO LIPPI

Draped woman

Metalpoint and white heightening on
salmon-pink prepared paper,
20.2 × 8.3 cm
Devonshire Collecion, Chatsworth. Reproduced
by permission of the Duke of Devonshire
and the Chatsworth Settlement Trustees, 887B recto

Scharf 1937, pp. 4–7; Shoemaker 1975, cat. no. 3,
pp. 135–6; Jaffé 1994, no. 35, p. 68.

PLR

Ghostly, but elegant, this figure is almost identical to the Virgin in the *Annunciation* painted by Fra Filippo Lippi for the nuns at the convent of Le Murate (now in the Alte Pinakothek, Munich). It is also similar to the Virgin in an *Annunciation* based on Fra Filippo's composition (formerly in the church of San Firenze, now in the Accademia, Florence). These repetitions not only demonstrate the way that Filippino was heir to his father's achievements, but also the way that Fra Filippo's works had established a model and a stylistic mode for sacred art which remained in demand. Its essential qualities are studied here in the general elongation of the form, the intricately looped folds of the drapery and the delicate luminosity of the different surfaces. The somewhat ethereal figure is conceived in terms of gracefulness and is meant to embody grace.

Filippino's drawing is not a mechanical copy; it is a free and creative assimilation of his father's annunciate Virgin. Metalpoint sketching seeks the outlines of the forms that shape the figure. Filippino also used metalpoint to model the deep shadows of the folds and to cover larger areas, or patches, of shadow in order to indicate the direction of the light. Fine white hatching, applied in vertical strokes, suggests a sheen on the fabric while emphasising the height of the figure. Disconnected and differentiated accents of white highlight create a sensation of moving light with an energetic force typical of Filippino. He seems to have been undecided or dissatisfied with some aspect of the underdrawing of the face, which he simply blotted out in white. Filippino's priority here was not facial expression, but a consideration of the textures of the drapery as described by light. The dramatically accentuated illumination and the physical coherence of the figure under the drapery are both characteristic of Filippino and not of Fra Filippo. Filippino's filial respect in no way hindered his independent vision or his innate ambition.

Cut down and damaged as it is, this drawing is still a striking demonstration of Filippino's early command of pen and brush. Throughout his career he favoured prepared paper for figure studies. Using the preparation, often grey as here, as the middle tone, Filippino illuminated and animated his figures with white heightening, which he applied with an unfaltering touch. The figures in such studies have the appearance of being designed by and formed out of light, a vibrant effect that characterises his painted figures as well.

The face, hands, feet and torso of the female figure and the neck and arms of the kneeling man – largely invisible to the naked eye – are dramatically revealed by ultraviolet light, so that the figures are complete (fig. 116).

One feature of Filippino's surviving corpus of drawings is that a high proportion of figure studies have no direct connection to specific works. Filippino seems to have used drawing to perfect motifs potentially serviceable in a variety of contexts. The figures could be drawn from a model in order to consider, or reconsider, a standard pose. The solid physicality of the kneeling man here suggests that he might be drawn from life. He is a standard figure of devotional desire, expressing humility and hope. The folds of drapery spreading out on the ground create a stable base, while the vertical lines of light articulating the back of the robe and the curving lines over the raised knee and around the arms give a momentum to the figure who turns towards a focus of devotion. The pose is similar to that of the kneeling kings in the National Gallery *Adoration* (cat. no. 69), or in the drapery of the lower part, to the fold vocabulary of the friar being presented to the Virgin in the painting from Budapest (cat. no. 71). The outline of a hood slung over the left shoulder of the drawn figure suggests that it may be meant to represent a layman rather than a king or cleric.

The gesturing woman is a nymph type with origins in Roman relief sculpture. Elongated, and composed of contrasting areas of falling, flowing and billowing drapery, she is the sort of wind-blown figure recommended as pleasing by Alberti in his treatise *On Painting*, with the body revealed under the side struck by the wind and whose clothing on the other sides is blown about and waves 'appropriately up in the air'. Used by Fra Filippo Lippi, as in the Bartolini tondo in the Pitti Palace, this graceful type also occurs in Botticelli's works, notably in the Uffizi panel showing Judith and her maid returning to Bethulia with the head of Holofernes (fig. 123). Filippino has given the figure a physical plausibility lacking in the draped constructions of his father's works, and the sculptural sensation of fabric against body seems to reassert the classical source. This drawing shows Filippino's critical and creative involvement with the figural legacy of the ancient as well as the immediate past as he sought to establish his own career, and his efforts to find a calligraphy of light that would embody and express both beauty and devotion.

74

FILIPPINO LIPPI

Studies of a female figure leaning forward and a kneeling man

Two sorts of white gouache and brown ink on grey prepared paper, 22.2 × 19 cm
Cambridge, Mass., Harvard University Art Museums, Fogg Art Museum, bequest of Meta and Paul J. Sachs, 1965.394

Berenson 1938, vol. 2, cat. no. 1271G, p. 140; Mongan and Sachs 1940, no. 21, fig. 20; Shoemaker 1975, cat. no. 4, pp. 137–8; Alberti, ed. Grayson/Kemp 1991, p. 81 (Book 2, chapter 45); Knipe 1998.

I would like to thank Craigen Bowen and Penley Knipe of the Straus Center for Conservation, Harvard University Art Museums, for discussing the results of the technical examination of this drawing with me.

PLR

Fig. 116. Ultraviolet photograph of cat. no. 74.

75

LEONARDO DA VINCI

Studies of figures, heads and various mechanical devices

Metalpoint and black chalk? (with some ink on verso) on deep pinky-orange prepared paper, 30.3 × 19.4cm (at widest points)
Florence, Galleria degli Uffizi,
Gabinetto Disegni e Stampe 447E recto

Inscribed on recto, along left edge:
questo è il modo del chalar degli uccelli; top centre *questa segniata 'a' è l'ultima*; along right edge: *questa ruota segniata 'A' a d'avere 16. denti*; bottom left: *questa è la gangheratura / de manichi delle tanaglie*
on verso, top right: *vuole essere a barbachane di nicholo d'ughulino Martgli all'orio lo . . .*

Pedretti 1957, pp. 211–16; Pedretti and Dalli Regoli 1985, pp. 15, 58–9 and 82; Galluzzi in *Il Disegno fiorentino*, exh. cat., Florence 1992, cat. no. 9.17, pp. 195; Popham, ed. Kemp 1994, p. 25.

A W

The choice of a highly coloured prepared paper and the orientation of the drawings suggest that Leonardo began using this sheet for figure studies and for the neck, wings and head of a dragon (the profile of a curly-headed youth at bottom right is by another hand). The paper was then turned 90 degrees clockwise and the surrounding space used for drawings of various hinged and cogged mechanisms for transmitting movement and a sketch of the flight path of birds descending, which are not directly related to the figures. The verso, which includes a bat-winged flying device, has an inscription referring to one Niccolò di Ugolino Martelli, a young member of a Florentine banking family, who may have been a patron. Leonardo's fascination with the flying machine, which he referred to as a bird, emerges here for the first time. This interest is symptomatic of the special kind of creative ingenuity to which Leonardo aspired and suggests an identification with the legendary ancient artist Dedalus who was not only a maker but a man of science who devised wings that allowed man to fly.

The main figure study on the recto is of a richly dressed figure of a man looking on as though part of a larger composition, perhaps an Adoration of the Magi. This connection is strengthened by his juxtaposition with an attacking dragon that can be related to Leonardo's thoughts for the background of the *Adoration of the Magi* (see cat. no. 64). Though there is no precise equivalent in Leonardo's unfinished Uffizi *Adoration* (fig. 78), the figure's conical hat with its long peak seems to characterise him as eastern, like one of the retinue of the Magi. Botticelli's horizontal painting of the same subject has a very similar figure viewed from behind appearing at the centre (cat. no. 68). This type of dress is also used for the learned astrologer who appears at the centre of the engraving of *Mercury* (fig. 50). Leonardo's initial idea, which shows the figure in a swaggering pose, hand on hip, with the right, booted, leg extended and the head in a lost profile seems to have been inspired by bystander figures shown from behind in the work of Antonio del Pollaiuolo. There are a number of variants on this type in similar dress in Pollaiuolo's designs for the Baptistery embroidery cycle (see for example cat. no. 49). Unlike most of Leonardo's surviving studies for the *Adoration*, this figure is seen principally as a support for drapery. Metalpoint, a subtle medium for the treatment of relief, has been used with selective emphasis to draw out the fold structure of the generous mantle and indicate the glimmering fall of light on the swags of cloth. This type of study is indebted to the metalpoint drawings of heavily draped figures by Fra Filippo Lippi and perhaps also to his son Filippino (cat. no. 73). It is characteristic of Leonardo that he gives a crystalline luminosity to the principal folds, reserving the highest tonal contrast to the area of drapery that swings over the hip in order to bring out the underlying articulation of the figure. Leonardo does not seem to have been entirely satisfied with the pose. He shifted the left arm and right leg inwards and then restudied the line of the back and the near leg in a separate sketch to the left, which partially overlaps a pre-existing profile of a youth with flowing hair. The principal study shows the young artist approaching the task of describing a beautifully draped figure with the graphic models of Antonio del Pollaiuolo and Filippo Lippi in mind. He also rethinks them, revealing his own concern with the description of the human form in space and with the evocation of a particular moment or mood. In this isolated figure, his sense for psychological interrelation excites the viewer's curiosity as to what is not shown, leading us to wonder at the object of this stranger's regard.

In addition to the drawings which can be regarded as preparatory for the unfinished *Adoration of the Magi* (figs. 53 and 78), Leonardo's musings on the theme of the Adoration of Christ include four surviving studies related to the subject of the Adoration of the Shepherds. There is a sheet in the Musée Bonnat, Bayonne, with a compositional drawing showing a Nativity with the shepherds and a young Saint John the Baptist (fig. 117), two fragments in the Accademia, Venice (one with the holy family, a shepherd and angels flying overhead; the other with a kneeling shepherd, an angel and figures of the infant Baptist and Christ) and this drawing, where Leonardo considered alternatives for the figure of Christ and pursued the conversation between Joseph and the shepherds. For Leonardo both moments of veneration – by the kings and by the shepherds – were also times when amazement and devotion were mixed with excitement, perplexity and reflection. Because he conceived of them as emotional as well as devotional histories there are some similar expressive motifs in the studies. They are, however, separate subjects. The Bayonne drawing represents a resolved idea for a painting which looks to be of a smaller scale than the San Donato *Adoration*. But it is futile to speculate about lost projects, unknown commissions or even changed intentions for one commission. A close examination of the Hamburg drawing reveals, instead, the fertility of Leonardo's imaginative speculation on the subject at hand.

The truncated sketch of a torso at the lower right edge of the sheet indicates that the drawing has been cut down or cut out of a larger sheet. Leonardo often used metalpoint for preliminary sketches and then fixed some outlines with pen (as in cat. nos. 37 and 64), but it was unusual for him to do so on coloured paper. Since this is just a portion of the original page, it could be that the preparation is incidental to the present sketches, but the muted middle tone seems to have suited his desire to see the figures more in terms of curving and sinuous lines than in forceful relief.

76

LEONARDO DA VINCI

Studies for an Adoration of the Shepherds

Metalpoint, pen and ink on lavender prepared paper, 17.3 × 11 cm
Hamburg, Kunsthalle, Kupferstichkabinett, inv. 21488

Berenson 1938, vol. 1, p. 171, vol. 2, p. 112, cat. no. 1021, vol. 3, fig. 483; Popham, ed. Kemp 1994, pp. 22, 110, no. 41; *Italienische Zeichnungen*, exh. cat., Hamburg 1995, pp. 93-4, cat. no. 27.

PLR

Fig. 117. LEONARDO DA VINCI, *Study for an Adoration of the Shepherds*. Metalpoint, pen and ink on paper, 22.2 × 15.2 cm. Bayonne, Musée Bonnat, 658.

Fig. 118. LEONARDO DA VINCI, *Study for an Adoration.*
Pen and ink on paper, 28.5 × 21.5 cm.
Paris, Musée du Louvre, Département des
Arts Graphiques, 1978RF.

opposite
Fig. 119. Ultraviolet photograph of cat. no. 76.

Even with the naked eye, it possible to see that his metalpoint pondering of the poses of the child on its belly in the centre and the one facing upwards at the right was particularly intense. That Leonardo was intrigued with these opposite notions is proven by the drawings in Venice, each with a variant of the belly up and belly down positions. Inspection with ultraviolet light reveals that Leonardo had reworked these two figures virtually to the point of obliteration, and that he had further thoughts regarding the upright figure at the lower edge (fig. 119). In this first stage he generated ideas with uninhibited creative furore: raising, lowering and extending limbs. Eventually he selected three distinct and distinctive solutions with pen, still undecided about the direction of the child's body and gaze. While the upward looking child holding one hand to his mouth retains some of the eager immediacy of the children studied for the Virgin and Child with cat, the turning and outstretched poses of the other two have an air of deliberate artifice. They are images of Christ conceived as an object of worshipful contemplation, as divinity incarnate.

The miraculous nature of the child is, one supposes, the subject that Joseph is urgently explaining to the attentive shepherds or attendant figures. The pen line of his staff is below that of the baby beneath him, so Leonardo must have sketched Joseph and his listeners in metalpoint before taking up the pen. The adults are also drawn with graceful, curving lines. Leonardo used the pen to describe and enforce rhythmically repeating lines. The two shepherds are intricately intertwined. The cross-legged stance that Leonardo is trying out here is found on ancient sarcophagi. It could be that the conscious formalism of the drawing reflects Leonardo's study of the statues in Lorenzo de' Medici's sculpture garden. The form is not divorced from the subject, but integrated with its message of the divine grace manifested by the birth of Christ.

77

ANTONIO DEL POLLAIUOLO

The eldest magus (Melchior) and his page

Pen and brown ink with two shades of brown
wash and traces of black chalk on paper,
12.6 × 22.8 cm
Florence, Galleria degli Uffizi, Gabinetto Disegni e
Stampe, inv. 369E

Busignani 1969, p. XXVI (as possibly autograph);
Angelini, exh. cat., Florence 1986, cat. no. 160,
pp. 116–17.

AW

The figure is recognisable from his pose and attributes as the eldest magus or wise man, traditionally identified as Melchior, for a composition of the Adoration of Magi. Balanced on his right knee he is shown making deep obeisance, as though before the Christ Child seated on the Virgin's lap. Still wearing his nobleman's gloves, he has removed his curly-brimmed hat as a sign of respect and holds the vessel containing his gift of gold in his left hand. His seniority and status are marked by the smaller-scale Moorish page who holds up the train of his heavy, layered robe.

The wise man's prostrate position and profile view are found in other Florentine treatments of the subject (cat. no. 68), yet the detailed and emphatic characterisation of his head and the treatment of dress are also reminiscent of Northern European paintings of the Adoration. No painting by Antonio del Pollaiuolo survives on this subject but two other drawings after Pollaiuolo, one of which shows another king, may be related to a lost composition, for which the Uffizi drawing would have been a highly finished study. The attribution to Antonio rests both on the accomplished use of pen and wash, based on traces of black chalk, and the treatment of the subject. The clarity of contour and the volumetric use of wash are characteristic of figure studies by Antonio's fellow goldsmith Maso Finiguerra. But the dramatic intensity conveyed by the old man's expression, the concern with courtly deportment – seen in the page and the elegantly extended little finger – and the decorative geometry of the cascading robe are typical of Antonio's mature draughtsmanship.

The magus is characterised by his improbably curling hat and long beard as an eastern (Greek?) sage and the black page, carrying a drinking horn, serves as his exotic attribute. The style of the figures is reminiscent of those devised by Antonio for the court scenes in the embroideries on the life of Saint John the Baptist in the 1460s and 1470s (cat. no. 48). The almost caricatural profile of the page recalls the moor's head appearing on the coat of arms of Antonio Pucci, the Pollaiuolo brothers' patron for the *Martyrdom of Saint Sebastian* altarpiece, but a connection with Pucci patronage for this Adoration study is entirely conjectural.

Antonio Pollaiuolo.

VII   'The Beautiful Chamber'

In the 1497 inventory of the Tornabuoni palace, the heading for Lorenzo di Giovanni's *camera* notes that it is 'beautiful'. Its contents included: a gold-framed tondo showing the Adoration of the Magi; two marriage chests with backboards – gilt and painted; two world maps, in gilded frames; two gilded infants, embracing, and a walnut chest and backboard with inlaid woodwork. The items, all richly decorated and glimmering with gold, are characteristic of the furnishings found in the rooms of the leading families of Florence in the later part of the fifteenth century. The ground-floor chamber of the Medici palace, identified in the 1492 inventory as Lorenzo's, had a canopied bed on a platform with intarsia panelling. Above it, in gilded frames, were dramatic paintings: a battle of lions and dragons, a hunt by Pesellino, a *Judgement of Paris* by Paolo Uccello and three large panels by Uccello showing the Battle of San Romano (one now in the National Gallery, NG 583). The room was lit by seven brass candelabra, hung with trophies – helmets and banners. Among the other paintings were a large gilt-framed tondo showing the *Adoration of the Magi* by Fra Angelico and portraits of the Duke of Urbino and of Galeazzo Maria Sforza (by Piero del Pollaiuolo; fig. 19). Botticelli's *Primavera* (fig. 15) was part of the decorative ensemble of the ground-floor chamber in the neighbouring palace of Lorenzo's cousin, Lorenzo di Pierfrancesco.

The word 'chamber' or *camera* designates a specific type of room. Typically a large house or palace was occupied by several generations of the male line of the family, namely the husband and wife with their sons and unmarried daughters, married sons with their families, and possibly widowed sisters. Large houses or palaces were generally divided into suites, or apartments, each assigned to a different family unit. A usual sequence of rooms was: *sala* (hall), antechamber, chamber and study. Halls were flexible spaces, and had benches, trestle tables and stools and could be used for public events or family dining. The standard furnishings for a chamber were a huge bed (*letto* or *lettiera*, which could be four metres square and was often set on a platform made of chests, used for seating and storage), an equally impressive daybed (*lettuccio*, also three or four metres long and with a panelled backboard), large storage chests, strong boxes and a pair of painted wedding chests. There were lavish bed hangings and tapestries. There could be maiolica and glass vessels. No chamber was complete without its holy image, usually a Virgin and Child. Holy figures were present to guide and to express the piety of the household, and to represent their welcome protection of the family.

Chambers were the nucleus of the domestic sphere, and therefore private; but in addition to their functions as bedrooms, the daily matters of family life were conducted there, guests received and business transacted. Their decoration involved an element of display and over the course of the fifteenth century these rooms came to hold an increasing number and variety of paintings and sculptures. The study (*studio*, *studiolo* or *scrittoio*) was the true inner sanctum or retreat – an almost exclusively male preserve, where private papers were kept, books and manuscripts read and the rarest objects appreciated.

Custom dictated the general distribution of spaces and their furnishing, but fashion determined the way they looked. Beds and daybeds were traditional furniture forms, for example, but once the shop of Giuliano and Benedetto da Maiano had established its mastery of intarsia design, woodwork inlaid with perspective designs, Petrarchan *Triumphs* and foliate patterns became popular. In his tax declaration of 1427 Niccolò da Uzzano already stated that 'more and more' household goods were required by someone of his standing. The multiplication of goods in the domestic setting is one of the noteworthy features of fifteenth-century Florence. The 1492 inventory of Lorenzo de' Medici's palace lists more than six times as many paintings and statues than the 1418 inventory of his great-grandfather's belongings, and that does not include the collected objects in the study or the sculpture garden. Accumulation does not alone account for the multiplication of decorative and beautiful possessions. The difference between generations caused Vespasiano da Bisticci to comment on the fact that in the earlier part of the century even a man of modest means like the learned Niccolò Niccoli could possess marble statues, antique vases and sculpture, crystal cups and pictures by distinguished masters, because things of the sort were not so highly prized at the time. By the later part of the century such beautiful things were more widely appreciated and to own them was generally considered a mark of distinction.

Lorenzo di Matteo Morelli, who commissioned sumptuous wedding chests with scenes from Livy in 1472 (cat. nos. 5, 78 and 79), had previously acquired, among other things, a picture of Petrarch, coloured plaster busts of Dante and the emperor Hadrian, a painted plaster relief showing Romulus and Remus, three painted plaster angels, two paintings of Saint George, one by Paolo Uccello (possibly like that in the National Gallery, NG 6294), a mirror with a woman's head in the frame, another gilded mirror surrounded by figures (like cat. no. 80). He also owned a small plaster statue of Hercules, which he traded with the painters who decorated his mirror. Morelli's purchases are significant because it could be said that their cultural worth was at least as great as their material value: his gallery of great men was not made of marble, but of painted plaster. Neither old nor antique, these 'modern' works betray the fact that poetry and history could be considered everyday pleasures in Morelli's generation. These pleasures could be satisfied and enhanced by artists like Antonio del Pollaiuolo and Botticelli who composed visual poetry on ancient and *all'antica* subjects (such as cat. nos. 88 and 86).

From the middle of the century the surfaces of walls and wedding chests were opportunities for informed viewing. Subjects from classical history and ancient poetry and mythology became standard features of the decorative repertoire, supplementing, if not supplanting, scenes of chivalric romance or courtly pleasures. Instruction was allied with amusement: a duality of purpose that could make the room exemplary as well as beautiful and bring virtue to ornament. Family history was also incorporated into the fabric of domestic life in the form of painted portraits and portrait busts.

The 'beautiful chamber' was a space where tradition and innovation were elegantly accommodated. Often furnished at the time of a marriage, its decoration related to the consolidation and propagation of the family and the lineage. Heraldic markers – arms and emblems – were on the picture and furniture frames. Wedding chests were literally monuments to marriage. Decorated birth trays predicted or proclaimed the safe arrival of hoped-for heirs. Function and convention determined the basic elements of the room and gave it a sense of solid continuity. The details of its decoration signalled a new chapter in a longer history. In the 1470s its topics and its visual vocabulary were enriched by artists eager to enhance their own prestige while satisfying their clients' honour.

PLR

78 and 79

BIAGIO DI ANTONIO AND JACOPO DEL SELLAIO

Pair of chests with scenes from Roman history

Tempera on poplar, with gilding,
205.5 × 193 cm (each chest, overall)
40.5 × 35.5 cm (each side panel)
40.5 × 1.37 cm (each front panel)
4.5 × 162.5 cm (each *spalliera*)
London, Courtauld Gallery, Lee Collection,
F1947LF4,5

Livy, trans. Foster 1919–24, vol. 1, pp. 6–7, 92–7,
160–7, vol. 2, pp. 250–3, 254–61; Callmann 1974,
p. 26, note 10; Lydecker 1987, pp. 112–23, 161, 167,
286–8 (for the Morelli documents); Callmann 1988,
pp. 8–9 (fig. 5 for the Savonarola woodcut);
Barriault 1994, pp. 34, 71–2, 108–110, 141–2;
Davies 1995, pp. 36–44; Bellosi and Haines 1999,
p. 68; Callmann 1999, pp. 342–4.

PLR

In September 1472 Lorenzo di Matteo Morelli (1446–1528) paid the woodworker Zanobi di Domenico twenty-one florins for a pair of chests (*forzieri*) with their backboards (*spalliere*) and plinth (*predella*). In November and December he registered payments of just over forty florins to the firm of Jacopo del Sellaio and Biagio di Antonio for painting the chests and backboards with histories and gilding them with fine gold. The fortunate survival of both Lorenzo's record books and the chests is unique. The chests have been restored, however. Most of the framing elements are modern, including the volutes at the edges of the *spalliera* panels and the lion's paw feet; the reconstruction, which was probably done in the nineteenth century, looks as though it was based on a fifteenth-century source, such as the woodcut showing a chamber in Savonarola's treatise on the *Art of Dying Well*. Though not totally original, the chests are extraordinarily complete and accurate in their impressiveness.

Lorenzo's record books permit a detailed view into his chamber. In 1466-7, Lorenzo had furnished his room with a daybed (*lettuccio*) and bed (*letto*), each four *braccia* long (232 cm) and with inlaid woodwork. The *lettuccio*, which was commissioned from Giuliano da Maiano, had three panels showing Triumphs. The combined cost of these large and elaborate beds was around forty-four florins. The first campaign of decoration was undertaken when Lorenzo became owner of the house he shared with his father. The pair of chests were commissioned at the time of his marriage to Vaggia di Tanai Nerli. The union is commemorated by the family arms on the volutes at the corners of the chests, the Morelli arms on one chest, the Nerli arms on the other.

As a type of furniture such decorated chests, known in the fifteenth century as *forzieri* (and now usually called *cassoni*), were specifically associated with marriage. They were generally made in pairs, and could be, as in Morelli's case, the costliest items in a room. Until the middle of the fifteenth century they had been supplied by the bride's family and were used to carry the dower goods she brought into her marital home. Lorenzo's purchases are representative of a shift in custom whereby the bride came with a larger dowry (Vaggia's was two thousand florins, a high but standard sum among the Florentine élite) and the furnishing was left to the groom and his family. This was not merely a matter of money, but of maintaining the balance of honour in the exchange between the families involved. It can also be connected to an increased interest in keeping control of lavish and co-ordinated decorative ensembles. Typically Lorenzo made no significant changes or additions to his chamber after his marriage. Useful for storage, these marriage chests became part of his family history and family identity.

The chests were a form of permanently open picture book for the household and Lorenzo chose very high-minded histories for its benefit. The scenes are all taken from the history of Rome written by Livy between *c.* 29 BC and AD 17. The scenes on the front panels are from Book 5 and record the bravery, justice and wisdom of Marcus Furius Camillus, who was hailed as the second founder of Rome after his defeat of the Gauls in 390 BC, which is shown on the chest with the Morelli arms (cat. no. 78).

Livy tells how Rome, which had been under siege, was going to settle with the Gauls for a ransom of a thousand pounds of gold. Insult was added to injury when the Gauls brought dishonest weights, and the Roman tribune's protests were answered by the Gallic leader adding his sword to the weight, saying 'Woe to the conquered' – the scene shown at the left of the panel, with its continuation as Camillus appears riding to the rescue. The Gauls were subsequently routed, as shown at the right. The chest with the Nerli arms (cat. no. 79) has a previous episode, that of the treacherous schoolmaster of the children of Rome's rivals, the Faliscans, who led his charges from the town of Falerii into the Roman camp – shown on the right side of the panel. Camillus – just and brave – was outraged at this violation of the 'rights of war'. The schoolmaster was bound and sent back, and he is depicted being scourged in the city at the centre. The Faliscans were so impressed at the Roman fair-dealing that they surrendered the town to Camillus, who receives its keys in the left foreground centre of the panel. His soldiers leave for home at the far left.

The episodes revealed by curtains in the *spalliere* are from Book 2. On the Morelli chest, the valiant Horatius Cocles is depicted as he defended Rome against the Etruscans by holding a bridge over the Tiber until it could be torn down (as is happening at the left), he then leapt off and swam away. The Virtues on the side panel of this chest are Justice and Fortitude. The *spalliera* story on the Nerli chest is that of Gaius Mucius Scaevola, a young Roman noble who set out to assassinate the Etruscan king Porsinna. He mistakenly slew Porsinna's secretary, a confusion explained by the similarity of their dress. Attempting to force a confession of further plots, the king ordered that he be flung into sacrificial flames, but Mucius thrust his hand in the fire, heedless of pain. He was freed and praised for his valour. Prudence and Temperance flank this chest.

Cat. no. 78.

The stories are not illustrated in a linear fashion, even though they follow Livy's accounts. The *spalliere* scenes are almost emblematic, with the courageous deeds at the centre. The panels are discursive, but the narrative is not in a simple left to right sequence. The observer must seek out the story and tell it by recognising the episodes. Through repeated looking more details of the story emerge. This intricate form of storytelling is typical of this type of painting. As is common with such objects, the overall mode is ornamental, with variety of action more important than clarity. Roman soldiers are identified with SPQR banners and in the tribute scene the Capitoline hill is represented, but generally the costumes and settings mix contemporary and past styles in a way meant to make the past immediate and relevant. For Livy and for his Renaissance readers the study of history was 'wholesome and profitable' because it provided examples for imitation and avoidance. Lorenzo Morelli, a silk merchant, had no intention of becoming a soldier, but he most certainly wanted to be seen as a prudent, wise, just and strong citizen and his intention would be to instruct his family, most particularly his sons, in virtuous behaviour. Leonardo Bruni's history of Florence was modelled on Livy's books. A similar translation of Roman glory to Florentine life takes place on these chests.

Cat. no. 79.

Fig. 120. Detail from the front of the
Morelli chest showing *Rome held ransom by the
Gauls and saved by Marcus Furius Camillus.*

Fig. 121. Detail from the front of the
Nerli chest showing *The schoolmaster of Falerii.*

80

UNKNOWN CRAFTSMAN

Mirror frame with reliefs of Venus and Mars and putti

Moulded component (stucco?), painted
and gilded, within a gilt wood frame,
50.8 cm diameter, *c*.5 cm deep
London, Victoria and Albert Museum, 5887-1859

Philostratus, *Imagines*, trans. A. Fairbanks 1931, Book 1,
9.3; Lydecker 1987, pp. 119–21 and p. 283; Spallanzani
and Bertelà 1992, p. 94; Thornton 1997, pp. 167–74.

AW

Made of blown glass or polished steel, mirrors were difficult to manufacture and consequently expensive. But their material brilliance and mysterious power made them desirable luxuries in the 1470s, worthy of being exchanged and collected. The patrician Lorenzo di Matteo Morelli, for example, is documented as owning two mirrors by 1465, anticipating by some years his property settlement and the furnishing of a new apartment (see cat. nos. 78 and 79).

In the example from the Victoria and Albert Museum, the blown glass that would have filled the central roundel has been lost. The character of this object would, however, always have been as much decorative as functional. Both the format and subject matter of the frame recall contemporary prints (cat. nos. 90 and 91), which frequently depicted amorous themes ingeniously composed in a circular field. It is conceivable that some of these designs might have been used as patterns for mirrors.

The sculpted stucco relief of the figured area becomes deeper towards the bottom of the composition and sometimes spills out over the border of the frame. The whole is extensively painted and gilded to create what would originally have been a colourful and gleaming object worthy of a beautiful domestic chamber. If the shield supported by putti ever contained a coat of arms it is no longer legible. However, a connection with the Medici family is possible since the outer frame is carved into a diamond ring, a device adopted by Piero de' Medici (d. 1469). A similar frame shape is recorded in the inventory of the Medici palace in 1492. The diamond ring, shown here binding together the reclining couple, was a symbol of eternity and could have referred to eternal love. Just as beauty was associated with virtue, the mirror which reflected an image of beauty was not morally neutral but construed as revealing inner truth. It could therefore be interpreted as a flattering gift to the beloved. This mirror frame has a male and a female side. At the bottom left the reclining figure of the nude Venus is surrounded by an entourage of winged putti or cupids, one of whom looks out of the frame as he crowns her, perhaps as a victor in love. Above them a putto rides a swan, perhaps alluding to Philostratus' *Imagines* (1, 9.3). On the male side of the mirror, cupids dominate a dragon while Mars, also vanquished by love, sleeps with his head thrown back. His pose is ultimately adopted from a classical sarcophagus in which the beautiful Endymion is shown asleep (compare also cat. no. 18). Both the composition and its playful associations are closely comparable to that of Botticelli's *Venus and Mars* panel (cat. no. 86) but probably predate it. It is not known who manufactured the mirror. The claim for a connection with Antonio del Pollaiuolo seems to rest on the muscular treatment of the torso of Mars, but the much softer modelling of the figures and the style of the faces suggest an artist more directly influenced by Lorenzo Ghiberti.

Tin-glazed earthenware, known in Italy as maiolica, was extensively exported from southern Spain. The luxury art of lustreware, the fruit of centuries of technological experiment, involving imported materials, repeated firings and a very high failure rate, had arrived in Islamic Spain from the Middle East in the tenth century. In the fifteenth it was much esteemed both for vessels and for floor tiles by Christian princes and prelates all over Europe. This piece was presumably commissioned through the Valencian branch of the Medici bank.

The shape of vase (*terrás* – a type of flower vase) and the decoration (ivy leaves of cobalt blue and gold lustre) belong to Islamic tradition but the decoration includes the Medici *impresa* of the diamond with two feathers on one side and the Medici arms with the *palle* (balls) on the other. The uppermost *palla* has a *fleur-de-lis* which King Louis XI of France in 1465 permitted Piero de' Medici to add to his coat of arms. The vessel was probably made in the decade following this event and very likely for Lorenzo whose appreciation of ceramic vases 'excellenti et rari' and of unfamiliar character ('nuovi a noi') is expressed in an undated letter written by him to a member of the Malatesta family. The maiolica which the Medici commissioned from local workshops – a notable example is the vase celebrating Lorenzo's marriage which is in the Detroit Institute of Arts (37.74) – imitate both the form and decoration of Spanish imports. A vase of this type appears in the cupboard behind the Virgin in the *Annunciation* of 1482–4 by Filippino Lippi in the Museo Civico, San Gimignano.

How vessels of this kind were used or displayed is uncertain. A pair appear in Lorenzo's inventory of 1492 valued at two florins and ten *soldi* – '2 orcioloni grandi con dua manichi da maiolicha, con l'arme' ('2 large maiolica jars, each with a pair of handles, with coat of arms') – in a *sala grande* of the villa at Careggi, listed together with candlesticks and other utensils of brass and copper.

81

VALENCIAN (SOUTHERN SPAIN)

Wing-handled vase

Tin-glazed earthenware decorated
in lustre and cobalt blue,
57 cm, height
London, British Museum, Department of
Medieval and Later Antiquities,
Godman Bequest 619

Caiger-Smith 1973, p. 7; Berardi 1984, pp. 42–3 (Lorenzo's letter); Caiger-Smith 1985, pp. 107–8; Wilson 1987, no. 16; Wilson 1989, pp. 129–30; Stratton in Levenson, ed., 1991–2, p. 171, cat. no. 53; Spallanzani and Bertelà 1992, p. 141 (for inventory, see p. 151 at note 128); Wilson 1995, p. 347.

This entry has been compiled with extensive help from Dora Thornton.

NP

82

ATTRIBUTED TO VERROCCHIO

Bust of a woman

White marble,
53 × 48.8 × 19.9 cm
Washington, DC, National Gallery of Art,
Samuel H. Kress Collection, 1939.1.326

Suida 1948, pp. 2 ff, and 1949, pp. 176 ff;
Pope-Hennessy 1958, p. 304; Seymour 1971, pp. 120–1
and p. 169; Middeldorf 1976, pp. 20–1; Luchs in
Italian Renaissance Sculpture in the Time of Donatello,
exh. cat., Detroit 1985, cat. no. 71, pp. 207–9.

AW

This sculpture belongs to a genre of sculpted portrait bust developed from the 1450s by Florentine sculptors such as Mino da Fiesole and Desiderio da Settignano in emulation of antique busts (fig. 85). The earliest surviving examples all represent patrician men (often men of learning such as Matteo Palmieri, fig. 27) who commissioned likenesses in marble, in emulation of the ancient Romans. The practice was soon extended to worthy (usually implying high-ranking and chaste) women and to production in other 'antique' materials such as bronze and terracotta (see cat. no. 17). Such busts are generally recorded in *camere* and might be placed high up where it would not always be possible to admire them in detail. An effect of bodily presence is enhanced in the Washington bust by the sculptor's impressive control of the bone structure in relation to the overlying flesh. The indication of slight pockets beneath the eyes and of characterful indentations at the corners of the mouth is of great subtlety and the flesh of the sitter's shoulders seems to swell out where it emerges from the stiff encasement of her dress. The attention both to underlying structure and surface texture are stylistic arguments in favour of Andrea del Verrocchio's authorship of the bust. This attribution has not been unanimously accepted, but those who favour Verrocchio point to the sitter's waving and deeply cut locks of hair, like those found on the Forteguerri monument (fig. 96). Luchs has drawn specific parallels with the bust of Giuliano de' Medici (cat. no. 17) with its 'remarkably similar long tapering eyes, bulging gently under sharp-edged lids and topped with a long fold above the upper lid'.

Although the marble is equally highly finished all round, the flat band of the woman's dress forms a type of base to the front of the bust that is absent at the back, a feature that reinforces the dominant frontal viewpoint. As in contemporary painted portraits of high-ranking young women, the subject is given an extremely erect posture, associated with nobility, which is here enlivened only by the slightest tilt of the sitter's head out of the central axis. In keeping with beliefs concerning external beauty as an expression of inner virtue, portraits of women are much more strongly idealised in the period than those of men and tend to mask individual personality behind generally admired norms for female representation. While the bust clearly depicts a particular individual, her extremely high hair line, broad, smooth forehead, and even her protruding upper lip, seem to have been fashionable for Florentine women in the 1460s and 70s (compare fig. 63) and they do not help to identify her. The suggestion that the bust represents Giuliano de' Medici's platonic mistress Simonetta Vespucci was first proposed by Suida on the basis of her resemblance to a presumed portrait of Simonetta by the young Ghirlandaio in the fresco in the Vespucci chapel at Ognissanti (fig. 39). The woman sheltering beneath the Virgin's mantle in the fresco is probably a member of the Vespucci family, but there is no certainty that she is Simonetta and the identity of the Washington subject remains unclear. There can be no question as to the sitter's status. Her hair is bound in a fine snood covering the ears, which then laces at the back near the nape of the neck, leaving neat waves of hair visible on the crown and brow. She is shown wearing the most fashionable and expensive type of cut silk brocaded velvet 'cotta', probably of Florentine manufacture, displaying a large pomegranate pattern. Clothing of such luxury fabric was restricted by sumptuary law, sanctioned to be worn only shortly before, and for a restricted period after, marriage. The precise date of the bust is difficult to gauge but the form and pattern of the dress seem to have been more popular in the 1460s and earlier 1470s than later. Simpler materials and more flowing garments were also represented in this decade (cat. no. 83). Verrocchio himself would exploit the

greater fluid potential of the summer indoor dress in his exquisite portrait of a woman holding flowers (fig. 67) datable to the mid-1470s. Using a less static formula, Verrocchio included the expressive feature of the displayed hands and implied movement in the hips. The result is an intimate image of feminine grace of a kind associated with the love object in lyric poetry (see cat. no. 88) and directed to a male viewer. Though less emotive, the type of the Washington bust remained the dominant form for the sculpted portrait, partly perhaps on account of its more general address to the dynastic and representational interests of the patrician family as a whole.

This woman, so tranquil as she meets the viewer's gaze, is one of the boldest inventions in Florentine fifteenth-century portraiture. The Italian word for portrait, *ritratto*, means copy; but Botticelli, whose portraits are remarkable for their variety, did not restrict himself to making a record of features. Nor did he keep to one format. Before the 1470s it was usual for Florentine women to be painted in profile. This position avoided the semblance of any immodest eye contact. They were also usually shown in the expensive garments and with the sort of jewellery a man would purchase for his bride, which were not given to the new wife, but which remained his property. Women were represented as objects of admiration – proud possessions, encoded as belonging to their husband's family and displaying its status and honour. None of these conventions was observed by Botticelli here; his sitter is an active subject.

The woman seems to come to the window, putting one hand on its frame with a spontaneous gesture. The strong diagonals and verticals of the window frames behind her reinforce her position in the foreground and through the compression of space add to her stature and dramatise her expressive features. Decently dressed, and holding a handkerchief (a sign of breeding and status), she is clothed in the simple garments worn at home. Not only is the woman represented, but the viewer is also constructed or construed as a friend, an intimate visitor to the household who is permitted this form of casual encounter. So when Marco Parenti went to inspect a potential bride for his brother-in-law Filippo Strozzi at the house of Francesco Tanagli, the girl was summoned to be seen as here, dressed 'en gamurra'. This circumstance was reported to Filippo as a testimony to the close friendship between the men and to the candour allowed by the visit. Florentine girls were carefully guarded from view, and this portrait is not to be thought of as a form of pre-nuptial snapshot. It is, however, a completely domestic painting: the woman is shown as wife, not bride. The pillar in the window may not be incidental, it was a familiar symbol of fortitude and constancy. The viewer is received into a private and well-ordered realm by the woman who is to be remembered respectfully and affectionately for her role as the dutiful manager of the household.

She would seem to be identified as Smeralda, the wife of Viviano Bandinelli, by the partly effaced inscription on the ledge in front of her. Smeralda was the grandmother of the socially ambitious sixteenth-century court sculptor Baccio Bandinelli. Baccio was the first to use the surname Bandinelli, which does not occur before the 1520s. The inscription has long been recognised as dating at least from that time, with the implication that it was added by Baccio as part of a self-advancing genealogy most extensively recorded in his autobiographical *Memoriale*. Louis Waldman has recently exposed this as a seventeenth-century pastiche by Baccio's grandson, undertaken as part of a comprehensive project of forgery intended to raise the status of the family. The handwriting on the ledge resembles that found in the forged documents and could well be part of Baccio the Younger's re-writing of his family history. The question remains as to whether the added inscription adopted the portrayed woman into the Bandinelli family or simply remembered and acknowledged her. Given the level of falsifying undertaken by Baccio the Younger, the former seems likely. It is also the case that portraits were rare items in the fifteenth century and paintings owned by artisans (like Viviano, who was a blacksmith) were generally limited to one or two holy images – a Virgin and Child or a Crucifixion. Still there are exceptions to every rule and Botticelli's discreetly smiling lady retains her mystery.

83

SANDRO BOTTICELLI

Portrait of a Woman, 'Smeralda Bandinelli'

Tempera on panel,
65.7 × 41 cm
London, Victoria and Albert Museum, CAI 100

Inscribed: *Smeralda di . . . Bandinelli moglie d . . . Bandinelli.* The two male christian names are illegible.

Strozzi 1877, pp. 444–5 (26 July 1465 letter about Parenti); Kauffmann 1973, vol. 1, pp. 37–9; Lightbown 1978, vol. 2, B15, pp. 28–9; Herald 1981, p. 220; Campbell 1990, p. 115.

I would like to thank Louis Waldman for generously sharing his Bandinelli discoveries with me; they will be published in a forthcoming edition of Bandinelli's *Memoriale*.

PLR

84

SANDRO BOTTICELLI

Madonna of the Magnificat

Egg tempera on wood (5 planks laid diagonally),
maximum diameter 62.6 cm
Private Collection

Lightbown 1978, vol. 2, pp. 42–4, B29;
Lightbown 1989, pp. 82–6; Puppi in Grabski 1990,
pp. 88–93, no. 13.

NP

Fig. 122. SANDRO BOTTICELLI, *Madonna of the Magnificat*,
late 1470s. Tempera on panel, 118 cm diameter.
Florence, Galleria degli Uffizi, inv. 1609.

The painting is a reduced version, almost exactly half size, of the famous tondo in the Uffizi. The Virgin appears to be writing the Latin text on the right-hand page – that of the Magnificat from Luke I, 46-48 ('magnificat a[n]i[m]a mea ... My soul doth magnify the Lord ...'). On the previous page may be discerned the story of Zacharias from Luke I, 72-76 referring to the Baptist as the prophet of the highest. It has been proposed that the painting was a monastic commission because these texts form part of a breviary prayer but the texts are not arcane and such tondi seem to have been made for domestic devotional use. Although Botticelli did not invent this type of painting, he did much to make it popular. His *Adoration of the Kings* (cat. no. 7) was more crowded and complex, and deeper in its pictorial space, than previous examples. Here the emphasis is rather on rich surface pattern. It is noticeable that he has also departed from the tender sentiment usual in such small devotional paintings to express the sublime awareness by both mother and child of the nature of their mission: the Virgin writes out the Magnificat with awe bordering on sorrow and the infant Christ, a precocious reader, looks up from the letters to the rays and tongues of divine light which fall on him – both touch the pomegranate, a symbol of the Passion. The youths who support the book and the ink are guided by an angel. The larger and presumably earlier painting, probably of about 1480, included angels holding a crown over the Virgin's head and more gilded ornaments. There are numerous minor variations in this version (the lips seem more open, the Virgin's thigh has a more clearly defined volume) and the artist has not reproduced the design mechanically but drawn it afresh. A very fine brush drawing, not always exactly followed, can be seen with infra-red reflectography. Other replicas of the Uffizi tondo are known (there is one in the Louvre and one in the Pierpont Morgan library) but they are full size and of lesser quality. Botticelli's workshop appears to have been very loosely organised and most of the replicas with variations made of his inventions are careless in composition or execution or both. This work, probably a special commission, is certainly an exception. It is slightly worn in some of the flesh areas but well preserved in all colours except for the darkened green.

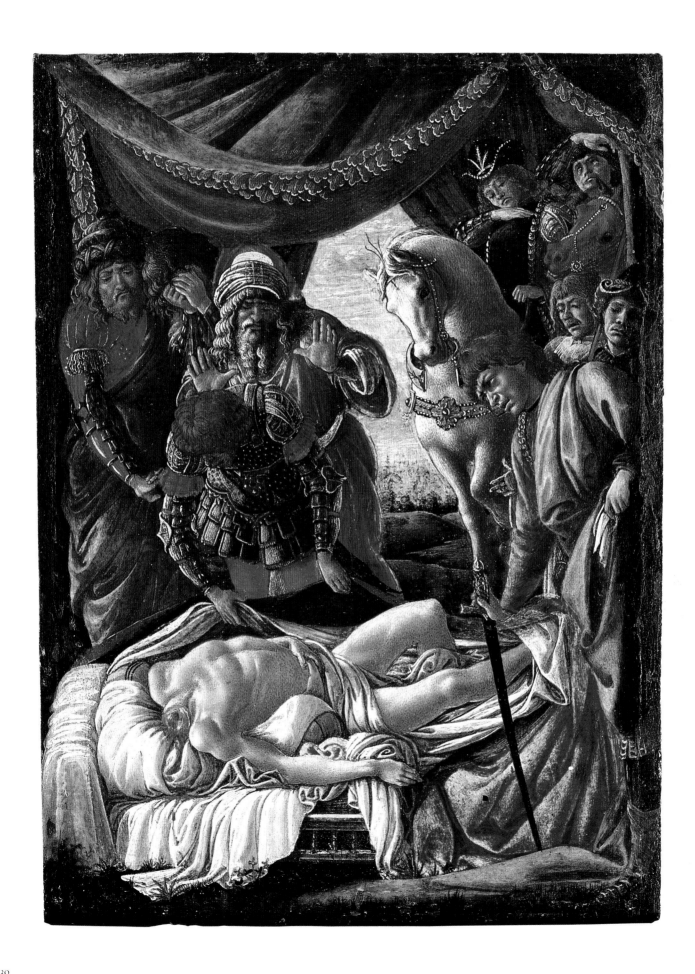

Unblemished, yet mutilated, the headless body of the Assyrian general Holofernes confronts the viewer as an awful revelation even as it is discovered by his men. The story in the Book of Judith tells how the chaste and beautiful Israelite widow saved her people by pretending to defect to the Assyrians. On her fourth day in the Assyrian camp she was invited to a banquet by Holofernes, who intended to seduce her. Instead he drank such quantities of wine that when they were left alone in his tent he was 'overcome with wine' and she was able to behead him with two strokes of his sword (Judith, 13:2-8).

Botticelli depicted the story in two panels. One shows Judith returning to her native town, Bethulia, Holofernes' bloodied sword in her right hand and an olive branch – symbol of peace – in her left (fig. 123). Her devoted maid follows carrying the head, the covering cloth blown back to reveal a bearded middle-aged face. This panel shows a subsequent moment when the general was found 'cast upon the floor dead, and his head … taken from him', a discovery which caused dismay and fear in his camp and which led to the flight of his men and the defeat of the Assyrians (Judith, 14:14–19; 15:1–7).

Judith was traditionally a symbol of the triumph of humility over pride, of the weak against the strong. Holofernes, by contrast, was a symbol of *lussuria* or lust. The inscription placed on the front of the column of the statue of *Judith slaying Holofernes* in the courtyard of the Medici palace was a reminder of how 'Kingdoms fall through luxury, cities rise through virtue.' Viewers were urged to 'Behold the proud neck severed by a humble hand.'

In the Renaissance, history was meant to delight as well as to instruct. Carefully wrought, these small pictures were precious objects, conceived to inspire pleasure and intended for close and repeated inspection. In the 1492 Medici inventory, for example, a 'tavoletta' of *Judith with the Head of Holofernes* by Squarcione was listed among those kept in the study along with the gems, medals and cameos. However pleasing as objects, Botticelli's images were also edifying histories. The spectacle of the headless body is a harsh warning against lust. The luxuriant display of the prostrate form arched up against pillows and cushions, blood coursing down the folds of the sheets, both attracts and repels. The youthful body is disturbingly at odds with the mature head carried by the maid. This disparity is one of the many disruptive elements in the composition that draw attention and that give warning. The perplexing, crowded space of the tent expresses the disorder and disarray of the Assyrian army, now metaphorically and actually without a head. The biblical account says that only one attendant found Holofernes. Botticelli included nine, and two horses, all looming over the corpse. In this case Botticelli's own *horror vacui* shows the horror of the event. Even more terrible in its way is the erotic invitation of the body laid across the luxurious bed. The story of Judith represented a potentially disturbing role reversal, with a woman having power over a man. This is reinforced here, where the male body has been shown as fatally vulnerable. To a Renaissance viewer this was itself a warning, one given in a different, but related, fashion in the *Venus and Mars* (cat. no. 86), where the contrast between active and passive gives Venus dominance over her warrior lover. Perversely desirable and commanding inspection, Botticelli's rendering of the dead Holofernes both gives the story its fitting moral and evokes the sexual desires which brought it to its inevitable conclusion.

85

SANDRO BOTTICELLI

The Discovery of the Dead Holofernes

Tempera on panel,
31 × 25 cm
Florence, Galleria degli Uffizi, inv. 1487

Horne 1908, pp. 24–6; Lightbown 1978, vol. 1, pp. 26–9, vol. 2, B7, p. 22; Florence, Uffizi, *Catalogo Generale*, 1979, P251, p. 176; Ciletti 1991, pp. 35–70; Spallanzani and Bertelà 1992, p. 51 (Medici inventory, Squarcione).

PLR

Fig. 123. SANDRO BOTTICELLI, *Judith and her Handmaiden returning to Bethulia*, c.1467–72. Tempera on panel, 31 × 24 cm. Florence, Galleria degli Uffizi, inv. 1484.

86

SANDRO BOTTICELLI

Venus and Mars

Egg tempera and oil on poplar,
70.6 × 176.8 cm
National Gallery, London NG 915

Horne 1908, pp. 140–1; Panofsky 1939, p. 63; Davies 1961, pp. 99–101; Wind 1968, pp. 89–91; Gombrich 1972, pp. 66–9; Lightbown 1978, vol. 2, pp. 55–6 (with bibliography); Bober and Rubinstein 1986, p. 130 (for the hermaphrodite statue); Penny in Dunkerton et al. 1991, pp. 336–7.

NP

As in many romances of the late Middle Ages, as well as in Ovid and other ancient Roman writers who influenced them, sexual passion is here depicted as involving the subjection of the male to female control. Mars, the god of war, is so completely subdued that satyr children can play with his armour. The wasps buzzing in their nest by one ear fail to rouse him, as does the conch shell blasted in his other. His limp right hand mimics the exhausted member. Venus calmly contemplates the scene. Although lightly and loosely clad, she is completely covered and her garment could not easily be removed (but it could be opened) since it is fastened to two plaits of her hair.

The god's sword, breastplate, helmet and lance are all modern in style but the image depends upon a knowledge of ancient literature, notably Lucian's description of a painting of the marriage of Alexander the Great in which cupids play with the hero's arms and armour. The satyrs also owe something to ancient sculpture and the striking way that the foot is caught in the drapery (seen also in the body of Holofernes, cat. no. 85) is derived from an antique statue of a sleeping hermaphrodite much admired in Florence (Ghiberti indeed praises this very feature of it). If both Mars' legs seem oddly feeble, Venus at first glance seems only to have one. Her right knee was perhaps originally more apparent beneath her skirts and her right foot below the tail of drapery (her toes are below Mars' right hand), but the distortion is extreme even for Botticelli who commonly ignored anatomical plausibility in the interest of elegant or expressive line.

The wasps (*vespe*) may refer to the Vespucci family for whom Botticelli is known to have worked. The large green fruit (an unripe lemon?) clutched by the child satyr on the right has not been explained (and is seldom noticed). The painting is likely to have been made as part of the redecoration of a Florentine *camera* at the time of a wedding when amatory and humorous imagery was often considered appropriate. It would have originally been incorporated in the wainscot of a room, as a *spalliera* above a bench or chest. Other early paintings of the nude are sometimes found in the inside of the lids of chests.

The paint is worn in some areas and some underdrawing is apparent, including a lock of the goddess's hair which was painted in a different position. The drapery behind Mars' hand is very damaged and some of the shell gold used extensively in the picture has been lost. The modelling of the flesh in the god's head and in the goddess' right hand is especially well preserved. The background is painted with little care and the ships are so faint that it is not obvious that the sea is depicted – the sea whence Venus (and the conch shell) came. The nearer band of green is distinguished as grass by rapid punctuation marks. The painting probably dates from the early 1480s.

87

SANDRO BOTTICELLI

Abundance or Autumn

Black chalk, pen and brown ink, brown wash,
white heightening on pink–tinted paper,
31.7 × 25.4 cm
London, British Museum,
Department of Prints and Drawings, 1895-9-15-447

Warburg 1932, vol. I, pp. 65–6; Popham and Pouncey
1950, no. 24, p. 16; Ovid, trans. Innes 1955, p. 205,
Book 9, lines 89ff; Lightbown 1978, vol. 2, D3, p. 162;
Dacos et al. 1980, no. 8, pp. 45–6, pl. VI (*Dionysius*
cameo); Bennett and Wilkins 1984, pp. 71–3
(Donatello's *Dovizia*); Royalton-Kisch et al.,
exh. cat., London 1996, no. 10, pp. 36–7.

PLR

Botticelli's *Abundance* violates every Renaissance rule of female decorum and ignores anatomical reality. Her forward glance and her revealing garment are openly tempting, and invite contemplation of her charms. Even though women, as irrational beings, were not regarded as having any set proportions, her arms are impossibly long. She is not, however, a monstrous image of depravity, but an explicitly poetic figure – a nymph. She represents the sort of allegorical and ornamental female that had become a fashionable component of domestic decoration in this period. Her classical origins are to be found in Book 9 of Ovid's *Metamorphoses* where the river god Achelous recounts how, having taken the form of a bull, one of his horns was ripped from his brow by Hercules. Sanctified, it became the horn of the goddess of Plenty. When Achelous had finished his story 'one of his attendants, a nymph dressed in the style of Diana, came forward, her hair streaming over her shoulders, and brought all autumn's harvest in the rich horn.' Similarly this nymph approaches, gently swaying, while a kind breeze gracefully rustles her diaphanous drapery and ruffles her long hair.

Abundance was as familiar as she was welcome in Florence. A monumental figure of *Dovizia* – meaning wealth and plenty – presided over the city's central marketplace from the top of a granite column. Sculpted in sandstone by Donatello in the 1420s, the exposed stone eroded over time and the statue was replaced in the eighteenth century. Programmatically *all'antica*, *Dovizia* was the first and the grandest of the nymphs gracing the city and doubtless did much to establish the norms or the expectations for the figure type. Generically inspired by the statue, this version of *Abundance* corresponds more closely to the descriptions of nymphs and idealised lovers found in contemporary poetry and also in the imagery of the Medici jousts. The 'gentle air' and light movements of this fair nymph are aspects of the stereotyped femininity of this poetic production. The precious qualities of the drawing demonstrate Botticelli's efforts to arrive at a pictorial parallel to the poet's art and artifice.

Like the cornucopia in Ovid's poem, this drawing is a product of metamorphosis: from rough, unformed and changing ideas to a refined image. The process is masked by the result, but indecisive moments can still be seen in the preliminary drawing. They are most easily found in the putto at the left, which was not worked up beyond this stage. Botticelli prepared his paper by brushing pink colour over the area he intended for the figures (which might first have been very lightly sketched in black chalk). This use of a middle tone indicates that from the outset Botticelli was thinking in terms of texture as much as line. Having put down the chalk, he picked up his pen to variously define curving, rippling and turning shapes. Brown wash models the form, and pen and ink hatching deepens and accentuates areas of shadow. Botticelli applied white both to create highlights and to represent transparent fabrics. His concern to evoke the light and flowing qualities of the nymph's robe meant that he nearly lost sight of the body it teasingly covers; a black chalk line reaffirms the right side.

The drawing is a virtuouso performance. The delicately shifting tones, the glimmering surfaces and rhythmic, sinuous patterns compare with those of cameos and gems. The motif of the putto in a tunic might have been inspired by the dressed cupids in a cameo of *Dionysius* once in the Medici collection (now in the Museo Nazionale in Naples). Botticelli painted one of the cameos in this collection (*Apollo and Marsyas*) as a pendant worn by a nymph-like lady now in the Städelsches Kunstinstitut, Frankfurt. This drawing shows how the study of those rare items influenced his creative ambitions and his creative procedures.

The exquisite qualities of this work suggest that it was to be viewed at close hand, perhaps in a small chamber or study. While scholars have proposed a relation to Florentine furniture painting, where the mythological theme of Apollo and Daphne makes its first appearance on panel, the degree of finish, excellent preservation and small scale of the painting indicate that it was probably an independent work, perceived as a precious object in its own right. The narrowness of the panel would seem to rule out the possibility that it served as the cover or reverse of a portrait. Pollaiuolo's use of glossy, saturated colour and treatment of landscape seem to emulate Northern European works in oil that Florentine patricians admired on their business travels and imported to Florence as collectors' pieces.

The story, one of the best known tales from Ovid's poem *Metamorphoses*, tells how, by Cupid's mischief, Apollo is spurred to love the nymph Daphne, who is equally bound to flee him. Appealing to her father, the fleeing Daphne is turned into a laurel tree, thus eluding her disappointed lover. Pollaiuolo ingeniously compressed the narrative of chase and metamorphosis into a single culminating moment, presenting Daphne as though lifted up in her pursuer's arms. Thus Apollo appears still to pursue his quarry and Daphne, one leg extended, to flee, even as she becomes rooted to the ground by her other leg. Daphne, proposed as a model of chastity with her eyes modestly downcast, is effectively pinned to the centre of the picture by the diagonals of her extended arms and leg. Apollo, in turn, looks up adoringly at his object of devotion in a profile view that follows the pictorial convention for a devotee established in religious images. In Pollaiuolo's rendering the mythological couple play out the contemporary conventions of ideal love formulated by chivalric culture and the poetry of Petrarch. Ovid's story was perfectly suited to such a treatment because, like the ideal beloved of Petrarch's poetry, Daphne remains forever beyond her lover's reach. Similarly, through the dominant motif of the laurel, Daphne could be associated with Petrarch's beloved Laura. Apollo is cast as a contemporary noble youth in courtly dress, but Pollaiuolo adopts Ovid's highly pictorial and sensual descriptions of Daphne with her bare arms, her flowing hair touched by Apollo's breath and the wind-blown drapery that reveals her limbs. This nymph type would have been familiar to a literate fifteenth-century viewer by her frequent appearance in Tuscan lyric poetry. Pollaiuolo seems to devise a pictorial equivalent to such poetry in his attentive description of the natural setting. The landscape sets the mood for the depiction of the bitter-sweet encounter and its misty distances could be read, as they are in Petrarch, as a metaphor for the lover's loss.

88

ANTONIO DEL POLLAIUOLO

Apollo and Daphne

Oil? and tempera on panel,
29.5 × 20 cm
London, National Gallery, NG 928

Cruttwell 1907, pp. 62–4; Davies 1961, p. 446; Schubring 1923, no. 334; Ettlinger 1978, p. 141.

AW

SIX ENGRAVINGS ON THEMES
OF LOVE AND CHASTITY

Warburg 1905, appendix to nos. 7–8, pp. 1–15;
Hind vol. 1, 1938, pp. 85–7; Swarzenski 1947, no. 261,
pp. 55–62; Oberhuber, 'Baccio Baldini' in
eds. Levenson, Oberhuber and Sheehan 1973,
pp. 13–21; Whitaker 1994, pp. 181–96.

A W

This selection of prints illustrates the diffusion of poetic subjects, of the kind developed in the paintings of Verrocchio, Antonio del Pollaiuolo and Botticelli, outside the luxury market. Though inexpensive and potentially reproducible in large numbers, these prints nonetheless reflect the cultural interests of the social élite and may be presumed to have appealed to the patrician class rather than to a strictly 'popular' market. The circular or oval prints (see also cat. no. 59) are almost unique survivals acquired from a single Florentine collection assembled by Baron von Stosch and subsequently owned by Peter Ernst Otto (d. 1799), from whom they derive their collective designation as the 'Otto prints'. The engraving technique, which employs deeply incised outlines and fine internal cross-hatching (often referred to as 'Fine Manner'), is dependent on nielloed designs on silver (see page 81), but was apparently intended to imitate the effects of pen and ink drawing with an internal wash. The prints have been convincingly attributed to the workshop of Baccio Baldini, a close follower of the goldsmith Maso Finiguerra. Baldini was in all likelihood the principal draughtsman of the encyclopaedic history in pictures known as the *Florentine Picture-Chronicle*, a book in the British Museum, now believed to have been produced in the first half of the 1470s. Motifs found in the *Chronicle* are recognisable in at least one of the prints.

The decorative function of the Otto prints has been deduced from their format. This suggests that they could have been pasted directly onto the lids of cylindrical toilet-or work-boxes. Such boxes would have been the poorer cousins of the larger versions with painted scenes and coats of arms which survive from the early fifteenth century. The recurrent pairings of courtly lovers on these prints and occasional inclusion of blank shields have encouraged the view that such boxes could have served as love tokens or marriage gifts for a woman. A couple of the surviving Otto prints include free-hand additions demonstrating how they could be 'customised' to the particular occasion by penning in the specific coats of arms in the central roundels or reserved shields. This suggests that the prints were produced speculatively rather than commissioned and that they were used as tokens of legitimate alliances. It is nonetheless to those conversant with the language of courtly love that they appeal.

The print is one of several in a circular format that depict young lovers. Here the pair, shown in profile and separated by the central roundel, reach forward to support an armillary sphere. They are further united by a winding scroll which reads, in translation, 'Love needs faith and where there is no faith there can be no love'. A version of this motto was associated with Lorenzo de' Medici's faithful love for Lucrezia Donati by Luigi Pulci in his poem *La giostra.* Their relationship, not entirely severed by Lucrezia's marriage in 1465, found public expression in the joust Lorenzo held in Lucrezia's honour in 1469, shortly before his own marriage to Clarice Orsini. Aby Warburg, who drew attention to the connection between the print, the poem and the joust claimed that the depiction of the Medici device of a ring and three feathers on the youth's sleeve identified the couple as Lorenzo de' Medici and Lucrezia Donati. In fact the idealised physiognomy of both youth and girl and the fantastic quality of their costume suggest that they are only indirectly linked with the historical persons of Lucrezia and Lorenzo. As in Pulci's poem, the pair are reconfigured into poetic models, one as a noble and faithful lover, the other as an inspiring nymph. Indeed even the motto on the scroll is non-specific, since as Pulci's poem declares, it was a 'detto antico' or old saying. It also appears, for example, in the print of a reclining nymph, cat. no. 93.

The armillary sphere, a three-dimensional model of the paths of the planets in the heavens, may have been included as a play on the Italian word *spero,* meaning 'I hope'. The heavens, which are constantly turning, were also a metaphor for fortune. Both readings would apparently refer to the lovers' desire which may or may not be fulfilled and over which they seem to have no control. The conceit seems particularly well adapted to the circular format of the print.

89

ATTRIBUTED TO
BACCIO BALDINI

Youth and nymph holding an armillary sphere

Engraving,
14.4 cm, diameter
Paris, Bibliothèque Nationale
Inscribed: *Amor vuol fe e dove fe nonne amor non puo*

Warburg 1905, pp. 1–15; Hind, vol. 1, 1938, pp. 86, 90 ; Dempsey 1992, pp. 111–12.

AW

90

ATTRIBUTED TO
BACCIO BALDINI

Chastisement of Cupid

Engraving,
16.5 cm, diameter
London, British Museum, Department of Prints and
Drawings, A.IV.8
Inscribed on sleeve of woman with sword: *Amor.vuol.fe*

Hind, vol. 1, 1938, p. 89; Lightbown 1978, vol. 2,
pp. 58–60.

AW

The young Cupid, mischievous god of love, is shown bound to a tree and violently assailed by a group of four nobly dressed women in an attempt to deprive him of his power. As well as plucking at his wings, they attack him with shears, a sword and a mace. The blindfold over his eyes is a conventional sign of Amor's arbitrariness in his choice of victims, one of the qualities that made him dangerous to maidenly virtue and contentment and for which the women wish to revenge their sex. The inscription on the sleeve of the woman with the sword 'love needs faith', which is part of a fidelity motto found in other Otto prints (see cat. no. 93), may be understood to indicate her love has been betrayed. The allegory of the Chastisement of Cupid has a literary source in Petrarch's *Triumphs* where Love is defeated and humiliated by Chastity and her devotees, who include the historical figures of Virginia and Judith. The bound Cupid also appeared on Giuliano de' Medici's banner painted by Botticelli for the joust of 1475 where his captivity results from Pallas's intervention as goddess of reason. In the print, the satirical and implicitly erotic charge of the poetic and visual invention resides in its obvious reversal of gender roles: a gang of fully clothed and dangerously equipped young noblewomen getting the better of a naked and disarmed young man. Another variant of this print shows Cupid with his hands bound above his head, a pose apparently adapted from a Northern European print of the martyred Saint Sebastian, another figure often shown as a beautiful youth.

In contrast to the bitter conflict of the *Chastisement of Cupid* (cat. no. 90) the theme of love is associated here with harmony and delight, in the form of music and dance. In the centre a courtly couple are shown dancing in a meadow beneath the beneficent rays of the sun. Their action is commented upon in the framing border where lively putti playing percussion and wind instruments set the rhythm. The outcome of the dancing scene is implied below where a pair of lovers are shown reclining. The reclining nude woman and noble youth recall similar figures sometimes found painted inside the lids of pairs of marriage chests. Like other prints in the Otto group, this design adopts a decorative vocabulary found in contemporary works of sculpture. The fish-scale outer border recalls those used in the della Robbia workshop, for example in the reliefs on the ceiling of the Cardinal of Portugal's Chapel (fig. 55) or in the Lisbon warrior tondo (cat. no. 62). The engraver's interest in qualities of relief is apparent both in the shading technique and in the ingenious design of the acanthus leaf scrolls that encircle the putti and wind around the central tondo.

91

ATTRIBUTED TO BACCIO BALDINI

Pair of dancers encircled in a wreath with music-making cupids and a reclining couple

Engraving,
c.20 cm, diameter
London, British Museum,
Department of Prints and Drawings, A.IV.13
Inscribed on the young man's sleeve: *Ame droit*

Hind, vol. 1, 1938, p. 91.

AW

92

ATTRIBUTED TO
BACCIO BALDINI

Seated woman with a unicorn

Engraving,
16 cm (diameter of outer border),
15. 3 cm (diameter of inner border)
London, British Museum,
Department of Prints and Drawings, A.IV.4
Inscribed on the woman's sleeve: *Marietta*

Hind 1938, vol. 1, p. 88; Ricciardi 1992, pp. 161–6;
Popham, ed. Kemp 1994, no. 27, p. 108, and no. 288,
p. 109 (for the Leonardo drawings).

AW

The legendary unicorn, believed to be able to purify a pool by dipping its horn in the water, was often represented as a symbol of purity and, by extension, female chastity. The same is true of the white-furred ermine, shown at the bottom right of this engraving, gazing in adoration at the seated woman from the edge of her skirts. The conceit of this print is that the noble lady is so much a friend to chastity that the unicorn nestles devotedly in her lap, even when released from the collar and chain that once kept him restrained. Two early drawings by Leonardo, now in the British Museum, London, and the Ashmolean Museum, Oxford, one of which is clearly a design for a painting of a seated woman caressing a unicorn, testify to the popularity of this formulation of a feminine ideal.

The decorative sleeves, garland headdress and long plait worn by the figure shown here in profile are extravagant variants of Northern European dress from the earlier fifteenth century. They evoked a desirable association with chivalric values and continued to be depicted in Florentine art into the 1470s. The empty shields were apparently designed to hold the coats of arms of families united by a marriage alliance; the name 'Marietta' on the sleeve may allude to the celebrated beauty Marietta Strozzi, ostentatiously courted by Bartolommeo Benci and his *brigata* – band of friends – in 1464.

The oval format, perhaps suggested by engraved gems, accommodates a reclining woman. She appears, from the inclusion of a stream in the background, to be a nymph of the spring. Her scroll bears the same motto found on cat. no. 89. The nymph as an object of love was a commonplace of contemporary lyric poetry that was also utilised in the imagery of Lorenzo de' Medici's joust of 1469. Verrocchio made a sleeping nymph approached by Cupid the subject of what appears to have been a design for a pageant banner (fig. 14). In this print the artfulness of the pose is enhanced by the sinuous curves of the nymph's veil and by her curling scroll.

93
ATTRIBUTED TO
BACCIO BALDINI

Reclining nude woman

Engraving,
5.4 × 9.8 cm
London, British Museum,
Department of Prints and Drawings, A.IV.9
Inscribed: *Amor vuol fe e dove fe nonne amor non puo*

Hind, vol. 1, 1938, p. 89.

AW

94

ATTRIBUTED TO
FRANCESCO ROSSELLI

Triumph of Love

Engraving,
26 × 17.3 cm
London, British Museum, Department of Prints and
Drawings, B.II.1.I
Inscribed: *Questo e colui chel mondo chiama amore/ Amaro
chome vedi & vedrai meglio/Quando fia tuo chome nostro
signore./ E i nacque docio & di lascivia humana/Nutrito di
pensier dolci & soavi/Facto signor & dio da gente vana*

Hind, vol. 1, 1938, pp. 131–3; Goldsmith Philipps 1955,
pp. 72–5; Oberhuber in eds. Levenson, Oberhuber
and Sheehan 1973, pp. 47–59.

AW

The *Triumph of Love* is one of a series of six engravings illustrating Francesco Petrarch's poem the *Triumphs*. Rather than an accompaniment to the whole text (see cat. no. 3), the prints were an independent production with quotations of two three-line verses inscribed below each image which refer to the personification and draw a moral. Here the verses, which are addressed to Petrarch in the poem, constitute a warning: 'This is he whom the world calleth Love: / Bitter, you see, and you will see more clearly/ When he shall be your lord, as he is ours./[…] Idleness gave him birth, and wantonness, /He was nursed by sweet and gentle thoughts/ And a vain people made him their lord and god.' Moving from left to right through the landscape, Cupid's chariot is shown pulled by four white horses while Love himself is lifted up on a burning vase, balanced on one foot like a verrocchiesque fountain figure. The chariot is surrounded by his victims, made captive or wounded by his power. The Triumph of Love was a popular subject on furniture painting and *deschi da parto* (decorated birth trays) kept in the domestic *camera*. Illustrations of the *Triumphs* were more closely dependent on visual traditions than on the poem itself and tend to vary little from one another, but the present print is unusual in that it includes the figure of Petrarch himself to the bottom left, questioning one of the unhappy lovers of antiquity as he does in the poem.

The engraving is executed in the so-called 'Broad Manner' which, in contrast to the 'Fine Manner' Otto prints, employs a more robust parallel hatching that could support a larger number of impressions taken from a single plate. The *Triumph* series was recognised as the work of Francesco Rosselli on the basis of the close similarity in the landscape background, with its long curved strokes for hills and tight parallel curves for trees, with the surviving engraved sheet from the *View of Florence with a Chain* (fig. 12). A very similar notation for distant trees was practised in the Verrocchio workshop as can be seen in Leonardo's Arno landscape drawing of 1473 (fig. 73) and in the background of the *Virgin and Child with Two Angels* (cat. no. 23).

Questo e colui: chel mondo chiama amore
Amaro chome uedi: & uedrai meglio
Quando fia tuo/chome nostro signore.

E i nacque docio/& di lasciuia humana/
Nutrito di pensier dolci & soaui/
Facto signor & dio da gente uana.

345

Bibliography

ABBATE, V., ed., *Maestri del Disegno nelle collezioni di Palazzo Abatellis*, Palermo 1995.

ACIDINI LUCHINAT, C., ed., *La Chiesa e il Convento di Santo Spirito a Firenze*, Florence 1996.

ADORNO, P., *Il Verrocchio. Nuove proposte nella civiltà artistica del tempo di Lorenzo il Magnifico*, Florence 1991.

ALBERTI, L.B., *On Painting*, trans. C. Grayson, ed. M. Kemp, London 1991.

ALBERTINI, F., *Memoriale di molte statue et picture sono nella inclyta cipta di Florentia*, Florence 1510.

ALSOP, J., *The Rare Art Traditions*, London 1982.

AMES-LEWIS, F., *Drawing in Early Renaissance Italy*, New Haven and London 1981.

AMES-LEWIS, F., and WRIGHT, J., *Drawing in the Italian Renaissance Workshop*, exh. cat., University Art Gallery, Nottingham, and Victoria and Albert Museum, London, London 1983.

ANDREWS, K., *National Gallery of Scotland. Catalogue of Italian Drawings*, 2 vols., Cambridge 1968.

ANGELINI, A., *Disegni italiani al tempo di Donatello*, exh. cat., Gabinetto Disegni e Stampe degli Uffizi, Florence 1986.

ARISTOTLE, *Nichomachean Ethics*, in *The Complete Works of Aristotle*, ed. J. Barnes, vol. 2, Princeton 1984.

ARMSTRONG ANDERSON, L., 'Copies of Pollaiuolo's Battling Nudes', *Art Quarterly*, XXXI, 1968, pp. 155–67.

ASTORRI, A., 'Note sulla Mercanzia fiorentina sotto Lorenzo dei Medici. Aspetti istituzionali e politici', *Archivio storico italiano*, vol. 150, 1992, pp. 965–93.

BAGEMIHL, R., 'Francesco Botticini's Palmieri altarpiece', *The Burlington Magazine*, 138, 1996, pp. 308–14.

BAKER, C., and HENRY, T., *The National Gallery. Complete Illustrated Catalogue*, London 1995.

BALDINI GIUSTI, L., and FALCHINETTI BOTTAI, F., 'Documento sulle prime fasi costruttive di Palazzo Pitti', in *Filippo Brunelleschi. La sua opera e il suo tempo*, vol. 2, Florence 1980, pp. 704–10.

BALDINUCCI, F., *Notizie degli Professori del Disegno*, Florence 1681–6.

BAMBACH CAPPEL, C., *The tradition of pouncing drawings in the Italian Renaissance workshop: Innovation and derivation*, PhD thesis, Yale University, New Haven 1988.

BAROCCHI, P., ed., *Il Giardino di San Marco. Maestri e compagni del giovane Michelangelo*, Florence 1992.

BARRIAULT, A.B., *Spalliera Paintings of Renaissance Tuscany. Fables of Poets for Patrician Homes*, University Park, Pa., 1994.

BARTOLI, R., in GREGORI, M., et al., eds., 1992.

BAXANDALL, M., *Painting and Experience in Fifteenth Century Italy*, Oxford 1972.

BECHERUCCI, L., and BRUNETTI, G., *Il Museo dell'Opera del Duomo*, 2 vols., Florence 1969.

BELLINAZZI, A., ed., *La casa del cancelliere. Documenti e studi sul palazzo di Bartolomeo Scala a Firenze*, Florence 1998.

BELLOSI, L., 'Un omaggio di Raffaello al Verrocchio', *Studi su Raffaello*, Urbino 1987, pp. 401–17.

BELLOSI, L., ed., *Pittura di Luce. Giovanni di Francesco e l'arte fiorentina di metà Quattrocento*, Florence 1990.

BELLOSI, L., and HAINES, M., *Lo Scheggia*, Florence and Siena 1999.

BEMPORAD, D.L., 'Il rapporto abito gioiello nel costume del Rinascimento', *Il costume nell'età del rinascimento*, Florence 1988, pp. 59–66.

BEMPORAD, D.L., ed., *Argenti fiorentini dal XV al XIX secolo. Tipologie e marchi*, vol. 1, Florence 1992.

BENNETT, B., and WILKINS, D., *Donatello*, Oxford 1984.

BERARDI, P., *L'antica maiolica di Pesaro*, Pesaro 1984.

BERENSON, B., 'Verrocchio e Leonardo. Leonardo e Credi', *Bollettino d'Arte*, 3rd series, 27, 1933, pp. 241–64.

BERENSON, B., *The Drawings of the Florentine Painters*, 3 vols., Chicago 1938 (Chicago and London 1970, reprint).

BESCHI, L., 'Le antichità di Lorenzo il Magnifico', in P. BAROCCHI and G. RAGIONIERI, eds., *Gli Uffizi quattro secoli di una galleria. Atti del Convegno Internazionale di Studi (Firenze 20–24 settembre 1982)*, Florence 1983, pp. 161–76.

BOBER, P., and RUBINSTEIN, R., *Renaissance Artists and Antique Sculpture*, London 1986.

BONGIORNO, L.M., 'A Fifteenth-Century Stucco and the Style of Verrocchio', *Allen Memorial Art Museum Bulletin*, 19, 1962, pp. 115–38.

BORSI, F., ed., *'Per bellezza, per studio, per piacere'. Lorenzo e gli spazi dell'arti*, Florence 1991.

BORSOOK, E., 'Documenti relativi alle cappelle di Lecceto e delle Selve di Filippo Strozzi', *Antichità Viva*, vol. 9, no. 3, 1970, pp. 3–20.

BORSOOK, E., 'Two Letters concerning Antonio Pollaiuolo', *The Burlington Magazine*, 115, 1973, pp. 464–8.

BORSOOK, E., *The Mural Painters of Tuscany*, 2nd edn, Oxford 1980.

BORSOOK, E., 'Ritratto di Filippo Strozzi il Vecchio', in *Palazzo Strozzi, metà millennio. 1489–1989. Atti del convegno di studi, Firenze, 3–6 luglio, 1989*, Rome 1991, pp. 1–14.

BOSKOVITS, M., *Tuscan Paintings of the Early Renaissance in Hungarian Museums*, Budapest 1969.

BOTTO, C., 'L'edificazione della Chiesa di Santo Spirito in Firenze', *Rivista d'Arte*, ser. 2, III, 1931, pp. 477–511.

BRIGSTOCKE, H., *Italian and Spanish Paintings in the National Gallery of Scotland*, Edinburgh 1993 (1st edn 1978).

BROCKHAUS, H., *Forschungen über Florentiner Kunstwerke*, Leipzig 1902.

BROWN, A., *Bartolomeo Scala, 1430–1497, Chancellor of Florence. The Humanist as Bureaucrat*, Princeton 1979.

BROWN, A., *The Medici in Florence. The Exercise and Language of Power*, Florence and Perth 1992, pp. 281–303.

BROWN, A., 'Piero's Infirmity and Political Power', in A. BEYER and B. BOUCHER, eds., *Piero de' Medici 'il Gottoso' (1416–1469). Kunst im Dienste der Mediceer. Art in the Service of the Medici*, Berlin 1993, pp. 9–19.

BROWN, A., 'Lorenzo and Public Opinion in Florence. The Problem of Opposition', in GARFAGNINI, G.C., ed., 1994, pp. 61–85.

BROWN, B., 'The Patronage and Building History of the Tribuna of SS. Annunziata in Florence: A reappraisal in light of new documentation', *Mitteilungen des Kunsthistorischen Institutes in Florenz*, vol. 25, 1981, pp. 59–146.

BROWN, B.L., 'L'"Entrata" fiorentina di Ludovico Gonzaga', *Rivista d'Arte*, XLII, 1991, pp. 211–19.

BROWN, D.A., *Leonardo da Vinci. Origins of a Genius*, New Haven and London 1998.

BRUGNOLI, M.V., 'Documenti, notizie e ipotesi sulla scultura di Leonardo', in A. MARAZZA, ed., *Leonardo. Saggi e ricerche*, Rome 1954, pp. 359–89.

BULLARD, M.M., 'In pursuit of honore et utile, Lorenzo de' Medici and Rome', in GARFAGNINI, G.C., ed., 1994, pp. 123–42.

BURKE, J., *Form and Power. Patronage and Visual Arts in Florence 1480–1512*, PhD thesis, Courtauld Institute, London 1999.

BUSIGNANI, A., *Pollaiuolo*, Florence 1969.

BUTTERFIELD, A., 'Verrocchio's Christ and St. Thomas: chronology, iconography and political context', *The Burlington Magazine*, 134, 1992, pp. 225–33.

BUTTERFIELD, A., *The Sculptures of Andrea del Verrocchio*, New Haven and London 1997.

BUTTERS, S., *The Triumph of Vulcan. Sculptors' Tools, Porphyry, and the Prince in Ducal Florence*, 2 vols., Florence 1996.

BYAM SHAW, J., *Drawings by Old Masters at Christ Church Oxford*, 2 vols., Oxford 1976.

BYAM SHAW, J., *The Italian Drawings of the Frits Lugt Collection*, Paris 1983.

CADOGAN, J., 'Linen drapery studies by Verrocchio, Leonardo and Ghirlandaio', *Zeitschrift für Kunstgeschichte*, 46, 1983, pp. 27–62.

CADOGAN, J., 'Reconsidering Some Aspects of Ghirlandaio's Drawings', *Art Bulletin*, 65, 1983, pp. 274–90.

CADOGAN, J., 'Verrocchio's Drawings Reconsidered', *Zeitschrift für Kunstgeschichte*, 46, 1983, pp. 367–400.

CAGLIOTI, F., 'Due restauratori per le antichità dei primi medici: Mino da Fiesole, Andrea del Verrocchio e il "Marsia rosso" degli Uffizi. I', *Prospettiva*, 72, 1993, pp. 17–42.

CAIGER-SMITH, A., *Tin-glazed Pottery in Europe and the Islamic World*, London 1973.

CAIGER-SMITH, A., *Lustre Pottery*, London 1985.

CALLMANN, E., *Apollonio di Giovanni*, Oxford 1974.

CALLMANN, E., 'Apollonio di Giovanni and painting for the early Renaissance room', *Antichità Viva*, 27, nos. 3–4, 1988, pp. 5–18.

CALLMANN, E., 'William Blundell Spence and the transformation of the Renaissance cassoni', *The Burlington Magazine*, 161, 1999, pp. 338–48.

CAMESASCA, E., *L'Opera completa del Perugino*, Milan 1969 (1st edn 1959).

CAMPBELL, L., *Renaissance Portraits. European Portrait-Painting in the 14th, 15th and 16th Centuries*, New Haven and London 1990.

CANEVA, C., 1992 see *Il Disegno fiorentino*.

CANTINI GUIDOTTI, G., *Orafi in Toscana tra XV e XVIII secolo: storie di uomini, di cose e di parole*, vol. 2, Florence 1994.

CARL, D., 'Zur Goldschmiede Familie Dei mit neuen Dokmenten zu Antonio Pollaiuolo und Andrea Verrocchio', *Mitteilungen des Kunsthistorischen Institutes in Florenz*, vol. 26, 1982, pp. 128–66.

CARL, D., 'Addenda zu Antonio Pollaiuolo und seiner Werkstatt', *Mitteilungen des Kunsthistorischen Institutes in Florenz*, vol. 27, 1983, pp. 285–301.

CECCHI, A., 'Una predella e altri contributi per l'Adorazione dei Magi di Filippino', in *Gli Uffizi. Studi e Ricerche*, 5, *I pittori della Brancacci agli Uffizi*, L. BERTI and A. PETRIOLI TOFANI, eds., Florence 1984.

CECCHI, A., 'Giuliano e Benedetto da Maiano ai servigi della Signoria fiorentina', in D. LAMBERINI, M. LOTTI and R. LUNARDI, eds., *Giuliano e la bottega dei da Maiano, Atti del convegno internazionale di studi, Fiesole, 1991*, Florence 1994, pp. 143–57.

CENNINI, CENNINO, *The Craftsman's Handbook: The Italian 'il Libro dell'arte'*. ed. and trans. D.V. THOMPSON, New York 1954.

CHERUBINI G., and FANELLI, G., eds., *Il Palazzo Medici Riccardi di Firenze*, Florence 1990.

CHIARINI, M., and MARABOTINI, A., eds., *Firenze e la sua immagine. Cinque secoli di vedutismo*, exh. cat., Forte di Belvedere, Florence 1994.

CHITI, A., 'Di una tavola ignota di Piero del Pollaiuolo', *Bollettino storico Pistoiese*, vol. 2, 1900, pp. 41–8.

CHRISTIANSEN, K., 'Leonardo's drapery studies', *The Burlington Magazine*, 132, 1990, pp. 572–3.

CIARDI DUPRÉ DAL POGGETTO, M.G., ed., *L'Oreficeria nella Firenze del Quattrocento*, Florence 1997.

CIASCA, R., *Statuti dell'arte dei Medici e Speziali*, Florence 1922.

CILETTI, E., 'Patriarchal Ideology in the Renaissance Iconography of Judith', in M. MIGIEL and J. SCHIESARI, eds., *Refiguring Woman. Perspectives on Gender and the Italian Renaissance*, Ithaca, NY, 1991, pp. 35–70.

CLARK, K., *Leonardo da Vinci. An Account of his Development as an Artist*, Cambridge 1939.

CLARK, K., *The Drawings of Leonardo da Vinci in the collection of Her Majesty the Queen at Windsor Castle*, 3 vols., London 1969.

CLARKE, P.C., *The Soderini and the Medici. Power and Patronage in Fifteenth-Century Florence*, Oxford 1991.

CLAYTON, M., *Leonardo da Vinci. A Curious Vision*, exh. cat., The Queen's Gallery, London 1996.

COHN JR, S.K., 'Donne in piazza donne in tribunale a Firenze nel Rinascimento', *Studi storici*, no. 3, 22, 1981, pp. 515–33.

COVI, D., 'A documented tondo by Botticelli', in M.G. CIARDI DUPRÉ DAL POGGETTO and P. DAL POGGETTO, eds., *Scritti di storia dell'arte in onore di Ugo Procacci*, I, Milan 1977, pp. 270–2.

COVI, D., 'Nuovi Documenti per Antonio del Pollaiuolo e Antonio Rossellino', *Prospettiva*, 12, 1978, pp. 61–71.

COVI, D., 'Four New Documents Concerning Andrea del Verrocchio', *Art Bulletin*, 48, 1966, pp. 97–103.

CRUTTWELL, M., *Verrocchio*, London 1904.

CRUTTWELL, M., *Antonio Pollaiuolo*, London 1907.

DACOS, N., GIULIANO, A., and PANNUTI, U., *Le Gemme: Il Tesoro di Lorenzo il Magnifico*, exh. cat., Palazzo Medici-Riccardi, Florence 1972.

DACOS, N., et al., see *Il Tesoro di Lorenzo il Magnifico*, 1980.

DALLI REGOLI, G., *Lorenzo di Credi*, Pisa 1966.

DALLI REGOLI, G., 'Il "piegar de' panni"', *Critica d'arte*, 22, new series no. 150, 1976, pp. 35–48.

DALTON, O.M., *Catalogue of the Engraved Gems of the Post-Classical Periods in the British Museum*, London 1914.

DARR, A.P., and BONSANTI, G., *Donatello e i suoi. Scultura fiorentina del primo Rinascimento*, exh. cat., Florence 1986.

DAVIES, M., *Paintings and drawings on the backs of National Gallery pictures*, London 1946.

DAVIES, M., *National Gallery Catalogues. The Earlier Italian Schools*, London 1961.

DEAN, T., and LOWE, K.J.P., eds., *Marriage in Italy 1300–1650*, Cambridge 1998.

DEGENHART, B., and SCHMITT, A., *Corpus der italienischen Zeichnungen, 1300–1450*, Berlin 1968–82.

DEGENHART, B., 'Unbekannte Zeichnungen Francesco di Giorgio', *Zeitschrift für Kunstgeschichte*, VIII, 1939, esp. pp. 125–35.

DEI, BENEDETTO, *La Cronica*, ed. R. BARDUCCI, Florence 1984.

DELLA TORRE, A., *Storia dell'Accademia Platonica de Firenze*, Florence 1902.

DEMPSEY, C., *The Portrayal of Love. Botticelli's Primavera and Humanist Culture in the Time of Lorenzo il Magnifico*, Princeton 1992.

DIONISOTTI, C., 'Fortuna del Petrarca nel 400', *Italian medioevale e umanistica*, XVII, 1974, pp. 61–113.

Il Disegno fiorentino al tempo di Lorenzo, ed. A. PETRIOLI TOFANI, exh. cat., Galleria degli Uffizi, Florence 1992.

DOLCINI, L., ed., *Verrocchio's Christ and St. Thomas. A Masterpiece of Sculpture from Renaissance Florence*, exh. cat., Palazzo Vecchio, Florence, and the Metropolitan Museum of Art, New York, 1992–3, New York 1992.

DORINI, U., *Statuti dell'Arte di Por Santa Maria del tempo della Repubblica*, Florence 1934.

DRAPER, J., 1986 see DARR, A.P. and BONSANTI, G.

DRAPER, J., *Bertoldo di Giovanni, Sculptor of the Medici Household. Critical Reappraisal and Catalogue Raisonné*, Columbia, Missouri, 1992.

DUNKERTON, J., FOISTER, S., GORDON, D., and PENNY, N., *From Giotto to Dürer*, London and New Haven 1991.

ECKSTEIN, N., *The District of the Green Dragon. Neighbourhood Life and Social Change in Renaissance Florence*, Florence 1995.

EDELEIN-BADIA, B., *La collection de tableaux de Lucien Bonaparte, Prince de Canino*, Paris 1997.

EDGERTON, S.Y., *Pictures and Punishment. Art and Criminal Prosecution during the Florentine Renaissance*, Ithaca, NY, 1985.

EDLER DE ROOVER, F., 'Per la storia dell'arte della stampa in Italia', *La Bibliofilia*, 55, 1953, pp. 107–17.

ELAM, C., 'Lorenzo de' Medici and the Urban Development of Renaissance Florence', *Art History*, I, 1978, pp. 43–66.

ELAM, C., 'Il Palazzo nel contesteo della città: strategie urbanistiche dei Medici nel gonfalone del Leon d'Oro, 1415–1530', in G. CHERUBINI and G. FANELLI, eds., *Il Palazzo Medici Riccardi di Firenze*, Florence 1990, pp. 44–57.

ELAM, C., 'Lorenzo de' Medici's Sculpture Garden', *Mitteilungen des Kunsthistorischen Institutes in Florenz*, vol. 36, 1992, pp. 41–83.

EMISON, P., 'The Word made Naked in Pollaiuolo's Battle of the Nudes', *Art History*, 13, no. 3, 1990, pp. 261–75.

Eredità del Magnifico, exh. cat., Museo Nazionale del Bargello, Florence 1992.

ETTLINGER, L.D., 'Hercules Florentinus', *Mitteilungen des Kunsthistorischen Institutes in Florenz*, vol. 16, 1972, pp. 119–42.

ETTLINGER, L.D., *Antonio and Piero Pollaiuolo*, Oxford 1978.

DE FABRICZY, C., 'Andrea del Verrocchio ai servizi de' Medici', *Archivio storico dell'arte*, 2nd series, I, 1895, pp. 165–76.

VON FABRICZY, C., 'Donatellos hl. Ludwig und sein Tabernakel an Or San Michele', *Jahrbuch der Königlich Preussischen Kunstsammlungen*, 21, 1900, pp. 242–61.

FALLETTI, F., ed., *I Medici, Il Verrocchio e Pistoia. Storia e restauro di due capolavori nella cattedrale di S. Zeno*, Livorno 1996.

FANELLI, G., *Le città nella storia d'Italia*, Firenze, Bari 1980.

FIORELLI MALESCI, F., *La chiesa di Santa Felicità a Firenze*, Florence 1986.

FIORILLI, C., 'I dipintori a Firenze nell'Arte del Medici Speziale e Merciai', *Archivio storico italiano*, LXXVIII, 1920, II, pp. 5–74.

FITTSCHEN, K., 'Ritratti antichi nella collezione di Lorenzo il Magnifico', in *Toscana al tempo di Lorenzo il Magnifico. Politica, economica, cultura, arte*, vol. 1, Pisa 1996, pp. 7–32.

FLORENCE, *Gli Uffizi. Catalogo Generale*, Florence 1979.

FOSTER, P., *A Study of Lorenzo de' Medici's Villa at Poggio a Caiano*, PhD thesis, Yale University, New Haven 1973.

FRANK, E., *Pollaiuolo Studies*, Phd thesis., New York University 1988.

FREY, C., ed., *Il Codice Magliabecchiano*, Berlin 1892.

FRIEDMANN, H., 'Two Paintings by Botticelli in the Kress Collection', in *Studies in the History of Art Dedicated to William E. Suida on his Eightieth birthday*, London 1959.

FUBINI, R., ed., *Lorenzo de' Medici. Lettere*, vol. 1, Florence 1977.

FUMAGALLI, E., 'Nuovi documenti su Lorenzo e Giuliano de' Medici', *Italia medievale e umanistica*, 23, 1980, pp. 141–64.

FUSCO, L.S., 'The Use of Sculptural Models by Painters in the Fifteenth Century', *Art Bulletin*, 64, 1982, pp. 196–9.

FUSCO, L.S., 'Pollaiuolo's Battle of the Nudes: A Suggestion for an Ancient Source and a New Dating', in *Scritti di storia dell'arte in onore de Federico Zeri*, vol. 1, Milan 1984, pp. 196–9.

GABORIT, J-R., Article on terracotta angels in *Revue du Louvre* (forthcoming).

GARDNER, G., 'Master of the Gardner Annunciation', in *The Dictionary of Art*, vol. 20, London 1996, pp. 679–80.

GARFAGNINI, G.C., ed., *Lorenzo il Magnifico e il suo mondo*, Florence 1994.

GARZELLI, A., *Il ricamo nell'attività artistica di Pollaiuolo, Botticelli, Bartolomeo di Giovanni*, Florence 1973.

GARZELLI, A., 'Arte del "Libro d'Ore" e committenza medicea (1484-1536)' in *Atti del Primo Congresso Nazionale di Storia dell'Arte (Roma 1978)*, Rome 1980, pp. 475–90.

GARZELLI, A., 'Smalti nelle botteghe fiorentina del Quattrocento: Donatello, Antonio Pollaiuolo, Francesco Rosselli, Paolo di Giovanni Sogliani', *Annali della Scuola normale Superiore di Pisa*, XIV, 1984, no. 2, pp. 690–5.

GARZELLI, A., *Miniatura fiorentina del rinascimento 1440–1525. Un primo censimento*, 2 vols., Florence 1985.

GERE, J., and POUNCEY, P., *Artists Working in Rome c.1550 to c.1640* London 1983.

GHIBERTI, *Lorenzo, I commentarii*, ed. L. BARTOLI, Florence 1998.

Il Giardino di San Marco see BAROCCHI, P., ed., 1992.

GILBERT, C., *Italian Art 1400–1500. Sources and Documents*, Englewood Cliffs, NJ, 1980.

Giovanni Rucellai e il suo Zibaldone, vol. 1, ed. A. PEROSA, London 1960

GIOVANNINI, P., *Il convento del Carmine, caratteri e documenti*, Florence 1981.

GLASSER, H., *Artists' Contracts of the Early Renaissance*, PhD thesis, Columbia University 1965.

GOLDNER, G., and BAMBACH, C., eds., *The Drawings of Filippino Lippi and His Circle*, exh. cat., Metropolitan Museum of Art, New York 1997.

GOLDSMITH PHILIPPS, J., *Early Florentine Designers and Engravers*, Cambridge, Mass., 1955.

GOLDTHWAITE, R., 'The Building of the Strozzi Palace: the Construction Industry in Renaissance Florence', *Studies in Medieval and Renaissance History*, 10, 1973, pp. 97–194.

GOLDTHWAITE, R., *Wealth and the Demand for Art in Italy*, Baltimore 1993.

GOMBRICH, E.H., 'The Early Medici as Patrons of Art' and 'Leonardo's Method for Working out Compositions', in *Norm and Form. Studies in the Art of the Renaissance*, London 1966, pp. 35–57, 58–63.

GOMBRICH, E.H., 'Tobias and the Angel', in *Symbolic Images. Studies in the Art of the Renaissance*, London 1972, pp. 26–30.

GOMBRICH, E.H., 'Light, Form and Texture in Fifteenth-Century Painting North and South of the Alps', in *The Heritage of Apelles*, Oxford 1976, pp. 19–38.

GORI, A.F., *Thesaurus*, Florence 1750.

GRABSKI, J., ed., *Opus Sacrum*, exh. cat., Collection of Barbara Piasecki Johnson, Royal Castle, Warsaw 1990.

GREGORI, M., PAOLUCCI, A., and ACIDINI LUCHINAT, C., eds., *Maestri e botteghe. Pittura a Firenze alla fine del Quattrocento*, exh. cat., Palazzo Strozzi, Florence 1992.

GRISWOLD, W.M., 'Drawings by Francesco Botticini', *Master Drawings*, vol. 32, 1994, pp. 151–4.

GRONAU, G., 'Über das sogenannte Skizzenbuch des Verrocchio', *Jahrbuch der Königliche Preussischen Kunstsammlungen*, XVII, 1896, pp. 65–72.

GROPPI, A., ed., *Il lavoro delle donne*, Rome and Bari 1996.

GROSSMAN, S., 'An Anonymous Florentine Drawing and the so-called "Verrocchio Sketchbook"', *Master Drawings*, X, 1972, pp. 15–19.

GROSSMAN, S., 'Ghirlandaio's "Madonna and Child" in Frankfurt and Leonardo's Beginnings as a Painter', *Städel – Jahrbuch*, NF, 7, 1979, pp. 101–25.

GUASTI, C., ed. see STROZZI, A., 1877.

GUICCIARDINI, F., *Storie fiorentine dal 1378 al 1509*, ed. R. PALMAROCCHI, Bari 1931.

HAINES, M., *La Sacrestia delle Messe del Duomo di Firenze*, Florence 1983.

HAINES, M., 'Una ricostruzione dei perduti libri di matricole del Medici e Speziale a Firenze dal 1353 al 1408', *Rivista d'Arte*, 4th series, anno XLI, V, 1989, pp. 173–207.

HARTT, F., CORTI, G., and KENNEDY, C., *The Chapel of the Cardinal of Portugal*, Philadelphia 1964.

HATFIELD, R., 'The Compagnia de' Magi', *Journal of the Warburg and Courtauld Institutes*, 33, 1970, pp. 107–61.

HATFIELD, R., *Botticelli's Uffizi 'Adoration'. A Study in Pictorial Content*, Princeton 1976.

HEMSOLL, D., 'Giuliano da Sangallo and the new Renaissance of Lorenzo de' Medici', in F. AMES-LEWIS, ed., *The Early Medici and their Artists*, London 1995, pp. 187–205.

HERALD, J., *Renaissance Dress in Italy 1400–1500*, London 1981.

HILL, G.F., *A Corpus of Italian Medals before Cellini*, 2 vols., London 1930.

HIND, A.M., *Early Italian Engraving*, vol. 1, London 1938.

HOLLAND, G., *Gemälde der Romanischen Schulen vor 1800 im Städel*, Frankfurt am Main 1997.

HOLMES, C., *Old Masters and Modern Art, The National Gallery Italian Schools*, London 1923.

HORNE, H.P., *Alessandro Filipepi, Commonly called Sandro Botticelli. Painter of Florence*, London 1908 (Princeton 1980, reprint ed. J. POPE-HENNESSY.).

HORSTER, M., *Andrea del Castagno*, Oxford 1980.

HUECK, I., 'Le matricole dei pittori fiorentini prima e dopo il 1320', *Bollettino d'Arte*, serie V, anno LVII, 1972, II, pp. 114–21.

Italian Primitives. The Case History of a Collection and its Conservation, exh. cat., Yale University Art Gallery, New Haven 1972.

Italian Renaissance Sculpture in the Time of Donatello, exh. cat., Detroit Institute of Arts, Detroit 1985.

Italienische Zeichnungen der Renaissance aus dem Kupferstichkabinett der Hamburger Kunsthalle, exh. cat., Hamburg 1995.

JACOBSEN, E., 'Studien zu einem Gemälde des Ghirlandaio Werkstatt', *Jahrbuch der Preussischen Kunstsammlungen*, XXV, 1904, pp. 185-95.

JAFFÉ, M., *The Devonshire Collection of Italian Drawings*, vol. 1, *Tuscan and Umbrian Schools*, London 1994.

KAUFFMANN, C.M., *Victoria and Albert Museum. Catalogue of Foreign Paintings*. vol. 1, *Before 1800*, London 1973.

KEMP, M., *Leonardo da Vinci. The Marvellous Works of Nature and Man*, Cambridge, Mass., 1981.

KEMP, M., ed., *Leonardo da Vinci. The Mystery of the 'Madonna of the Yarnwinder'*, exh. cat., National Gallery of Scotland, Edinburgh 1992.

KEMP, M., 'Verrocchio's "San Donato" and the Chiesina della Vergine in Piazza in Pistoia', *Pantheon*, LVI, 1998, pp. 25–34.

KENT, F.W., '"Più superba di quella di Lorenzo": Courtly and Family Interest in the Building of Filippo Strozzi's Palace', *Renaissance Quarterly*, 30, 1977, pp. 311–23.

KENT, F.W., 'Lorenzo de' Medici's Acquisition of Poggio a Caiano in 1474 and an Early Reference to His Architectural Expertise', *Journal of the Warburg and Courtauld Institutes*, 42, 1979, pp. 250–7.

KENT, F.W., 'The Making of a Renaissance Patron of the Arts', in *Giovanni Rucellai ed il suo Zibaldone, II, A Florentine Patrician and his Palace*, London 1981, pp. 9–98.

KENT, F.W., 'Palaces, Politics and Society in Fifteenth-Century Florence', *I Tatti Studies*, 2, 1987, pp. 41–70.

KENT, F.W., 'Patron-Client Networks in Renaissance Florence and the Emergence of Lorenzo as "Maestro della Bottega"', in B. TOSCANI, ed., *Lorenzo de' Medici. New Perspectives*, New York 1993, pp. 279–314.

KENT, F.W., 'Individuals and Families as Patrons of Culture in Quattrocento Florence', in A. BROWN, ed., *Language and Images in Renaissance Italy*, Oxford 1995.

KENT, F.W., 'Lorenzo de' Medici, Madonna Scolastica Rondinelli e la politica di mecenatismo architettonico nel convento delle Murate a Firenze (1471–72)', in A. ESCH and C.L. FROMMEL, eds., *Arte, committenza ed economia a Roma e nelle corti del Rinascimento*, Turin 1995, pp. 353–82.

KENT, F.W., 'The Young Lorenzo, 1449–69', in M. MALLETT and N. MANN, eds., *Lorenzo the Magnificent. Culture and Politics*, London 1996, pp. 1–22.

KENT, F.W., *'A Hunger for beauty': Lorenzo de' Medici, Amateur and Patron of Art*, Baltimore (forthcoming).

KLAPISCH-ZUBER, C., *Women, Family and Ritual in Renaissance Italy*, Chicago 1985.

KNIPE, P., 'Grounds on paper: An Examination of Eight Early Drawings', unpublished paper, Straus Center for Conservation, Harvard University Art Museums, Cambridge, Mass., 1998.

KOVESI KILLERBY, C., 'Practical problems in the enforcement of Italian sumptuary law 1200–1500' in T. DEAN and K.J.P. LOWE, eds., *Crime Society and the Law in Renaissance Italy*, Cambridge 1994, pp. 99–120.

KRAUTHEIMER, R., *Lorenzo Ghiberti*, Princeton 1970.

KURZ, O., 'A Group of Florentine Drawings for an Altar', *Journal of the Warburg and Courtauld Institutes*, 18, 1955, pp. 35–53.

KWAKKELSTEIN, M., *Leonardo da Vinci as a Physiognomist. Theory and Drawing Practice*, Leiden 1994.

LAFITTER, M.P., 'Il Codice Ital. 548 della Biblioteca Nazionale di Parigi', in A. LENZUNI, ed., *All'Ombra del Lauro. Documenti librari della cultura in età Laurenziana*, Florence 1992, pp. 161–5.

LANDUCCI, LUCA, *A Florentine Diary*, trans. A. DE ROSEN JERVIS, London 1927.

LANGEDIJK, K., *Portraits of the Medici. 15th–18th Centuries*, Florence 1982.

LEITHE-JASPER, M., 'Inkunabeln der Bronzeplastik der Renaissance', *Die Weltkunst*, XXI, 1981, p. 3190.

Leonardo da Vinci, exh. cat., Hayward Gallery, London 1989.

Léonard de Vinci. Les études de draperie, exh. cat., Paris 1989.

LEVENSON, J.A., OBERHUBER, K., and SHEEHAN, J.L., *Early Italian Engravings from the National Gallery of Art*, Washington 1973.

LEVENSON, J.A., ed., *Circa 1492. Art in the Age of Exploration*, exh. cat., National Gallery of Art, Washington 1991–2.

LEVI D'ANCONA, M., *Miniatura e minitori a Firenze dal XIV al XVI secolo*, Florence 1962.

LIGHTBOWN, R., *Sandro Botticelli*, 2 vols., London 1978 (rev. edn, 1 vol., London 1989).

LILLIE, A., et al., 'The Palazzo Strozzi and Private Patronage in Fifteenth-Century Florence' in H. MILLON and V. LAMPUGNANI, eds., *The Renaissance from Brunelleschi to Michelangelo. The Representation of Architecture*, London 1994, pp. 518–21.

LIPPINCOTT, K., 'The Art of Cartography in Fifteenth-Century Florence', in *Lorenzo the Magnificent. Culture and Politics*, London 1996, pp. 131–49.

LIVY, trans. B.O. FOSTER, 14 vols., Cambridge, Mass., and London 1919.

LORENZO DE' MEDICI, *The Autobiography of Lorenzo de' Medici the Magnificent. A Commentary on my Sonnets*, trans. and ed. J.W. COOK, Binghamton, NY, 1995.

LUCIAN, trans. A.M. HARMON, vol. 1, London and New York 1913.

LUCRETIUS CAIUS, TITUS, *De rerum natura*, trans. W.H.D. ROUSE, 3rd edn, London 1975.

LYDECKER, J.K., *The domestic setting of the arts in Renaissance Florence*, PhD thesis, The Johns Hopkins University, Baltimore 1987.

MACANDREW, H., *Old Master Drawings from the National Gallery of Scotland*, exh. cat., National Gallery of Art, Washington 1990.

MACHIAVELLI, N., *Florentine Histories*, trans. L.F. BANFIELD and H.C. MANSFIELD, JR., Princeton 1988.

Maestri e botteghe. Pittura a Firenze alla fine del Quattrocento, see GREGORI, M., et al., eds., 1992.

MALLETT, M., 'Horse-racing and Politics in Lorenzo's Florence', in N. MANN and M. MALLETT, eds., *Lorenzo the Magnificent, Culture and Politics*, London 1996, pp. 253–62.

MANCINI, G., 'Il bel S. Giovanni e le feste patronali di Firenze descritte nel 1475 da Piero Cennini', *Rivista d'Arte*, VI, 1st series, nos. 3–4, 1909, pp. 185–227.

MARANI, P.C., *Leonardo. Catalogo completo*, Florence 1989.

MARKS, L.F., 'The Financial Oligarchy in Florence under Lorenzo', in E.F. JACOBS, ed., *Italian Renaissance Studies*, pp. 123–47.

MARLE, R. van, *The Development of the Italian Schools of Painting*, 19 vols., The Hague 1923–39.

MARRESE, E., ed., *Marco Parenti, Lettere*, Florence 1996.

MASCALCHI, S., 'Giovan Carlo de Medici – an outstanding but neglected collector in seventeenth-century Florence', *Apollo*, 120, 1984, pp. 268–72.

Master European Drawings from the collection of the National Gallery of Ireland, Washington 1983.

MELLER, P., 'Two Drawings of the Quattrocento in the Uffizi. A Study in Stylistic Change', *Master Drawings*, XII, 1974, esp. pp. 261–78.

MESNIL, J., 'Les Figures de Vertus de la Mercanzia. Piero del Pollaiuolo et Botticelli', *Miscellanea dell'Arte*, 1, 1903, pp. 43–6.

MIDDLEDORF, U., 'Su alcuni bronzetti all'antica del Quattrocento', *Il mondo antico nel rinascimento, Atti del V convegno internazionale di studi sul rinascimento, Florence, 1956*, Florence 1958, pp. 167–77.

MIDDLEDORF, U., *Complete Catalogue of the Samuel H. Kress Collection, European Sculpture XIV–XIX centuries*, London 1976.

MIDDLEDORF, U., 'Die Zwölf Caesaren von Desiderio da Settignano', *Mitteilungen des Kunsthistorischen Institutes in Florenz*, vol. 23, 1979, pp. 297–312.

MÖLLER, E., 'Leonardo e il Verrocchio. Quattro rilievi di capitani antichi lavorati per Re Mattia Corvino', *Raccolta Vinciana*, XIV, 1930–4, pp. 3–38.

MÖLLER, E., 'Verrocchio's last drawing', *The Burlington Magazine*, 66, 1935, pp. 193–5.

MONGAN, A., and SACHS, P., *Drawings in the Fogg Museum of Art*, Cambridge, Mass., 1940.

MORELLI TIMPANARO, M.A., MANNO TOLU, R., and VITI, P., eds., *Consortorie politiche e mutamenti istituzionali in età laurenziana*, exh. cat., Archivio di Stato, Florence 1992.

MOSCATO, A., *Il Palazzo Pazzi a Firenze*, Rome 1963.

MÜNTZ, E., *Les collections de Medicis au XVe siècle*, Paris, 1888.

NAJEMY, J., *Corporatism and Consensus in Florentine Electoral Politics, 1280–1400*, Chapel Hill, NJ, 1982.

NATALI, A., ed., *Lo Sguardo degli Angeli. Verrocchio, Leonardo e il 'Battesimo di Cristo'*, Milan 1998.

NATHAN, J., *The Working Methods of Leonardo da Vinci and their relation to previous artistic practice*, PhD thesis., Courtauld Institute of Art, University of London 1995.

NATHAN, J., review of 'Palermo and Rome. Maestri del Disegno nelle collezioni di Palazzo Abatellis', *The Burlington Magazine*, 138, 1996, pp. 712–13.

NERI DI BICCI, *Le Ricordanze 1453–1475*, ed. B. SANTI, Pisa 1976.

NEWBIGIN, N., 'Piety and Politics in the Feste of Lorenzo's Florence', in GARFAGNINI, G.C., ed.,1994, pp. 17–41.

NEWBIGIN, N., 'Politics in the Sacre Rappresentazione of Lorenzo's Florence', in M. MALLET and N. MANN, eds., *Lorenzo the Magnificent. Culture and Politics*, London 1996, pp. 117–30.

NEWBIGIN, N., *Feste dell'Oltrarno. Plays in Churches in fifteenth-century Florence*, 2 vols., Florence 1996.

NUTTALL, P., 'The Patrons of Chapels at the Badia di Fiesole', *Studi di Storia dell'Arte*, 3, 1992, pp. 97–112.

O'MALLEY, M., 'Late fifteenth- and early sixteenth-century painting contracts and the stipulated use of the artist's hand', in E. MARCHAND and A. WRIGHT, eds., *With and Without the Medici. Studies in Tuscan Art and Patronage 1434–1530*, Aldershot 1998, pp. 155–178.

ORTALLI, G., '…pingatur in palatio…', *La pittura infernante nei secoli XIII–XVI*, Rome 1979.

OVID, *Metamorphoses*, trans. M.M. INNES, London 1955.

OWEN HUGHES, D., 'Representing the Family: Portraits and Purposes in Early Modern Europe', in R.I. ROTBERG and T.K. RABB, eds., *Art and History. Images and their Meaning*, Cambridge, Mass., 1988, pp. 7–38.

PADOA RIZZO, A., 'La cappella della Compagnia di Santa Barbara della "nazione tedesca" alla Santissima Annunziata di Firenze nel secolo XV. Cosimo Rosselli e la sua "impresa" artistica', *Antichità Viva*, 26, no. 3, 1987, pp. 3–18.

PADOA RIZZO, A., 'Cosimo e Bernardo Rosselli per la Compagnia di Sant'Andrea dei Purgatori a Firenze', *Studi di Storia dell'Arte*, 2, 1991, pp. 265–70.

PADOA RIZZO, A., 'Botticini, Francesco', *The Dictionary of Art*, vol. 4, London 1996, pp. 505–7.

PALMIERI, MATTEO, *Vita civile*, ed. G. BELLONI, Florence 1982.

PANOFSKY, E., *Studies in Iconology*, London, 1939.

PANOFSKY, E., *Renaissance and Renascences in Western Art*, Stockholm 1960.

PAOLOZZI STROZZI, B., 'An unpublished crucifix by Andrea del Verrocchio', *The Burlington Magazine*, 126, 1994, pp. 808–15.

PARRONCHI, A., 'The Language of Humanism', *Journal of the Warburg and Courtauld Institutes*, 27, 1964, pp. 108–36.

PASSAVANT, G., *Andrea del Verrocchio als Maler*, Dusseldorf 1959 (English trans., *Verrocchio*, Oxford 1969).

PASSAVANT, G., *Verrocchio: Sculptures, Paintings and Drawings. Complete Edition*, London 1969.

PEDRETTI, C., 'Il foglio 447E degli Uffizi a Firenze' in *Studi Vinciani. Documenti, Analisi e Inediti Leonardeschi*, Geneva 1957, pp. 211–16.

PEDRETTI, C., *The Drawings and Miscellaneous Papers of Leonardo da Vinci in the Collection of Her Majesty the Queen at Windsor Castle*, vol. 2, New York 1987.

PEDRETTI, C., and DALLI REGOLI, G., *I disegni di Leonardo da Vinci e della sua cerchia nel Gabinetto Disegni e Stampe della Galleria degli Uffizi a Firenze*, Florence 1985.

PELLECCHIA, L., 'The Patron's Role in the Production of Architecture: Bartolomeo Scala and the Scala Palace', *Renaissance Quarterly*, 42, 1989.

PEROSA, A., ed., *Giovanni Rucellai e il suo Zibaldone*, vol. 1, London 1960.

PETRIOLI TOFANI, A., *Gabinetto disegni e stampe degli Uffizi. Inventario. 1. Disegni esposti*, Florence 1986.

PETRIOLI TOFANI, A., *Gabinetto disegni e stampe degli Uffizi. Inventario. 1. Disegni di figura*, Florence 1991.

PHILOSTRATUS THE YOUNGER, *Imagines*, 16, trans. A. FAIRBANKS, London and New York 1931.

PIGLER, A., *Katalog der Galerie Alter Meister*, Budapest 1967.

PLINY THE ELDER, *Natural History*, trans. H. RACKHAM, vol. 9, Cambridge, Mass., 1968.

The Elder Pliny's Chapters on the History of Art, ed. K. JEX-BLAKE, Chicago 1968.

POGGI, G., 'Mino da Fiesole e la Badia Fiorentina', *Miscellanea d'Arte*, II, 1903, pp. 98–103.

POGGI, G., *Catalogo del Museo dell'Opera del Duomo*, Florence 1904.

POGGI, G., *Il Duomo di Firenze: documenti sulla decorazione della chiesa e del campanile tratti dall'archivio dell'opera*, Florence 1909.

POLIZIANO, A., *The 'Stanze' of Angelo Poliziano*, trans. D. QUINT, Amherst, Mass., 1979.

POPE-HENNESSY, J., *Italian Renaissance Sculpture*, London 1958.

POPE-HENNESSY, J., *Catalogue of Italian Sculpture in the Victoria and Albert Museum*, vol. 1, London 1964.

POPE-HENNESSY, J., *Luca della Robbia*, Oxford 1980.

POPHAM, A.E., and POUNCEY, P., *Italian Drawings in the Department of Prints and Drawings in the British Museum: the fourteenth and fifteenth centuries*, London 1950.

POPHAM, A.E., 'The Dragon-Fight', in A. MARAZZI, ed., *Leonardo Saggi e ricerche*, Rome 1954, pp. 223–7.

POPHAM, A.E., *The drawings of Leonardo da Vinci*, ed. M. KEMP, London 1994 (1st edn 1946).

PREYER, B., 'The Rucellai Palace', in *Giovanni Rucellai e il suo Zibaldone*, vol. 2, London 1981.

PREYER, B., 'The "chasa overo palagio" of Alberto di Zanobi: A Florentine Palace of About 1400 and Its Later Remodeling', *Art Bulletin*, 65, 1983, pp. 387–401.

PREYER, B., 'Florentine Palaces and Memories of the Past', in G. CIAPPELLI and P. RUBIN, eds., *Art, Memory, and Family in Early Renaissance Florence*, Cambridge 1999.

PULCI, L., 'La Giostra', in P. ORVIETO, ed., *Opere Minori*, Milan 1986.

QUATTROCCHI, E.B., *Disegni toscani e umbri del primo rinascimento dalle collezioni del Gabinetto Nazionale delle Stampe*, exh. cat., Rome 1979.

QUINTERIO, F., *Giuliano da Maiano 'Grandissimo Domestico'*, Rome 1996.

RADCLIFFE, A., 1985 see *Italian Renaissance Sculpture*.

RAGGHIANTI, C.L., 'La giovinezza e lo svolgimento artistico di Domenico Ghirlandaio', *L'Arte*, 1935, pp. 167–98.

RANDOLPH, A.W.B., *Public Women. The Visual Logic of Authority and Gender in Fifteenth-Century Florence*, PhD thesis, Harvard University 1995.

RICCIARDI, L., 'Col senno, col tesoro e colla lancia,' in *Riti e giochi cavallereschi nella Firenze del Magnifico Lorenzo*, Florence 1992.

RICHARDS, L., 'Antonio Pollaiuolo, Battle of Naked Men', *Bulletin of the Cleveland Museum of Art*, 55, March 1968, pp. 63–70.

RICHARDSON, E.P., 'Bertoldo and Verrocchio: Two Fifteenth-Century Florentine Bronzes', *Art Quarterly*, XXII, 1959, pp. 205–15.

RICHTER, J.P., *The Literary Works of Leonardo da Vinci*, vol. 1, London 1970.

RINUCCINI, *Lettere ed orazioni*, ed. V. GIUSTINIANI, Florence 1953.

ROCHON, A., *La jeunesse de Laurent de Médicis (1449–1478)*, Paris 1963.

ROHLMANN, M., 'Ein Flämisches Vorbild für Ghirlandaios "prime pitture"', *Mitteilungen des Kunsthistorischen Institutes in Florenz*, vol. 36, 1992, pp. 388–96.

ROHLMANN, M., 'Zitate flämischer landschaftsmotive in Florentiner Quattrocento-malerei' in J. POESCKE, ed., *Italienische Frührenaissance und nordeuropaishes mittelalter*, Munich 1993.

ROHLMANN, M., *Auftragskunst und Sammlerbild. Altniederländische Tafelmalerei im Florenz des Quattrocento*, Alfter 1994.

ROLFI, G., SEBREGONDI, L., and VITI, P., eds., *La Chiesa e la Città a Firenze nel XV secolo*, Florence 1992.

ROMBY, G.C., *Descrizioni e rappresentazioni della città di Firenze nel XV secolo con trascrizione inedita dei manoscritti di Benedetto Dei e un indice ragionato dei manoscritti utili per la storica di Firenze*, Florence 1976.

ROSENTHAL, E., 'The Position of Women in Renaissance Florence: neither autonomy nor subjection', in P. DENLEY and C. ELAM, eds., *Florence and Italy: Renaissance Studies in Honour of Nicolai Rubinstein*, London 1988, pp. 369–81.

ROYALTON-KISCH, M., CHAPMAN, H., CAPPEL, S., *Old Master Drawings from the Malcolm Collection*, exh. cat., British Museum, London 1996.

RUBIN, P., 'Art and the Imagery of Memory', in G. CIAPPELLI and P. RUBIN, eds., *Art, Memory, and Family in Early Renaissance Florence*, Cambridge 1999 (forthcoming).

RUBINSTEIN, N., *The Government of Florence under the Medici 1434 to 1494*, Oxford 1966.

RUBINSTEIN, N., *The Palazzo Vecchio 1298–1532. Government, Architecture and Imagery in the Civic Palace of the Florentine Republic*, Oxford 1995.

Rucellai e il suo Zibaldone SEE GIOVANNI RUCELLAI.

SABATINI, A., 'Appunti sul Pollaiuolo', *Rivista d'Arte*, 23, 1941, pp. 72–98.

SALE, J.R., *The Strozzi Chapel by Filippino Lippi in Santa Maria Novella*, PhD thesis, University of Pennsylvania, Philadelphia 1976.

SCHARF, A., 'Two Neglected Works by Filippino Lippi', *The Burlington Magazine*, 71, 1937, pp. 4–7.

SCHER, S., ed., *The Currency of Fame. Portrait Medals of the Renaissance*, New York 1994.

SCHOLTEN, F., 'Technical aspects of Verrocchio's Candelabrum', *Bulletin van het Rijksmuseum*, 44, no. 2, 1996, pp. 123–9.

SCHUBRING, P., *Cassoni. Truhen und Truhenbilder der italienischen Frührenaissance*, Leipzig 1923.

SCHULZE ALTCAPPENBERG, H-T., *Die italienischen Zeichnungen des 14. und 15. Jahrhunderts im Berliner Kupferstichkabinett*, Berlin 1995.

SCHWABAHER, S., *Die Stickerein nach Entwurfen des Antonio Pollaiuolo in der Opera di S. Maria del Fiore zu Florenz*, Strasburg 1911.

SETTESOLDI, E., 'Il Gonfalone del comune di Carrara dipinto da Andrea del Verrocchio', *Paragone*, 31, no. 363, 1980, pp. 87–91.

SEYMOUR, C., *Masterpieces of Sculpture from the National Gallery of Art*, New York 1949.

SEYMOUR, C., *Early Italian Painting in the Yale University Art Collection*, New Haven and London 1970.

SEYMOUR, C., *The Sculpture of Andrea del Verrocchio*, Greenwich, Conn., 1971.

SHAPLEY, F.R., *Catalogue of the Italian Paintings*, National Gallery of Art, Washington 1979.

SHOEMAKER, I.H., *Filippino Lippi as a Draughtsman*, PhD thesis, Columbia University, New York 1975.

SIRÉN, O., *A Descriptive Catalogue of the Pictures in the Jarves Collection belonging to Yale University*, New Haven, London and Oxford 1916.

SISI, C., 1992, see *Il Disegno fiorentino*.

SPALLANZANI, M., and BERTELÀ, G.G., eds., *Libro d'inventario dei beni di Lorenzo il Magnifico*, Florence 1992.

STEDMAN SHEARD, W., '"Asa Adorna": The Prehistory of the Vendramin Tomb', *Jahrbuch der Berliner Museen*, 20, 1978, pp. 117–56.

STEDMAN SHEARD, W., 'Verrocchio's Medici Tomb and the Language of Materials; with a Postscript on his Legacy in Venice', in S. BULE, A.P. DARR and F. SUPERBI GIOFFREDI, eds., *Verrocchio and Late Quattrocento Italian Sculpture*, Florence 1992, pp. 63–90.

STROZZI, A., *Lettere di una gentildonna fiorentina*, ed. C. GUASTI, Florence 1877.

SUIDA, W., *Leonardo und sein Kreis*, Munich 1929.

SUIDA, W., 'La Bella Simonetta', *Art Quarterly*, XI, 1948, pp. 2–8, 'Again the Simonetta bust' *Art Quarterly*, XII, 1949, pp. 176–9.

SUIDA, W., 'Leonardo's Activity as a Painter: A Sketch', in A. MARAZZA, ed., *Leonardo: saggi e ricerche*, Rome 1954, pp. 315–29.

SUTTON, D., *Drawings from the National Gallery of Ireland*, London 1967.

SWARZENSKI, G., 'A Marriage Casket and its Moral', *Bulletin of the Museum of Fine Arts, Boston*, XLV, no. 261, 1947, pp. 55–62.

TAIT, H., ed., *Seven Thousand Years of Jewellery*, London 1986.

TEMPESTI, A.F., *I grandi disegni italiani degli Uffizi di Firenze*, Milan n.d. [1973].

Il Tesoro di Lorenzo il Magnifico. Repertorio delle gemme e dei vasi, eds. N. DACOS, A. GROTE, A. GIULIANO, D. HEIKAMP and U. PANNUTI, Florence 1980.

THOMAS, A., *The Painter's Practice in Renaissance Tuscany*, Cambridge and New York 1995.

THOMAS, A., 'Neri di Bicci in the Compagnia di San Frediano detta la Bruciata and a Painting of a deacon saint', *Arte Cristiana*, 85, no. 778, 1997, pp. 27–34.

THOMAS, A., 'Restoration or Renovation: Remuneration and Expectation in Renaissance "acconciatura"', in C. SITWELL and S. STANIFORTH, eds., *Studies in the History of Painting Restoration*, National Trust 1996, pp. 5–9.

THORNTON, D., *The Scholar in his Study. Ownership and Experience in Renaissance Italy*, New Haven and London 1997.

TRAPP, J.B., 'The Iconography of Petrarch in the Age of Humanism', *Quaderni Petrarcheschi*, IX–X, 1992–3, esp. pp. 29–30 and 39–65.

TREXLER, R., 'Lorenzo de' Medici and Savonarola, Martyrs for Florence', *Renaissance Quarterly*, 31, 1978, pp. 292–308.

TRIONFI HONORATI, M., 'Il Palazzo degli Antinori', *Antichità Viva*, vol. 7, no. 2, 1968, pp. 65–80.

TROTTA, G., *Palazzo Cocchi Serristori a Firenze*, Florence 1995.

ULLMANN, H., 'Bilder und Zeichnungen der Brüder Pollaiuoli', *Jahrbuch der Preussischen Kunstsammlungen*, 15, 1894, pp. 230–47.

VALENTINER, W.R., 'Leonardo as Verrocchio's Coworker', *Art Bulletin*, 12, 1930, pp. 43–89.

VALENTINER, W.R., *Detroit Institute of Arts, Italian Sculpture 1250–1500*, Detroit 1938.

VASARI, *Le opere*, ed. MILANESI, vol. 4, Florence 1878–85.

VENTRONE, P., ed., 'Le tems revient. Il tempo si rinuova'. *Feste e spettacoli nella Firenze di Lorenzo il Magnifico*, exh. cat., Palazzo Medici Riccardi, Florence 1992.

VENTRONE, P., 'Lorenzo's politica festiva' in M. MALLETT and N. MANN, eds., *Lorenzo the Magnificent. Culture and Politics*, Florence 1996, pp. 105–66.

VENTURINI, L., *Francesco Botticini*, Florence 1994.

VESPASIANO DA BISTICCI, *The Vespasiano Memoirs. Lives of Illustrious Men of the XVth Century*, trans. W.G. and E. WATERS, New York 1963.

VIATTE, F., 1989 see *Léonard de Vinci, Les études du draperie*.

VIATTE, F., 'Verrocchio et Leonardo da Vinci: à propos des "têtes idéales"', in E. CROPPER, ed., *Florentine Drawing at the Time of Lorenzo the Magnificent*, Florence 1992, pp. 45–53.

WACKERNAGEL, M., *The World of the Florentine Renaissance Artist*, trans. A. LUCHS, Princeton 1981.

WALKER, J., 'Ricostruzione d'un incisione Pollajolesca', *Dedalo*, 13, 1933, Part 1, pp. 229–37.

WARBURG, A., 'Delle "Imprese Amorose" nelle più antiche incisioni fiorentine', *Rivista d'Arte*, III, 1905, appendix to nos. 7–8, pp. 1–15.

WARBURG, A., *Gesammelte Schriften*, 2 vols., Leipzig and Berlin 1932.

WARD-JACKSON, P., *Victoria and Albert Museum Catalogues. Italian Drawings*, vol. 1, *14th–16th century*, London 1979.

WHITAKER, L., 'Maso Fineguerra, Baccio Baldini and The Florentine Picture Chronicle', in E. CROPPER, ed., *Florentine Drawing at the Time of Lorenzo the Magnificent*, Villa Spelman Colloquia, vol. 4, Bologna and Baltimore 1994, pp. 181–96.

WIECK, R.S, *Painted Prayers. The Book of Hours in Medieval and Renaissance Art*, New York 1997.

WIEMERS, M., *Bildform und Workgenese. Studien zur Zeichnerischen Bildvorbereitung in der italienischen Malerei zwischen 1450 und 1490*, Munich 1996.

WILDER, E., KENNEDY, C. and BACCI, P., *The Unfinished Monument by Andrea del Verrocchio to the Cardinal Niccolò Forteguerri at Pistoia*, Northampton, Mass., 1932.

WILSON, T.H., *Ceramic Art of the Italian Renaissance*, exh. cat., British Museum, London 1987.

WILSON, T.H., 'Maioliche rinascimentali armoriate con stemmi fiorentini' in *L'Araldica. Fonti e Metodi*, Florence 1989, pp. 128–38.

WILSON, T.H., 'Spanish Pottery in the British Museum' in C. GERRARD, A. GUTIÉRRES and A.G. VINCE, eds., *Spanish Medieval Ceramics in Spain and the British Isles*, Oxford 1995, pp. 339–51.

WIND, E., *Pagan Mysteries in the Renaissance*, London 1968.

WOLOHOJIAN, S.S., 'Francesco di Simone Ferrucci's Fogg "Virgin and Child" and the Martini Chapel in S. Giobbe, Venice', *The Burlington Magazine*, 139, December 1997, pp. 867–9.

WRIGHT, A., 'Antonio Pollaiuolo, "maestro di disegno"' in E. CROPPER, ed., *Florentine Drawing at the Time of Lorenzo the Magnificent*, Villa Spelman Colloquia, vol. 4, Bologna and Baltimore 1994, pp. 131–46.

WRIGHT, A., *Studies in the Paintings of the Pollaiuolo*, PhD thesis, Courtauld Institute, London 1992.

WRIGHT, A., 'A Portrait for the Visit of Galeazzo Maria Sforza to Florence in 1471', in M. MALLET and N. MANN, eds., *Lorenzo the Magnificent. Culture and Politics*, London 1996, pp. 65–92.

WRIGHT, A., 'Dancing Nudes in the Lanfredini villa at Arcetri', in E. MARCHAND and A. WRIGHT, eds., *With and Without the Medici. Studies in Tuscan Art and Patronage 1434–1530*, Aldershot 1998, pp. 47–77.

ZAMBRANO in ZAMBRANO and NELSON (forthcoming).

ZERI, F., 'Il Maestro dell'Annunciazione Gardner', *Bollettino d'Arte*, 4th series, 38, 1953, pp. 125–39.

ZERVAS, D.F, '"quos volent et eo modo quo volent": Piero de' Medici and the Operai of SS. Annunziata, 1445–55', in P. DENLEY and C. ELAM, eds., *Florence and Italy. Renaissance Studies in Honour of Nicolai Rubinstein*, London 1988, pp. 465–79.

ZURAW, S.E., 'The Public Commemorative Monument: Mino da Fiesole's Tombs in the Florentine Badia', *Art Bulletin*, LXXX, no. 3, 1998, pp. 452–77.

Acknowledgements

The authors wish to thank the National Gallery for inviting them to collaborate with Nicholas Penny in organising an exhibition devoted to Renaissance Florence and in writing the accompanying catalogue. They are deeply grateful for having had the opportunity to participate in such an exciting project and are appreciative of the expertise, energy and enthusiasm that went into realising it on the part of the curatorial, conservation, exhibitions and editorial staff of the National Gallery, and of National Gallery Publications. The comments made by our readers at the National Gallery and by Caroline Elam were invaluable to our text.

The preparation of book and catalogue benefited from the resources of the Courtauld Institute, University College London and Villa I Tatti and the authors are grateful to their friends and colleagues at those institutions for their support. The authors and Nicholas Penny are immeasurably thankful to all of the lending institutions and the curators and conservators of those collections who greatly facilitated their visits to study the relevant works of art. They would like to mention their gratitude to the following individuals who assisted them with special access to objects, information and expertise: Candace Adelson, François Avril, Christopher Baker, Antonia Boström, Craigen Bowen, Helen Braham, Bodo Brinkmann, David Alan Brown, Andrew Butterfield, Alessandro Cecchi, Isabelle Chabot, Hugo Chapman, Martin Clayton, Helen Cooper, Dominique Cordellier, James Cuno, Michael Daley, Alan Phipps Darr, Peter Day, Jean-Luc Dufresne, Chris Fischer, Jean-René Gaborit, Rudolf Hiller von Gaertringen, Hannah Hohl, Charlotte Hubbard, Penley Knipe, Michael Knuth, Alison Luchs, Hugh MacAndrew, Pietro Marani, D.P. Mortlock, Peta Motture, Antonio Natali, Charles Newton, Joachim Pissarro, Marie-Hélène de Ribou, Edward Saywell, Erich Schleier, Luke Syson, Dora Thornton, Anna Maria Petrioli Tofani, Marie-Louise Van der Pol, Ernst Vegelin, Françoise Viatte and Paul Williamson. Many scholars freely shared their insights with us and we want specifically to acknowledge those who have allowed us to refer to as yet unpublished material: Mark Aronson, Rolf Bagemihl, Roberta Bartoli, Jill Burke, Ellen Callmann, Pietro Marani, Jonathon Nelson, Louis Waldman and Patrizia Zambrano. Our own research was constantly and generously sustained by the hospitality of our friends and families, most notably Debby and James Brice, Eckart Marchand, Nan Ross, Barbara Santocchini, Barbara and Allen Schoen and Pat and Ian Wright.

As discussed at various points throughout this book, collaboration was a key characteristic of the art of Florence during the 1470s. It was a precious experience for the authors to work collaboratively on a book about this period and we repeat our thanks to everyone who made it possible.

Patricia Lee Rubin and Alison Wright

Lenders

Her Majesty Queen Elizabeth II
cat. nos. 9, 24, 30, 45, 64

His Grace The Duke of Devonshire
and the Chatsworth Settlement
Trustees cat. no. 73

The Earl of Leicester and the Trustees
of the Holkham Estates cat. no. 4

J. H. Kagan cat. no. 2

Amsterdam, Rijksmuseum cat. no. 12

Berlin, Staatliche Museen Preussischer
Kulturbesitz, Skulpturensammlung
cat. no. 18

Berlin, Staatliche Museen Preussischer
Kulturbesitz, Kupferstichkabinett cat.
nos. 32, 44, 49

Budapest, Szépmüvészeti Múzeum
cat. no. 71

Cambridge, Massachusetts, Harvard
University Art Museums, Fogg Art
Museum cat. nos. 56, 74

Cherbourg, Musée d'Art Thomas
Henry cat. no. 72

Detroit, The Detroit Institute of Arts
cat. no. 58

Dublin, The National Gallery of
Ireland cat. no. 52

Edinburgh, The National Gallery of
Scotland cat. nos. 19, 25

Florence, Galleria degli Uffizi
cat. no. 85

Florence, Galleria degli Uffizi,
Gabinetto Disegni e Stampe
cat. nos. 10, 22, 33, 34, 35, 39, 75, 77

Florence, Museo degli Argenti
cat. no. 5

Florence, Museo dell'Opera del
Duomo cat. no. 48

Frankfurt am Main, Städelsches
Kunstinstitut cat. no. 27

Hamburg, Kunsthalle
Kupferstichkabinett cat. no. 76

London, British Museum cat. nos. 2,
6, 16, 26, 29, 37, 38, 41, 47, 51, 55, 57, 59,
63, 67, 81, 87, 90, 91, 92, 93, 94

London, Courtauld Gallery, Lee
Collection cat. nos. 78, 79

London, Victoria and Albert Museum
cat. nos. 11, 13, 28, 54, 80, 83

Lisbon, Museu Nacional de Arte
Antiga cat. no. 62

New Haven, Yale University Art
Gallery cat. no. 46

Oxford, Ashmolean Museum
cat. no. 53

Oxford, Christ Church Picture Gallery
cat. nos. 31, 60

Paris, Bibliothèque Nationale de
France cat. nos. 3, 66, 89

Paris, Institut Néerlandais, Collection
Frits Lugt cat. no. 40

Paris, Musée du Louvre, Département
des Arts Graphiques cat. nos. 20, 36,
42, 50

Paris, Musée du Louvre, Département
des Sculptures cat. nos. 14, 15,

Rome, Istituto Nazionale per la
Grafica, Gabinetto Nazionale delle
Stampe cat. no. 8

Washington, National Gallery of Art
cat. nos. 1, 17, 61, 65, 82

as well as a private owner who wishes
to remain anonymous cat. no. 84

Photographic Credits

AMSTERDAM
Rijksmuseum (© Rijksmuseum-Stichting Amsterdam): cat. no. 12

BAYONNE
Musée Bonnat (© photos RMN-R.G.Ojeda): figs. 4, 111; (© photo RMN): fig. 117

BERLIN
Staatliche Museen zu Berlin-Preussischer Kulturbesitz-Skulpturensammlung (photo: Jorg P. Anders): cat. no. 18

Staatliche Museen zu Berlin-Preussischer Kulturbesitz-Kupferstichkabinett (photos: Jorg P. Anders): cat. nos. 32, 44, 49; figs. 2, 93, 101, 102

BUDAPEST
Szépmüvészeti Múzeum: cat. no. 71

CAMBRIDGE
Fitzwilliam Museum (© University of Cambridge): fig. 42

CAMBRIDGE, MASS.
Courtesy of the Fogg Art Museum, Harvard University Art Museums, © President and Fellows of Harvard College, Harvard University (photo: Rick Stafford): cat. no. 56; (photo: photographic services): cat. no. 74; (photos: David Mathews): figs. 36, 116

CHATSWORTH
Devonshire Collection, Chatsworth (Reproduced by permission of the Duke of Devonshire and the Chatsworth Settlement Trustees): cat. no. 73

CHERBOURG
Musée d'Art Thomas Henry: cat. no. 72

CLEVELAND
The Cleveland Museum of Art (© The Cleveland Museum of Art purchased from the J.H. Wade Fund): fig. 114

DETROIT
Detroit Institute of Art: figs. 22, 37; (photo: Dirk Bakker): cat. no. 58

DUBLIN
The National Gallery of Ireland: cat. no. 52; fig. 112

EDINBURGH
National Gallery of Scotland: cat. nos. 19, 25; fig. 98

FLORENCE
Antonio Quattrone: fig. 39

Archivi Alinari: figs. 5, 7,12, 29, 33, 44, 54, 66, 96, 113

Galleria degli Uffizi, Gabinetto Disegni e Stampe (photos: Paolo Tosi): figs. 14, 53, 59, 73, 76, 83, 90

Galleria degli Uffizi (photo: Archivi Alinari): fig. 107; (photos: The Bridgeman Art Library): figs. 10, 11, 78, 81; (photos: Antonio Quattrone): fig. 74; (photos: SCALA): figs. 15, 38, 61, 62, 72; (photos: Paolo Tosi): cat. nos. 10, 22, 33, 34, 35, 39, 75, 77, 85; figs. 19, 30, 80, 82, 108, 122, 123

Museo degli Argenti (photo: Paolo Tosi): cat. no. 5

Museo dell' Opera del Duomo: figs. 31, 32; (photo: Nicolò Orsi Battaglini): fig. 58

Museo Nazionale del Bargello (photo: Archivi Alinari): fig. 20; (photos: Nicolò Orsi Battaglini): figs. 68, 69, 85; (photo: Conway Library, Courtauld Institute of Art): fig. 17; (photo: Hirmer Fotoarchiv): fig. 67; (photo: private collection): fig. 97; (photos: SCALA): figs. 18, 27, 64

Nicolò Orsi Battaglini: cat. no. 48

SCALA: figs. 1, 8, 9, 13, 26, 55, 56, 57, 70

Soprintendenza per I Beni Artistici e Storici: fig. 46

FRANKFURT
Städelsches Kunstinstitut: cat. no. 27

HAMBURG
Hamburg Kunsthalle, Kupferstichkabinett: cat. no. 76, fig. 119; (photo: Elke Walford Fotowerkstatt): fig. 52

HOLKHAM
Holkham Hall (© The Earl of Leicester and the Trustees of the Holkham Estate): cat. no. 4

LISBON
Museu Nacional de Arte Antiga: cat. no. 62

LONDON
The British Museum (© The British Museum): cat. nos. 2 (obverse), 6, 16, 26, 29, 37, 38, 41, 47, 51, 55, 57, 59, 63, 67, 81, 87, 90, 91, 92, 93, 94; figs. 50, 103, 104

Courtauld Gallery, Lee Collection: cat. nos. 78, 79; (photos: The Bridgeman Art Library): figs. 120, 121

Courtauld Institute of Art, Conway Library: figs. 86, 95

Courtauld Institute of Art, Witt Library: figs. 35, 48, 49

The National Gallery (© The National Gallery): cat. nos. 7, 21, 23, 43, 68, 69, 70, 86, 88; fig. 28

The Royal Collection (© 1999, Her Majesty Queen Elizabeth II): cat. nos. 9, 24, 30, 45, 64; figs. 94, 115

The Victoria and Albert Museum (© V&A Picture Library): cat. nos. 11, 13, 28, 54, 80, 83; fig. 84

The Warburg Institute: figs. 3, 45, 47

Photo: private collection: fig. 43

MILAN
Museo Poldi-Pezzoli (photo: SCALA): fig. 63

NAPLES
Museo Nazionale (photo: private collection): fig. 21

NEW HAVEN
Yale University Art Gallery (photo: Carl Kaufman): cat. no. 46

NEW YORK
J.H. Kagan: cat. no. 2 (reverse)

OXFORD
Bodleian Library: figs. 24, 25

Christ Church Picture Gallery: cat. nos. 31, 60

PARIS
Bibliothèque Nationale de France: cat. nos. 3, 66, 89; figs. 91, 92

Institut Néerlandais, Collection Frits Lugt: cat. no. 40

Musée du Louvre (© photos: RMN): figs 79, 118; (© photo: RMN-C. Jean): fig. 23; (© photos: RMN-J.G. Berizzi): figs. 89, 105; (© photos: RMN- Ojeda / Hubert): cat. nos. 14, 15; (© photo: RMN- R. G. Ojeda): cat. no. 36; (© photos: RMN- Michèle Bellot): cat. nos. 20, 42, 50; figs. 71, 106; (© photo: RMN-Arnaudet): fig. 65

ROME
Gabinetto Nazionale delle Stampe (By kind permission of il Ministero per I Beni e le Attività Culturali): cat. no. 8

ST PETERSBURG
Hermitage (photo: SCALA): fig. 77

TURIN
Galleria Sabauda (photo: The Bridgeman Art Library): fig. 60

WASHINGTON
National Gallery of Art (© 1999 Board of Trustees): cat. nos. 1, 17, 61, 65; figs. 75, 88; (© 1999 Board of Trustees, photo: Philip A. Charles): cat. no. 82

VATICAN
Biblioteca Apostolica (Archivio Fotografico Musei Vaticani): fig. 6

PRIVATE COLLECTION
(© Prudence Cuming): cat. no. 84

Index

Pages including illustrations are shown in *italic*. Buildings, institutions etc. in Florence are listed under their own names; those outside Florence are under their place-names. Many Florentine palaces are listed with their name first (e.g. Pitti palace).